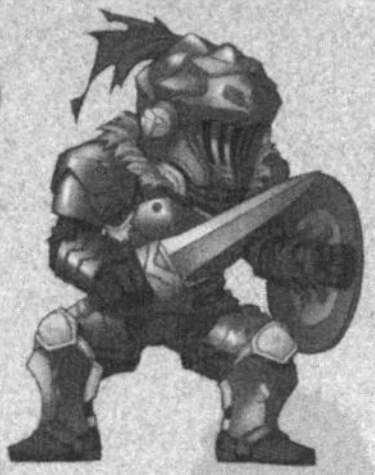

HE DOES NOT LET ANYONE ROLL THE DICE.

A young Priestess joins her first adventuring party, but blind to the dangers, they almost immediately find themselves in trouble. It's Goblin Slayer who comes to their rescue—a man who has dedicated his life to the extermination of all goblins by any means necessary. A dangerous, dirty, and thankless job, but he does it better than anyone. And when rumors of his feats begin to circulate, there's no telling who might come calling next...

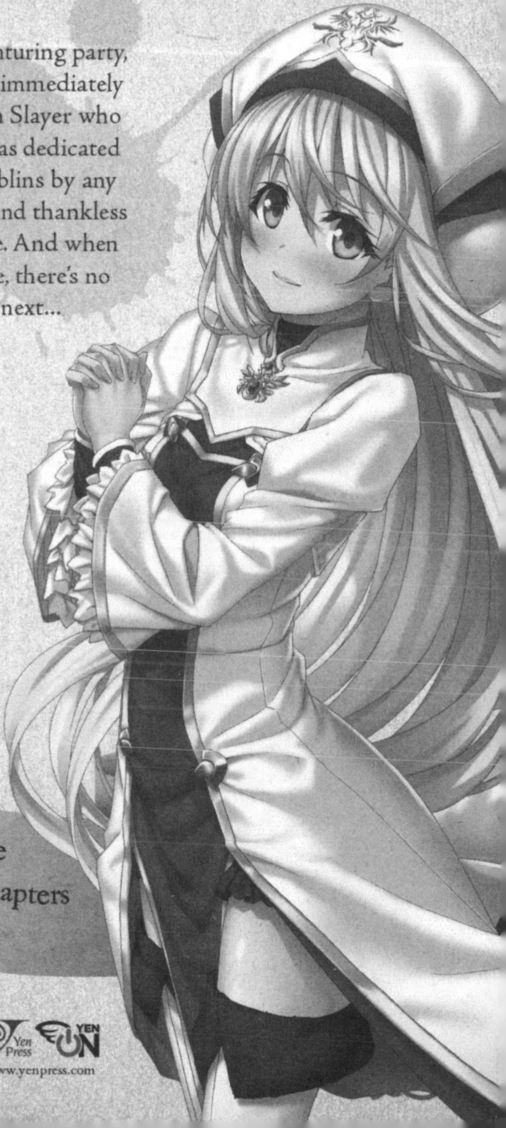

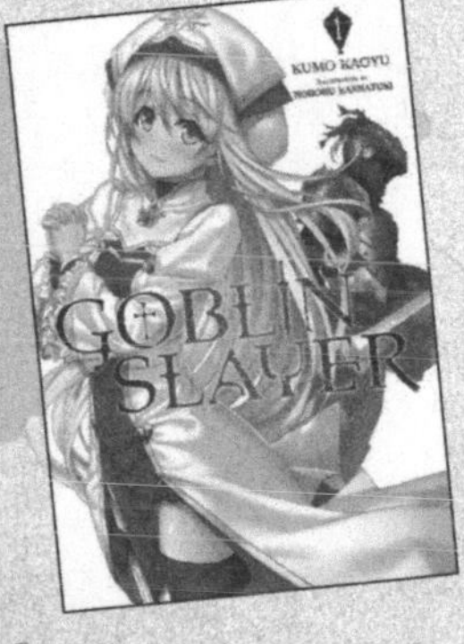
KUMO KAGYU
GOBLIN SLAYER

Light Novel
V. 1-2
Available
Now!

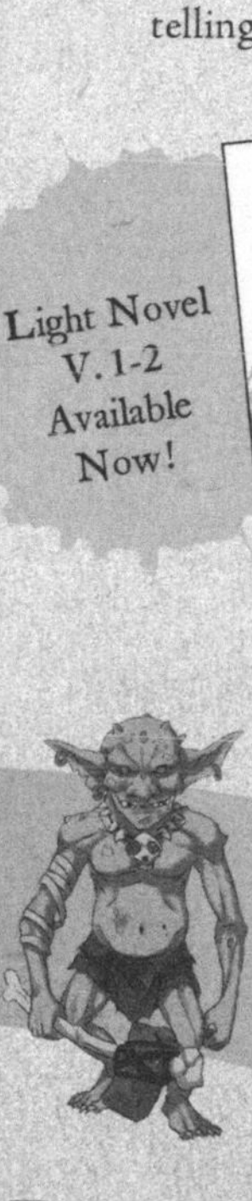

Check out the
simul-pub manga chapters
every month!

Yen Press Yen On

www.yenpress.com

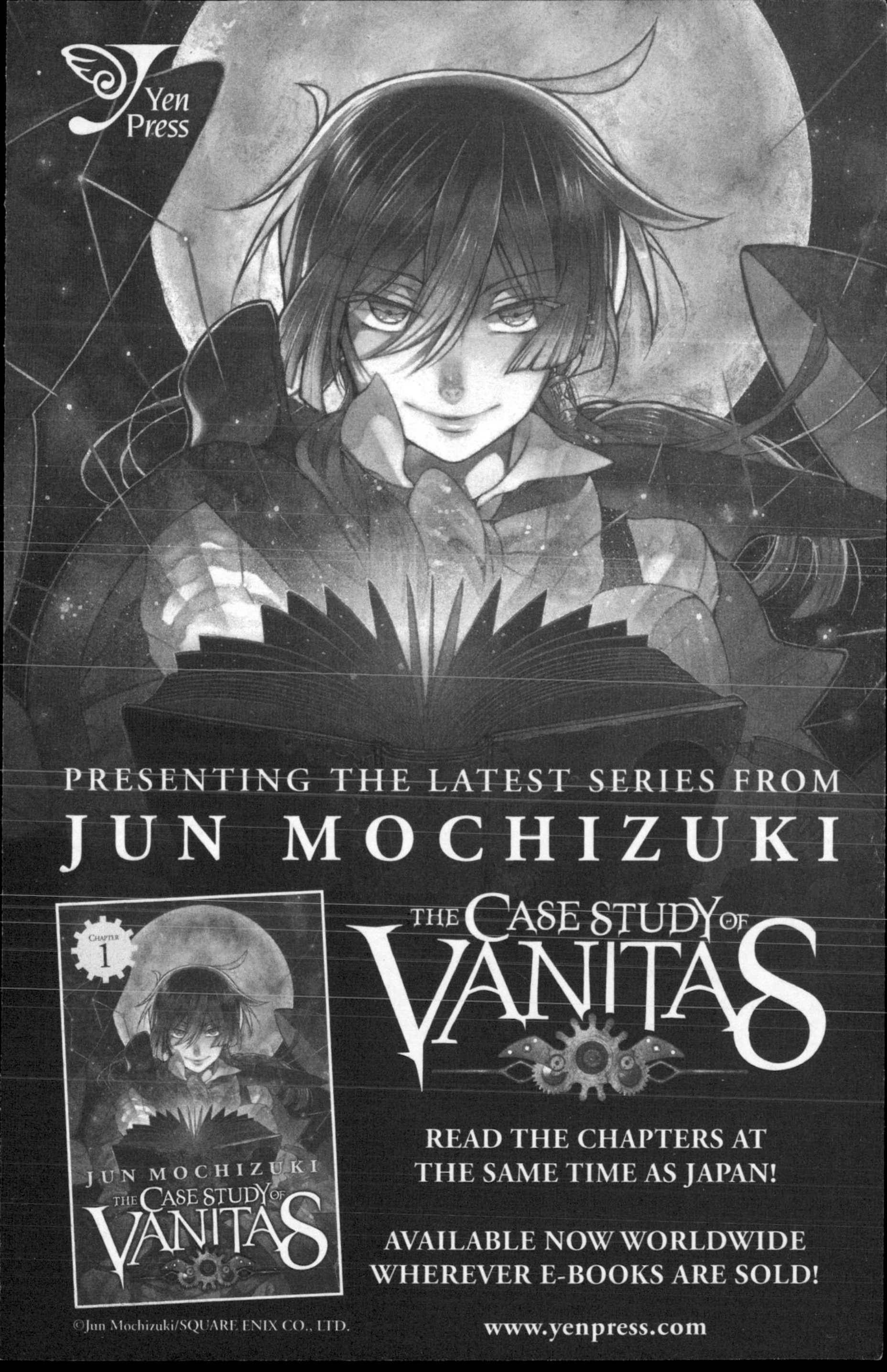
Yen Press
PRESENTING THE LATEST SERIES FROM
JUN MOCHIZUKI
THE CASE STUDY OF VANITAS
CHAPTER 1
JUN MOCHIZUKI
THE CASE STUDY OF VANITAS
READ THE CHAPTERS AT THE SAME TIME AS JAPAN!
AVAILABLE NOW WORLDWIDE WHEREVER E-BOOKS ARE SOLD!
©Jun Mochizuki/SQUARE ENIX CO., LTD.
www.yenpress.com

MURDERER
IN THE STREETS, KILLER
IN THE SHEETS!

MURCIÉLAGO

VOLUME I AVAILABLE NOW!

Mass murderer Kuroko Koumori has two passions in life: taking lives and pleasuring ladies. This doesn't leave her with many career prospects, but Kuroko actually has the perfect gig—as a hit woman for the police!

In the latest series from *New York Times*-bestseller Daisuke Hagiwara (*Horimiya*)...

Will love blossom between an odd couple ?!

Married off to a man more than twenty years her senior, Koyuki has no idea what her new life has in store for her. She's so in the dark, in fact, that she hasn't even seen her husband's face! But Koyuki isn't alone in fumbling through the intricacies of wedded bliss. Mask-donning Shin might have many years on his young wife, but as it turns out, he's just as naïve as she is! Will this pair of innocents ever get past their awkwardness (and the age gap)?!

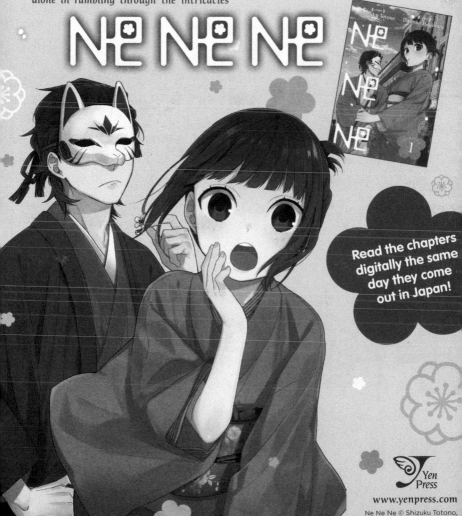

Read the chapters digitally the same day they come out in Japan!

THANKS.

AO JYUMONJI-SENSEI
EIRI SHIRAI-SENSEI

STAFF.

OGAWA-SAN   NOMOTO-SAN
URYUU-SAN   WATANABE-SAN

THANKS TO MY SUPERVISOR AND EVERYONE ELSE INVOLVED
WITH THE PUBLISHING OF THIS SERIES DURING IT'S ORIGINAL RUN.
ALSO, THANKS TO MY ASSISTANTS, WHO PRESSED ON
WHILE RUBBING THE SLEEP OUT OF THEIR EYES, AND TO MY
SUPPORTIVE MOTHER, FATHER, FRIENDS, AND ALL THE READERS
OUT THERE WHO STUCK WITH THIS SERIES TO THE VERY END!

-MUTSUMI OKUBASHI
AUGUST 2016

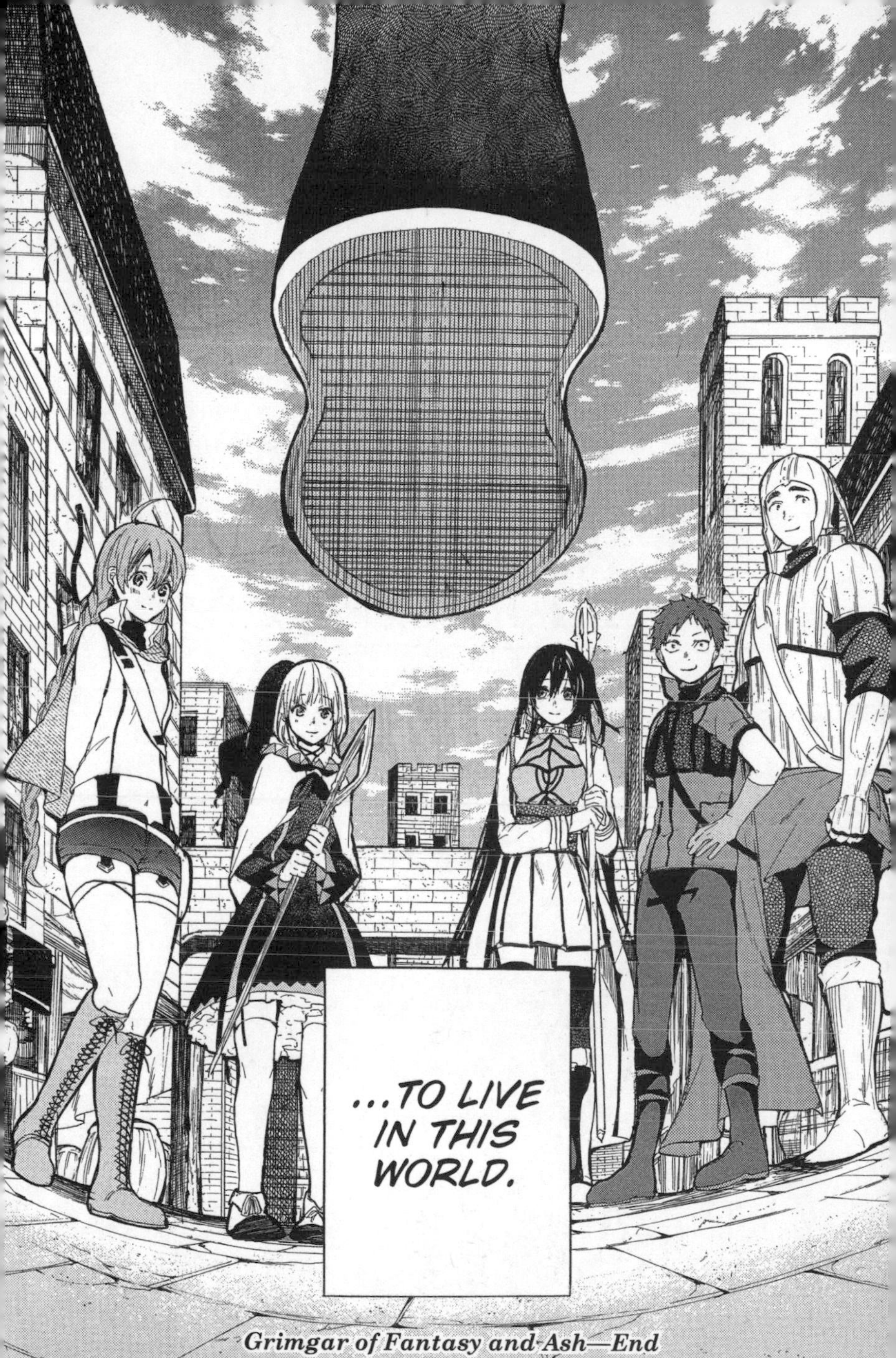
...TO LIVE IN THIS WORLD.

Grimgar of Fantasy and Ash—End

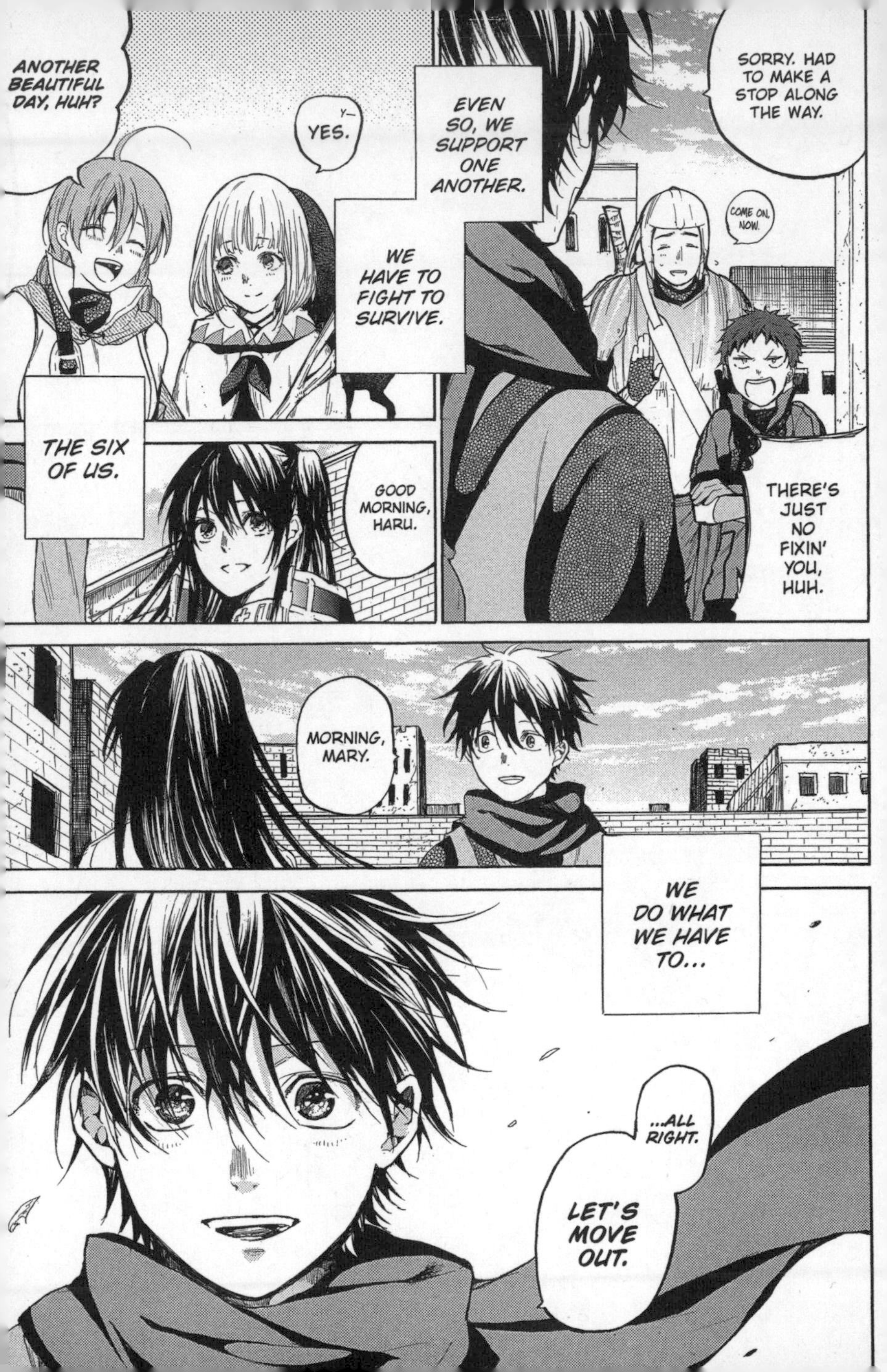
SORRY. HAD TO MAKE A STOP ALONG THE WAY.
COME ON, NOW.
EVEN SO, WE SUPPORT ONE ANOTHER.
WE HAVE TO FIGHT TO SURVIVE.
THERE'S JUST NO FIXIN' YOU, HUH.
Y— YES.
ANOTHER BEAUTIFUL DAY, HUH?
GOOD MORNING, HARU.
THE SIX OF US.
MORNING, MARY.
WE DO WHAT WE HAVE TO...
...ALL RIGHT.
LET'S MOVE OUT.

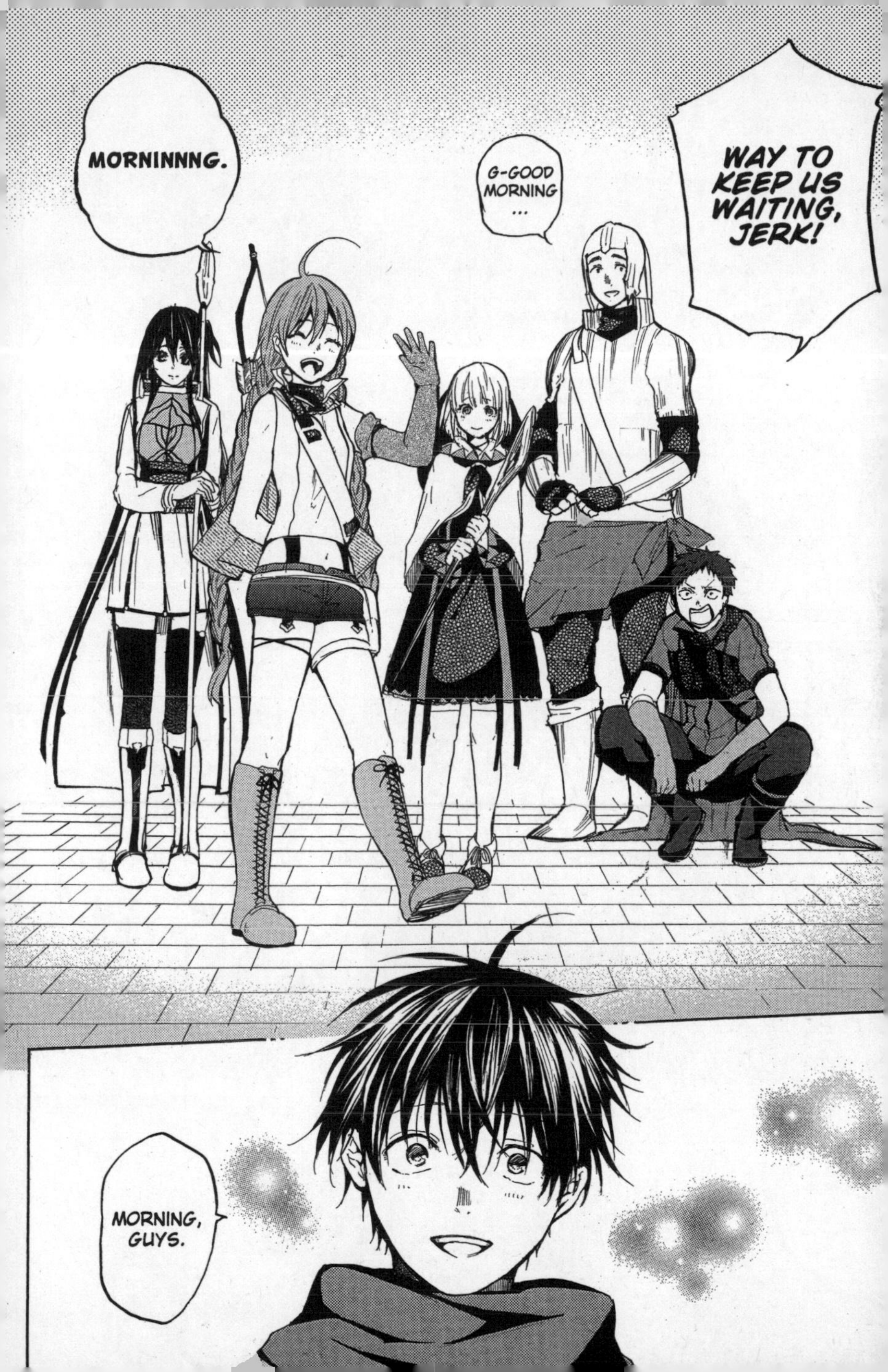
WAY TO KEEP US WAITING, JERK!
G-GOOD MORNING ...
MORNINNNG.
MORNING, GUYS.

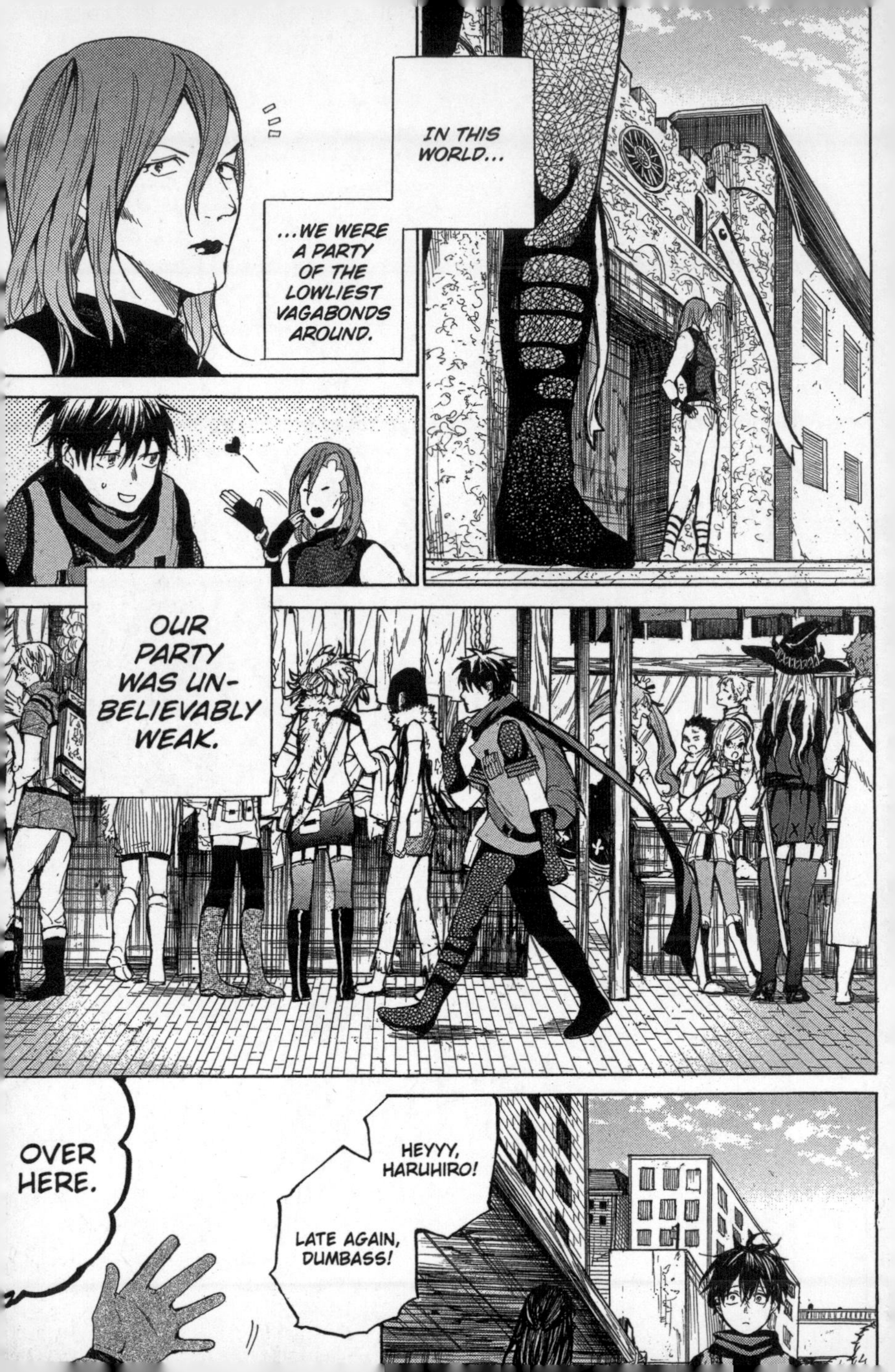
IN THIS WORLD...
...WE WERE A PARTY OF THE LOWLIEST VAGABONDS AROUND.
OUR PARTY WAS UN-BELIEVABLY WEAK.
HEYYY, HARUHIRO!
LATE AGAIN, DUMBASS!
OVER HERE.

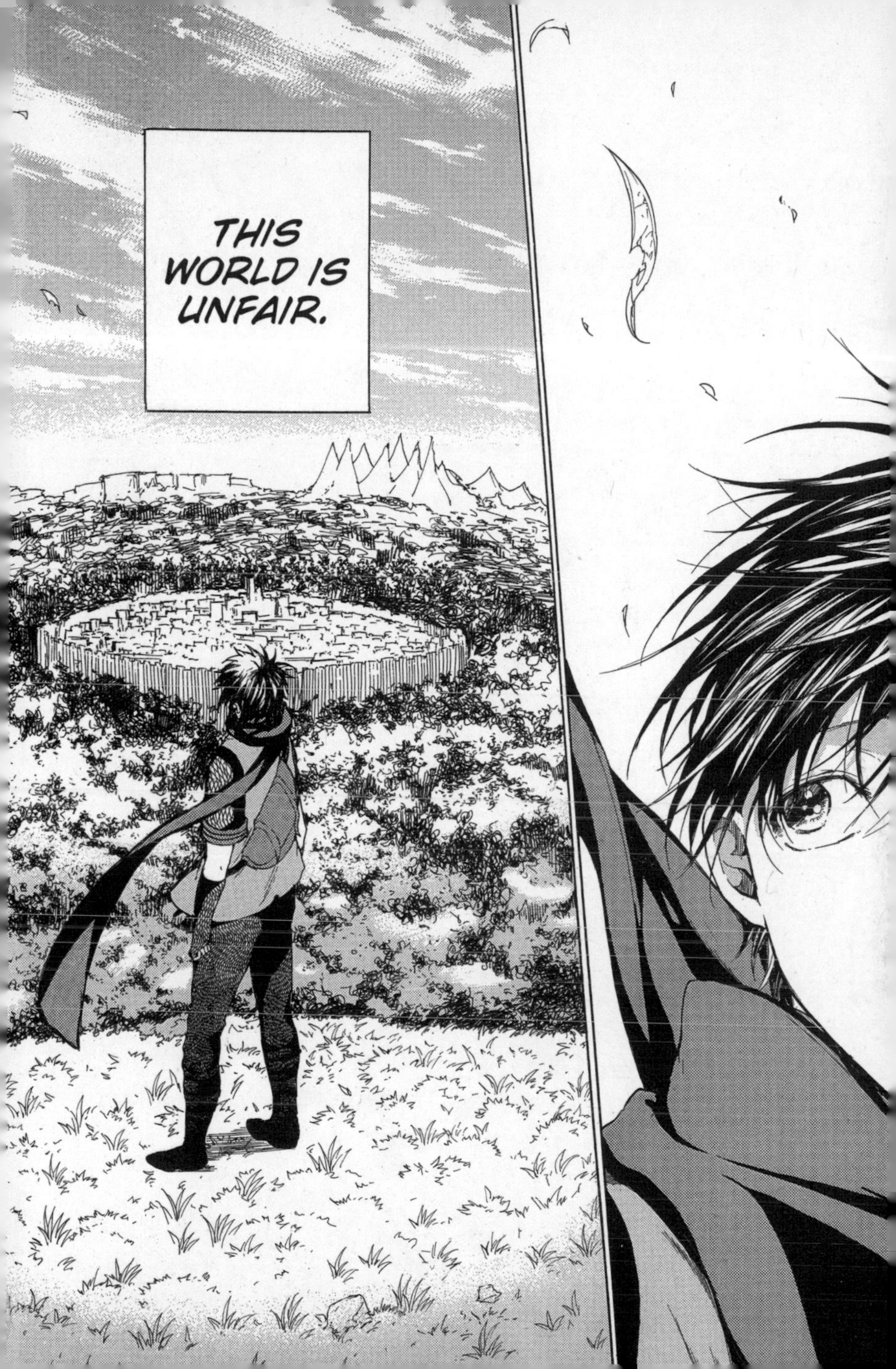
THIS WORLD IS UNFAIR.

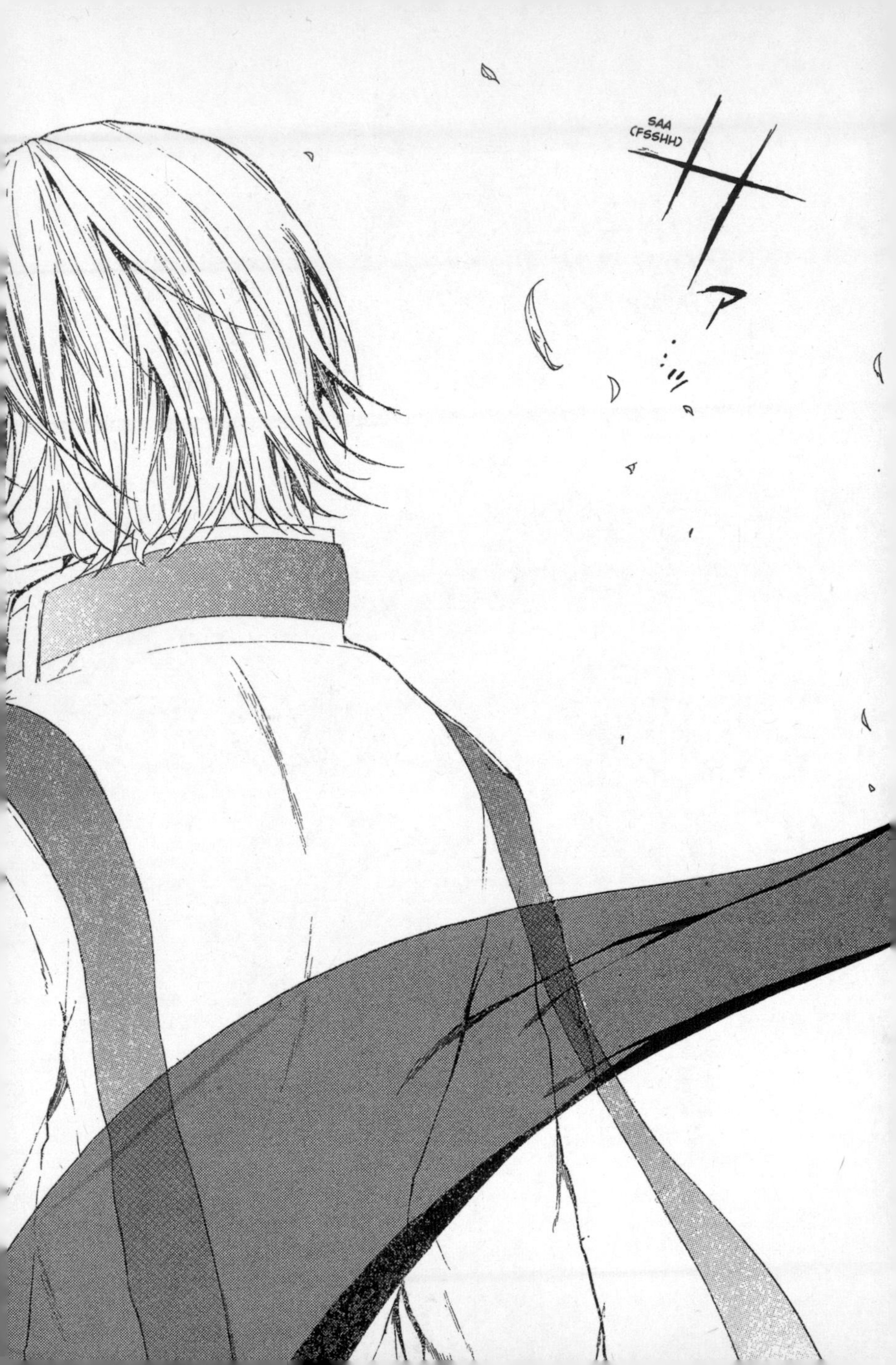
SAA
(FSSHH)

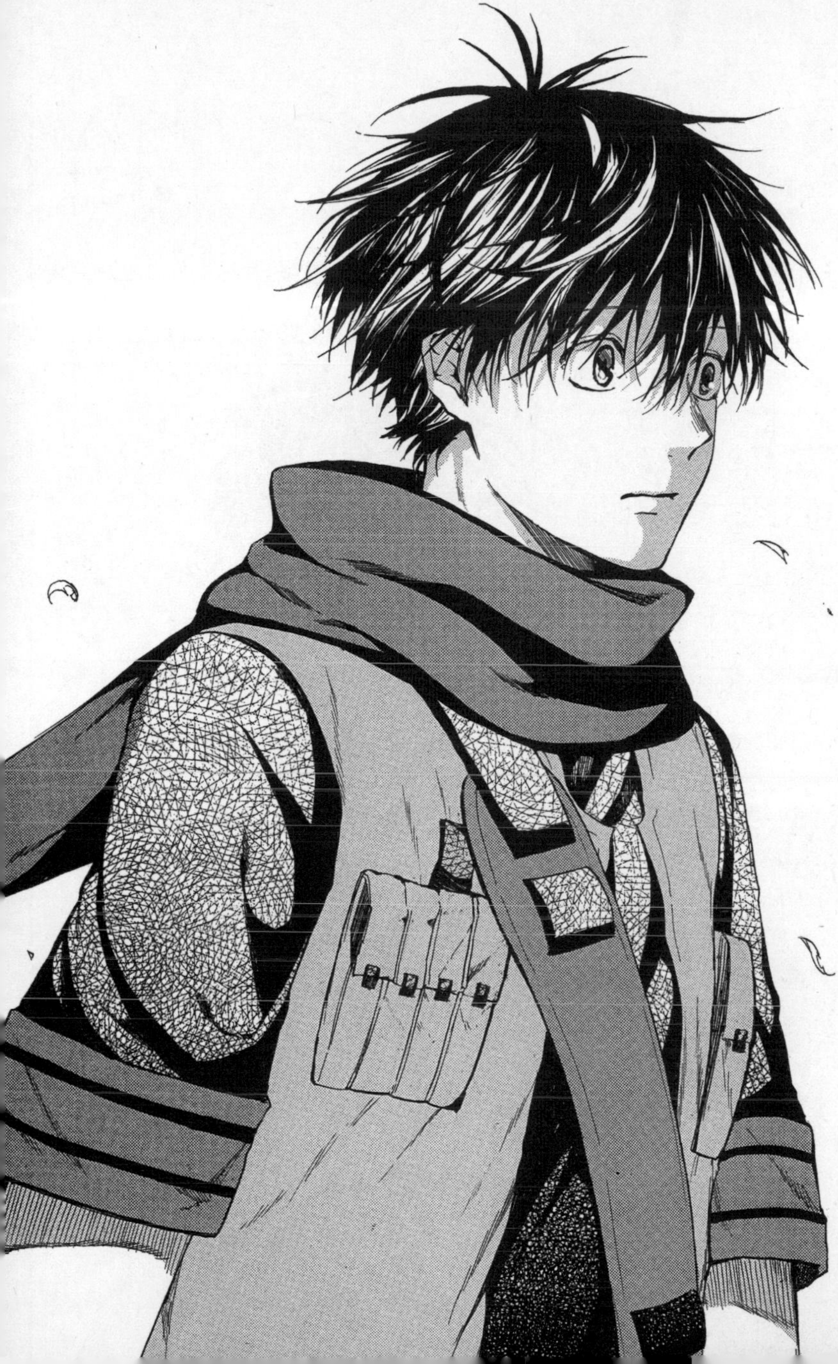

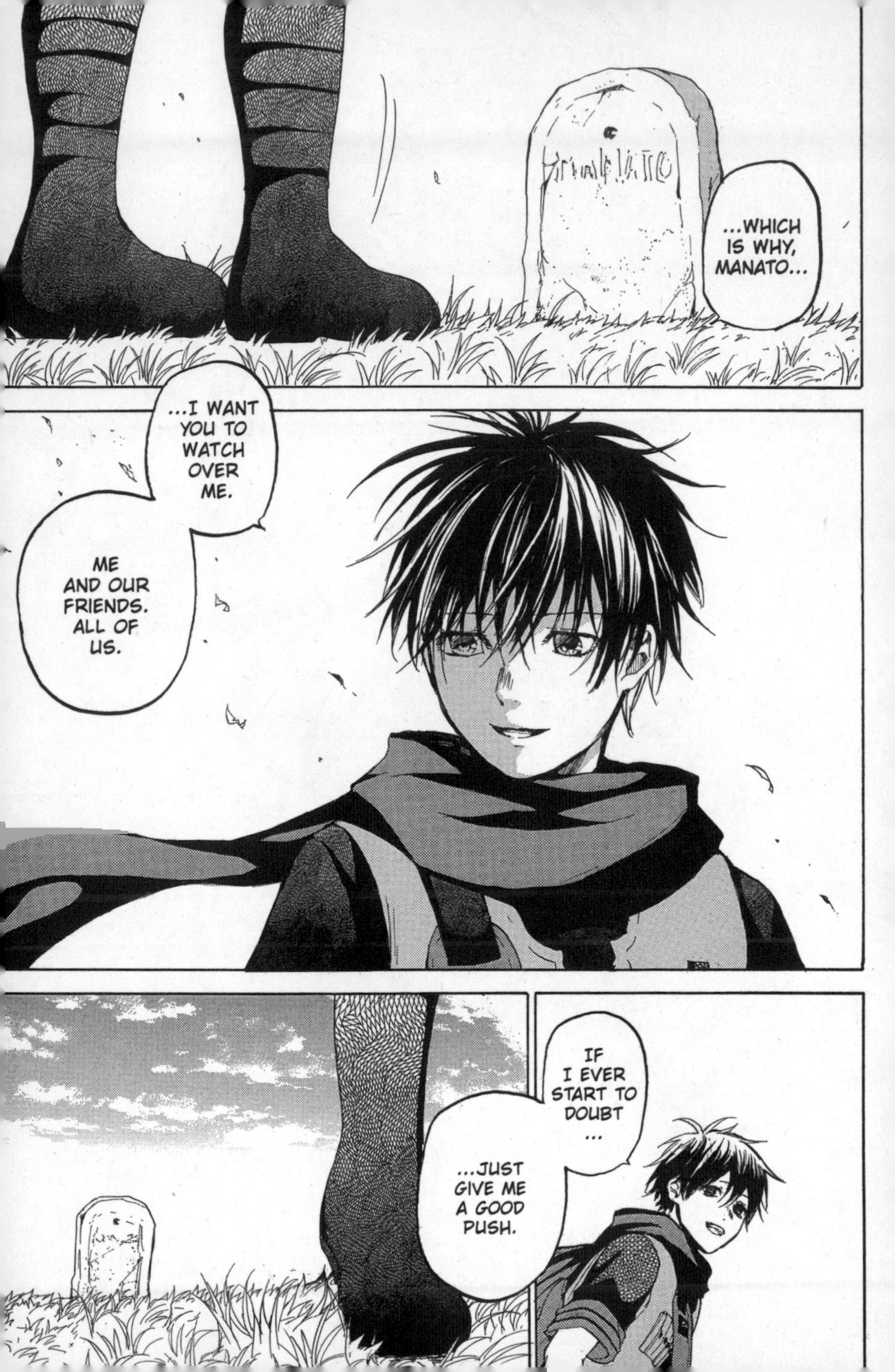
...WHICH IS WHY, MANATO...
...I WANT YOU TO WATCH OVER ME.
ME AND OUR FRIENDS. ALL OF US.
IF I EVER START TO DOUBT...
...JUST GIVE ME A GOOD PUSH.

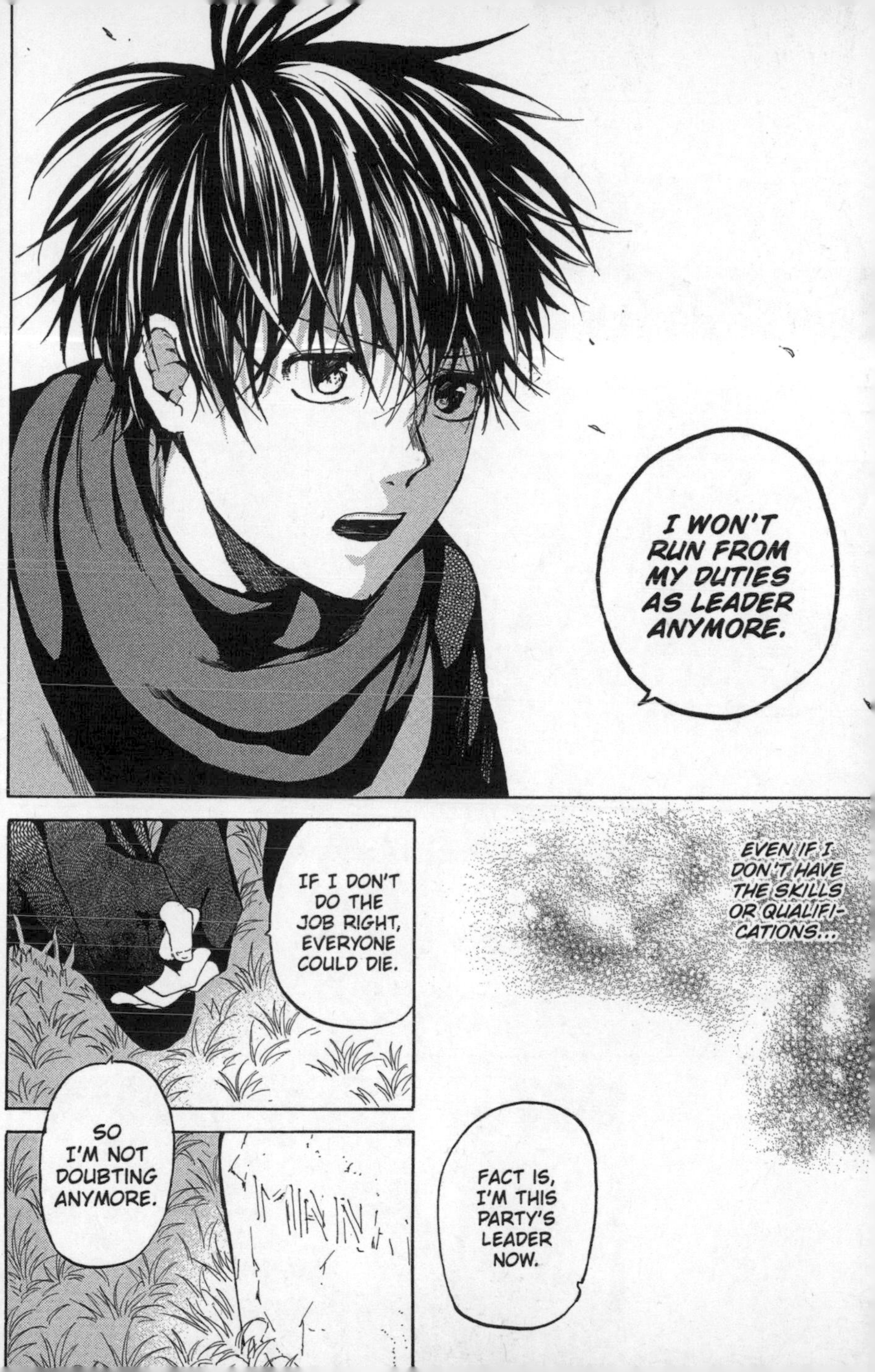
I WON'T RUN FROM MY DUTIES AS LEADER ANYMORE.
EVEN IF I DON'T HAVE THE SKILLS OR QUALIFI-CATIONS...
IF I DON'T DO THE JOB RIGHT, EVERYONE COULD DIE.
FACT IS, I'M THIS PARTY'S LEADER NOW.
SO I'M NOT DOUBTING ANYMORE.

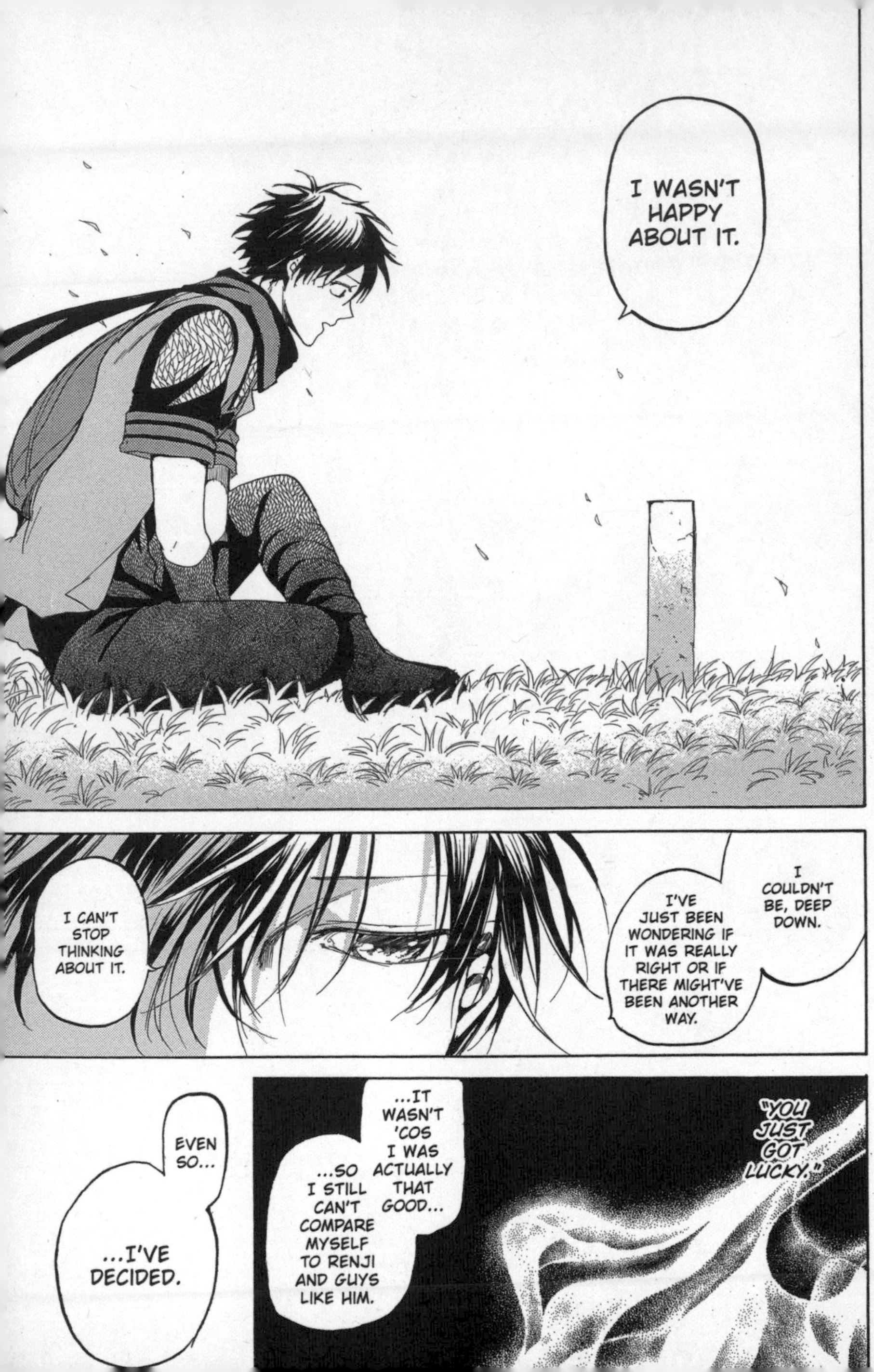
I WASN'T HAPPY ABOUT IT.
I COULDN'T BE, DEEP DOWN.
I'VE JUST BEEN WONDERING IF IT WAS REALLY RIGHT OR IF THERE MIGHT'VE BEEN ANOTHER WAY.
I CAN'T STOP THINKING ABOUT IT.
"YOU JUST GOT LUCKY."
...IT WASN'T 'COS I WAS ACTUALLY THAT GOOD...
...SO I STILL CAN'T COMPARE MYSELF TO RENJI AND GUYS LIKE HIM.
EVEN SO...
...I'VE DECIDED.

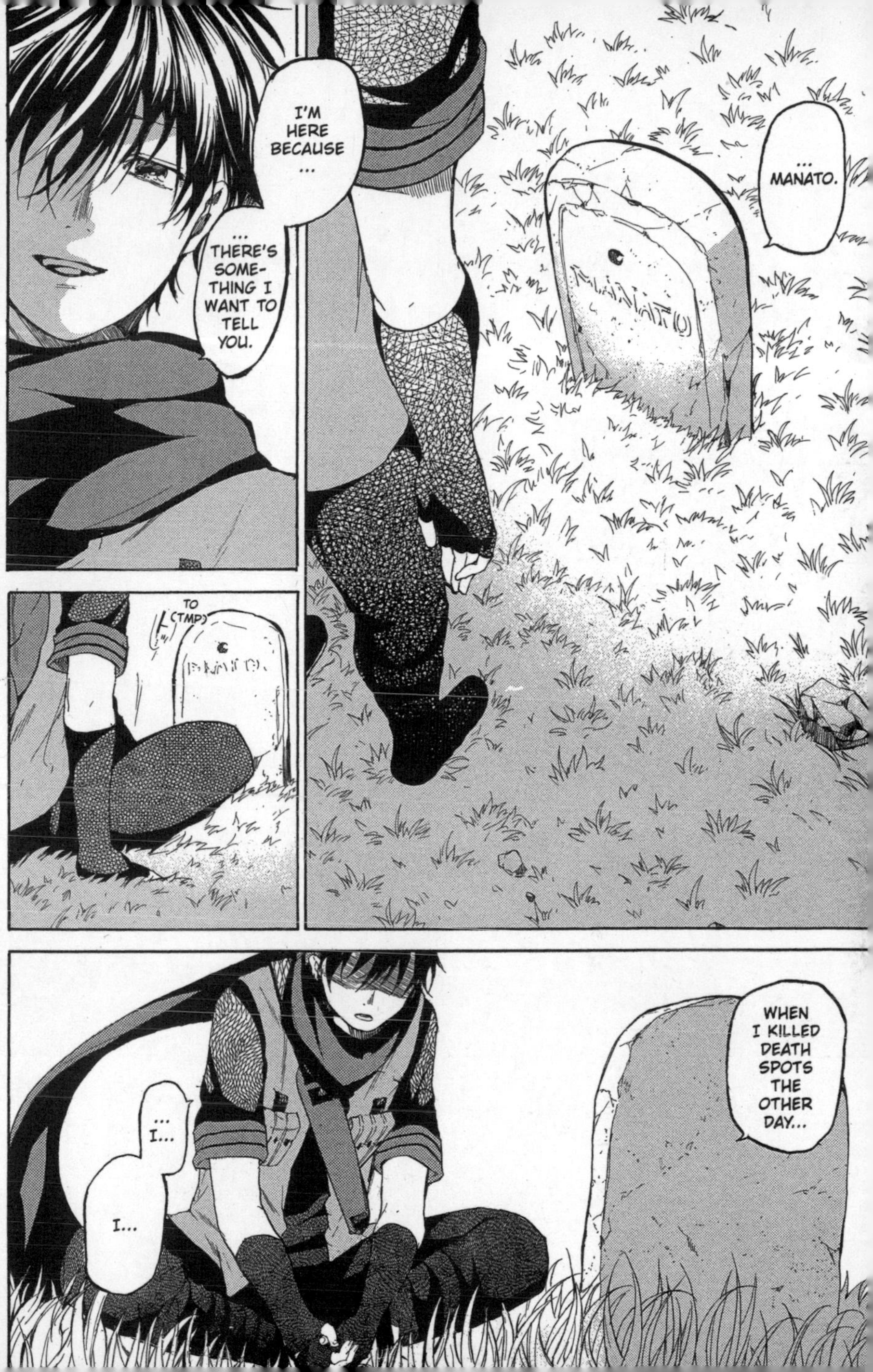
... MANATO.
I'M HERE BECAUSE ...
... THERE'S SOME-THING I WANT TO TELL YOU.
TO (TMP)
WHEN I KILLED DEATH SPOTS THE OTHER DAY...
... I...
I...

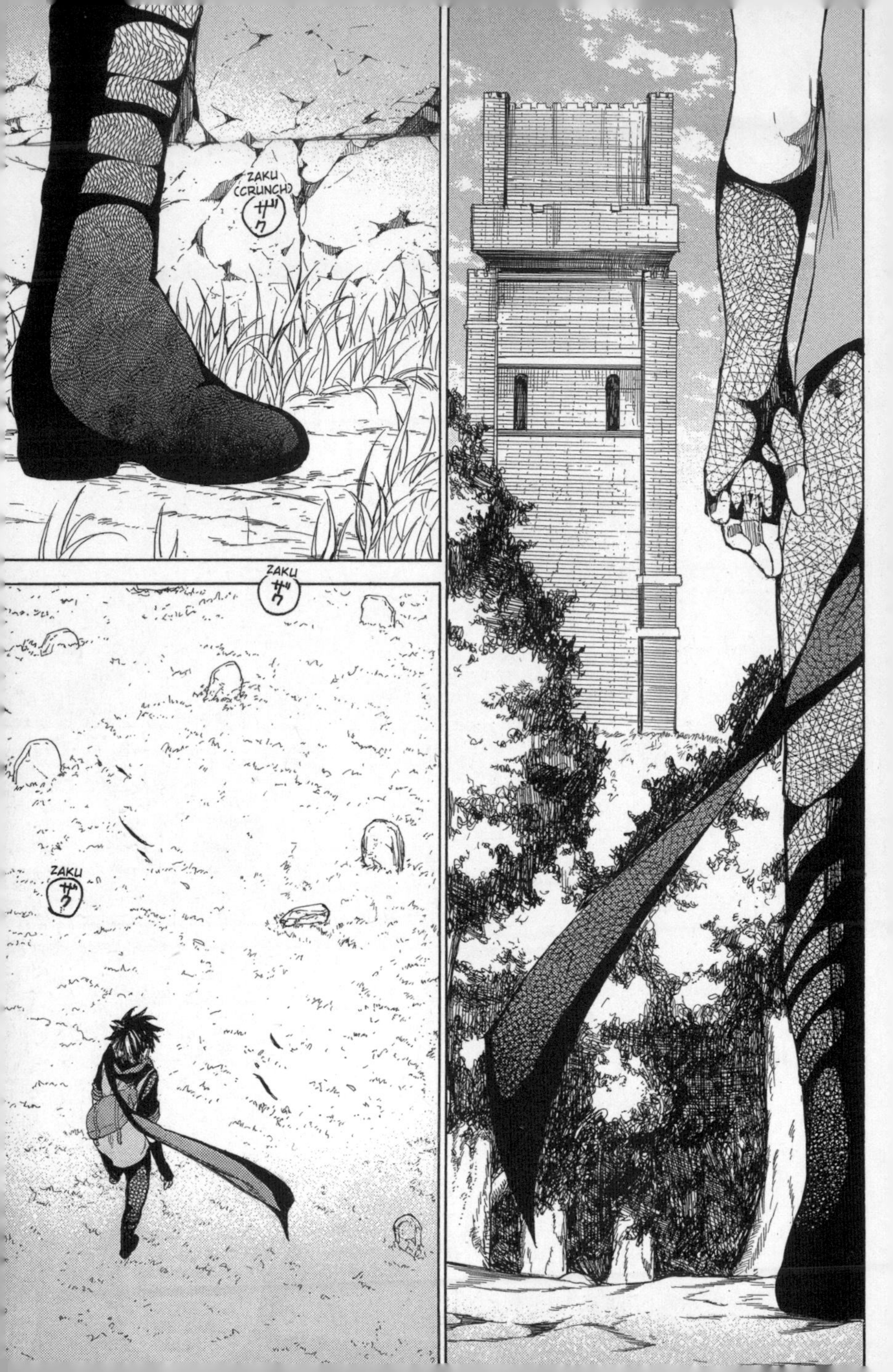
ZAKU (CRUNCH)
ザク
ZAKU
ザク
ZAKU
ザク

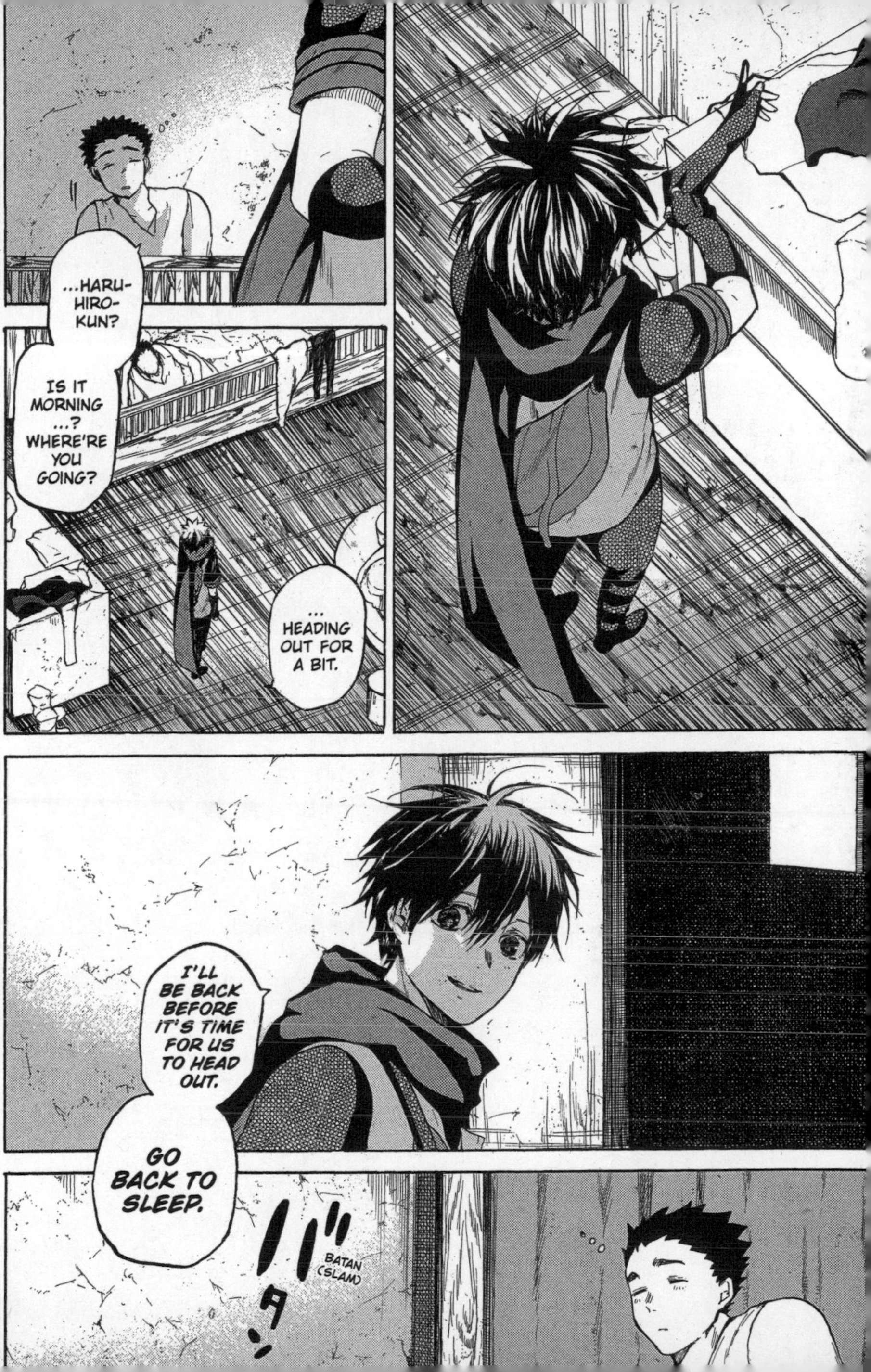
...HARU-HIRO-KUN?
IS IT MORNING ...? WHERE'RE YOU GOING?
... HEADING OUT FOR A BIT.
I'LL BE BACK BEFORE IT'S TIME FOR US TO HEAD OUT.
GO BACK TO SLEEP.
BATAN (SLAM)

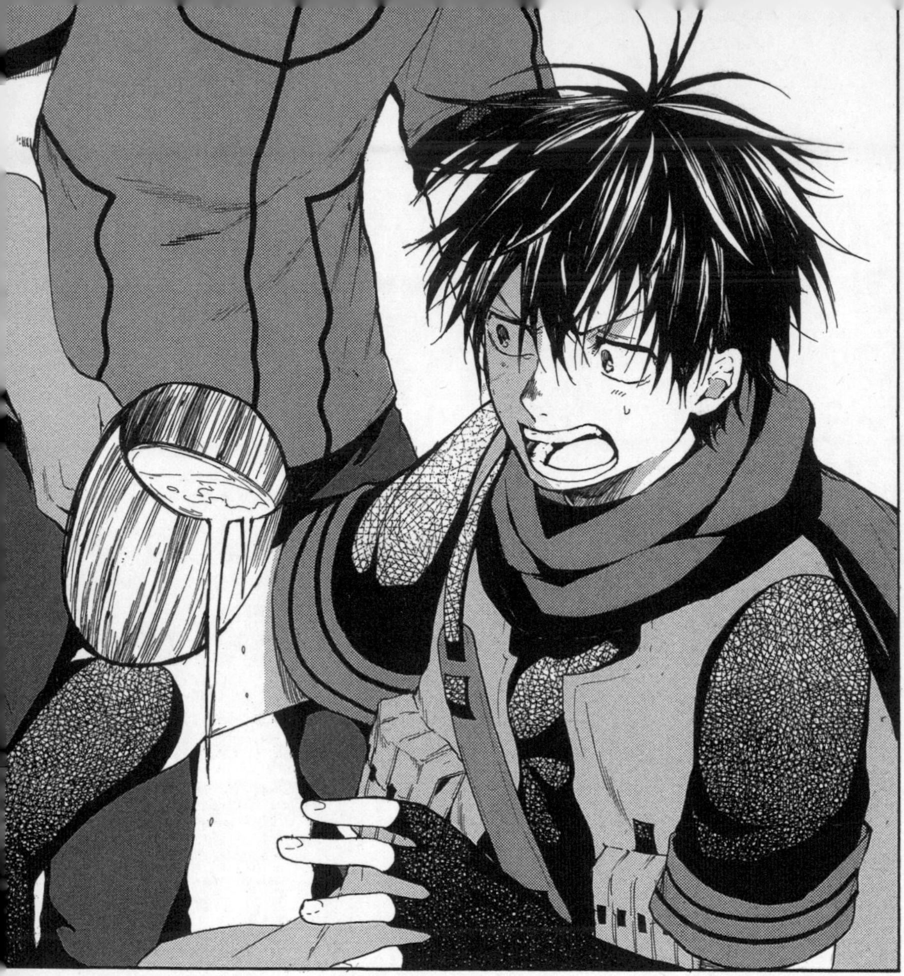
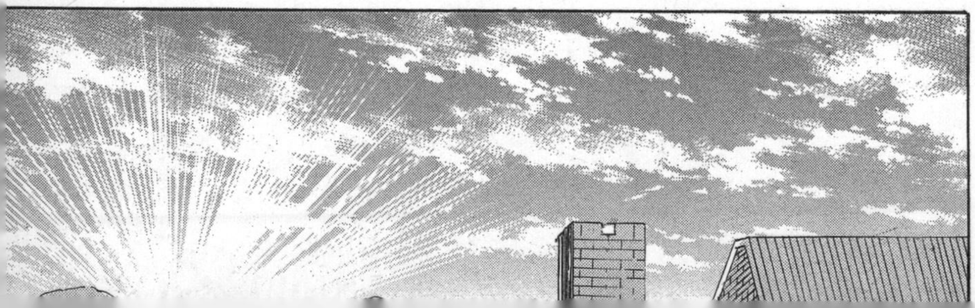

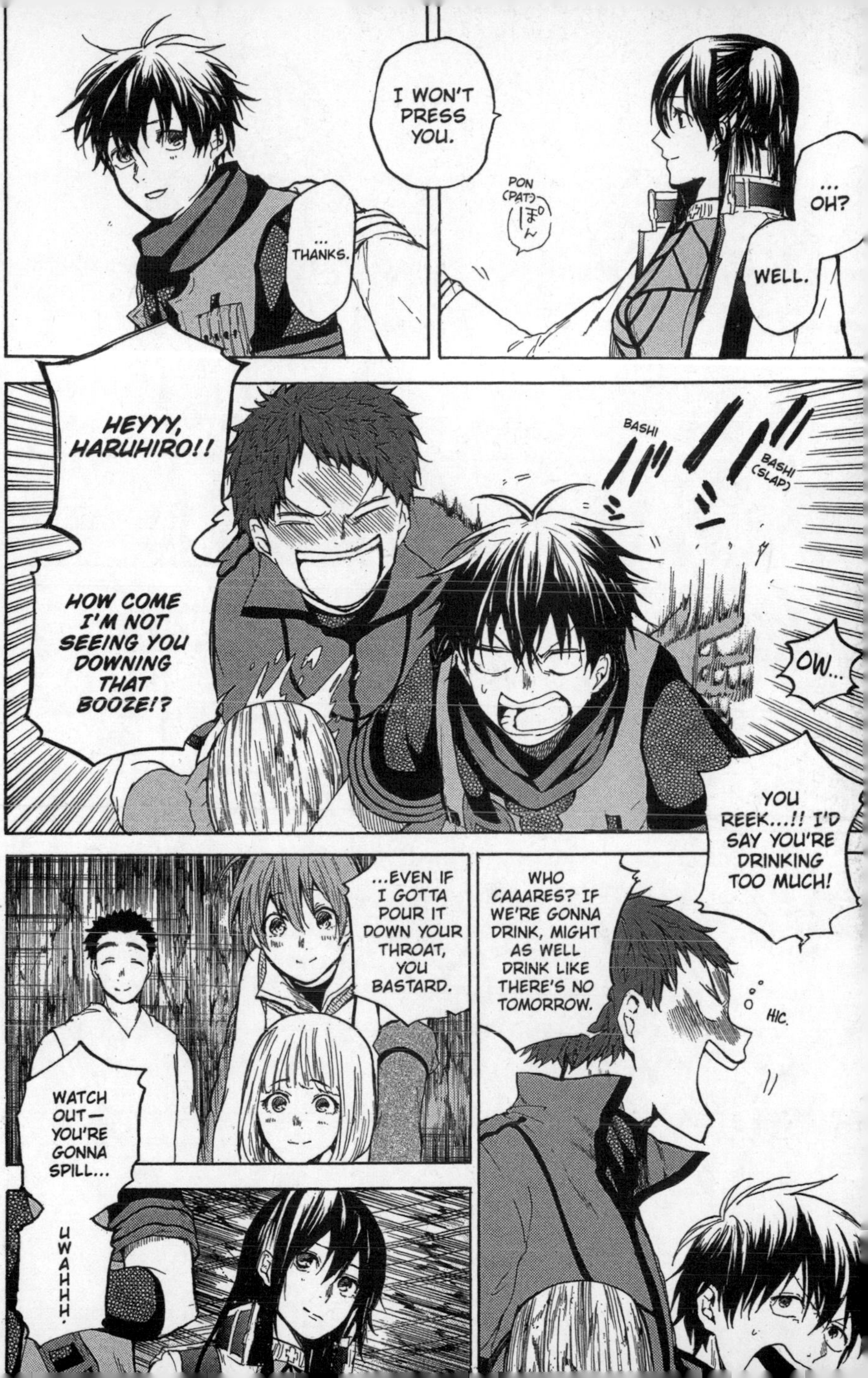
... OH?
WELL.
I WON'T PRESS YOU.
PON (PAT) ぽん
... THANKS.
BASHI
BASHI (SLAP)
HEYYY, HARUHIRO!!
HOW COME I'M NOT SEEING YOU DOWNING THAT BOOZE!?
OW...
YOU REEK...!! I'D SAY YOU'RE DRINKING TOO MUCH!
WHO CAAARES? IF WE'RE GONNA DRINK, MIGHT AS WELL DRINK LIKE THERE'S NO TOMORROW.
HIC.
...EVEN IF I GOTTA POUR IT DOWN YOUR THROAT, YOU BASTARD.
WATCH OUT— YOU'RE GONNA SPILL...
UWAHHH.

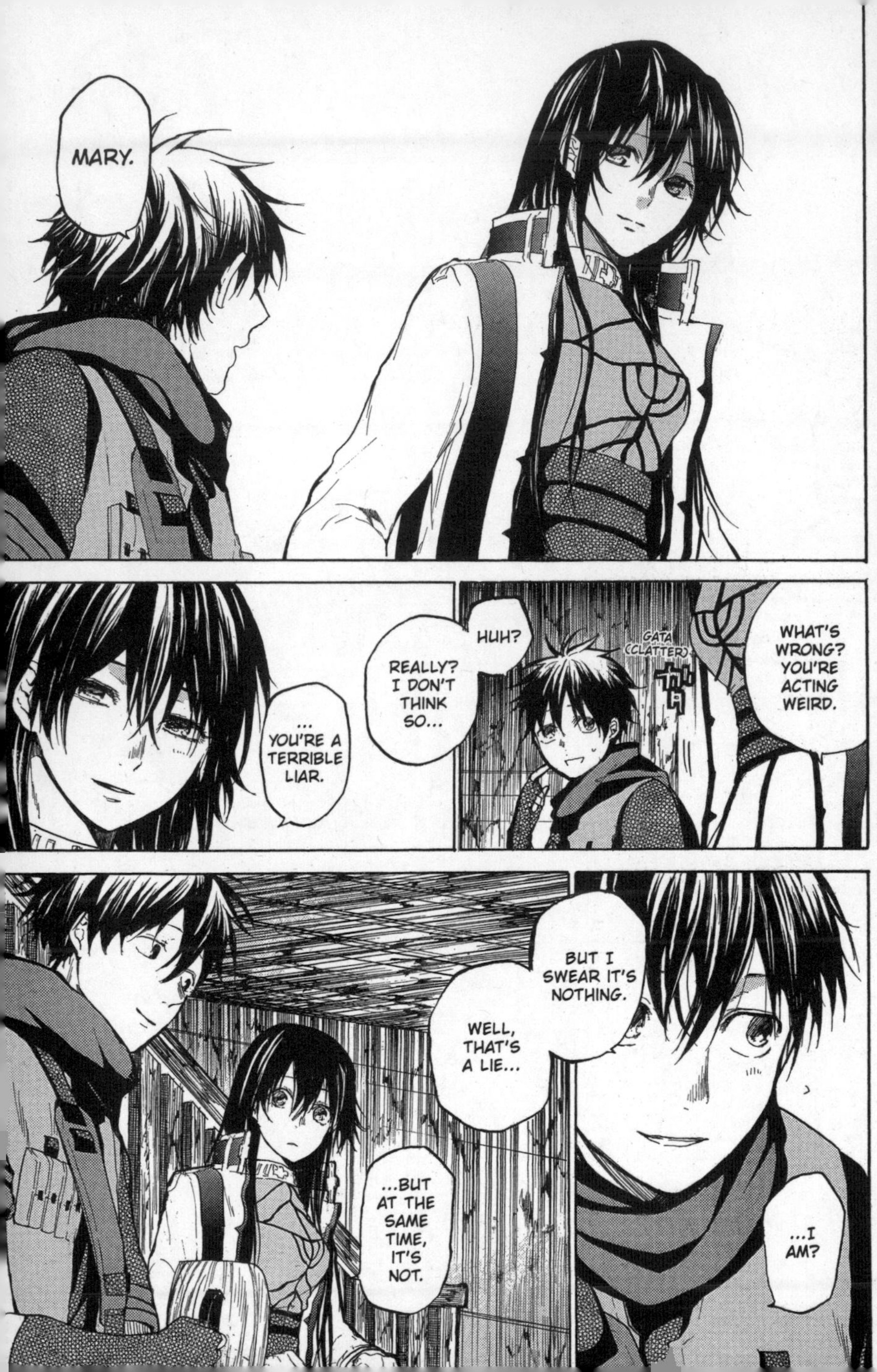
MARY.
WHAT'S WRONG? YOU'RE ACTING WEIRD.
GATA (CLATTER)
HUH?
REALLY? I DON'T THINK SO...
... YOU'RE A TERRIBLE LIAR.
...I AM?
WELL, THAT'S A LIE...
BUT I SWEAR IT'S NOTHING.
...BUT AT THE SAME TIME, IT'S NOT.

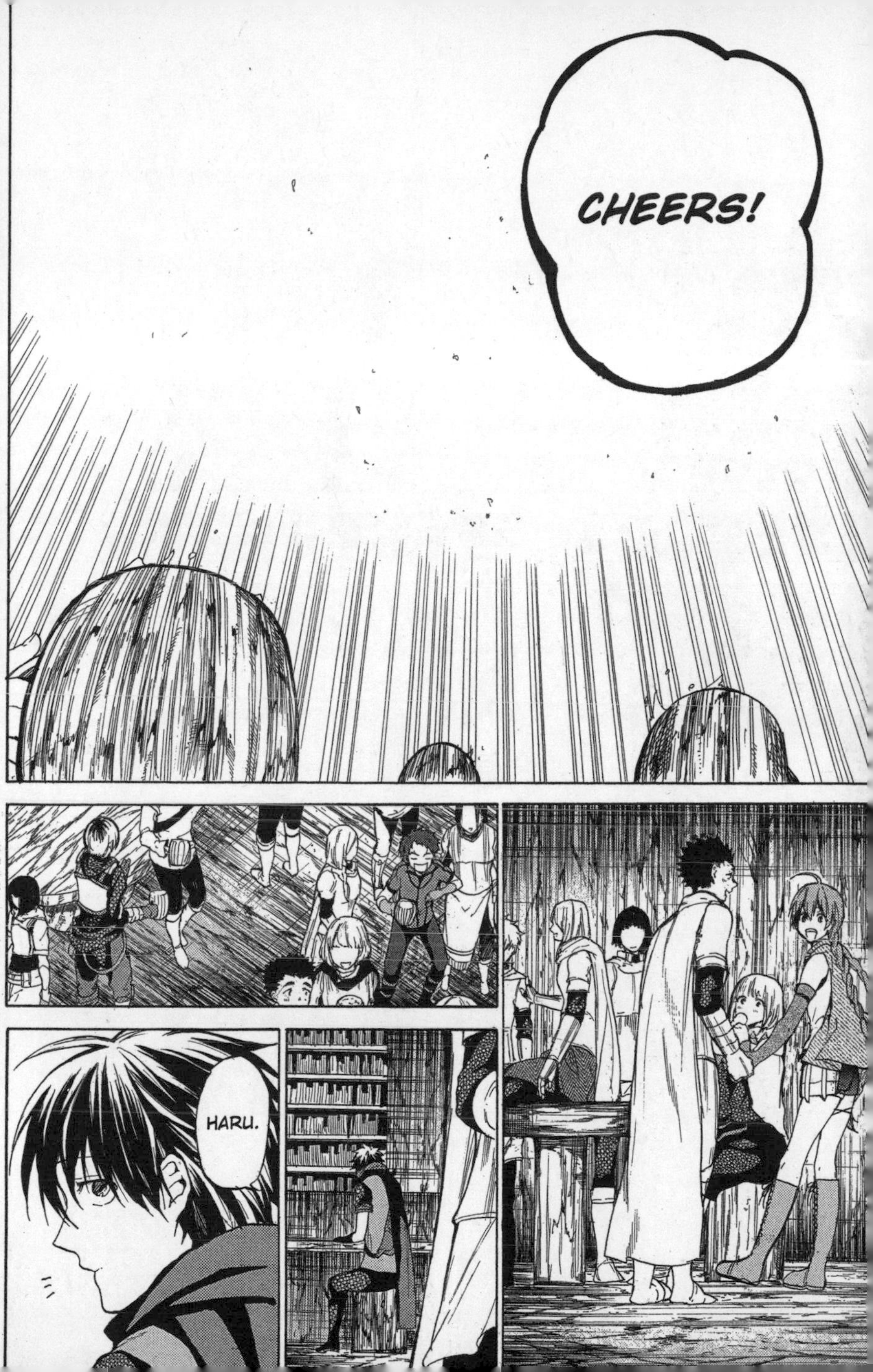
CHEERS!
HARU.

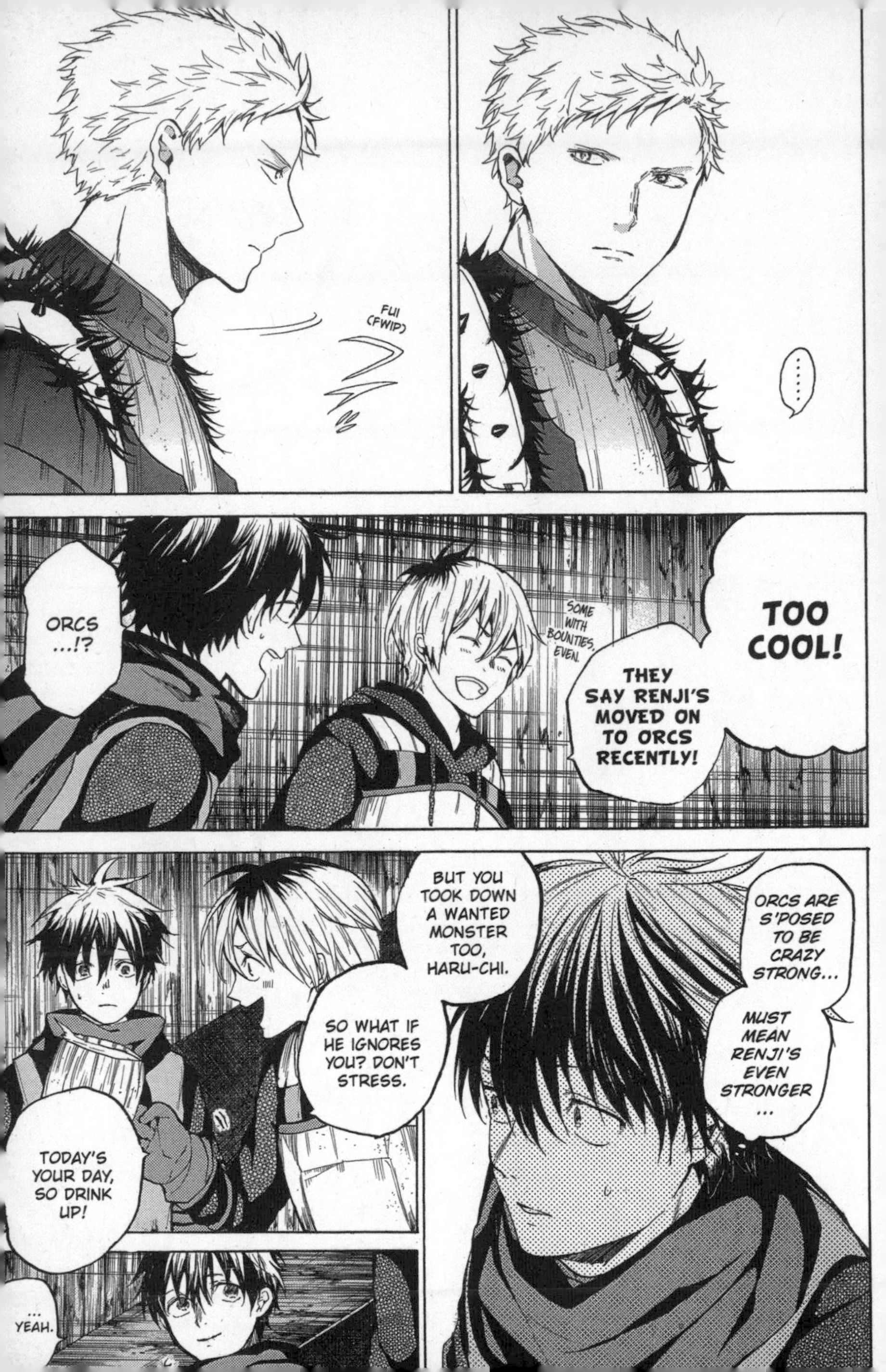
……
FUI (FWIP)
TOO COOL!
THEY SAY RENJI'S MOVED ON TO ORCS RECENTLY!
SOME WITH BOUNTIES, EVEN.
ORCS …!?
ORCS ARE S'POSED TO BE CRAZY STRONG…
MUST MEAN RENJI'S EVEN STRONGER …
BUT YOU TOOK DOWN A WANTED MONSTER TOO, HARU-CHI.
SO WHAT IF HE IGNORES YOU? DON'T STRESS.
TODAY'S YOUR DAY, SO DRINK UP!
… YEAH.

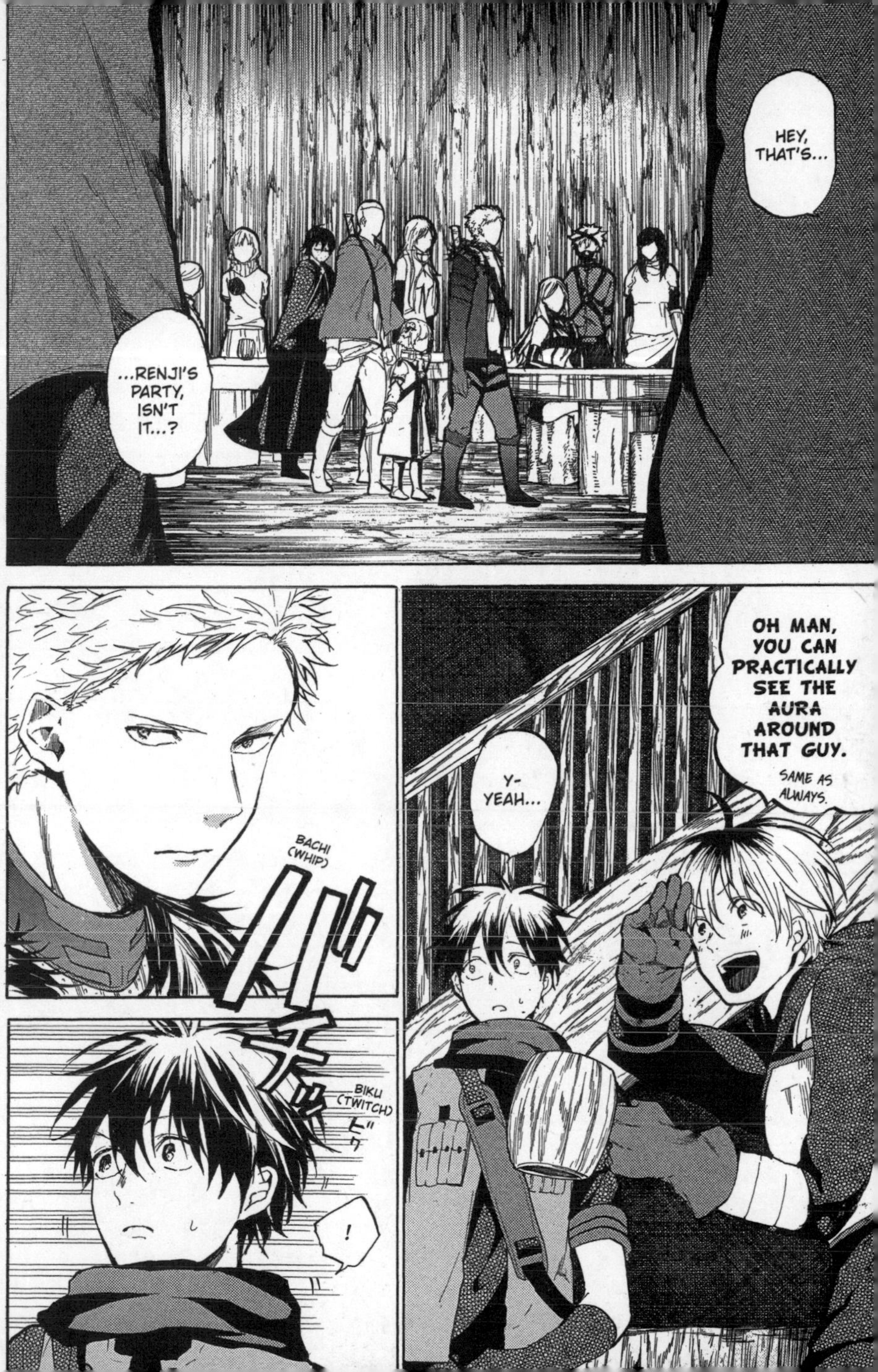
HEY, THAT'S...
...RENJI'S PARTY, ISN'T IT...?
OH MAN, YOU CAN PRACTICALLY SEE THE AURA AROUND THAT GUY.
SAME AS ALWAYS.
Y-YEAH...
BACHI (WHIP)
BIKU (TWITCH)
!

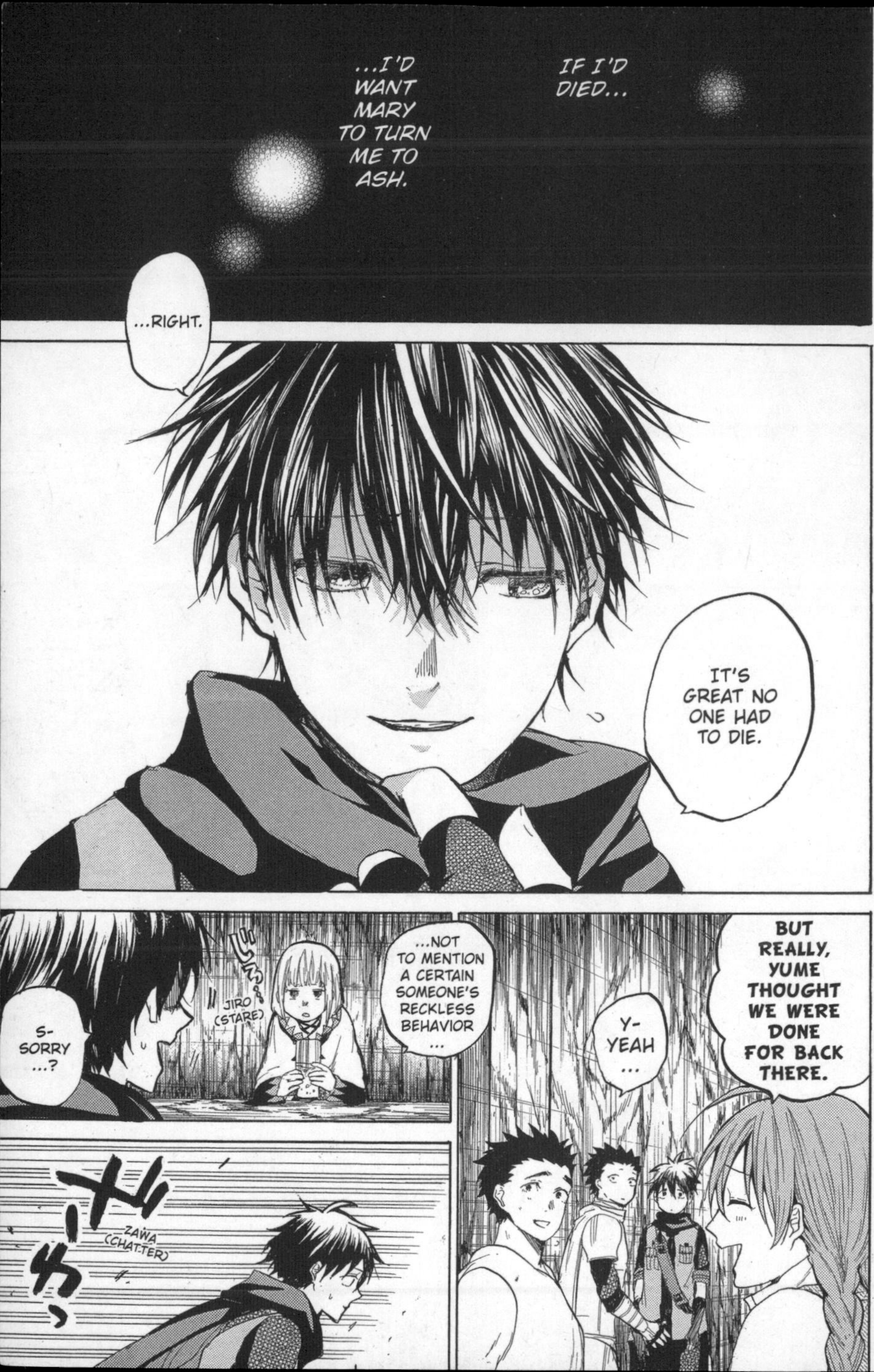
IF I'D DIED...
...I'D WANT MARY TO TURN ME TO ASH.
...RIGHT.
IT'S GREAT NO ONE HAD TO DIE.
BUT REALLY, YUME THOUGHT WE WERE DONE FOR BACK THERE.
Y-YEAH...
...NOT TO MENTION A CERTAIN SOMEONE'S RECKLESS BEHAVIOR...
JIRO (STARE)
S-SORRY...?
ZAWA (CHATTER)

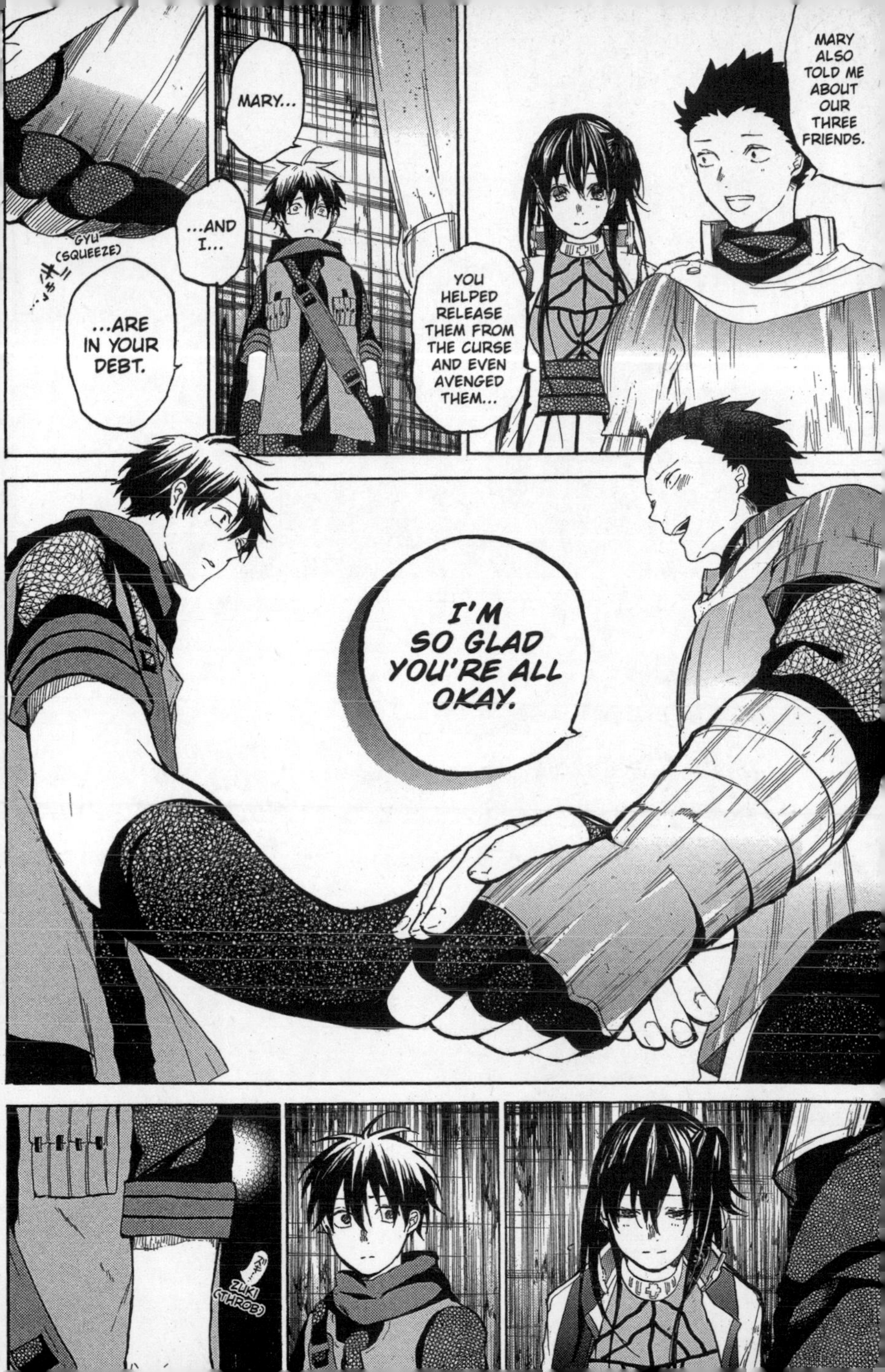
MARY ALSO TOLD ME ABOUT OUR THREE FRIENDS.
YOU HELPED RELEASE THEM FROM THE CURSE AND EVEN AVENGED THEM...
MARY...
...AND I...
GYU (SQUEEZE)
...ARE IN YOUR DEBT.
I'M SO GLAD YOU'RE ALL OKAY.
ZUKI (THROB)

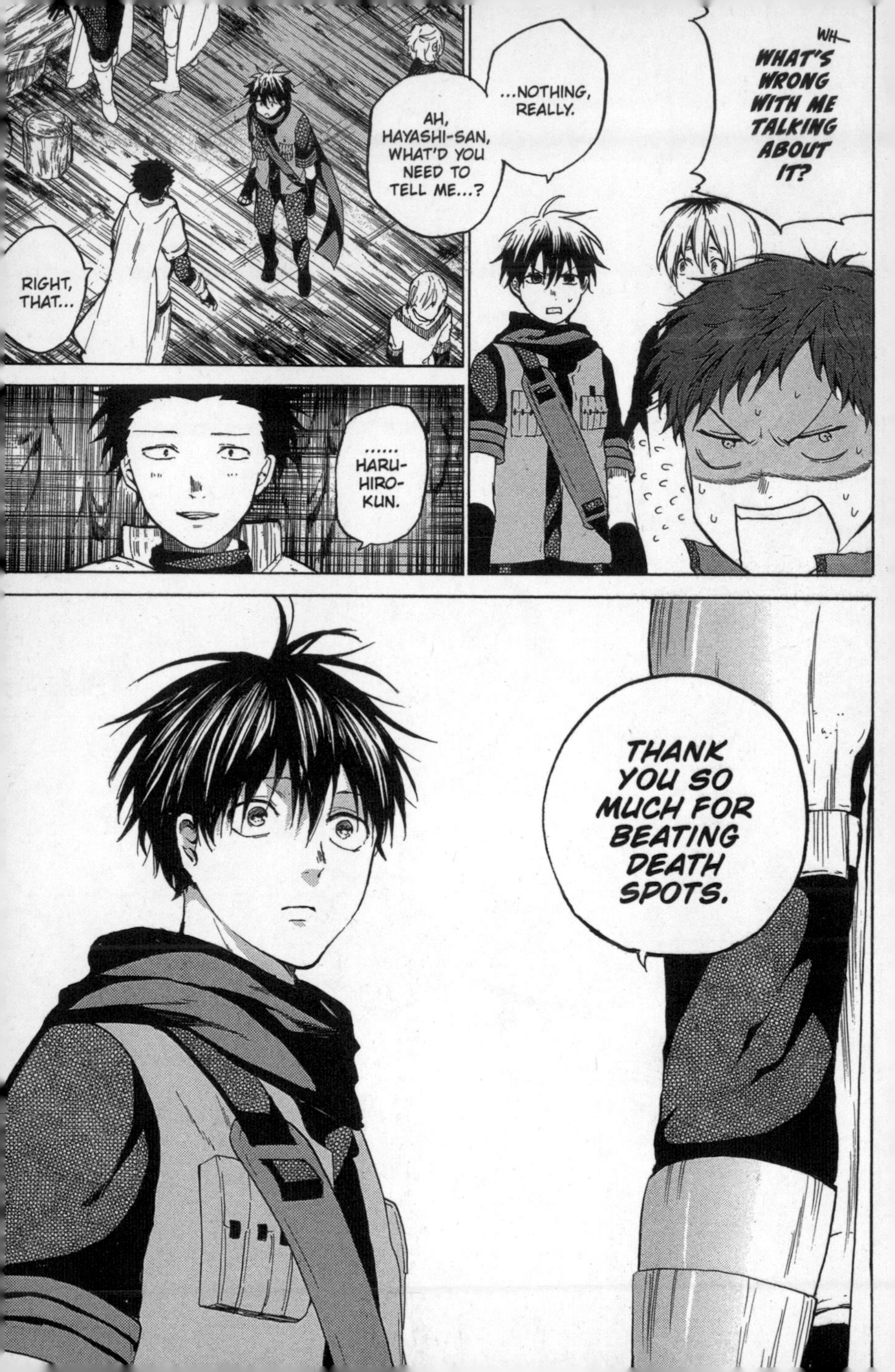
WH-
WHAT'S WRONG WITH ME TALKING ABOUT IT?
...NOTHING, REALLY.
AH, HAYASHI-SAN, WHAT'D YOU NEED TO TELL ME...?
RIGHT, THAT...
......
HARUHIRO-KUN.
THANK YOU SO MUCH FOR BEATING DEATH SPOTS.

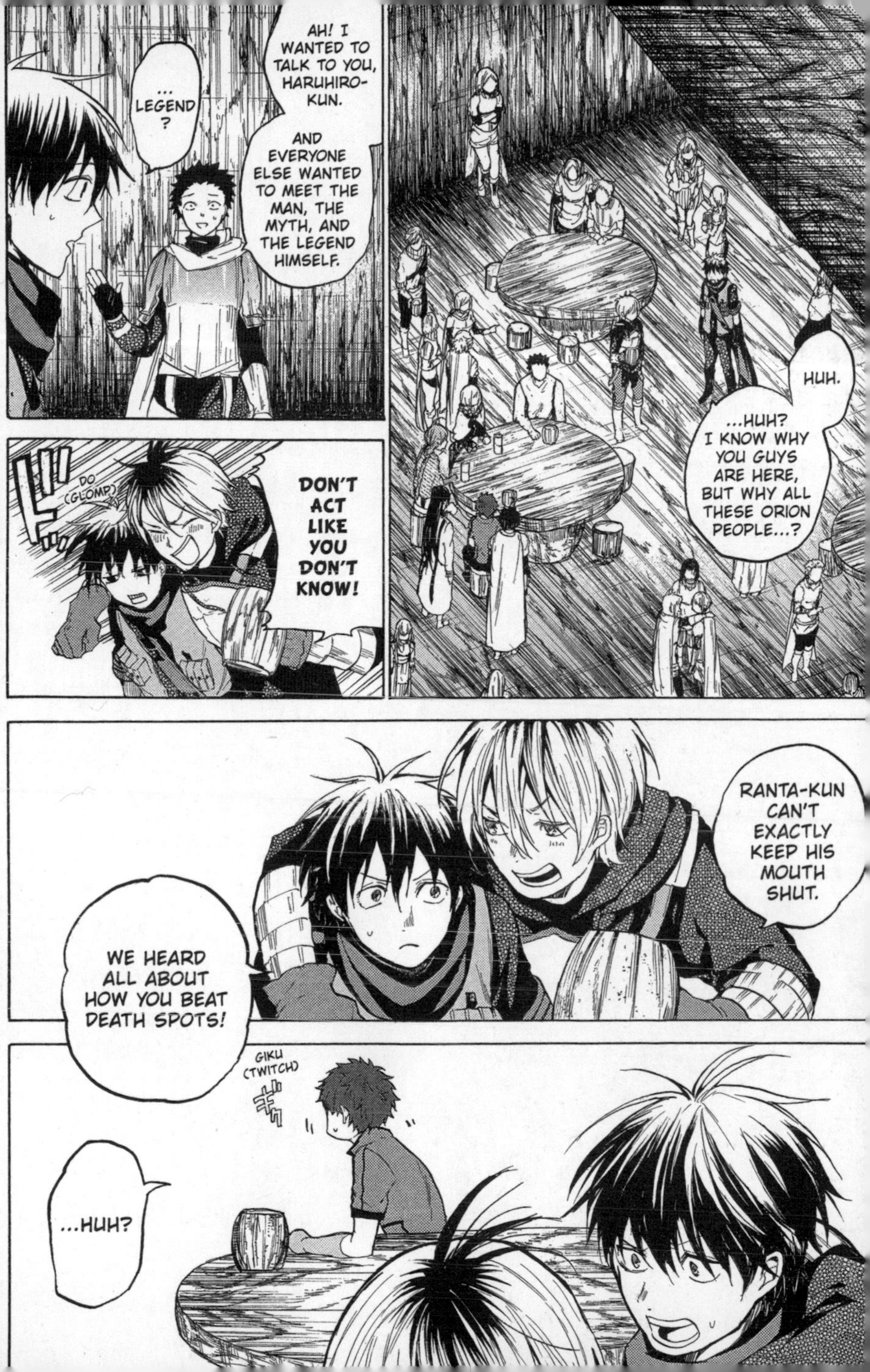
HUH.
...HUH? I KNOW WHY YOU GUYS ARE HERE, BUT WHY ALL THESE ORION PEOPLE...?
AH! I WANTED TO TALK TO YOU, HARUHIRO-KUN.
AND EVERYONE ELSE WANTED TO MEET THE MAN, THE MYTH, AND THE LEGEND HIMSELF.
...LEGEND?
DO (GLOMP)
DON'T ACT LIKE YOU DON'T KNOW!
RANTA-KUN CAN'T EXACTLY KEEP HIS MOUTH SHUT.
WE HEARD ALL ABOUT HOW YOU BEAT DEATH SPOTS!
GIKU (TWITCH)
...HUH?

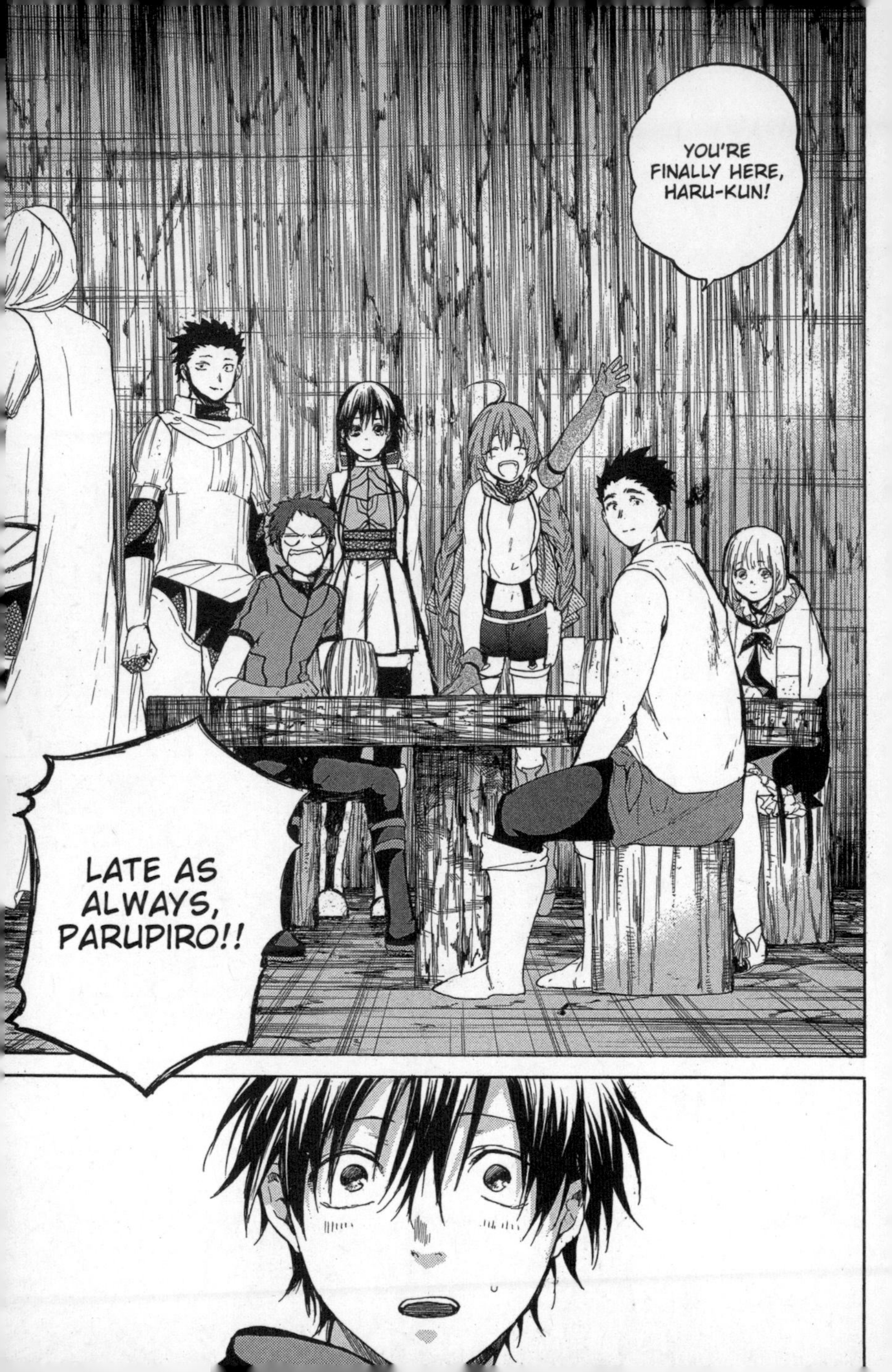
YOU'RE FINALLY HERE, HARU-KUN!
LATE AS ALWAYS, PARUPIRO!!

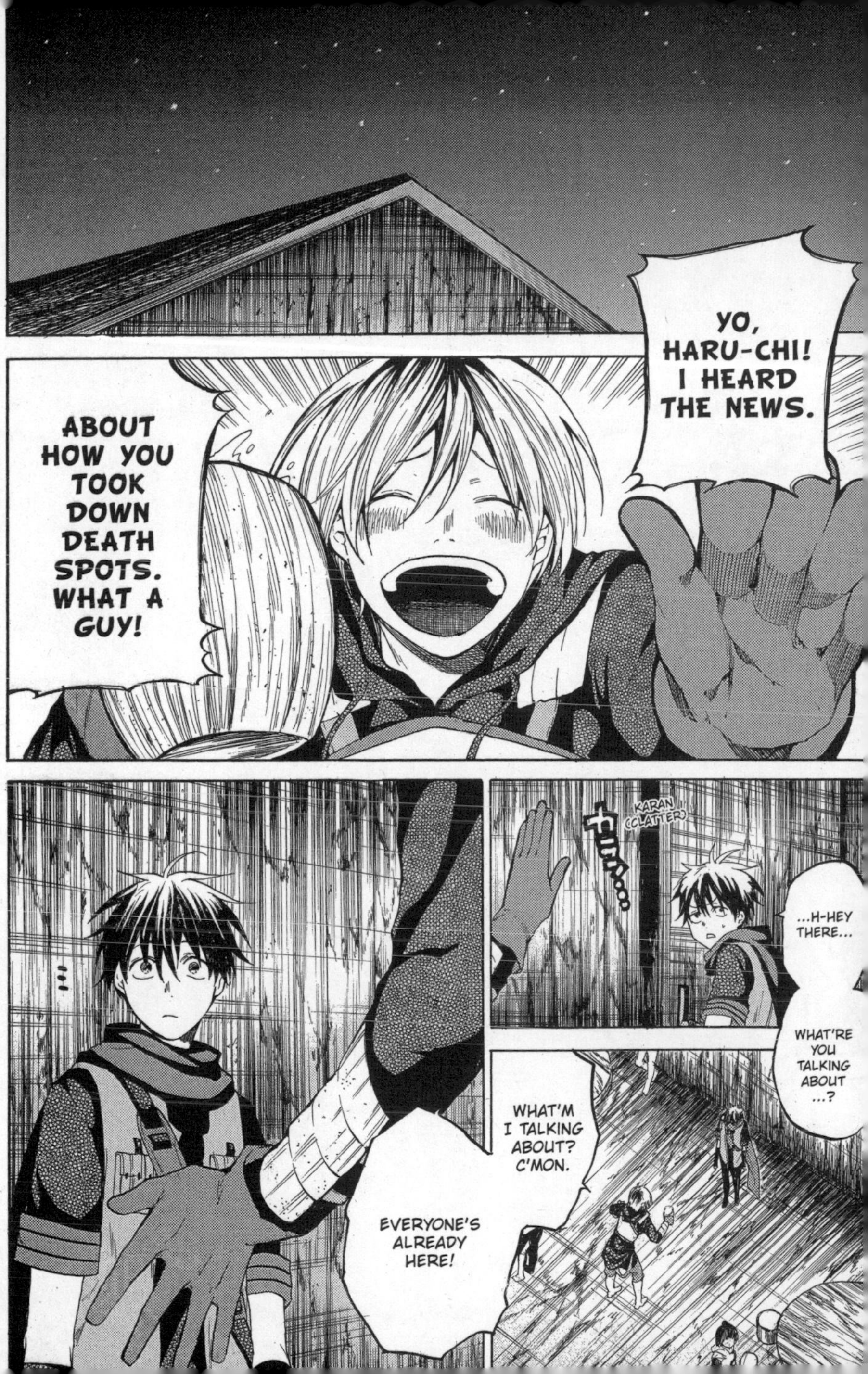
YO, HARU-CHI! I HEARD THE NEWS.
ABOUT HOW YOU TOOK DOWN DEATH SPOTS. WHAT A GUY!
KARAN (CLATTER)
...H-HEY THERE...
WHAT'RE YOU TALKING ABOUT ...?
WHAT'M I TALKING ABOUT? C'MON.
EVERYONE'S ALREADY HERE!

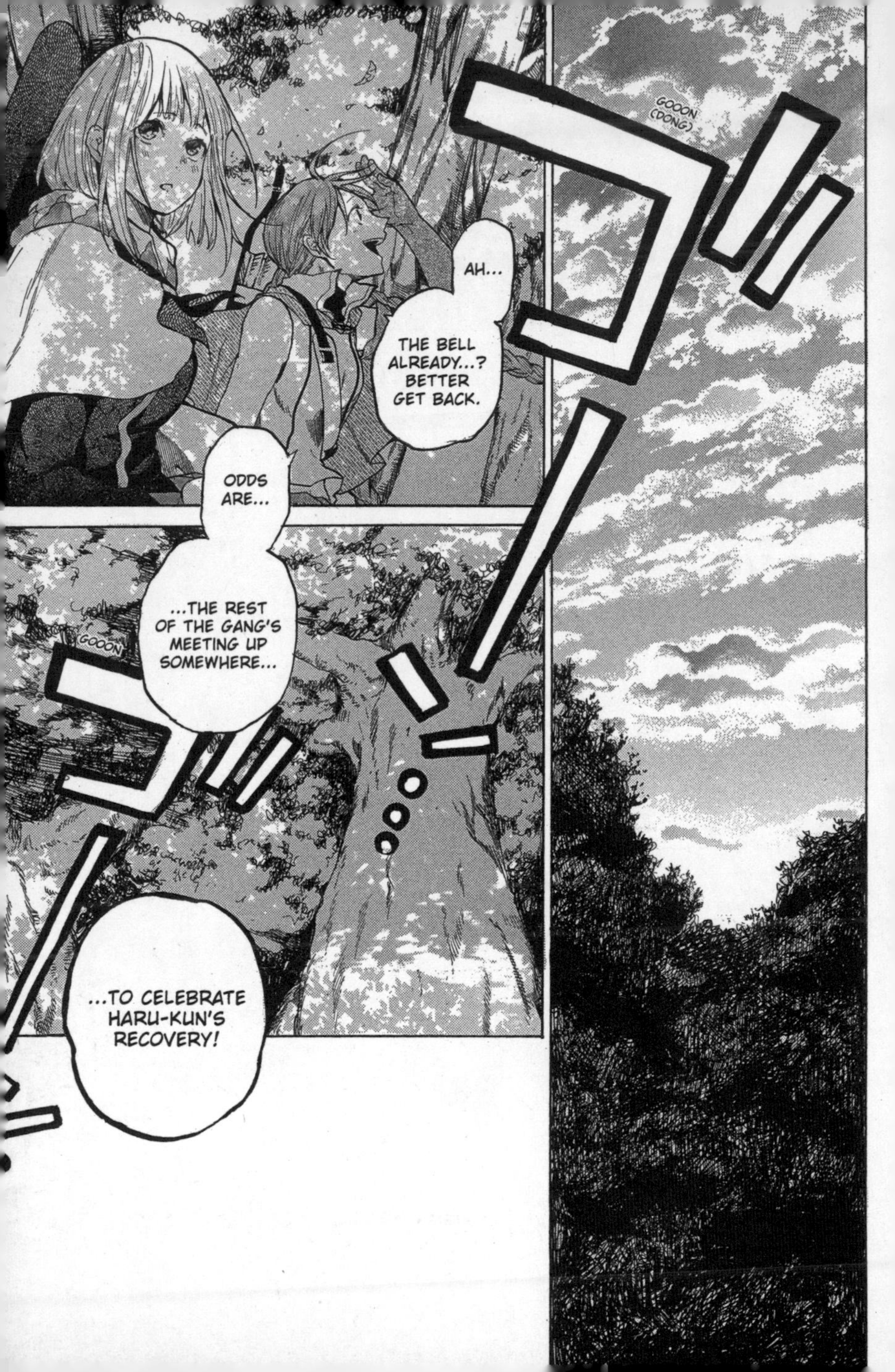
GOOON (DONG)
AH...
THE BELL ALREADY...? BETTER GET BACK.
ODDS ARE...
...THE REST OF THE GANG'S MEETING UP SOMEWHERE...
GOOON
...TO CELEBRATE HARU-KUN'S RECOVERY!

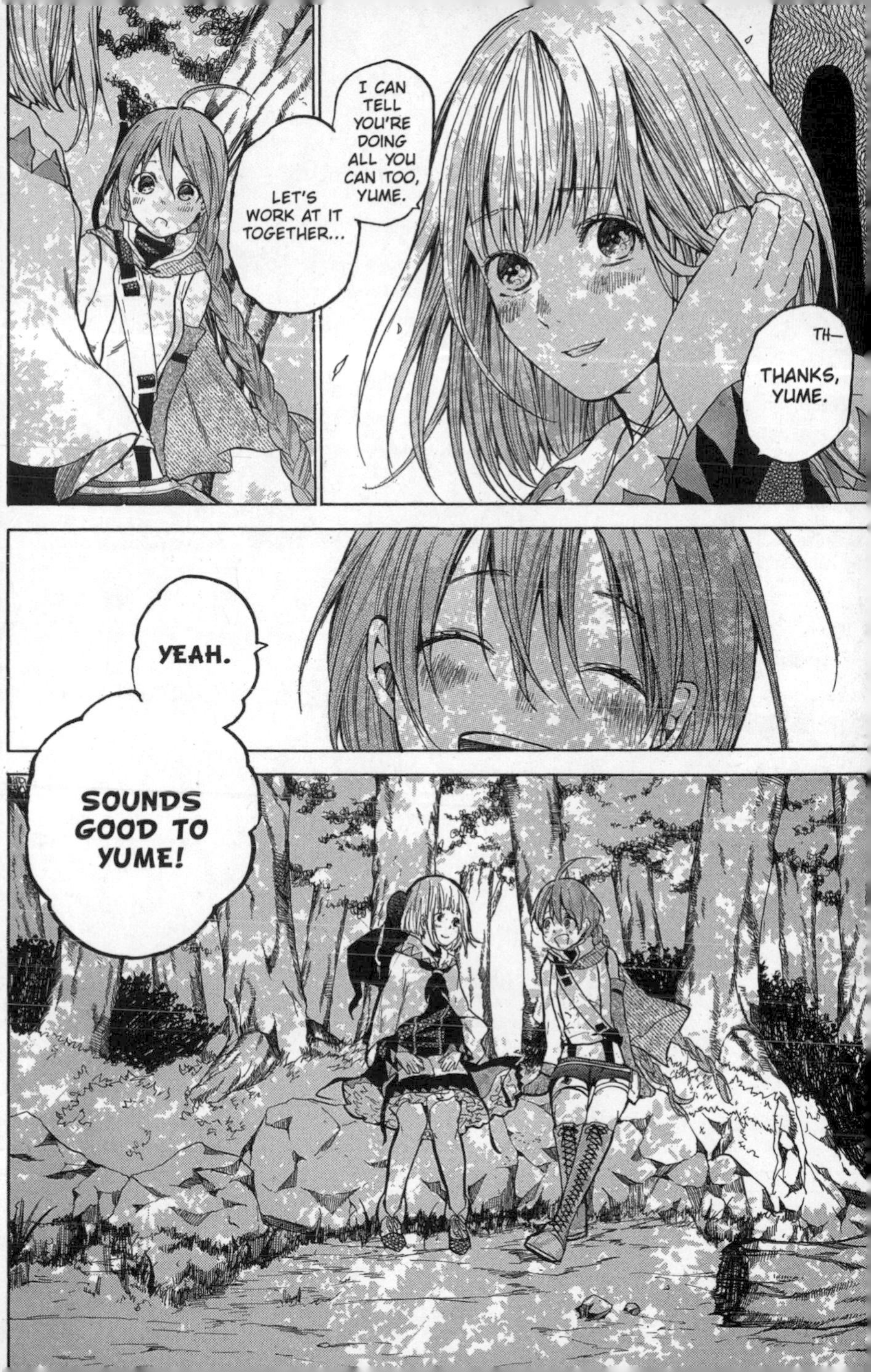
TH—
THANKS, YUME.
I CAN TELL YOU'RE DOING ALL YOU CAN TOO, YUME.
LET'S WORK AT IT TOGETHER...
YEAH.
SOUNDS GOOD TO YUME!

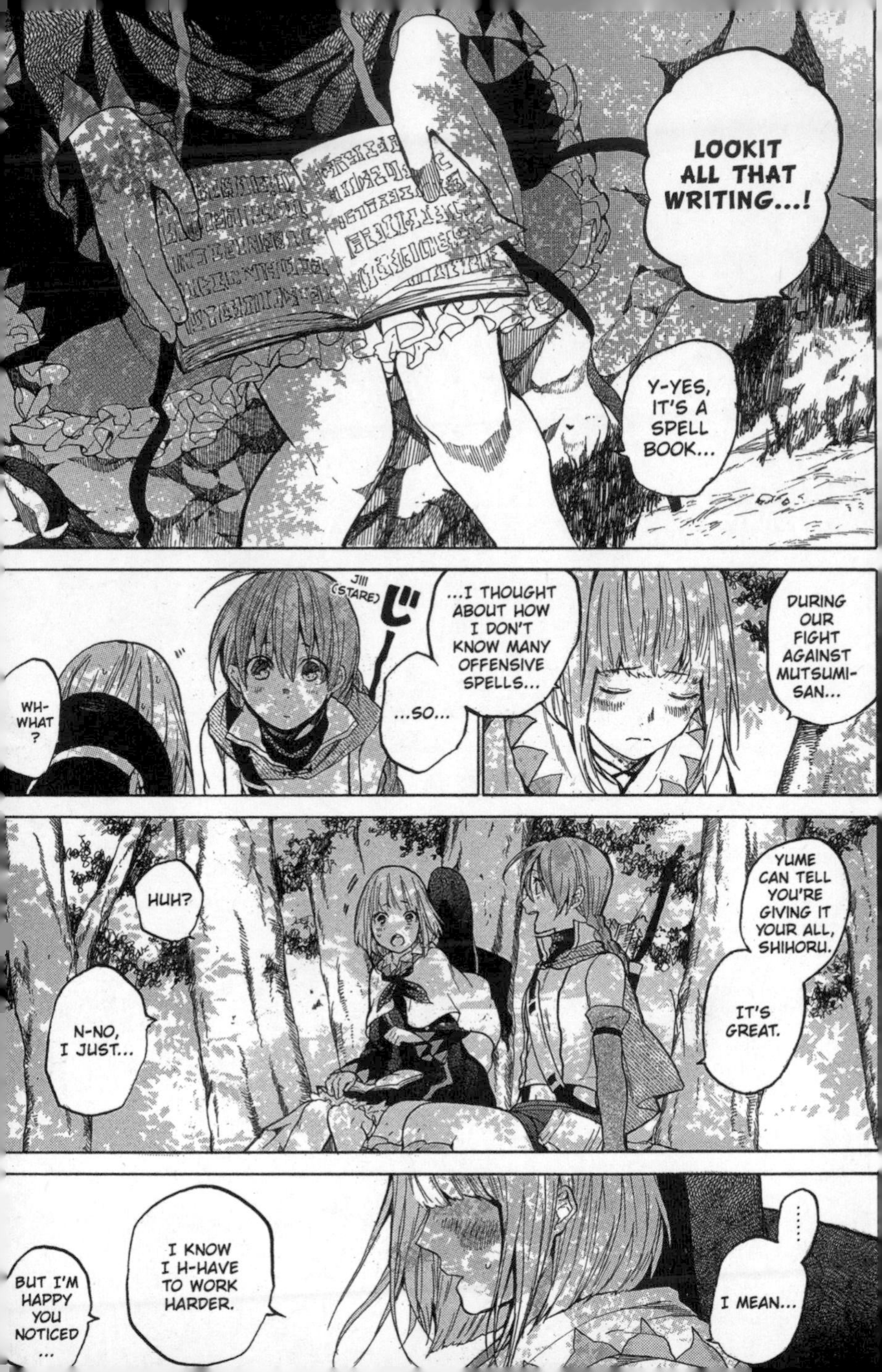
LOOKIT ALL THAT WRITING...!
Y-YES, IT'S A SPELL BOOK...
DURING OUR FIGHT AGAINST MUTSUMI-SAN...
...I THOUGHT ABOUT HOW I DON'T KNOW MANY OFFENSIVE SPELLS...
...SO...
JIII (STARE)
じ
WH-WHAT?
YUME CAN TELL YOU'RE GIVING IT YOUR ALL, SHIHORU.
IT'S GREAT.
HUH?
N-NO, I JUST...
......
I MEAN...
I KNOW I H-HAVE TO WORK HARDER.
BUT I'M HAPPY YOU NOTICED...

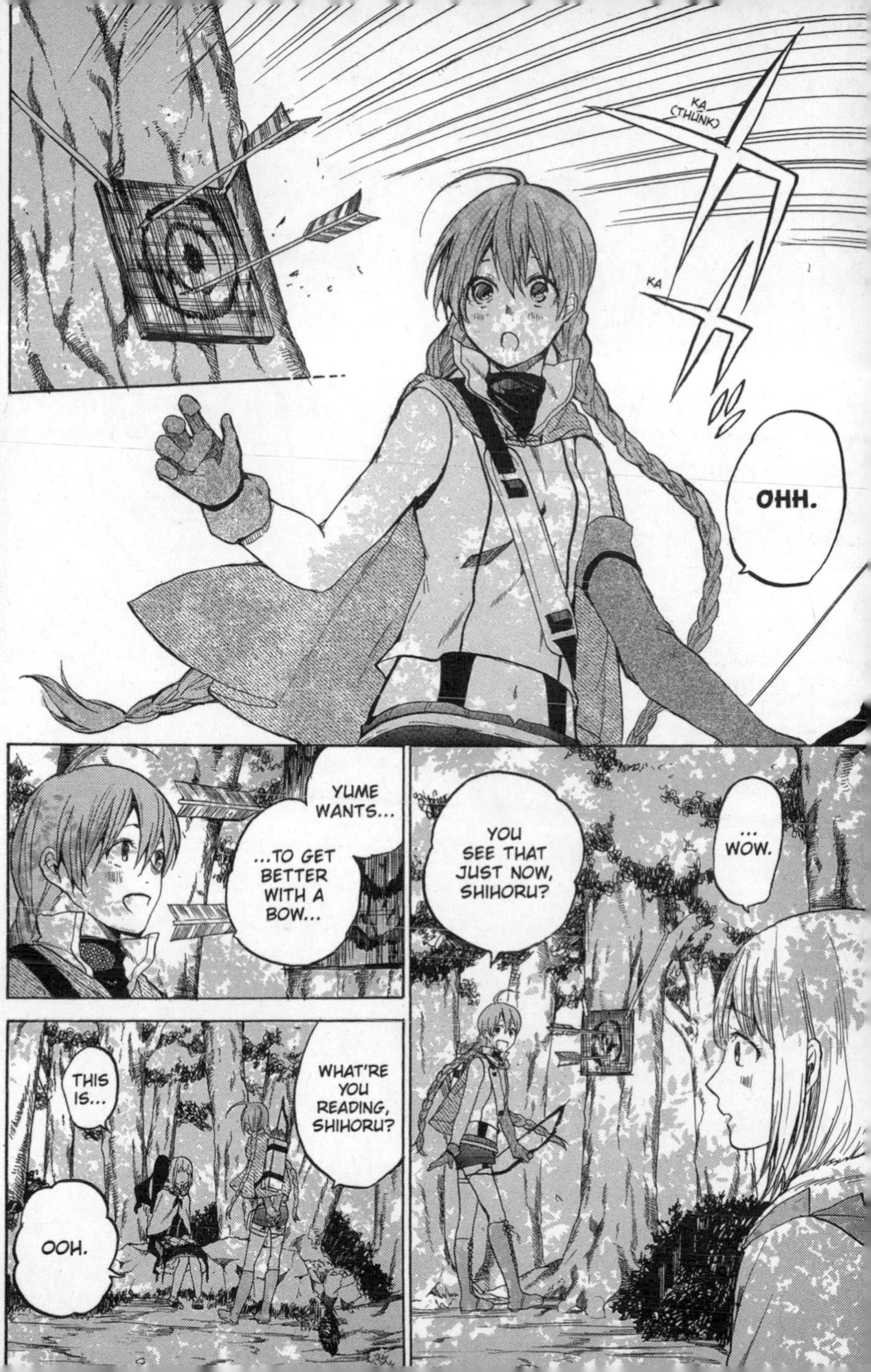
KA (THUNK)
KA
OHH.
... WOW.
YOU SEE THAT JUST NOW, SHIHORU?
YUME WANTS...
...TO GET BETTER WITH A BOW...
WHAT'RE YOU READING, SHIHORU?
THIS IS...
OOH.

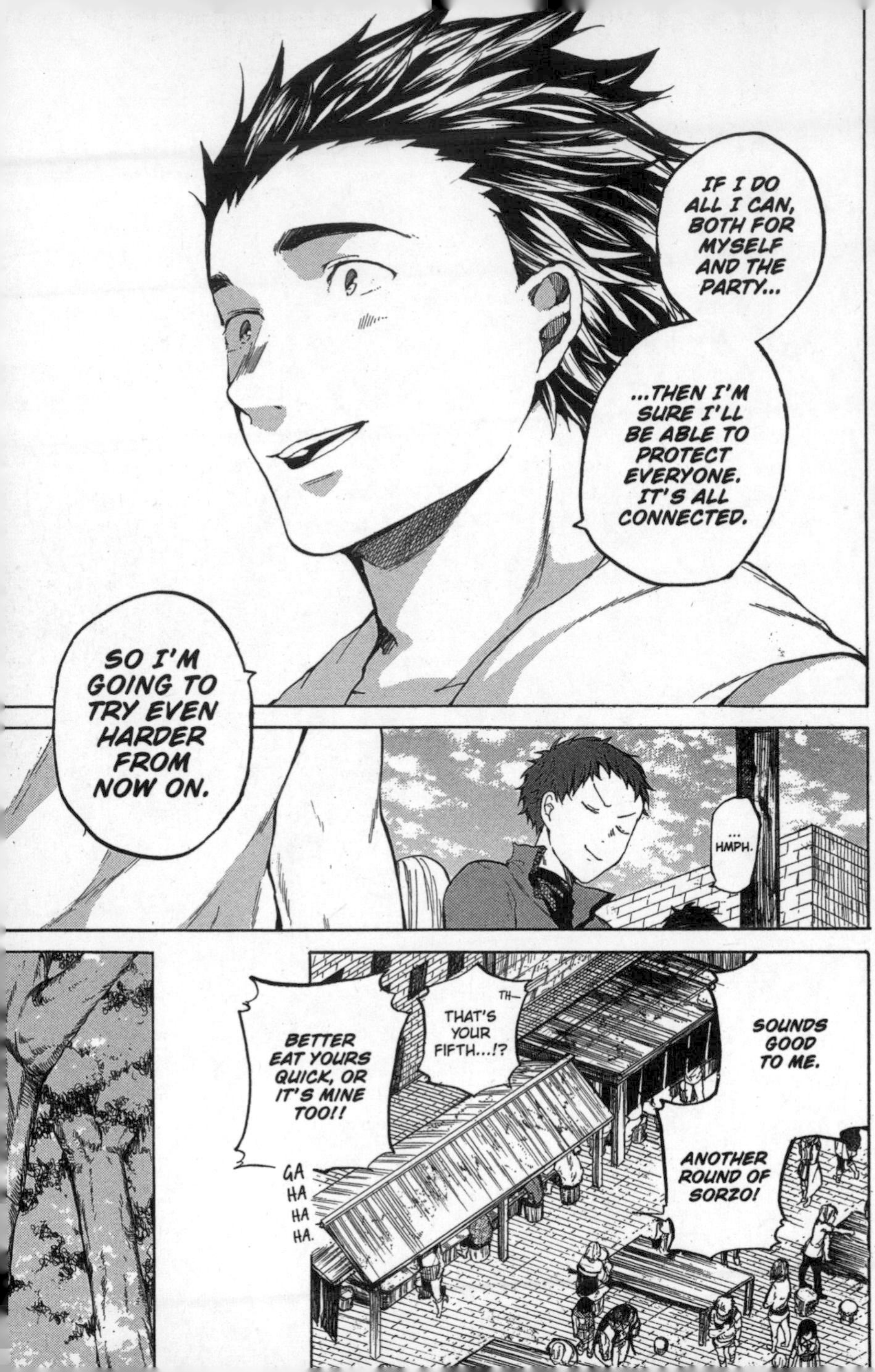
IF I DO ALL I CAN, BOTH FOR MYSELF AND THE PARTY...
...THEN I'M SURE I'LL BE ABLE TO PROTECT EVERYONE. IT'S ALL CONNECTED.
SO I'M GOING TO TRY EVEN HARDER FROM NOW ON.
...HMPH.
SOUNDS GOOD TO ME.
ANOTHER ROUND OF SORZO!
TH— THAT'S YOUR FIFTH...!?
BETTER EAT YOURS QUICK, OR IT'S MINE TOO!!
GA HA HA HA.

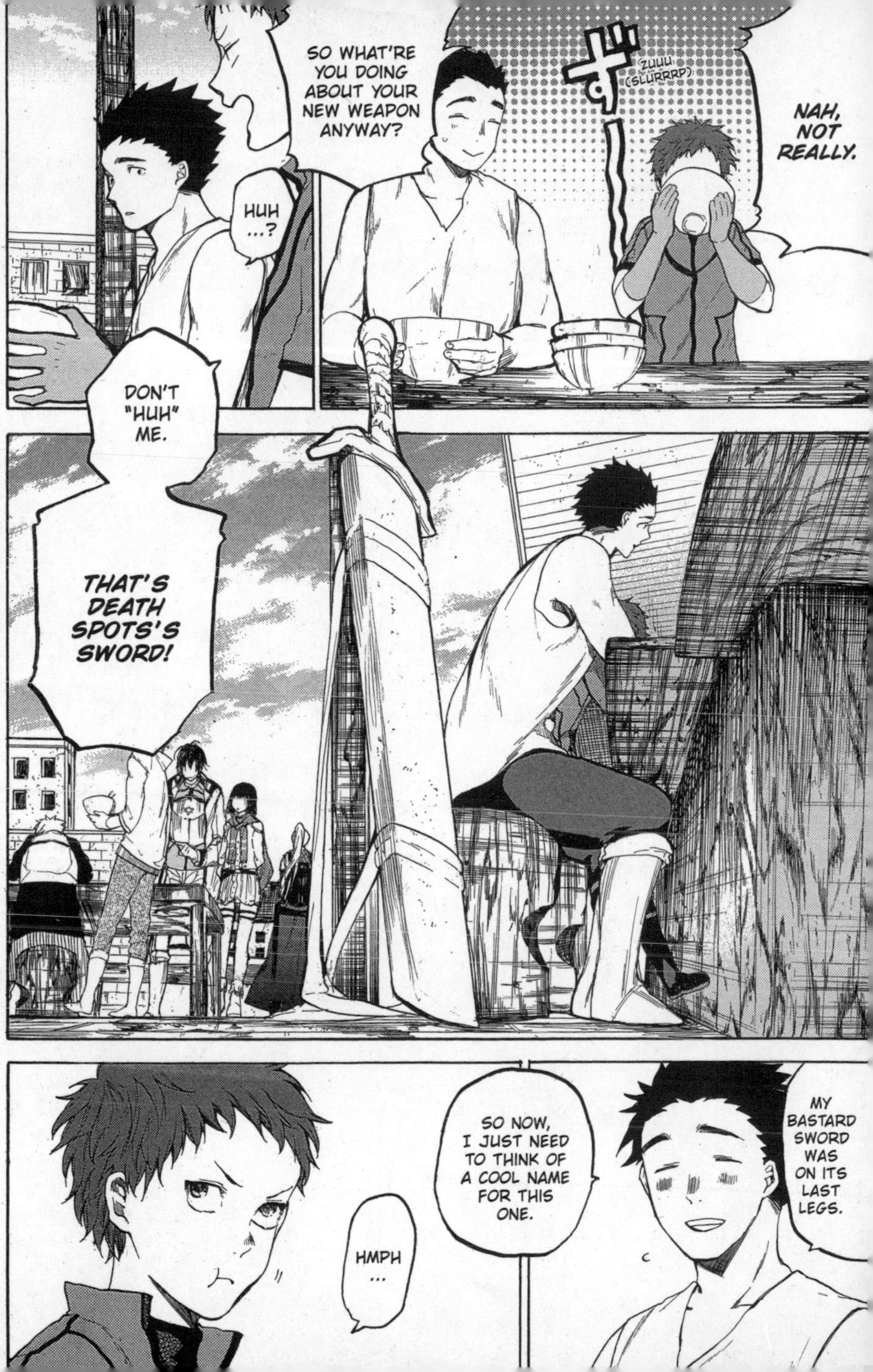
NAH, NOT REALLY.
ZUUU (SLURRRP)
SO WHAT'RE YOU DOING ABOUT YOUR NEW WEAPON ANYWAY?
HUH ...?
DON'T "HUH" ME.
THAT'S DEATH SPOTS'S SWORD!
MY BASTARD SWORD WAS ON ITS LAST LEGS.
SO NOW, I JUST NEED TO THINK OF A COOL NAME FOR THIS ONE.
HMPH ...

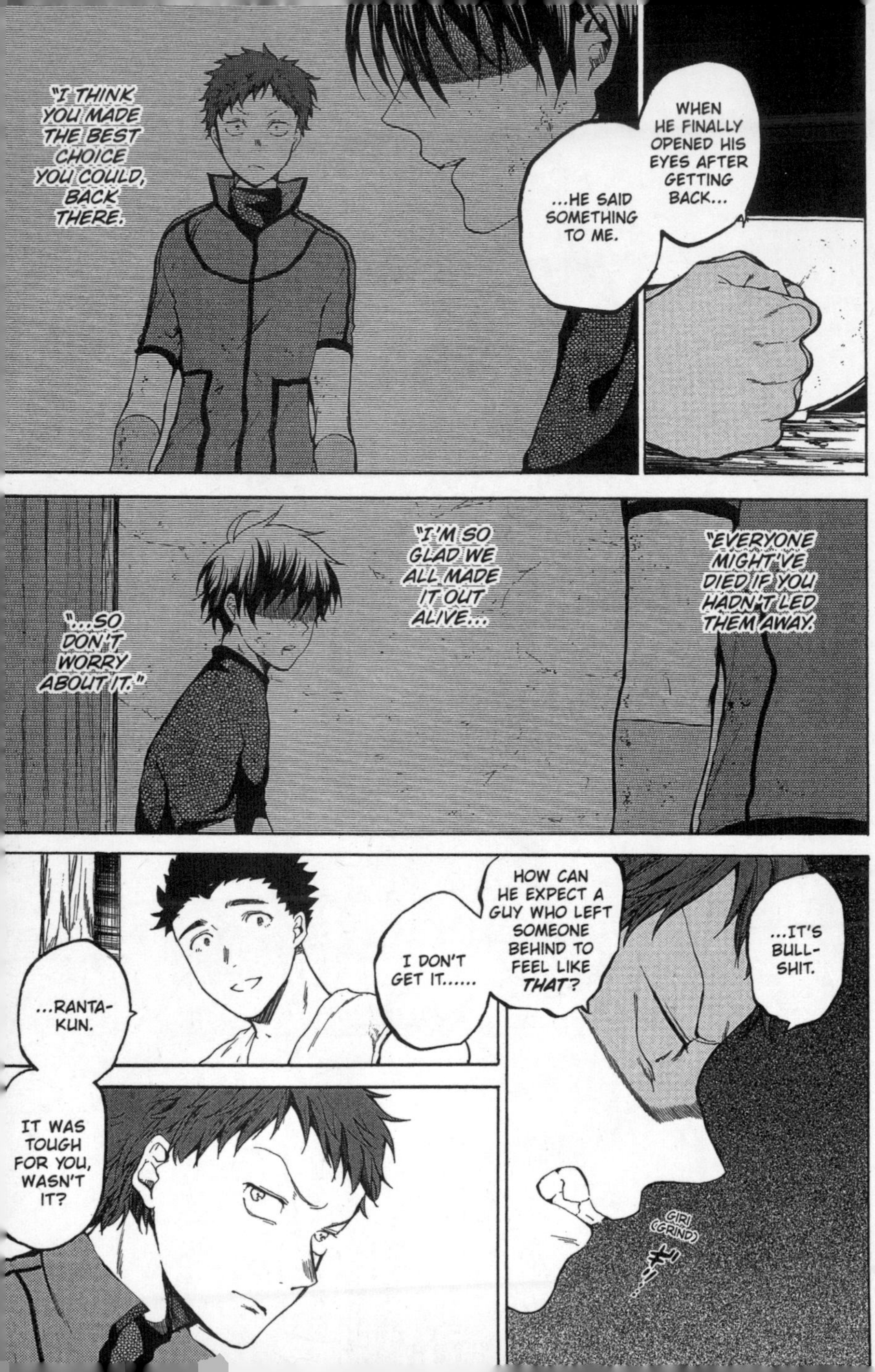
WHEN HE FINALLY OPENED HIS EYES AFTER GETTING BACK...
...HE SAID SOMETHING TO ME.
"I THINK YOU MADE THE BEST CHOICE YOU COULD, BACK THERE.
"EVERYONE MIGHT'VE DIED IF YOU HADN'T LED THEM AWAY.
"I'M SO GLAD WE ALL MADE IT OUT ALIVE...
"...SO DON'T WORRY ABOUT IT."
...IT'S BULLSHIT.
HOW CAN HE EXPECT A GUY WHO LEFT SOMEONE BEHIND TO FEEL LIKE *THAT*?
I DON'T GET IT......
...RANTA-KUN.
IT WAS TOUGH FOR YOU, WASN'T IT?
GIRI (GRIND)

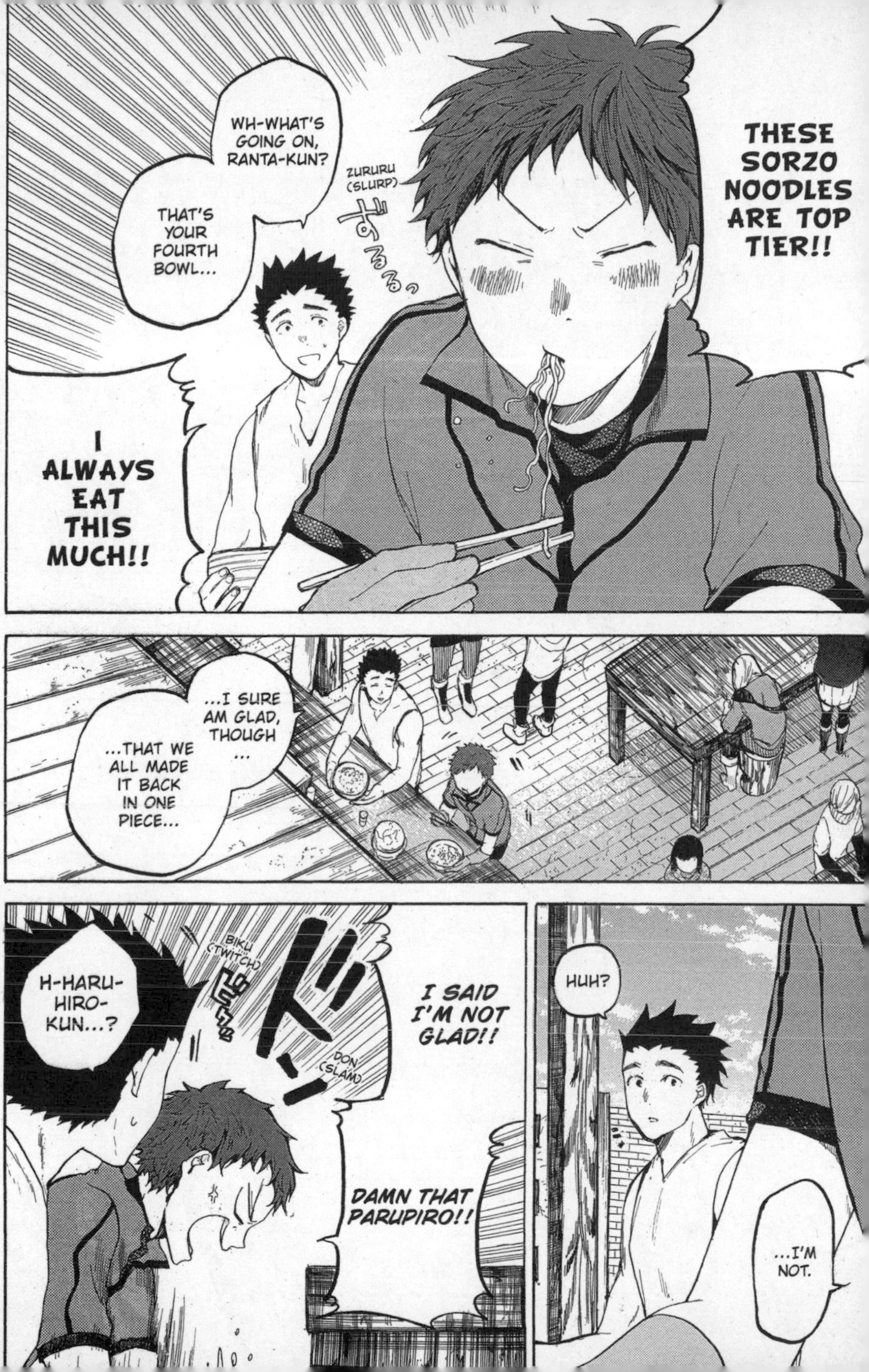
THESE SORZO NOODLES ARE TOP TIER!!
ZURURU (SLURP)
ずるるっ
WH-WHAT'S GOING ON, RANTA-KUN?
THAT'S YOUR FOURTH BOWL...
I ALWAYS EAT THIS MUCH!!
...I SURE AM GLAD, THOUGH...
...THAT WE ALL MADE IT BACK IN ONE PIECE...
HUH?
...I'M NOT.
I SAID I'M NOT GLAD!!
DON (SLAM)
BIKU (TWITCH)
H-HARU-HIRO-KUN...?
DAMN THAT PARUPIRO!!

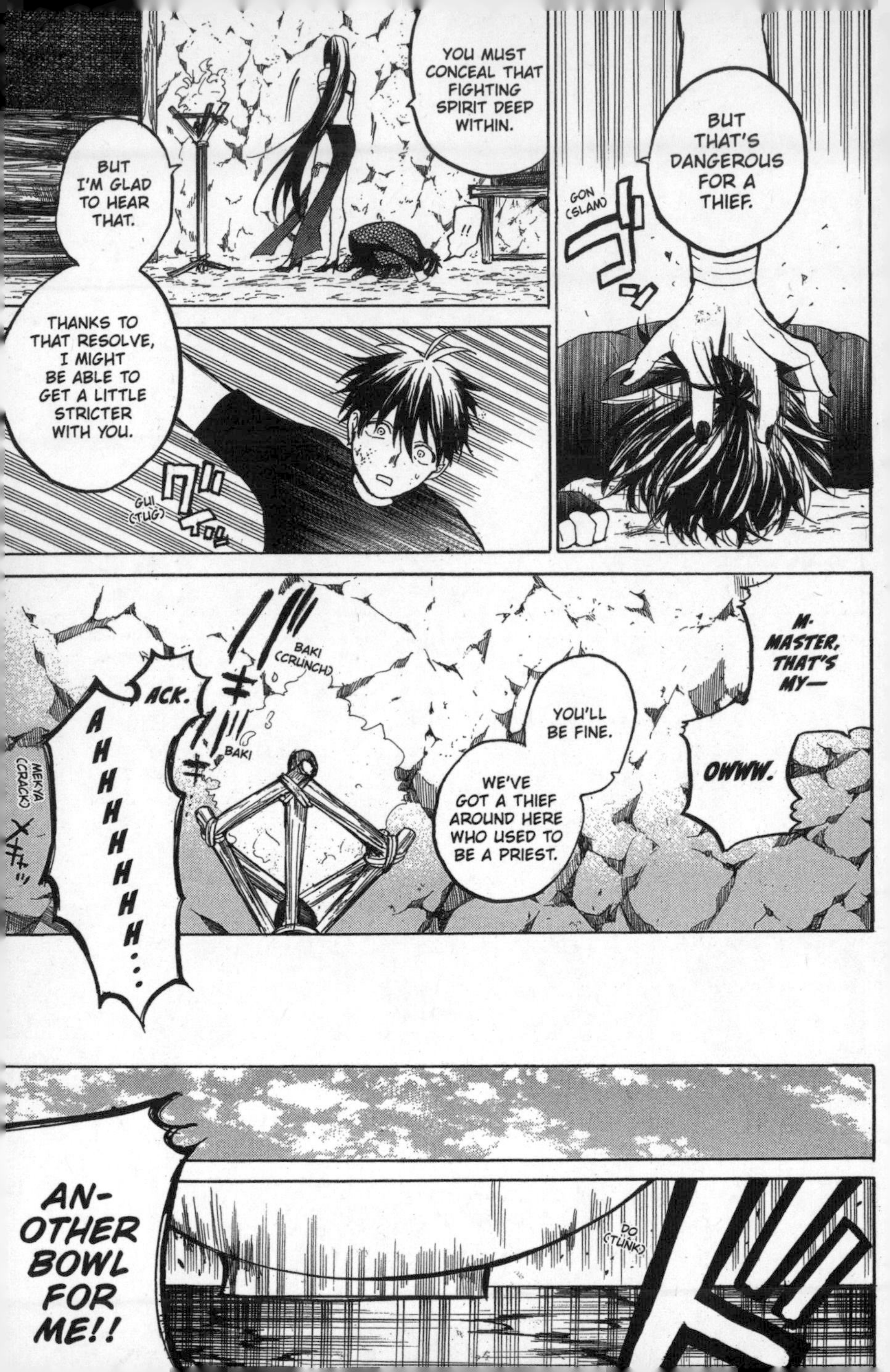

YOU MUST CONCEAL THAT FIGHTING SPIRIT DEEP WITHIN.
BUT THAT'S DANGEROUS FOR A THIEF.
GON (SLAM)
!!
BUT I'M GLAD TO HEAR THAT.
THANKS TO THAT RESOLVE, I MIGHT BE ABLE TO GET A LITTLE STRICTER WITH YOU.
GUI (TUG)
M-MASTER, THAT'S MY—
OWWW.
YOU'LL BE FINE.
WE'VE GOT A THIEF AROUND HERE WHO USED TO BE A PRIEST.
BAKI (CRUNCH)
BAKI
ACK.
AHHHHHHH...
MEKYA (CRACK)
DO (TUNK)
AN-OTHER BOWL FOR ME!!

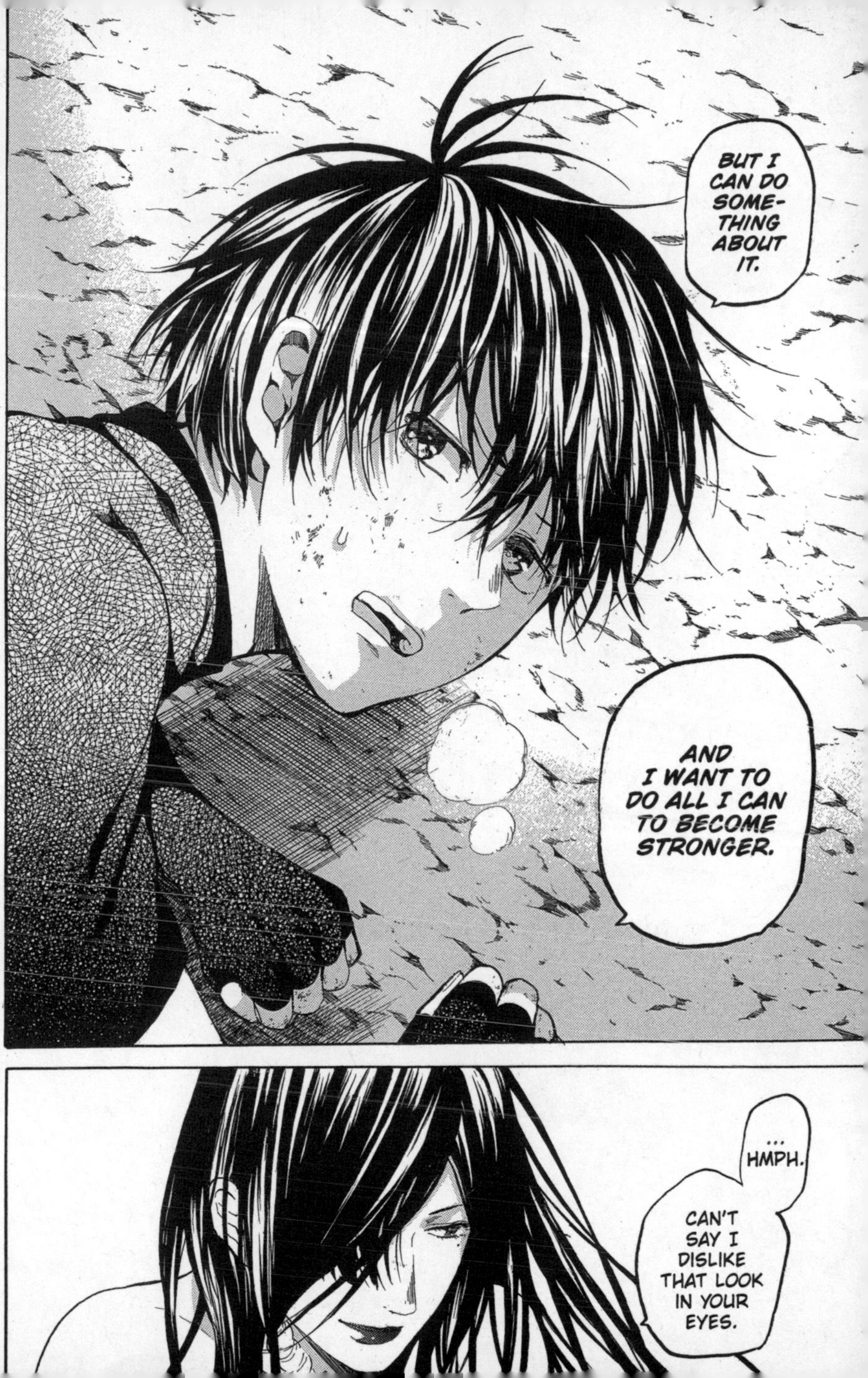
BUT I CAN DO SOME-THING ABOUT IT.
AND I WANT TO DO ALL I CAN TO BECOME STRONGER.
...HMPH.
CAN'T SAY I DISLIKE THAT LOOK IN YOUR EYES.

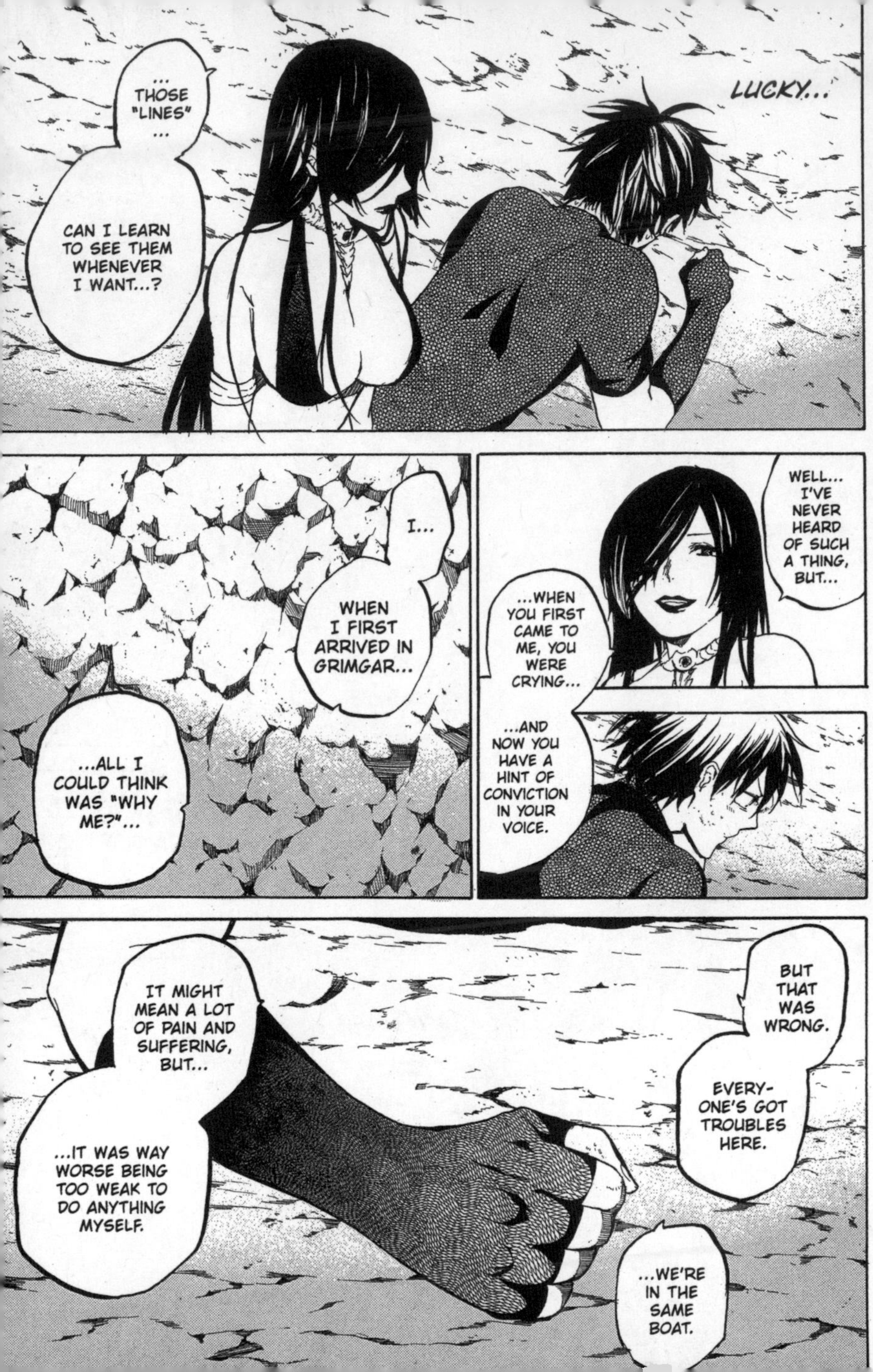
LUCKY...
...THOSE "LINES"...
CAN I LEARN TO SEE THEM WHENEVER I WANT...?
WELL... I'VE NEVER HEARD OF SUCH A THING, BUT...
...WHEN YOU FIRST CAME TO ME, YOU WERE CRYING...
...AND NOW YOU HAVE A HINT OF CONVICTION IN YOUR VOICE.
I...
WHEN I FIRST ARRIVED IN GRIMGAR...
...ALL I COULD THINK WAS "WHY ME?"...
BUT THAT WAS WRONG.
EVERY-ONE'S GOT TROUBLES HERE.
...WE'RE IN THE SAME BOAT.
IT MIGHT MEAN A LOT OF PAIN AND SUFFERING, BUT...
...IT WAS WAY WORSE BEING TOO WEAK TO DO ANYTHING MYSELF.

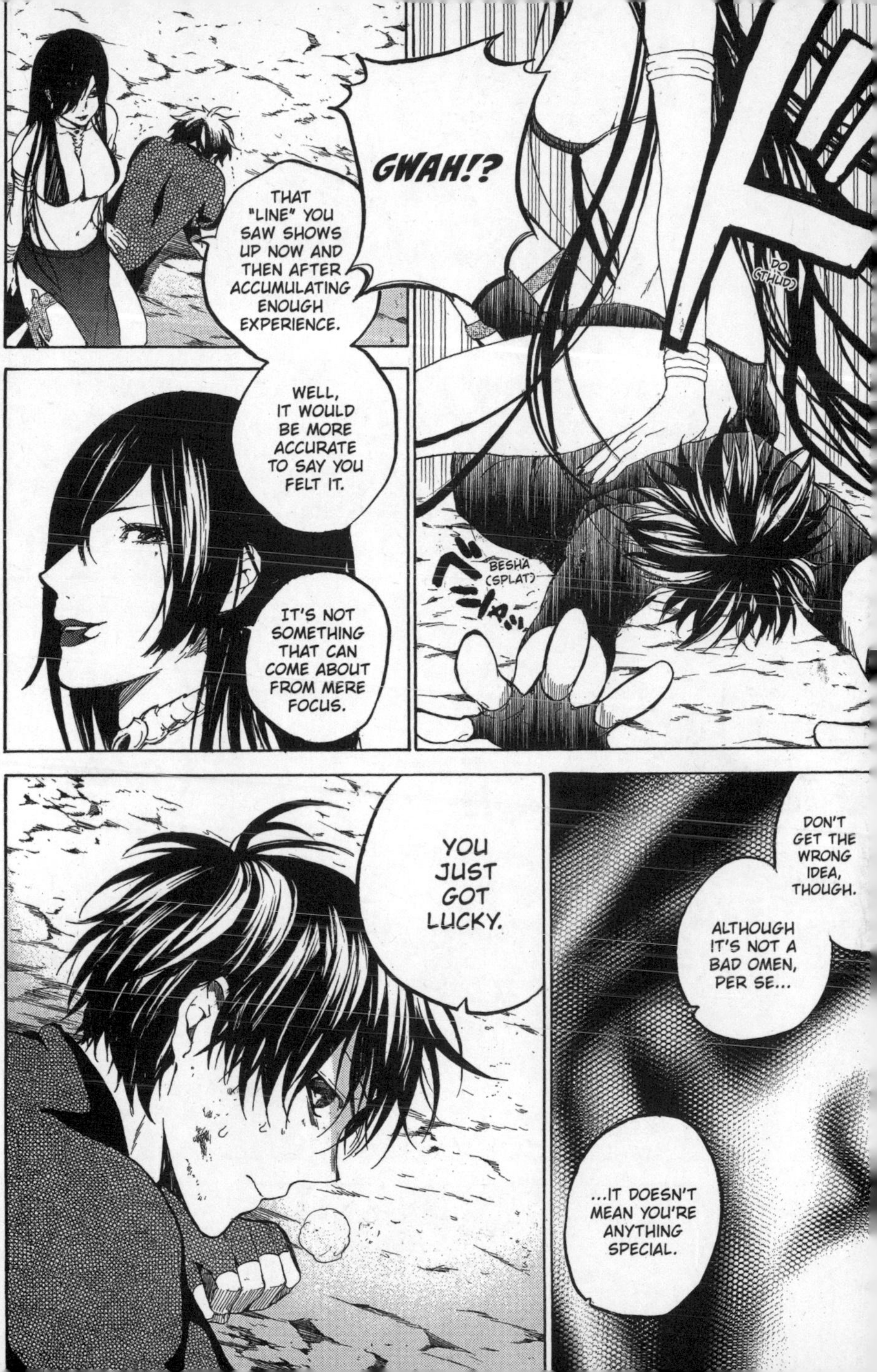
GWAH!?
DO (THUD)
BESHA (SPLAT)
THAT "LINE" YOU SAW SHOWS UP NOW AND THEN AFTER ACCUMULATING ENOUGH EXPERIENCE.
WELL, IT WOULD BE MORE ACCURATE TO SAY YOU FELT IT.
IT'S NOT SOMETHING THAT CAN COME ABOUT FROM MERE FOCUS.
DON'T GET THE WRONG IDEA, THOUGH.
ALTHOUGH IT'S NOT A BAD OMEN, PER SE...
...IT DOESN'T MEAN YOU'RE ANYTHING SPECIAL.
YOU JUST GOT LUCKY.

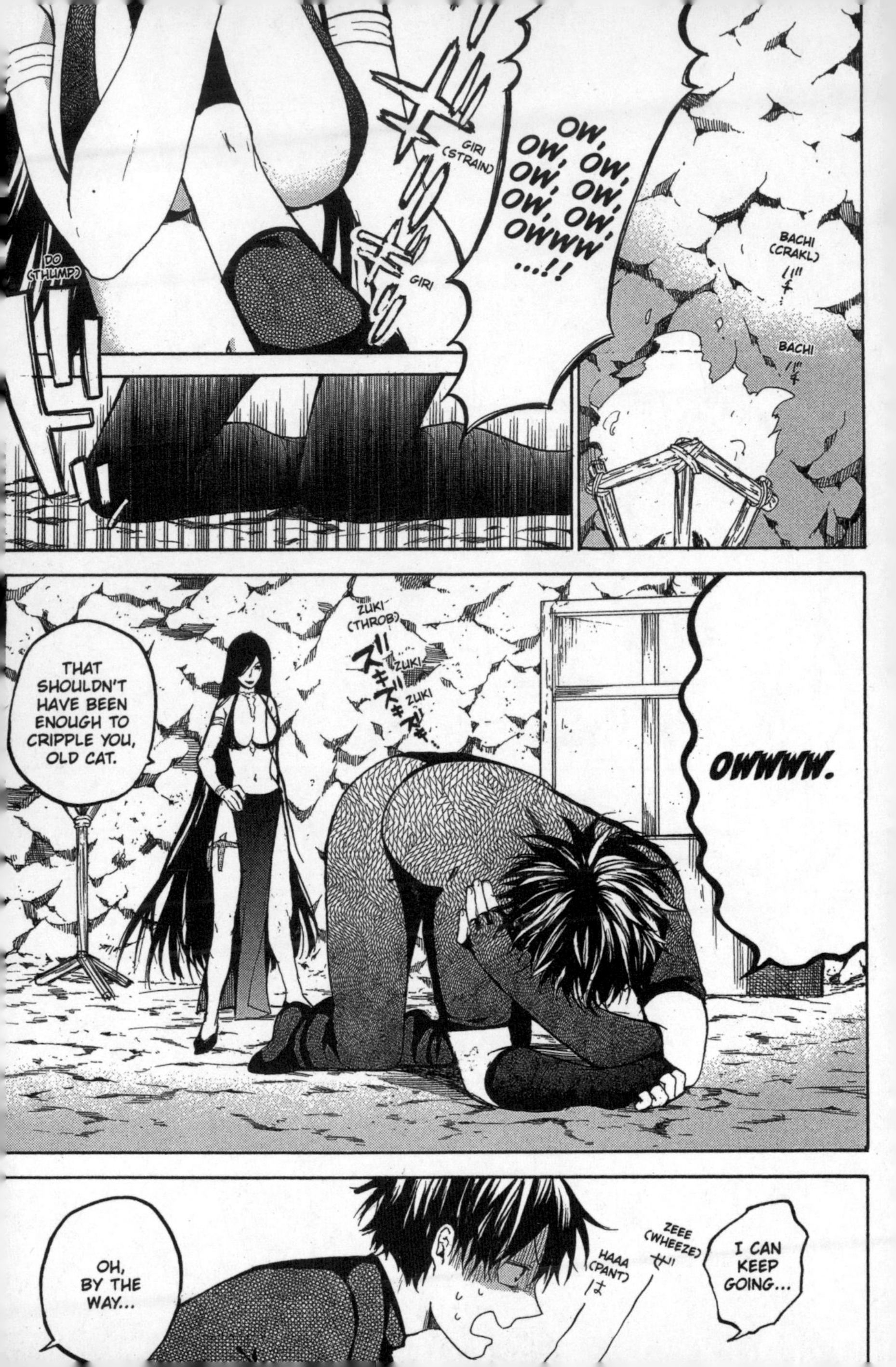

BACHI (CRAKL)
BACHI
OW, OW, OW, OW, OW, OW, OW, OWWW...!!
GIRI (STRAIN)
GIRI
DO (THUMP)
OWWWW.
ZUKI (THROB)
ZUKI
ZUKI
THAT SHOULDN'T HAVE BEEN ENOUGH TO CRIPPLE YOU, OLD CAT.
I CAN KEEP GOING...
ZEEE (WHEEZE)
HAAA (PANT)
OH, BY THE WAY...

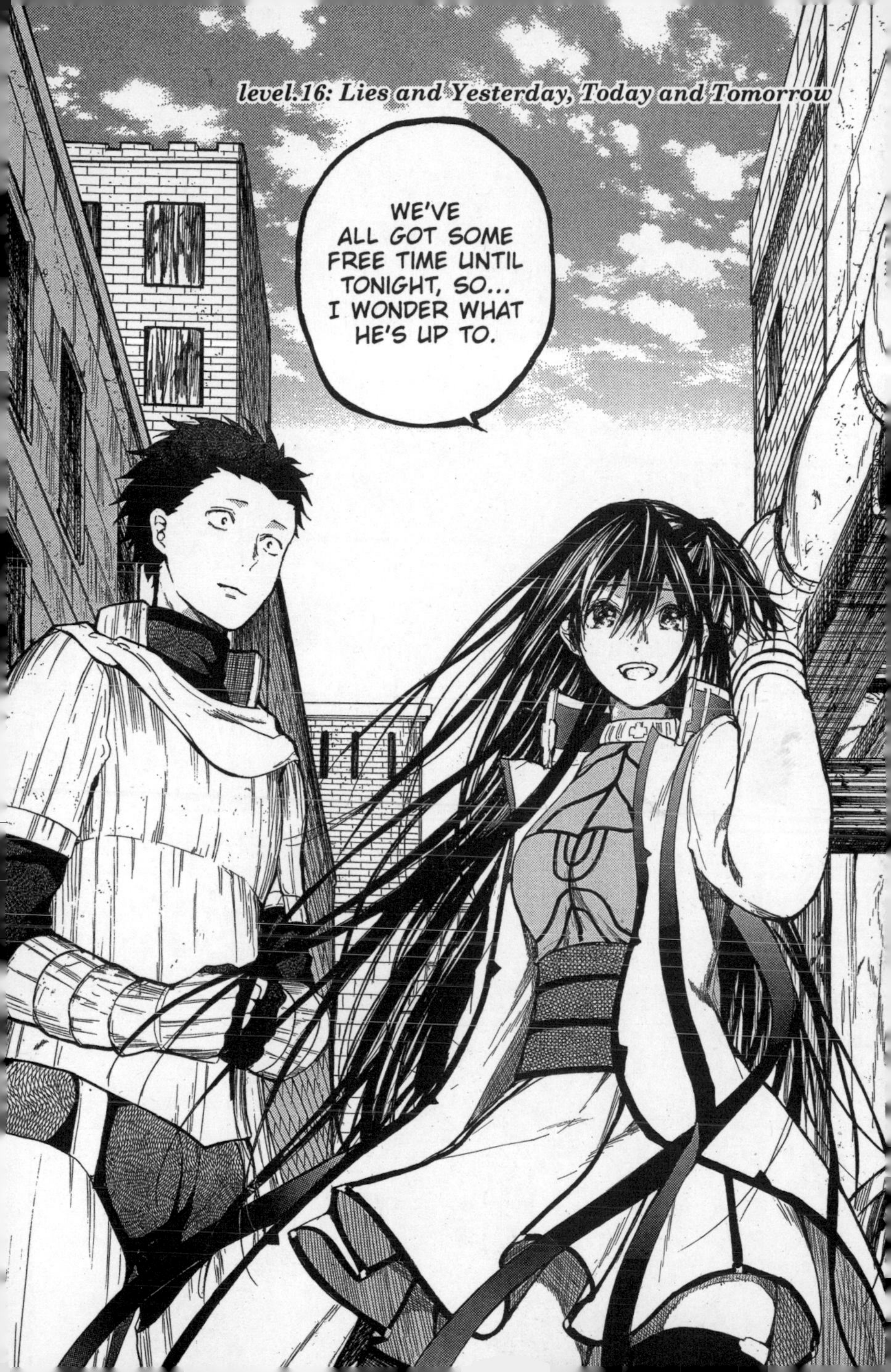
level.16: Lies and Yesterday, Today and Tomorrow
WE'VE ALL GOT SOME FREE TIME UNTIL TONIGHT, SO... I WONDER WHAT HE'S UP TO.

level.16

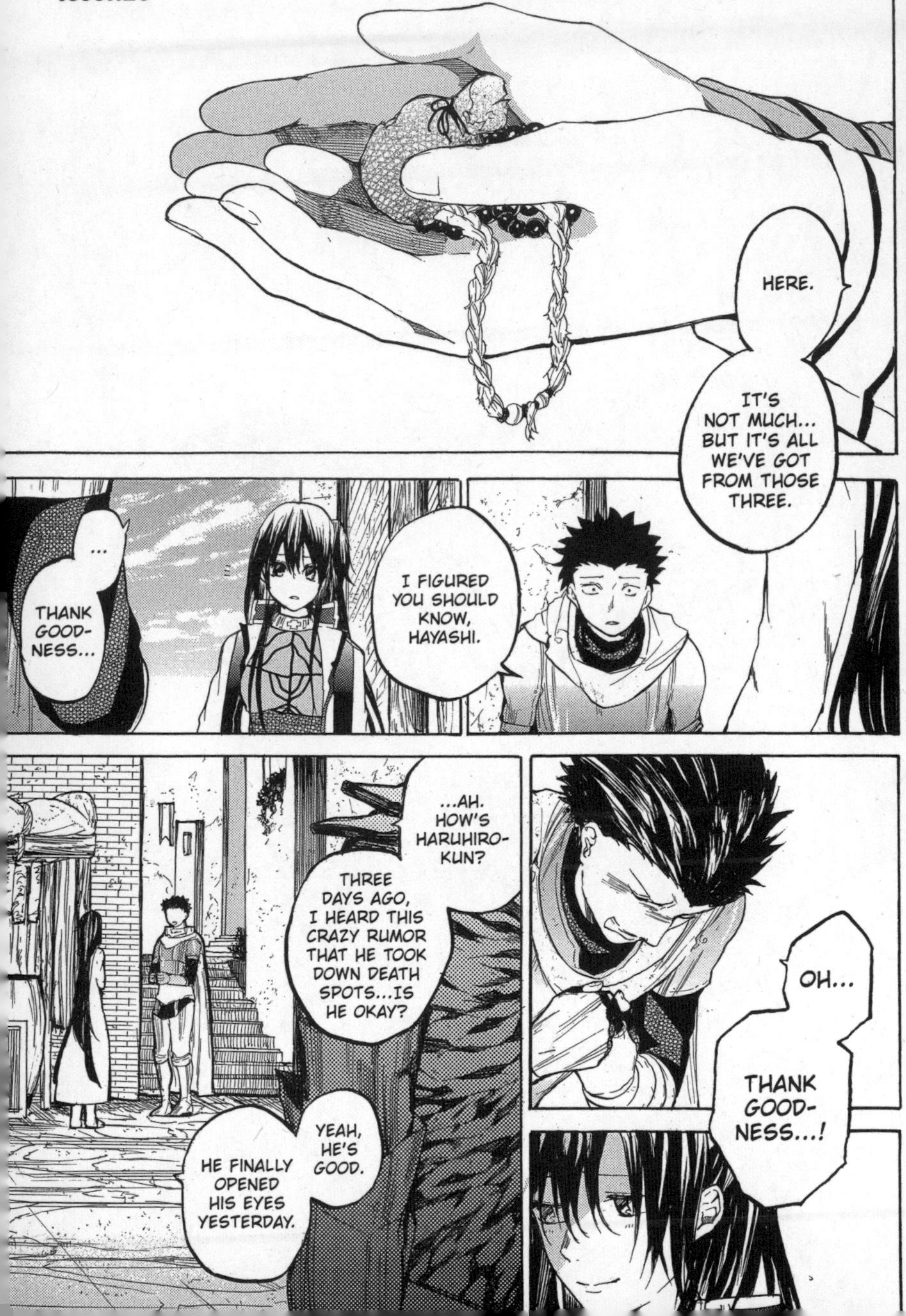
HERE.
IT'S NOT MUCH... BUT IT'S ALL WE'VE GOT FROM THOSE THREE.
I FIGURED YOU SHOULD KNOW, HAYASHI.
...
THANK GOOD-NESS...
OH...
THANK GOOD-NESS...!
...AH. HOW'S HARUHIRO-KUN?
THREE DAYS AGO, I HEARD THIS CRAZY RUMOR THAT HE TOOK DOWN DEATH SPOTS...IS HE OKAY?
YEAH, HE'S GOOD.
HE FINALLY OPENED HIS EYES YESTERDAY.

Grimgar
of Fantasy and Ash

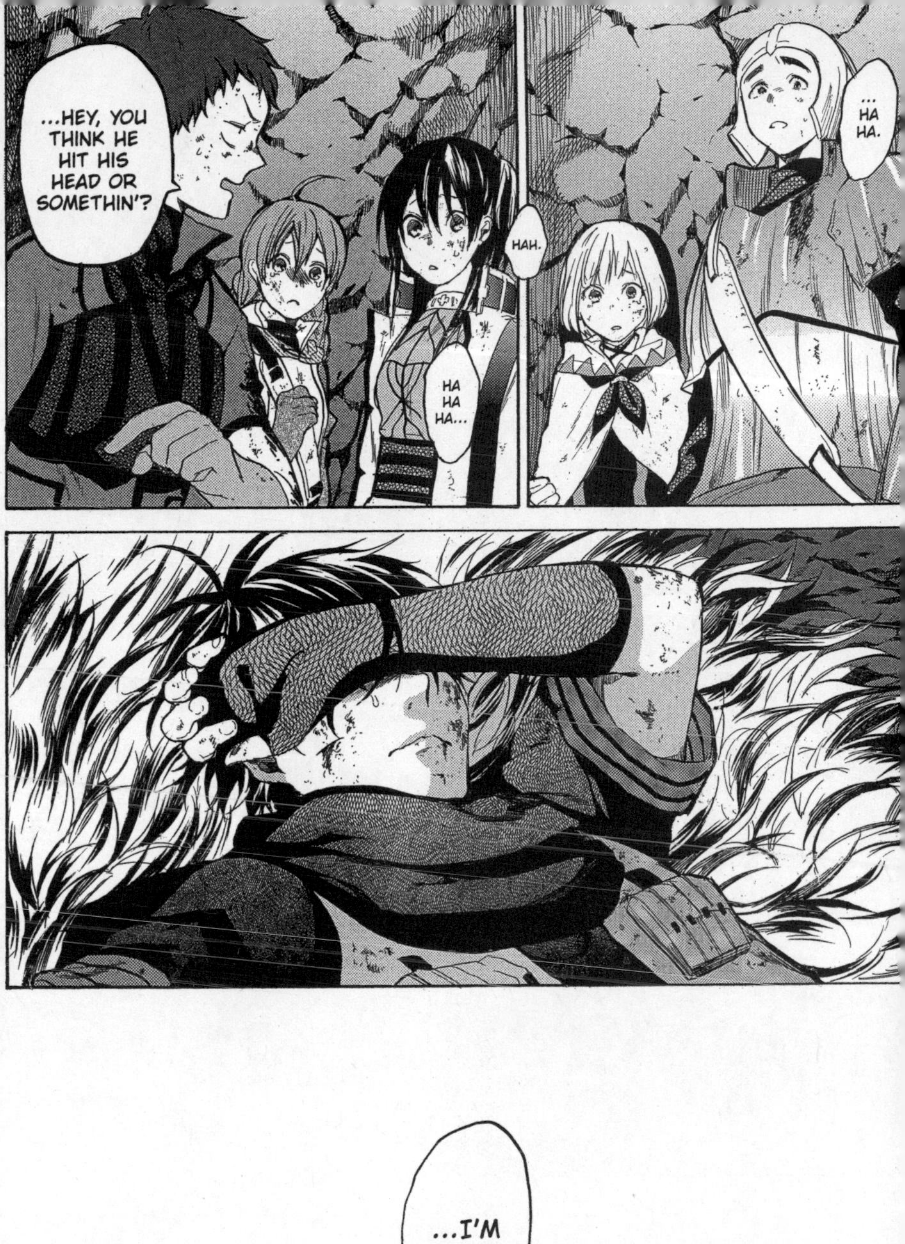
...HA HA.
HAH.
HA HA HA...
...HEY, YOU THINK HE HIT HIS HEAD OR SOMETHIN'?
...I'M ALIVE.

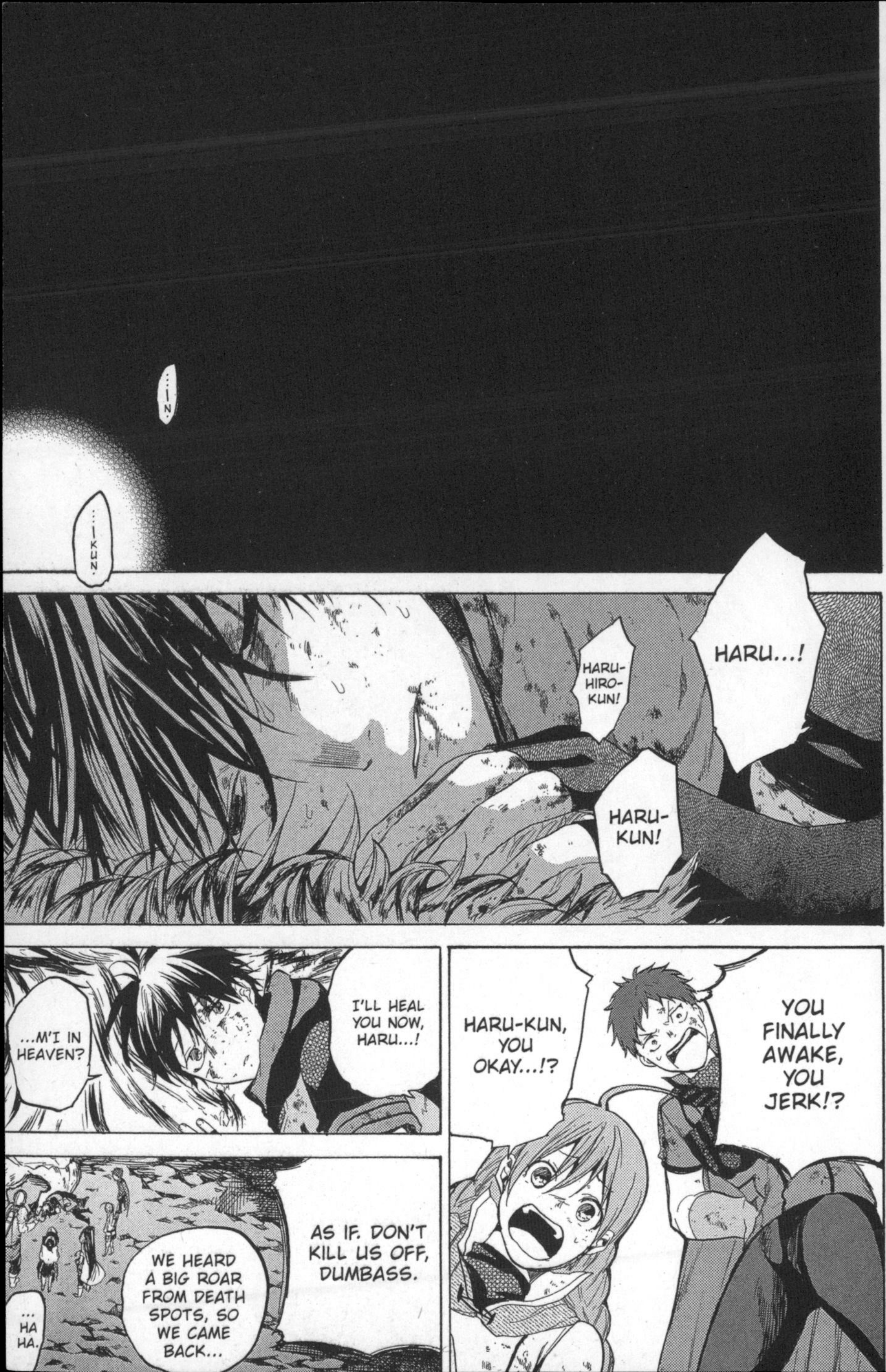

...-N.
...-KUN.
HARU...!
HARU-HIRO-KUN!
HARU-KUN!
YOU FINALLY AWAKE, YOU JERK!?
HARU-KUN, YOU OKAY...!?
I'LL HEAL YOU NOW, HARU...!
...M'I IN HEAVEN?
AS IF. DON'T KILL US OFF, DUMBASS.
WE HEARD A BIG ROAR FROM DEATH SPOTS, SO WE CAME BACK...
...HA HA.

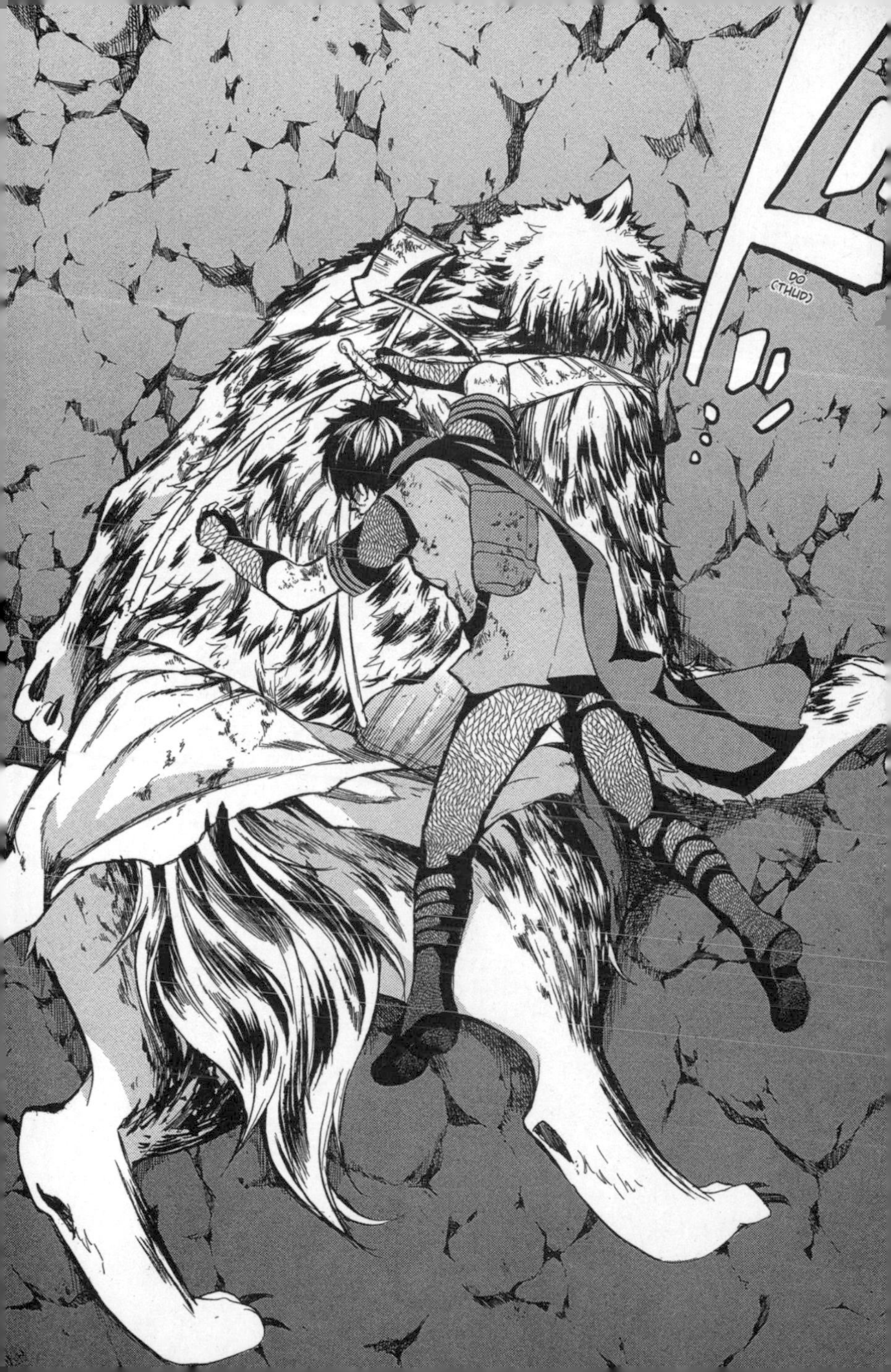
DO (THUD)

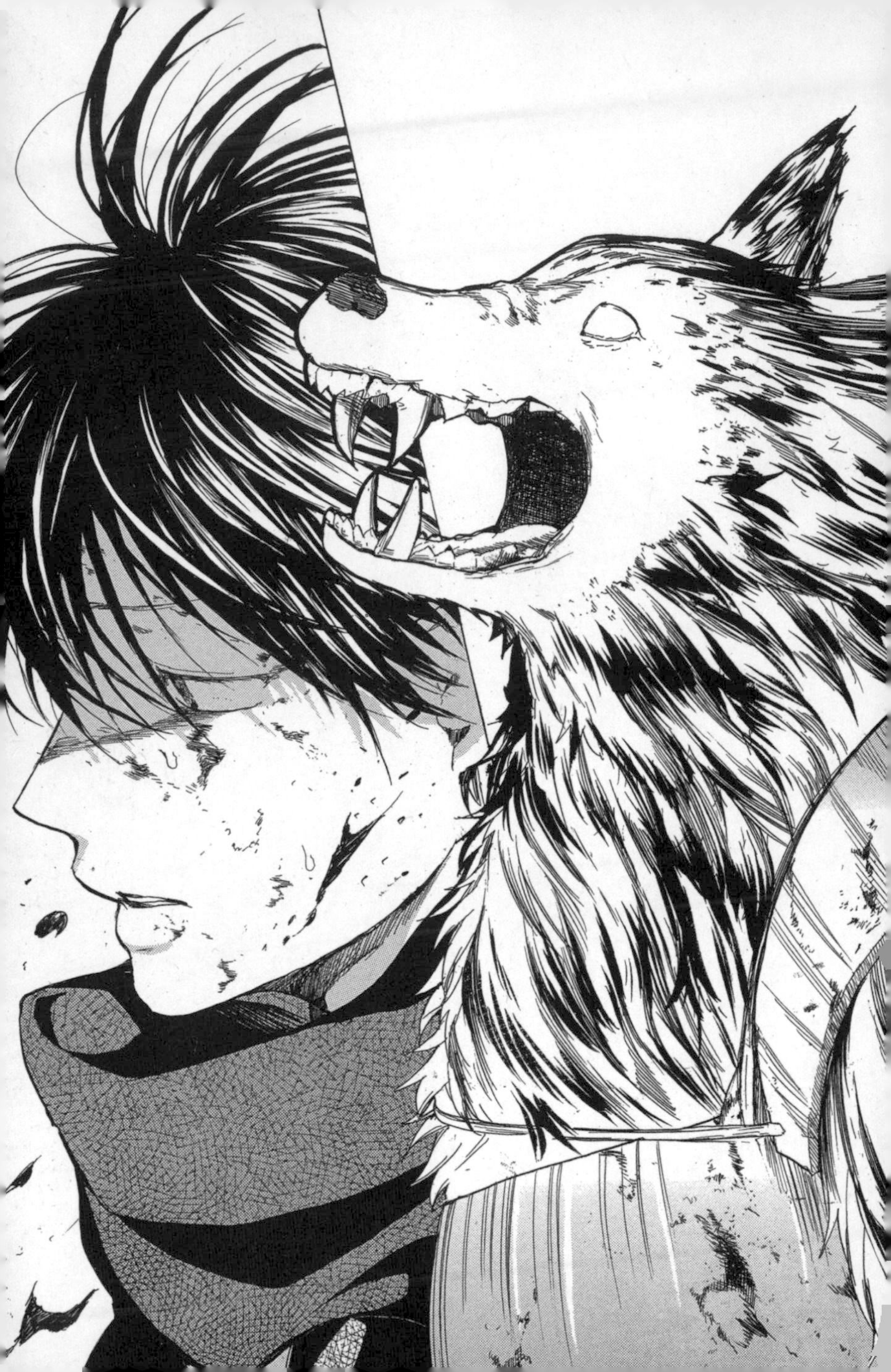

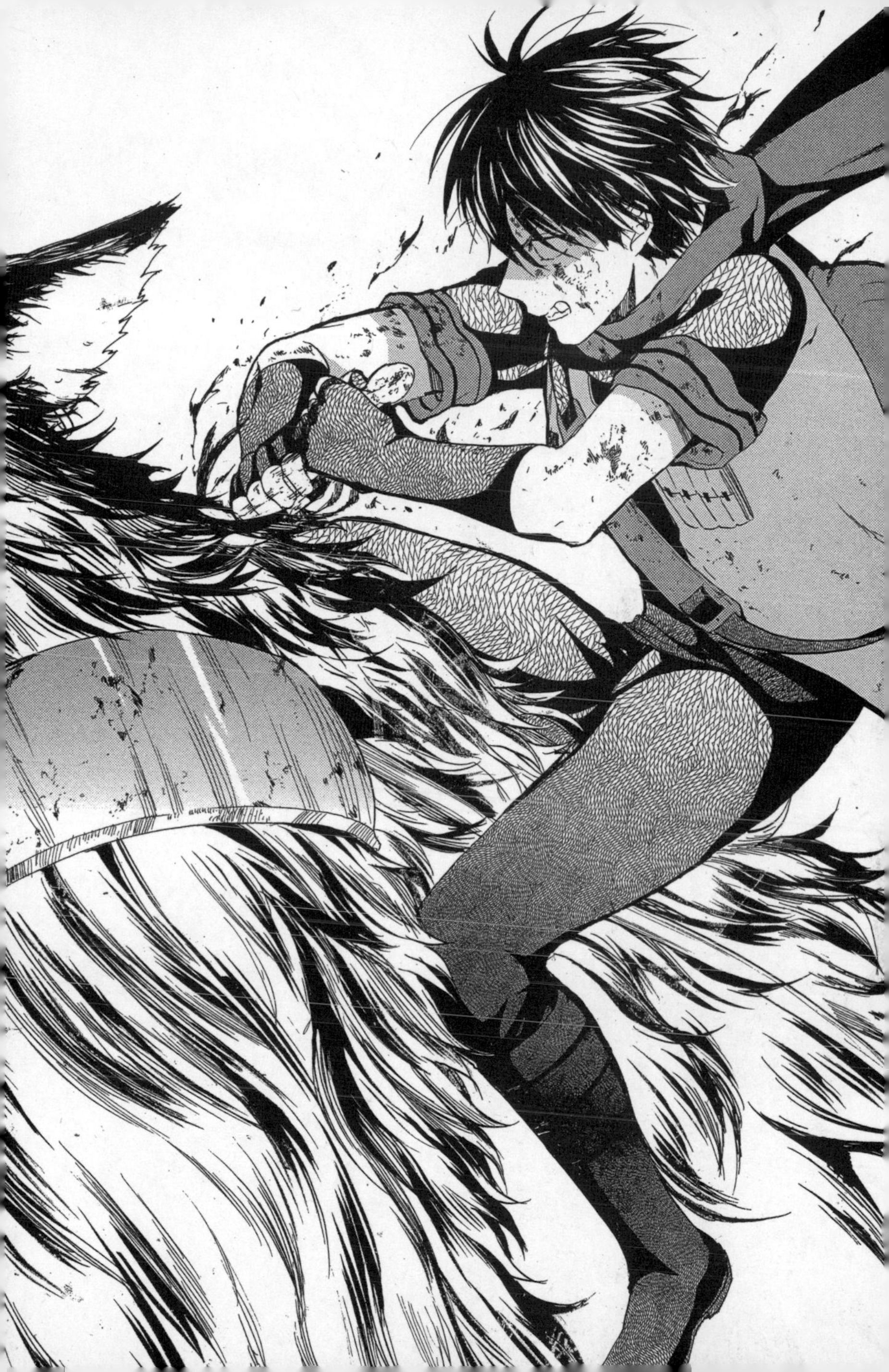

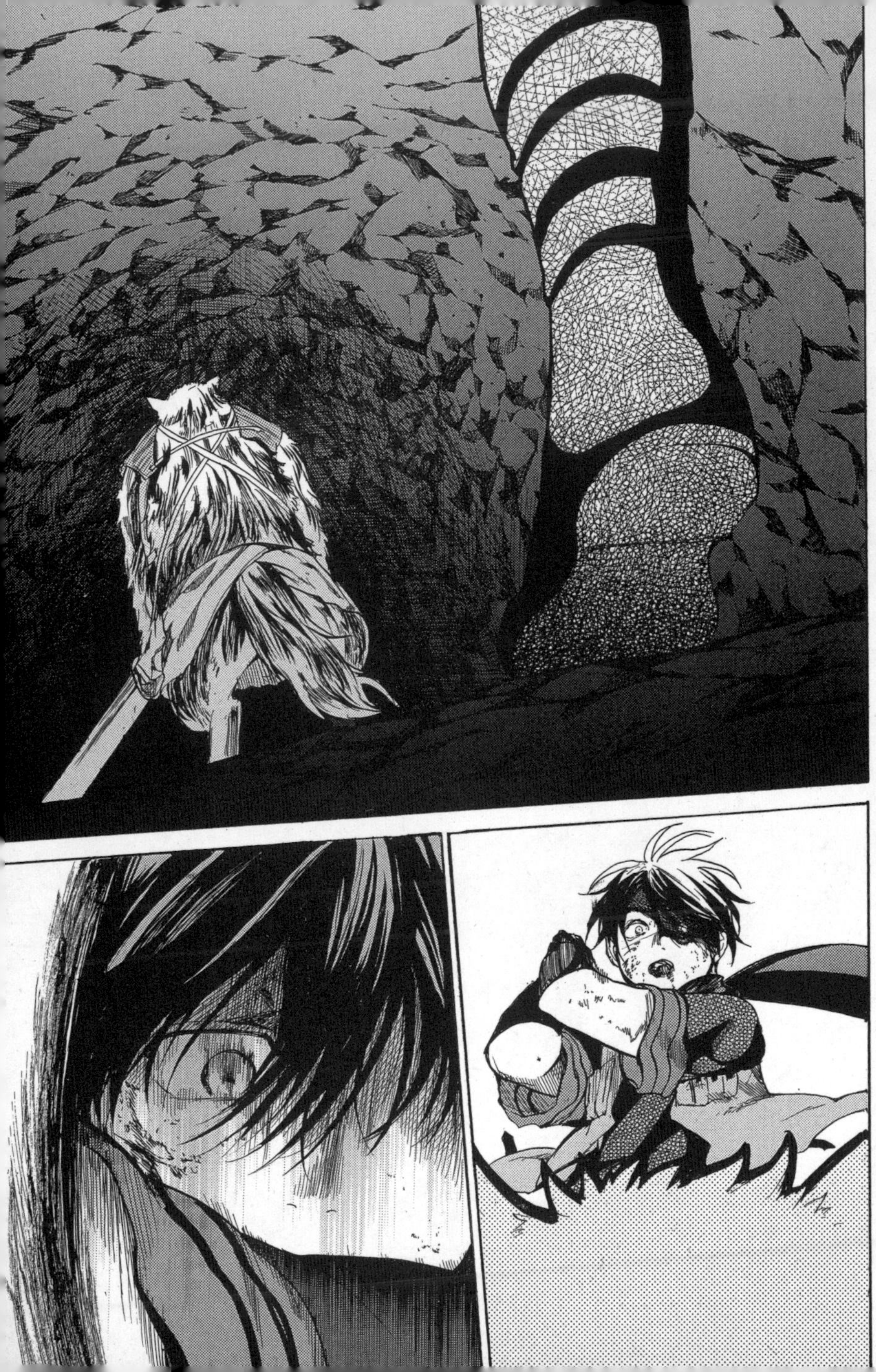

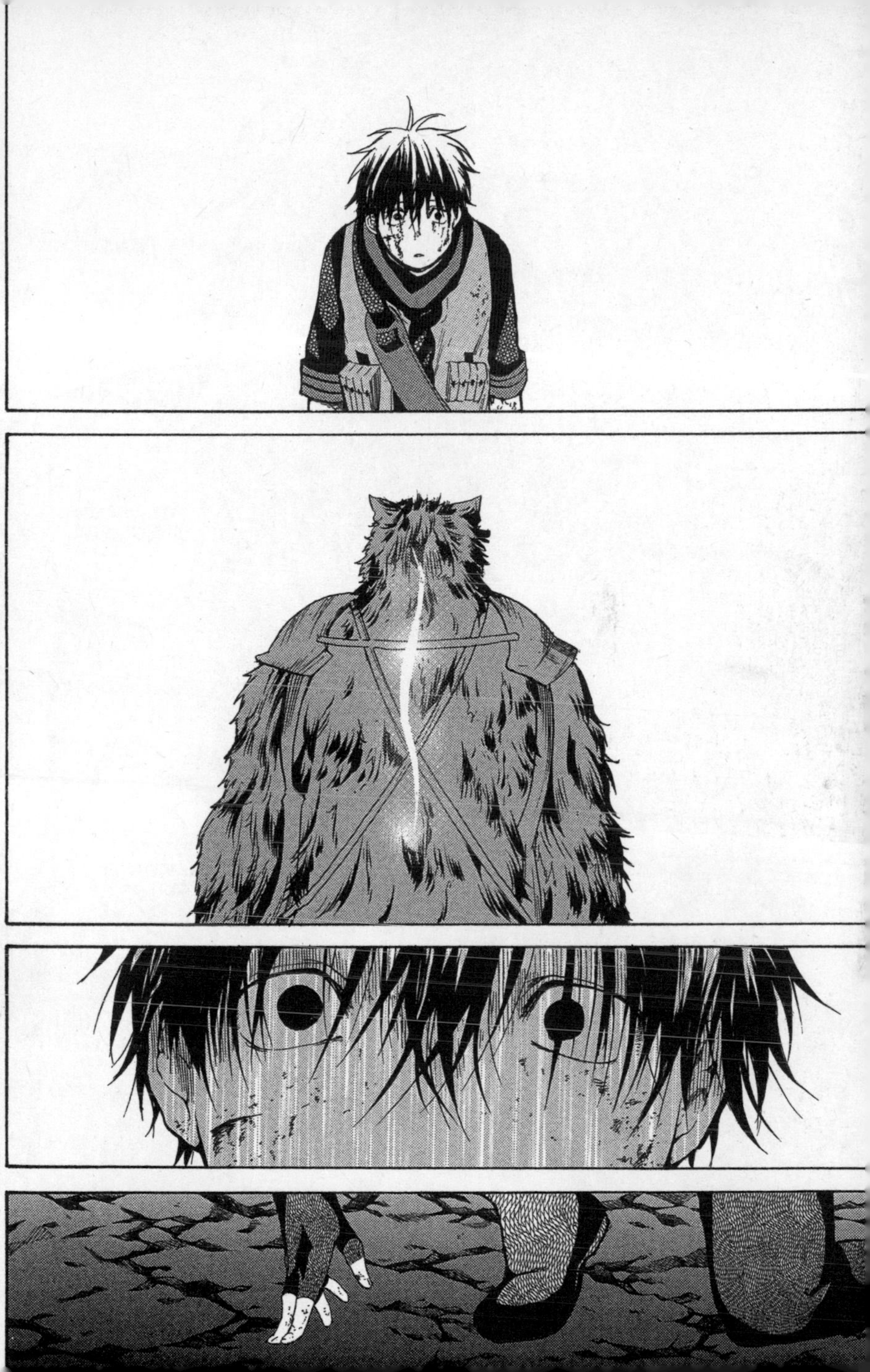

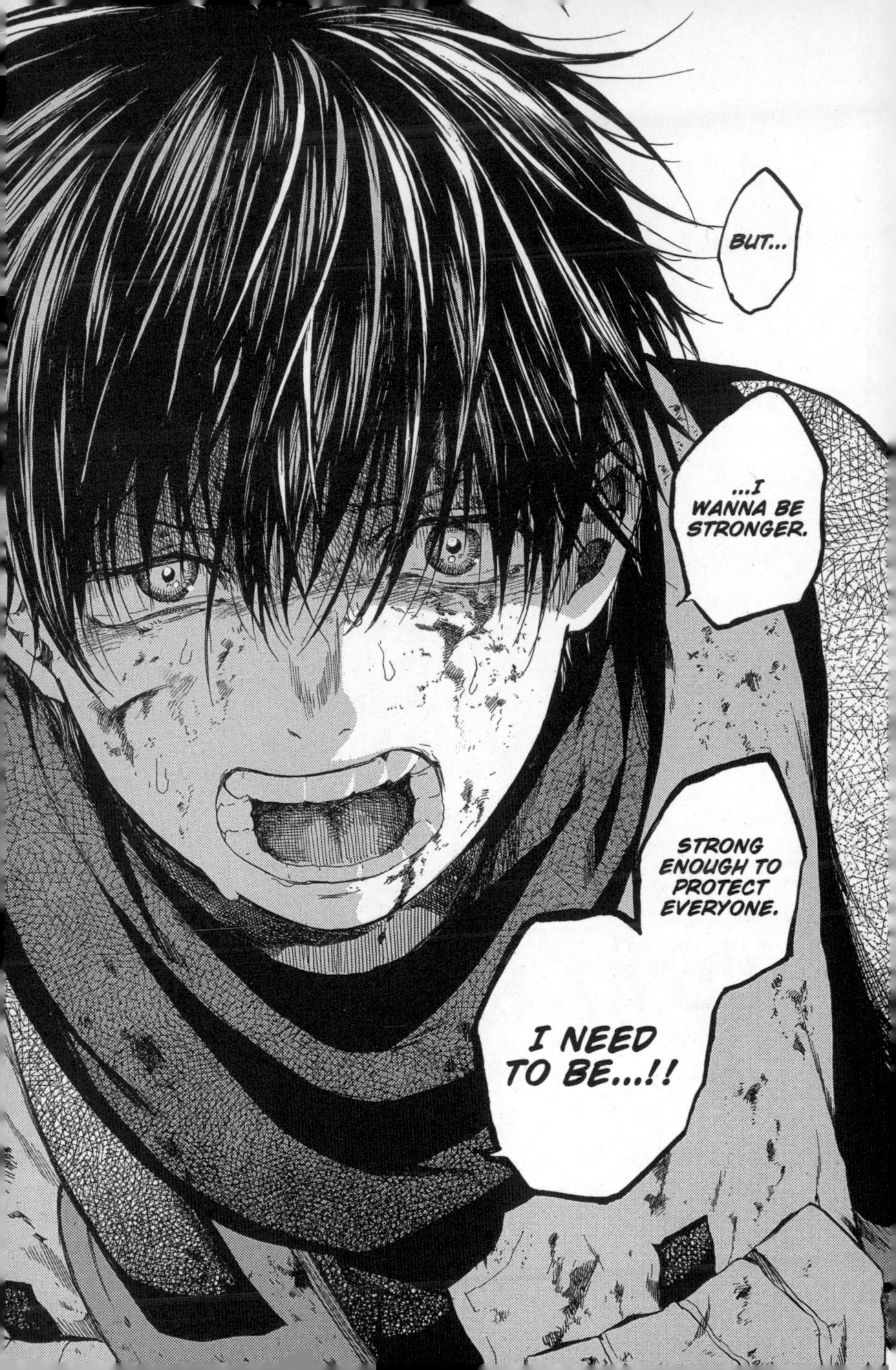
BUT...
...I WANNA BE STRONGER.
STRONG ENOUGH TO PROTECT EVERYONE.
I NEED TO BE...!!

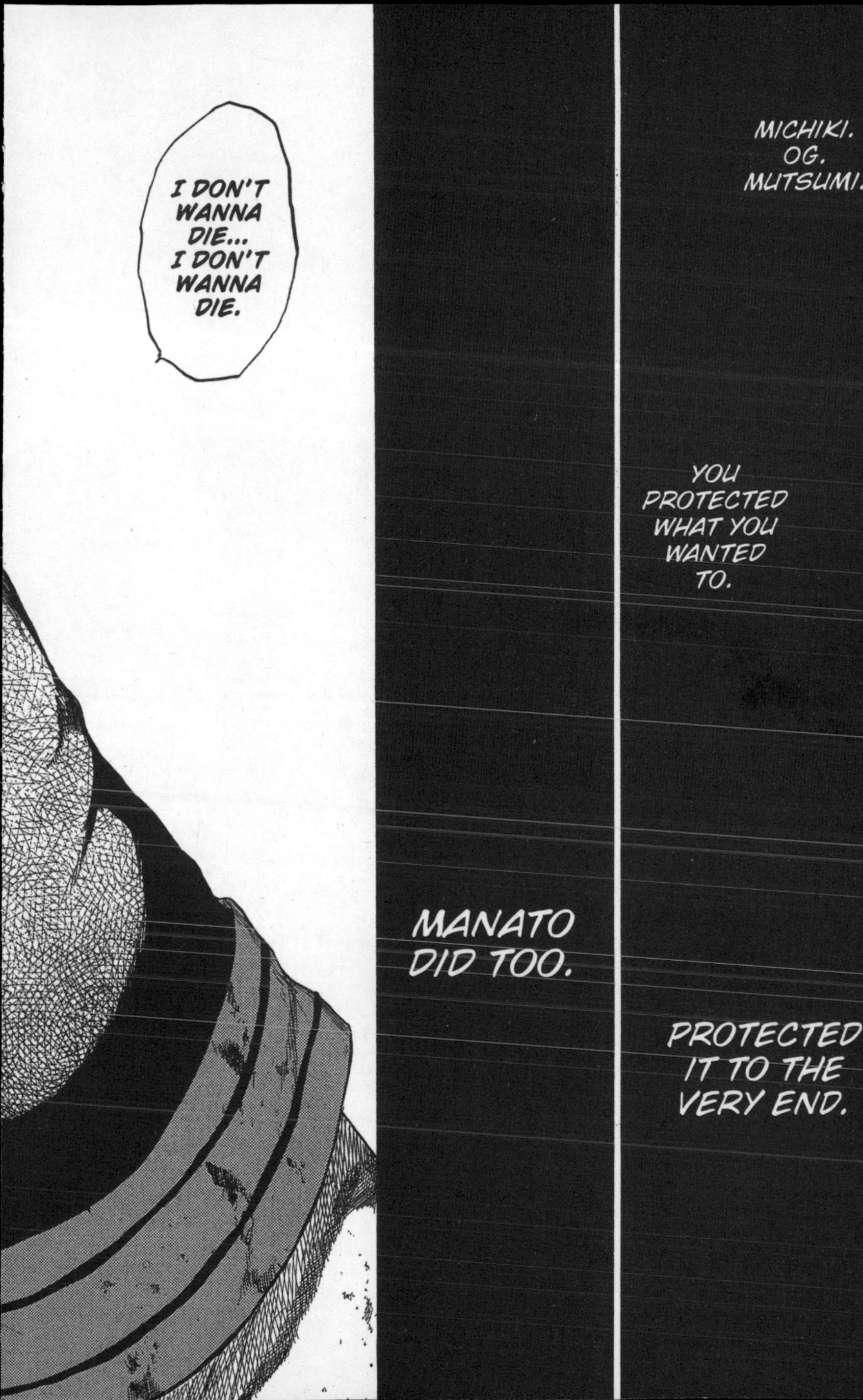
MICHIKI. OG. MUTSUMI.
YOU PROTECTED WHAT YOU WANTED TO.
PROTECTED IT TO THE VERY END.
MANATO DID TOO.
I DON'T WANNA DIE... I DON'T WANNA DIE.

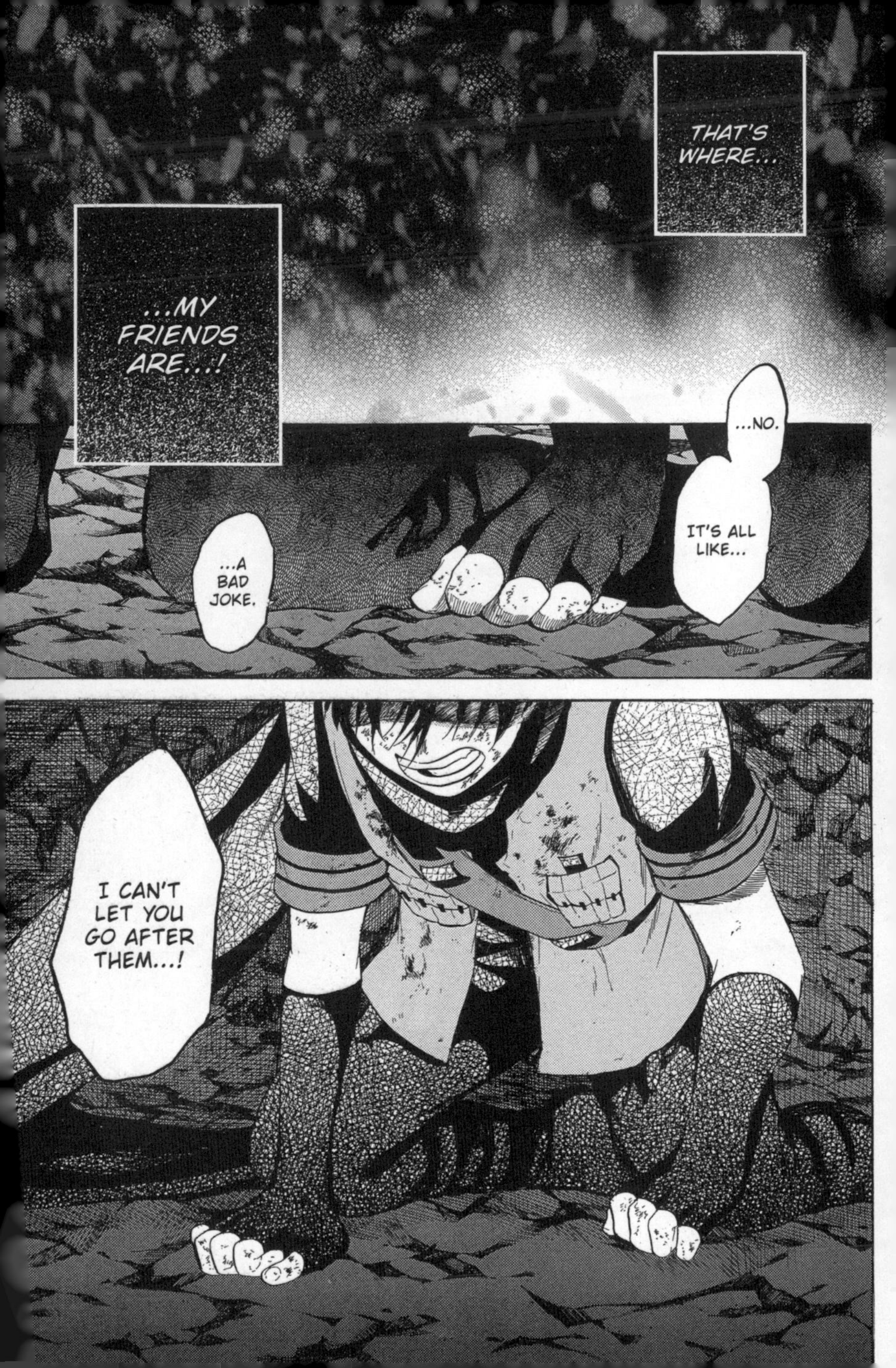
THAT'S WHERE...
...MY FRIENDS ARE...!
...NO.
IT'S ALL LIKE...
...A BAD JOKE.
I CAN'T LET YOU GO AFTER THEM...!

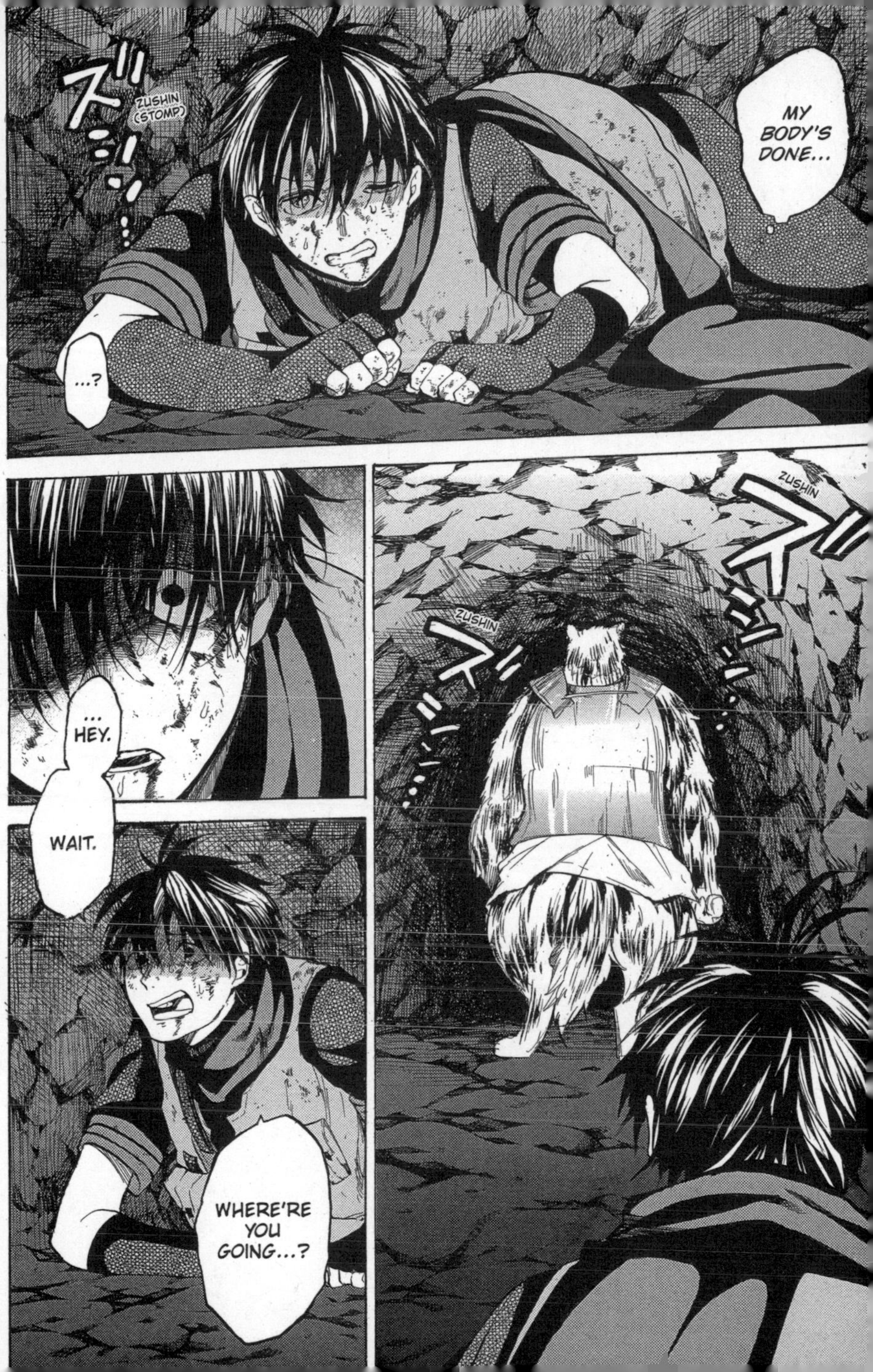
ZUSHIN (STOMP)
MY BODY'S DONE...
...?
ZUSHIN
ZUSHIN
... HEY.
WAIT.
WHERE'RE YOU GOING...?

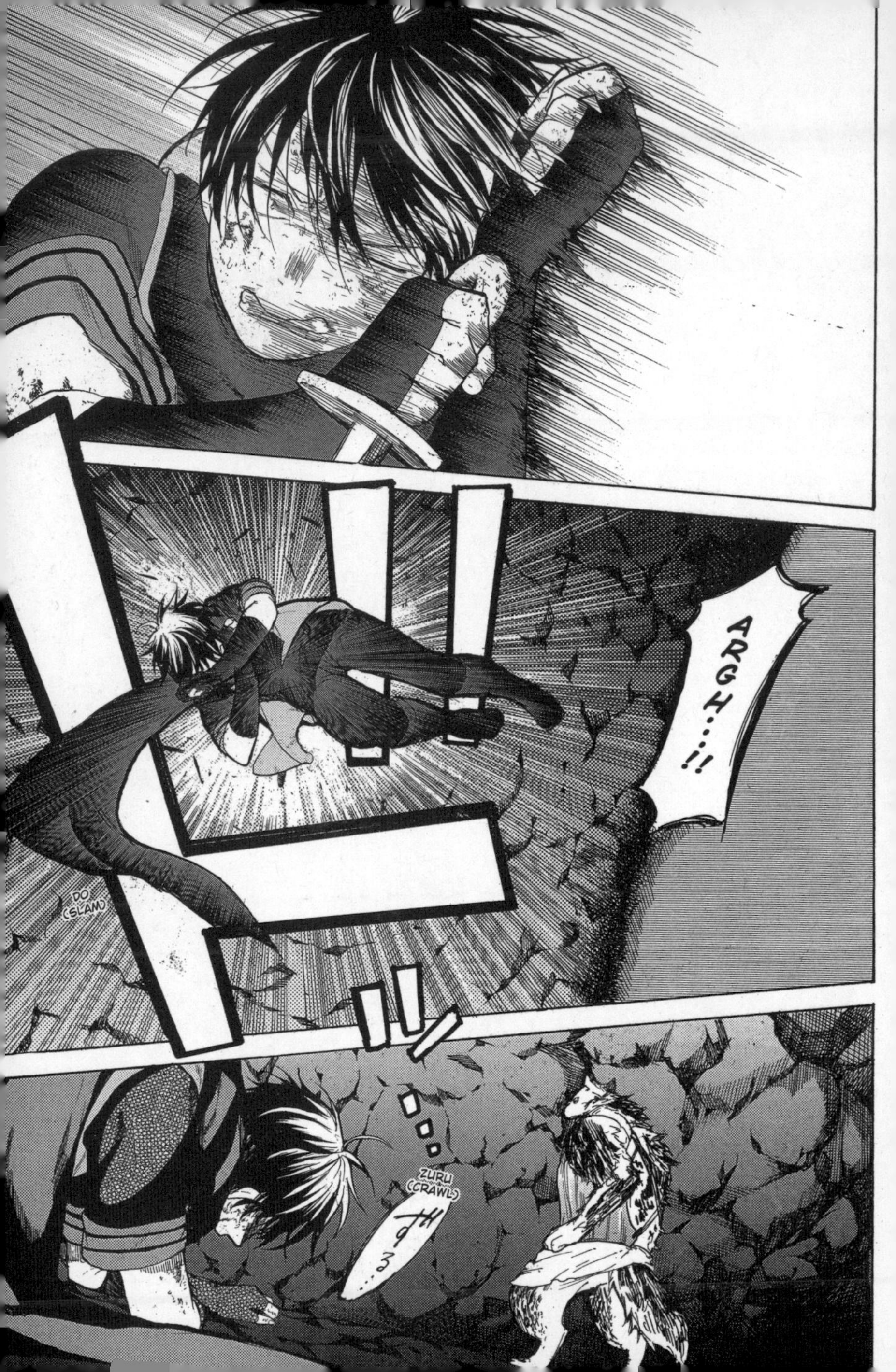
ARGH...!!
DO (SLAM)
ZURU (CRAWL)
ずるっ...

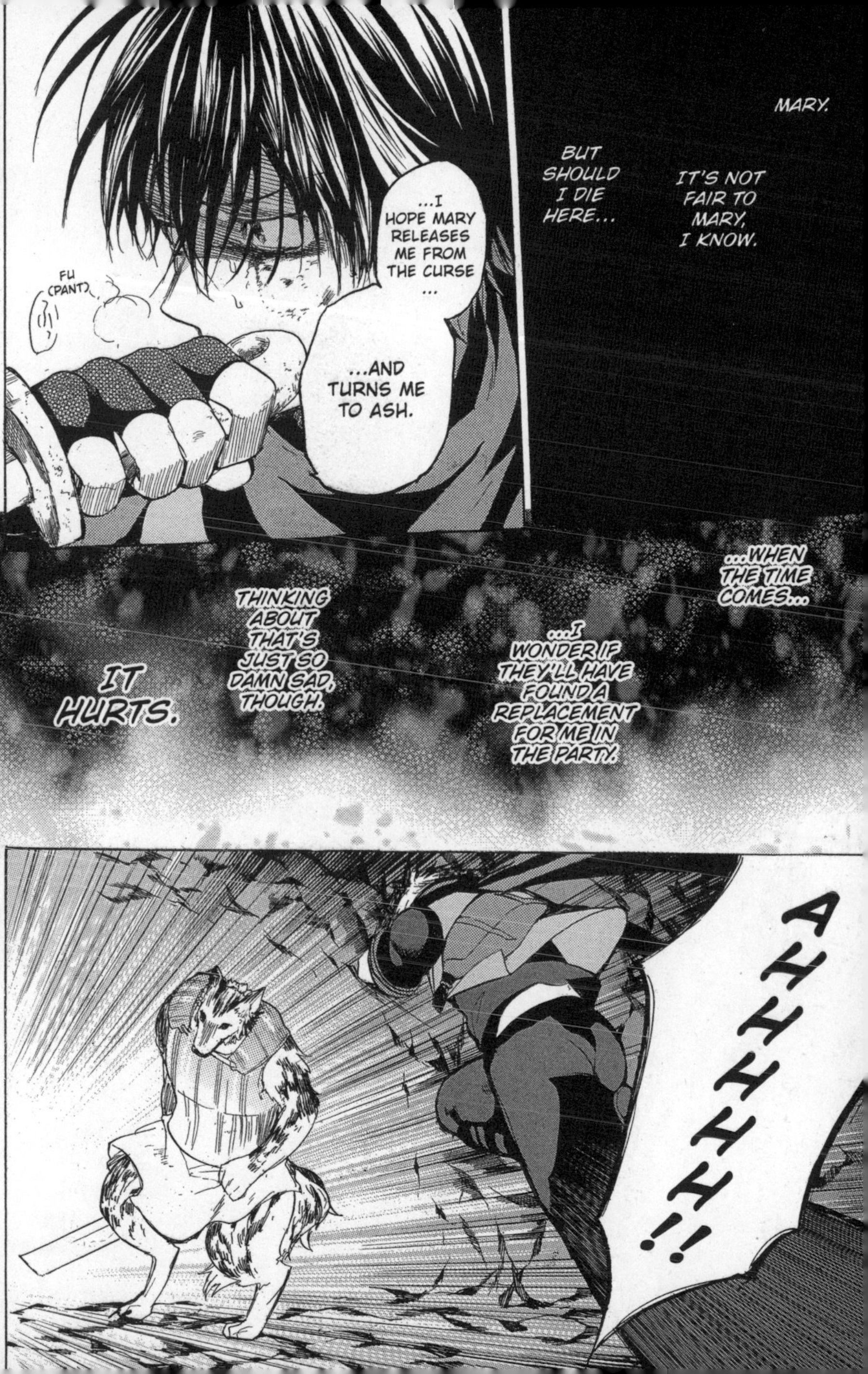
MARY.
IT'S NOT FAIR TO MARY, I KNOW.
BUT SHOULD I DIE HERE...
...I HOPE MARY RELEASES ME FROM THE CURSE...
...AND TURNS ME TO ASH.
FU (PANT)
...WHEN THE TIME COMES...
...I WONDER IF THEY'LL HAVE FOUND A REPLACEMENT FOR ME IN THE PARTY.
THINKING ABOUT THAT'S JUST SO DAMN SAD, THOUGH.
IT HURTS.
AHHHHH!!

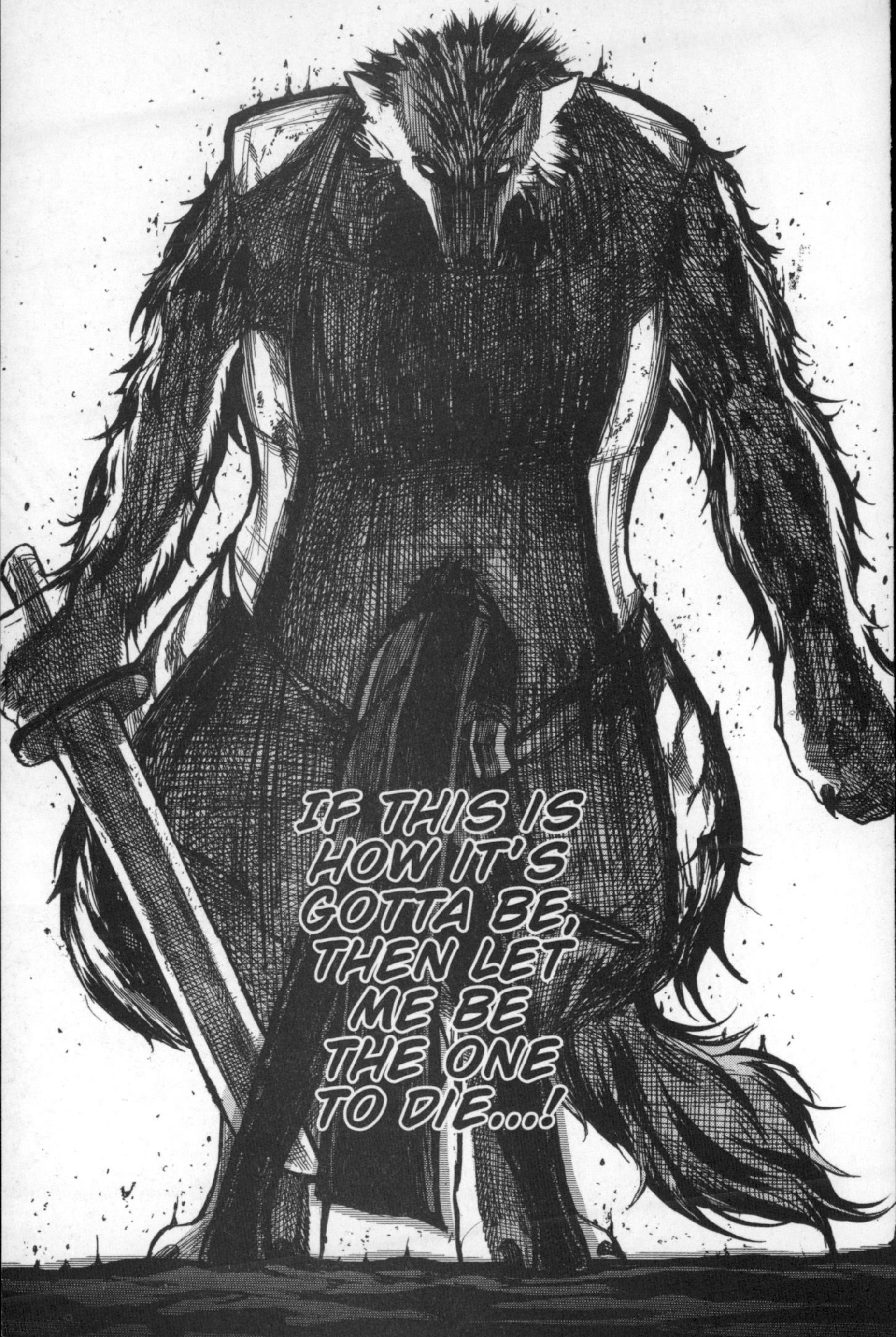
IF THIS IS HOW IT'S GOTTA BE, THEN LET ME BE THE ONE TO DIE...!

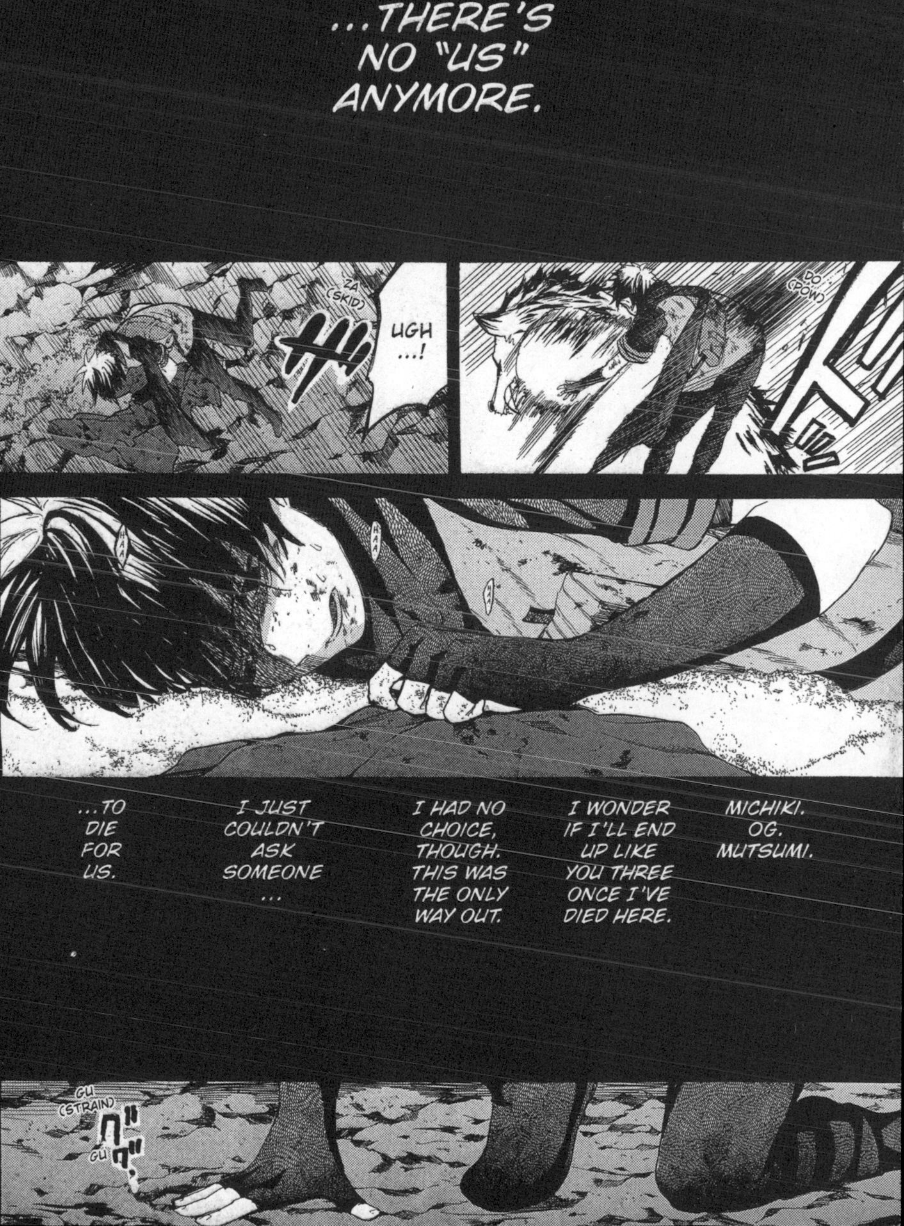
...THERE'S NO "US" ANYMORE.
DO (POW)
ZA (SKID)
UGH ...!
HAA
HAA
MICHIKI. OG. MUTSUMI.
I WONDER IF I'LL END UP LIKE YOU THREE ONCE I'VE DIED HERE.
I HAD NO CHOICE, THOUGH. THIS WAS THE ONLY WAY OUT.
I JUST COULDN'T ASK SOMEONE ...
...TO DIE FOR US.
GU (STRAIN)
GU

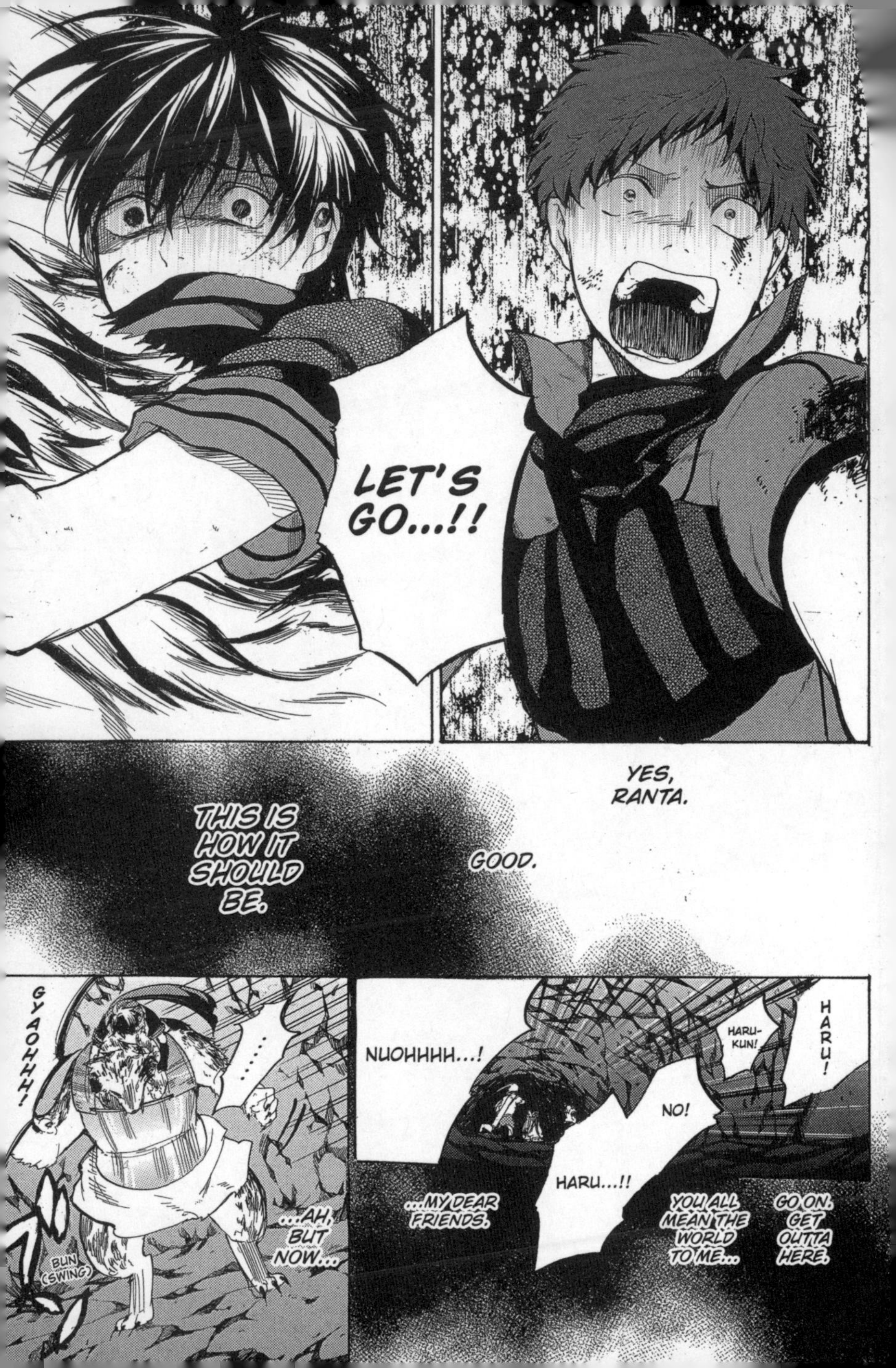

LET'S GO...!!
YES, RANTA.
GOOD.
THIS IS HOW IT SHOULD BE.
HARU!
HARU-KUN!
NUOHHHH...!
NO!
HARU...!!
GO ON. GET OUTTA HERE.
YOU ALL MEAN THE WORLD TO ME...
...MY DEAR FRIENDS.
...AH, BUT NOW...
...
GYAOHHH!
BUN (SWING)

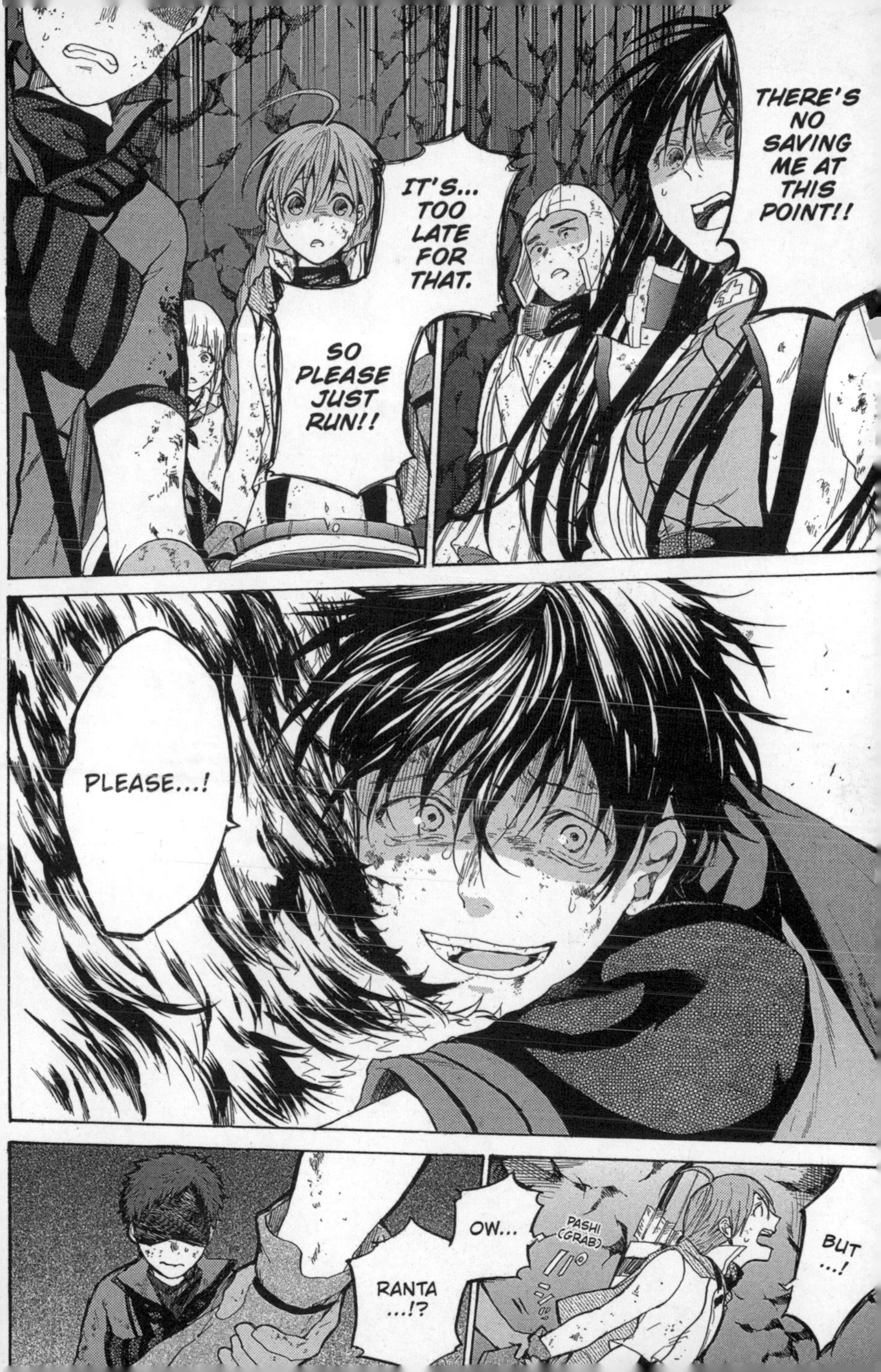
THERE'S NO SAVING ME AT THIS POINT!!
IT'S... TOO LATE FOR THAT.
SO PLEASE JUST RUN!!
PLEASE...!
BUT ...!
PASHI (GRAB)
OW...
RANTA ...!?

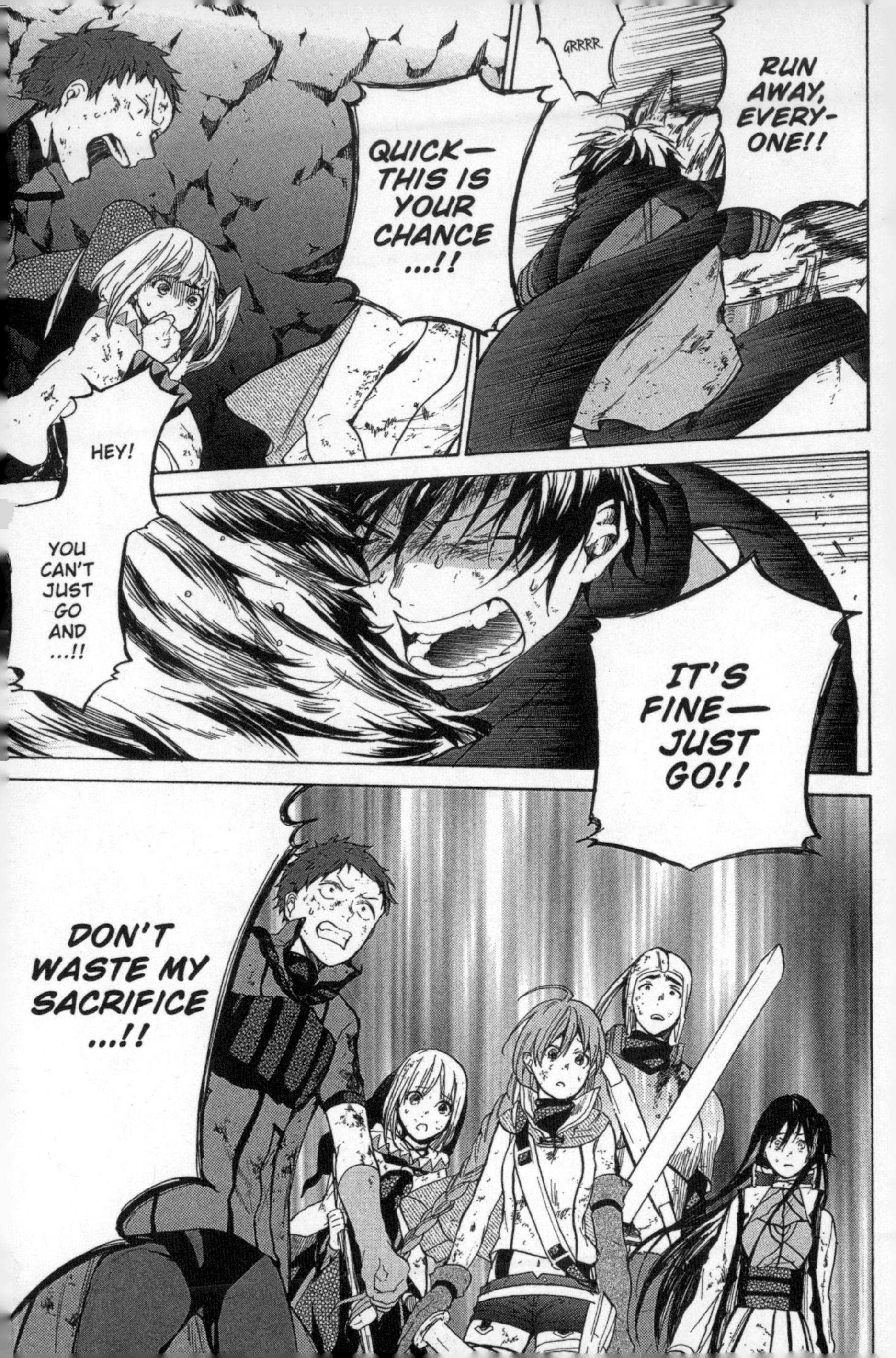
GRRRR.
RUN AWAY, EVERY-ONE!!
QUICK—THIS IS YOUR CHANCE...!!
HEY!
YOU CAN'T JUST GO AND ...!!
IT'S FINE—JUST GO!!
DON'T WASTE MY SACRIFICE...!!

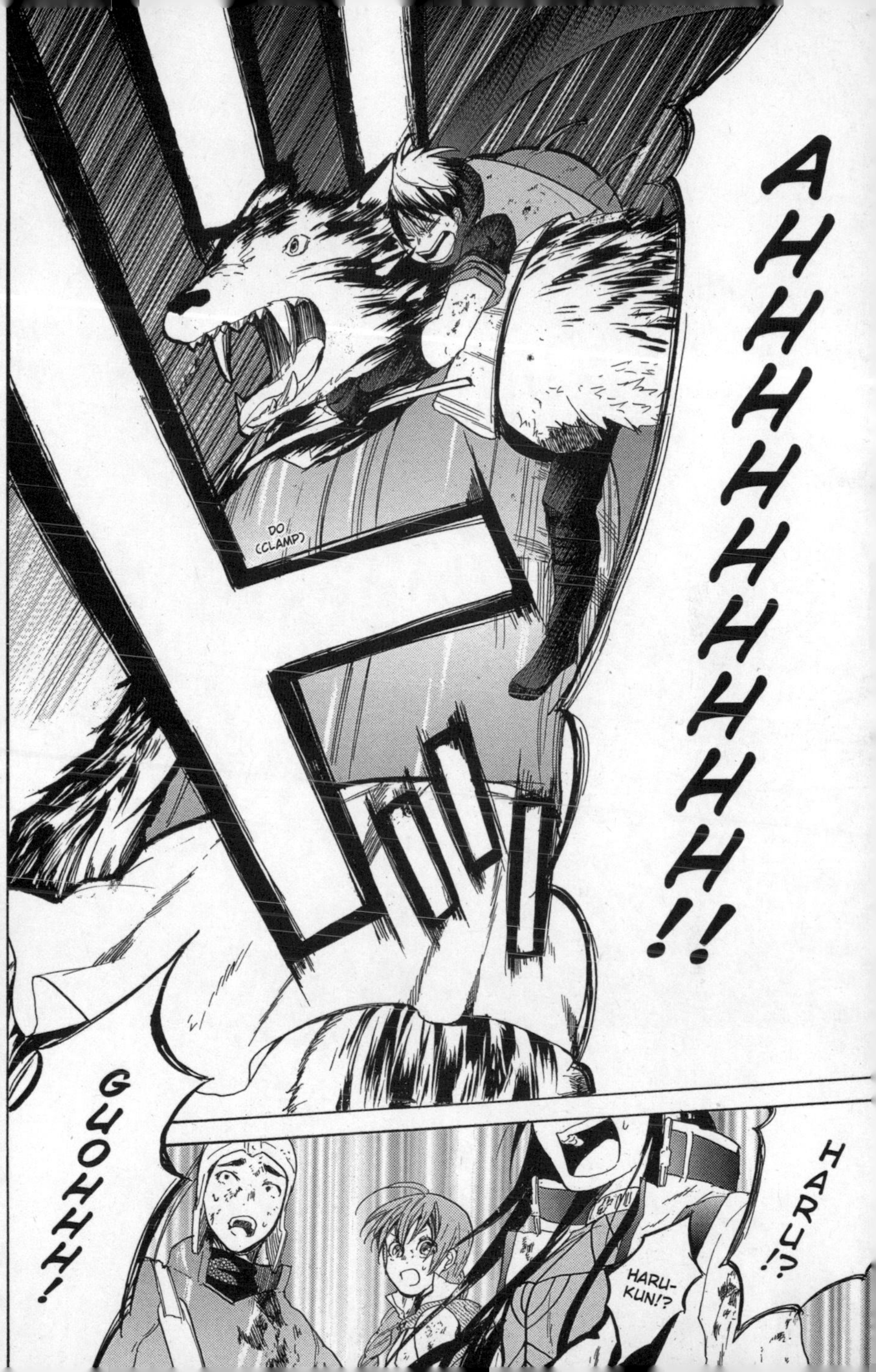
AHHHHHHHHHH!!
DO (CLAMP)
GUOHHH!
HARU!?
HARU-KUN!?

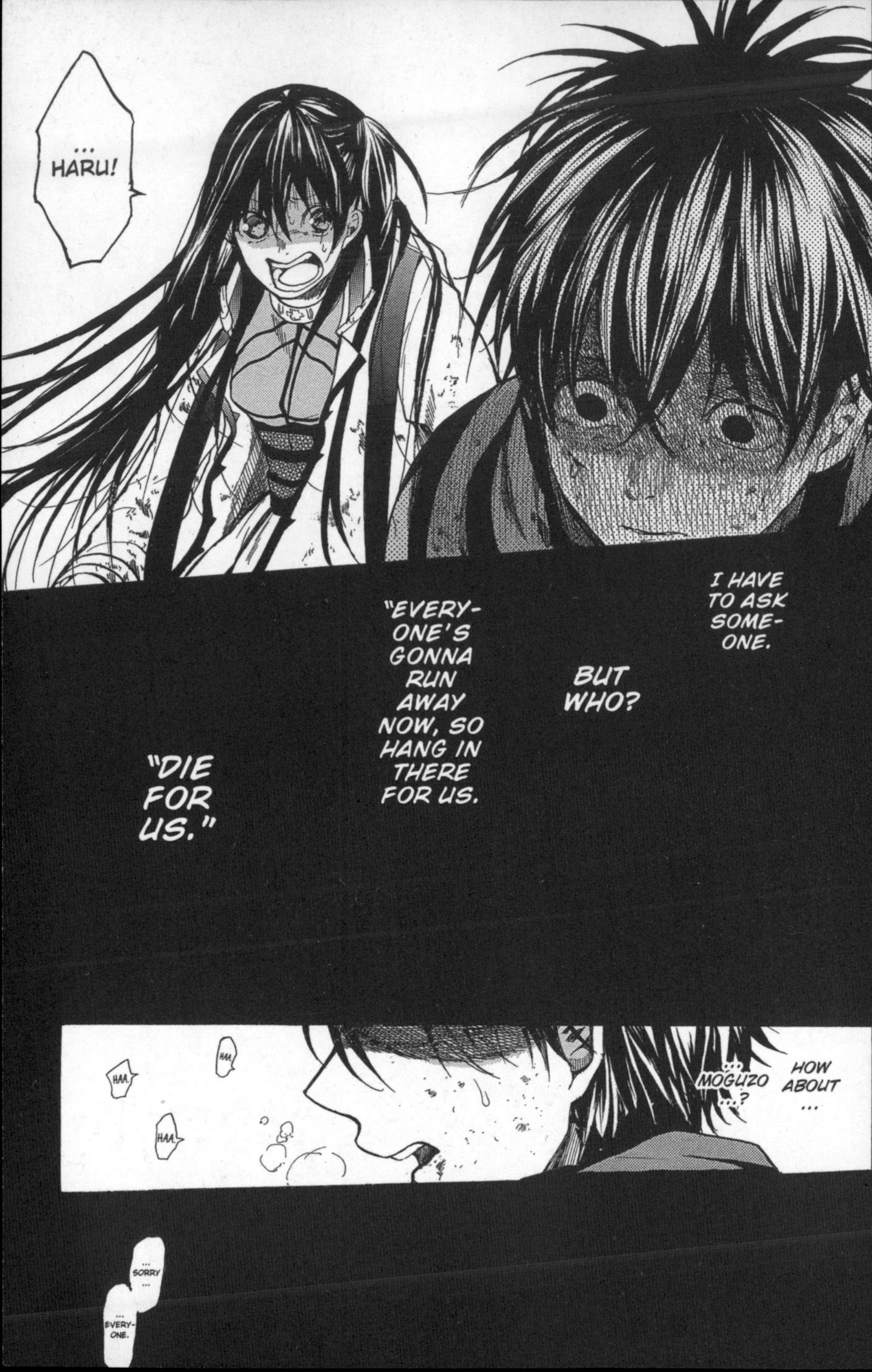

...HARU!
I HAVE TO ASK SOME-ONE.
BUT WHO?
"EVERY-ONE'S GONNA RUN AWAY NOW, SO HANG IN THERE FOR US.
"DIE FOR US."
HOW ABOUT ...
...MOGUZO ...?
HAA.
HAA.
HAA.
...SORRY ...
...EVERY-ONE.

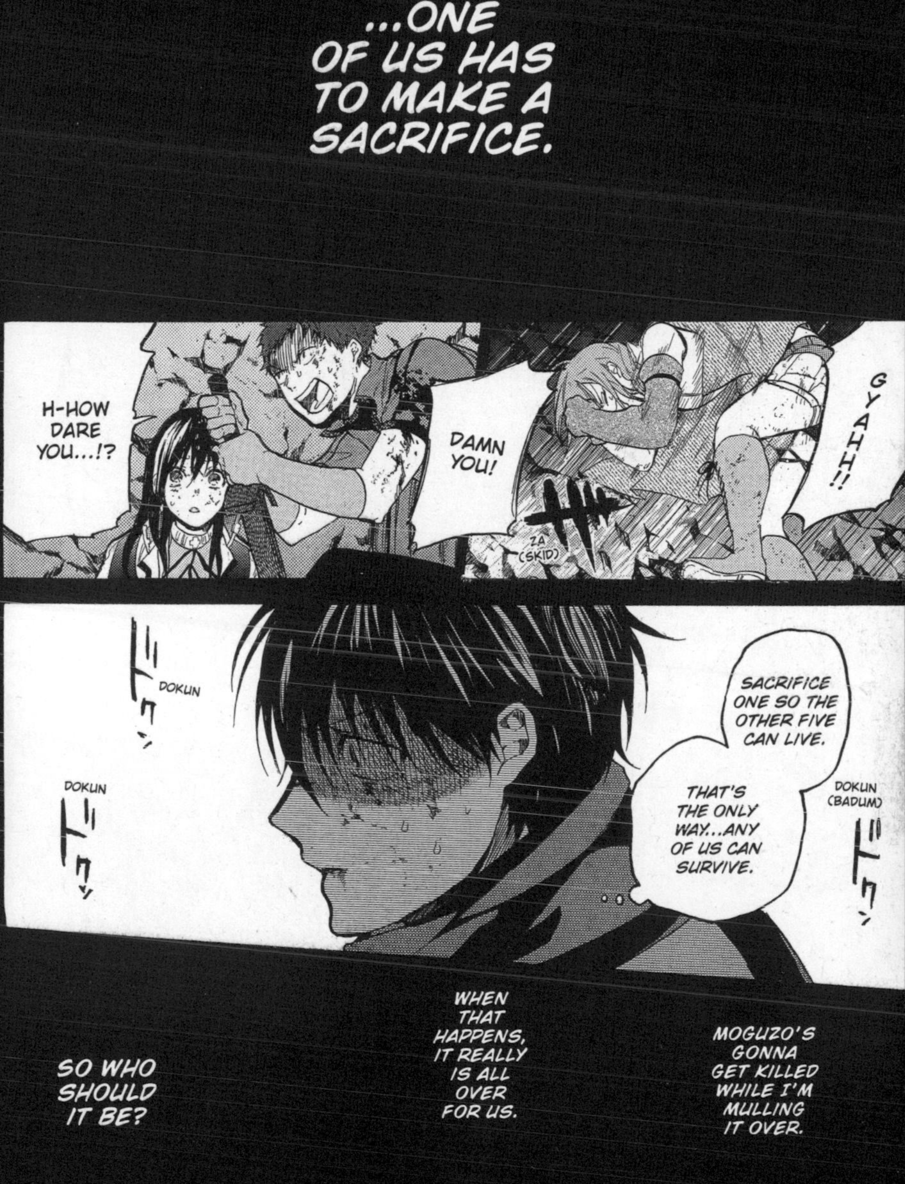
...ONE OF US HAS TO MAKE A SACRIFICE.
GYAHH!!
ZA (SKID)
DAMN YOU!
H-HOW DARE YOU...!?
SACRIFICE ONE SO THE OTHER FIVE CAN LIVE.
THAT'S THE ONLY WAY...ANY OF US CAN SURVIVE.
DOKUN (BADUM)
DOKUN
DOKUN
MOGUZO'S GONNA GET KILLED WHILE I'M MULLING IT OVER.
WHEN THAT HAPPENS, IT REALLY IS ALL OVER FOR US.
SO WHO SHOULD IT BE?

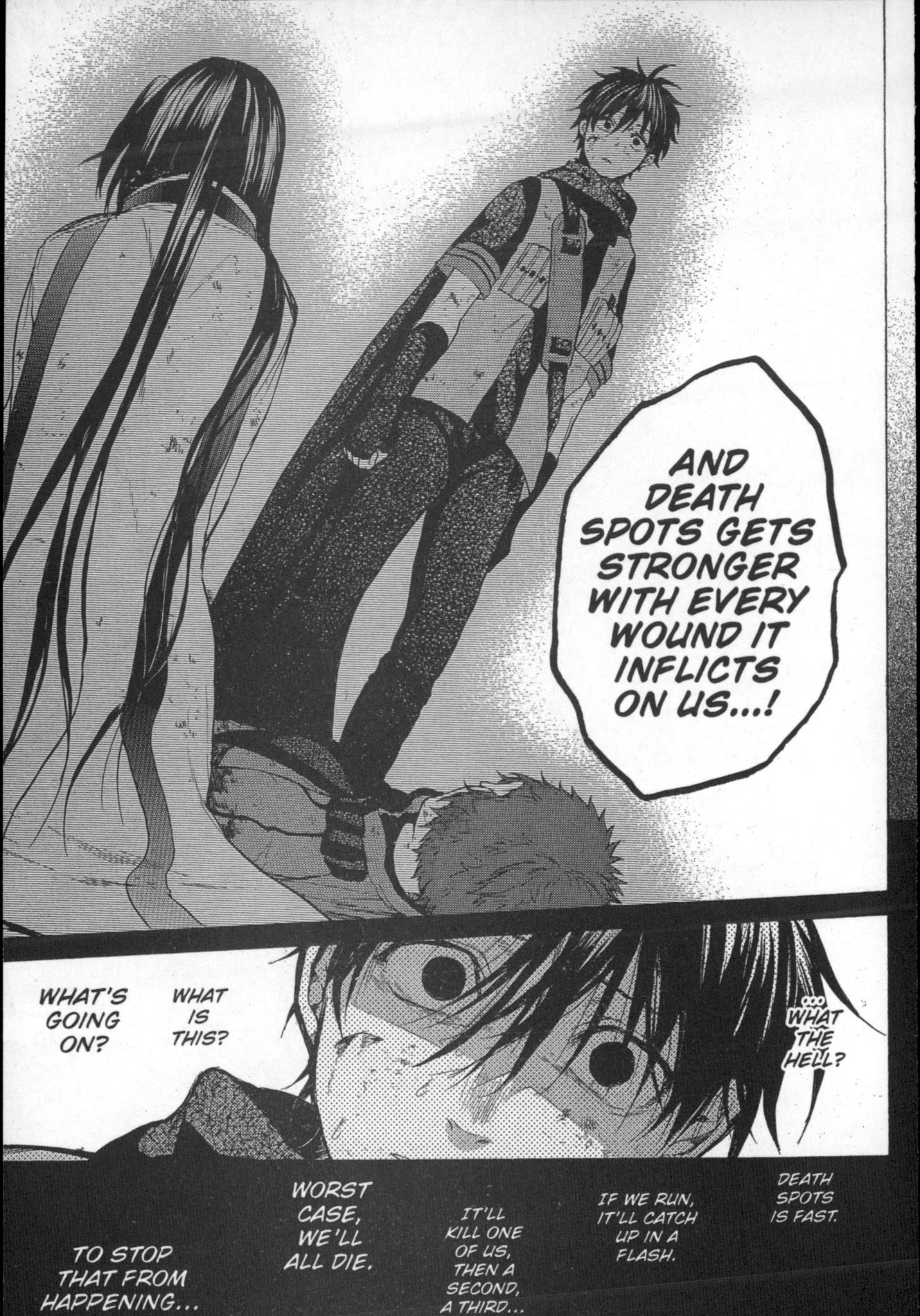
AND DEATH SPOTS GETS STRONGER WITH EVERY WOUND IT INFLICTS ON US...!
...WHAT THE HELL?
WHAT IS THIS?
WHAT'S GOING ON?
DEATH SPOTS IS FAST.
IF WE RUN, IT'LL CATCH UP IN A FLASH.
IT'LL KILL ONE OF US, THEN A SECOND, A THIRD...
WORST CASE, WE'LL ALL DIE.
TO STOP THAT FROM HAPPENING...

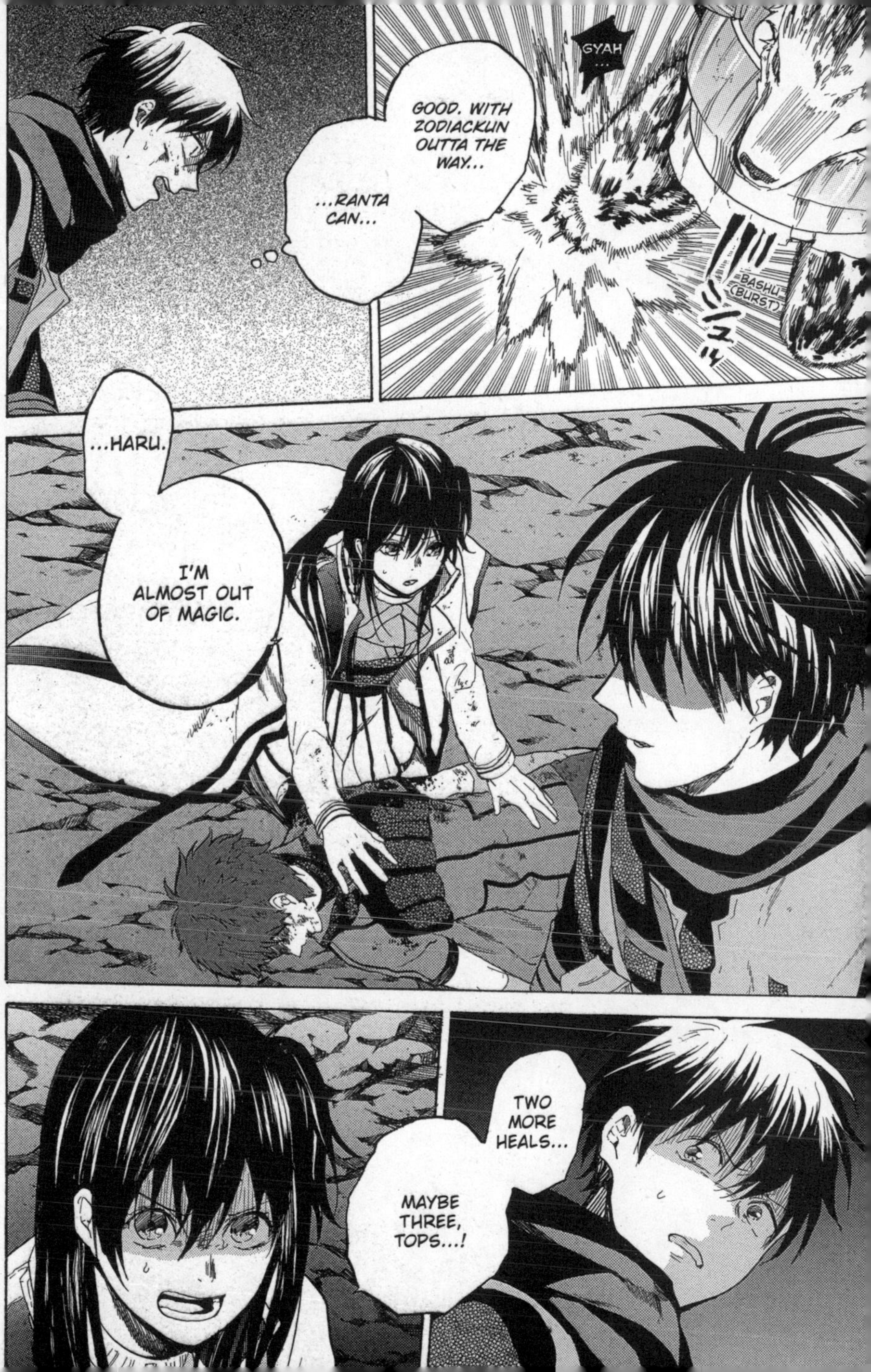
GYAH...
BASHU (BURST)
GOOD. WITH ZODIACKUN OUTTA THE WAY...
...RANTA CAN...
...HARU.
I'M ALMOST OUT OF MAGIC.
TWO MORE HEALS...
MAYBE THREE, TOPS...!

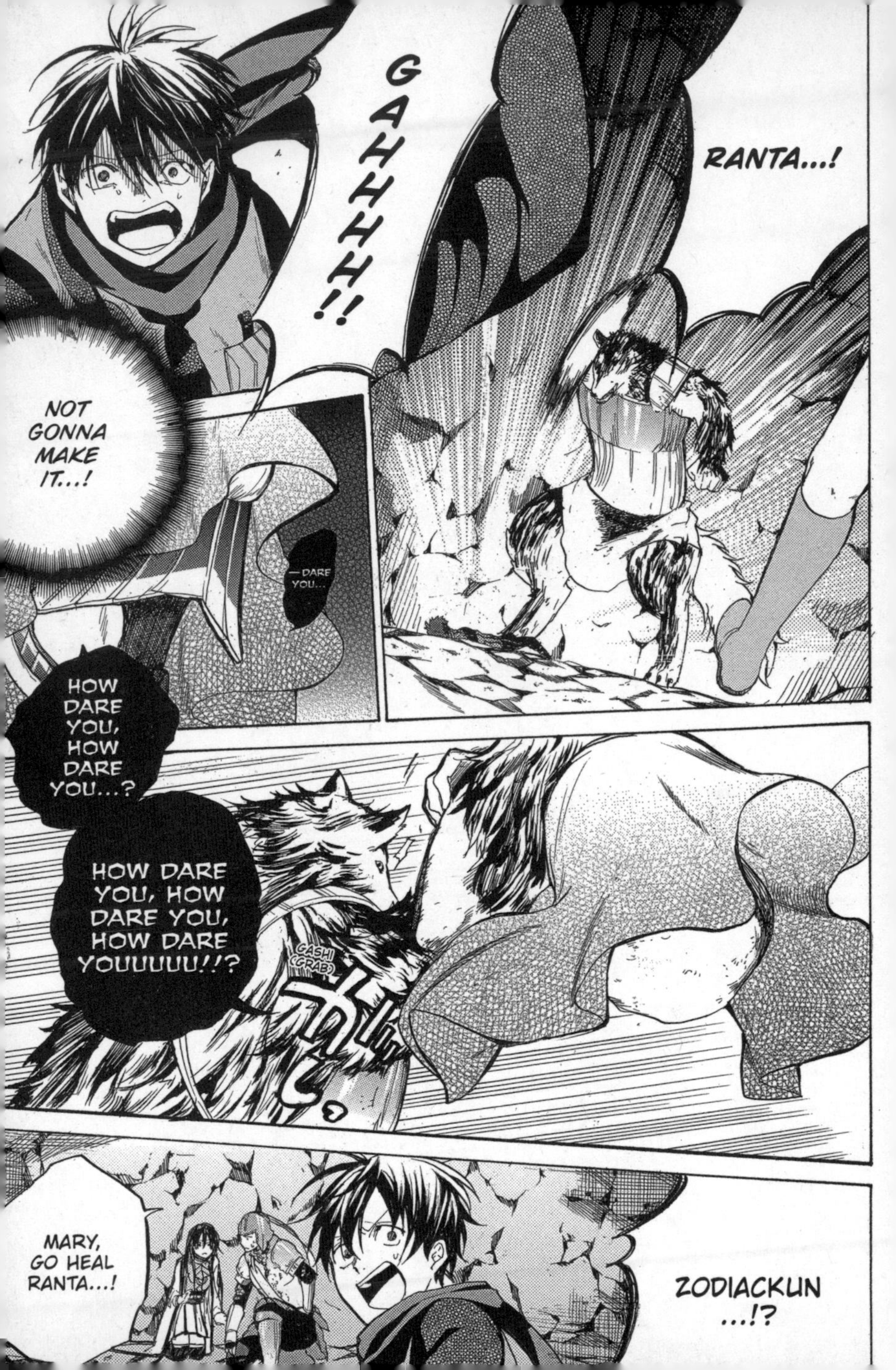
RANTA...!
GAHHHHH!!
NOT GONNA MAKE IT...!
—DARE YOU...
HOW DARE YOU, HOW DARE YOU...?
HOW DARE YOU, HOW DARE YOU, HOW DARE YOUUUUU!!?
GASHI (GRAB)
ZODIACKUN ...!?
MARY, GO HEAL RANTA...!

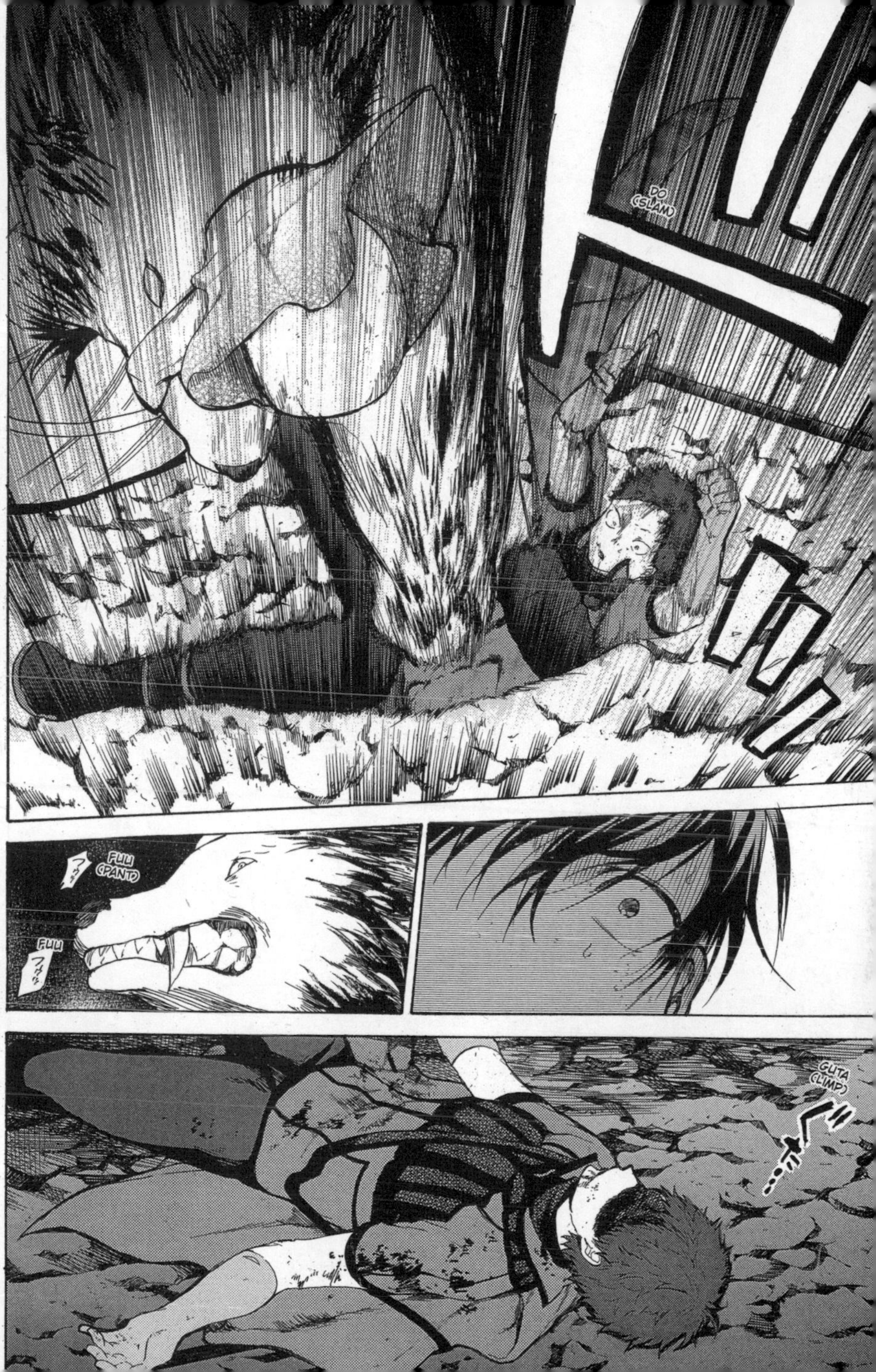
DO (SLAM)
FUU (PANT)
FUU
GUTA (LIMP)

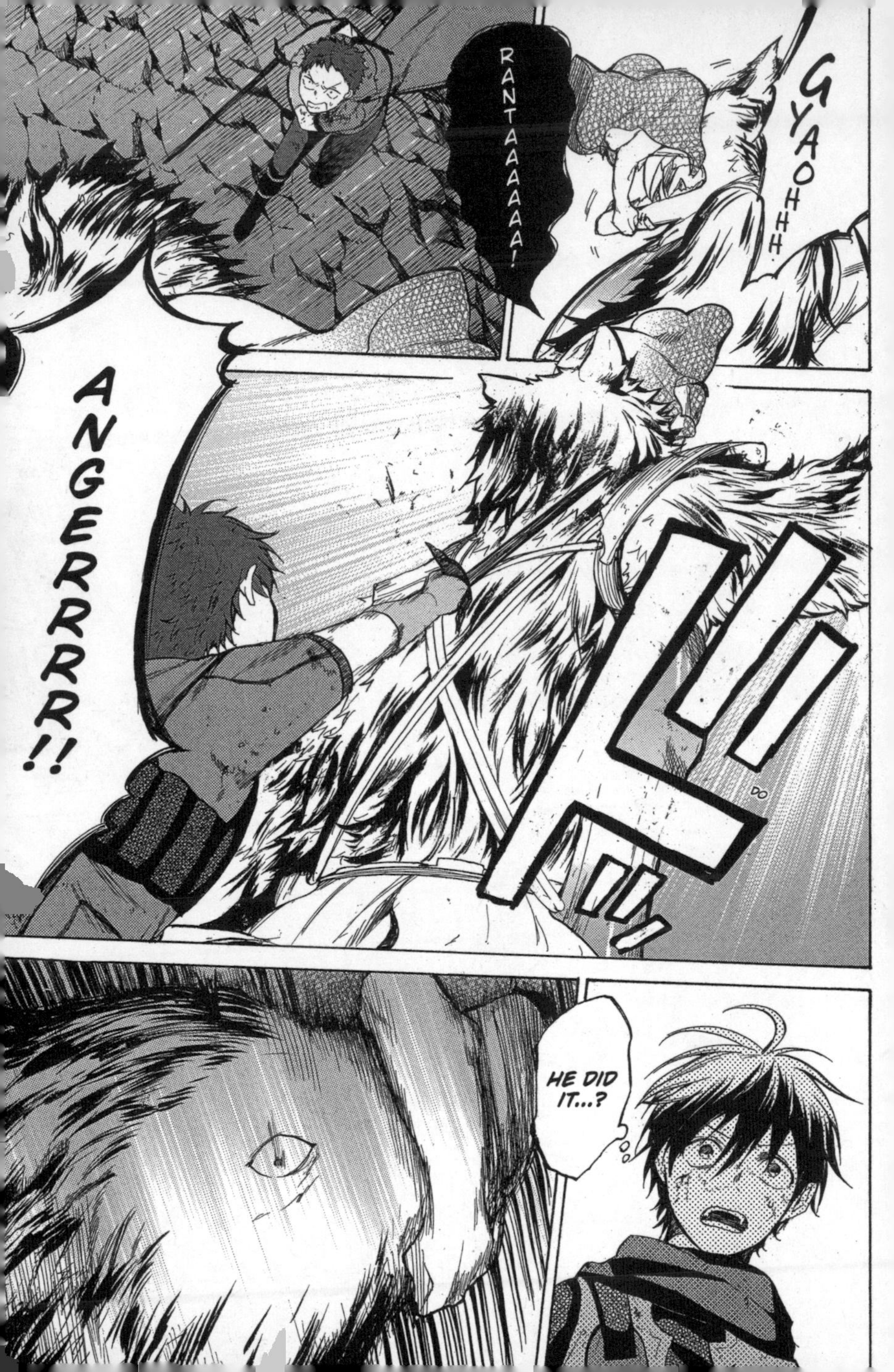

GYAOHHH
RANTAAAAAAA!
ANGERRRRR!!
DO
HE DID IT...?

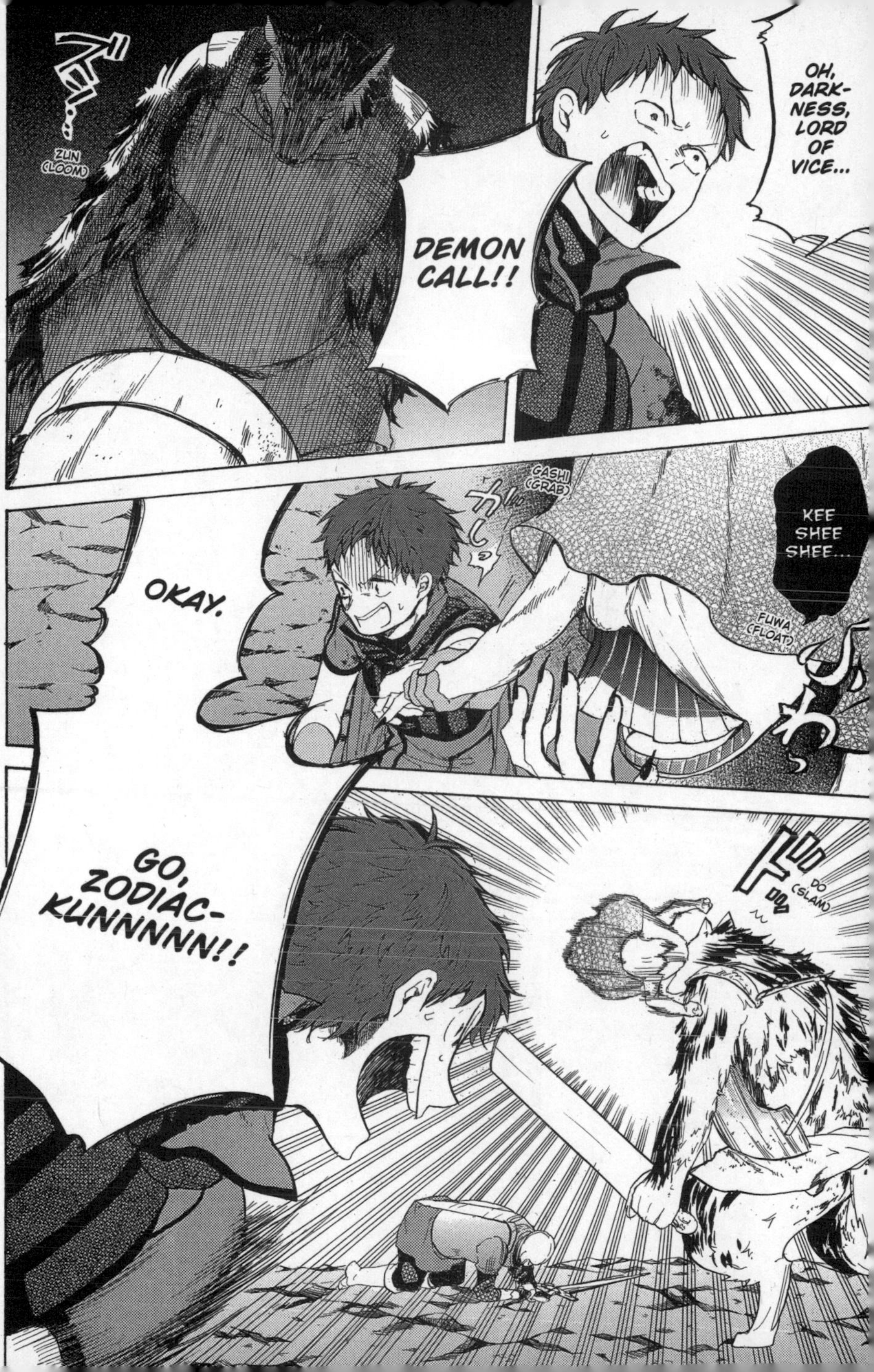

OH, DARKNESS, LORD OF VICE...
DEMON CALL!!
ZUN (LOOM)
KEE SHEE SHEE...
FUWA (FLOAT)
GASHI (GRAB)
OKAY.
DO (SLAM)
GO, ZODIAC-KUNNNNNN!!

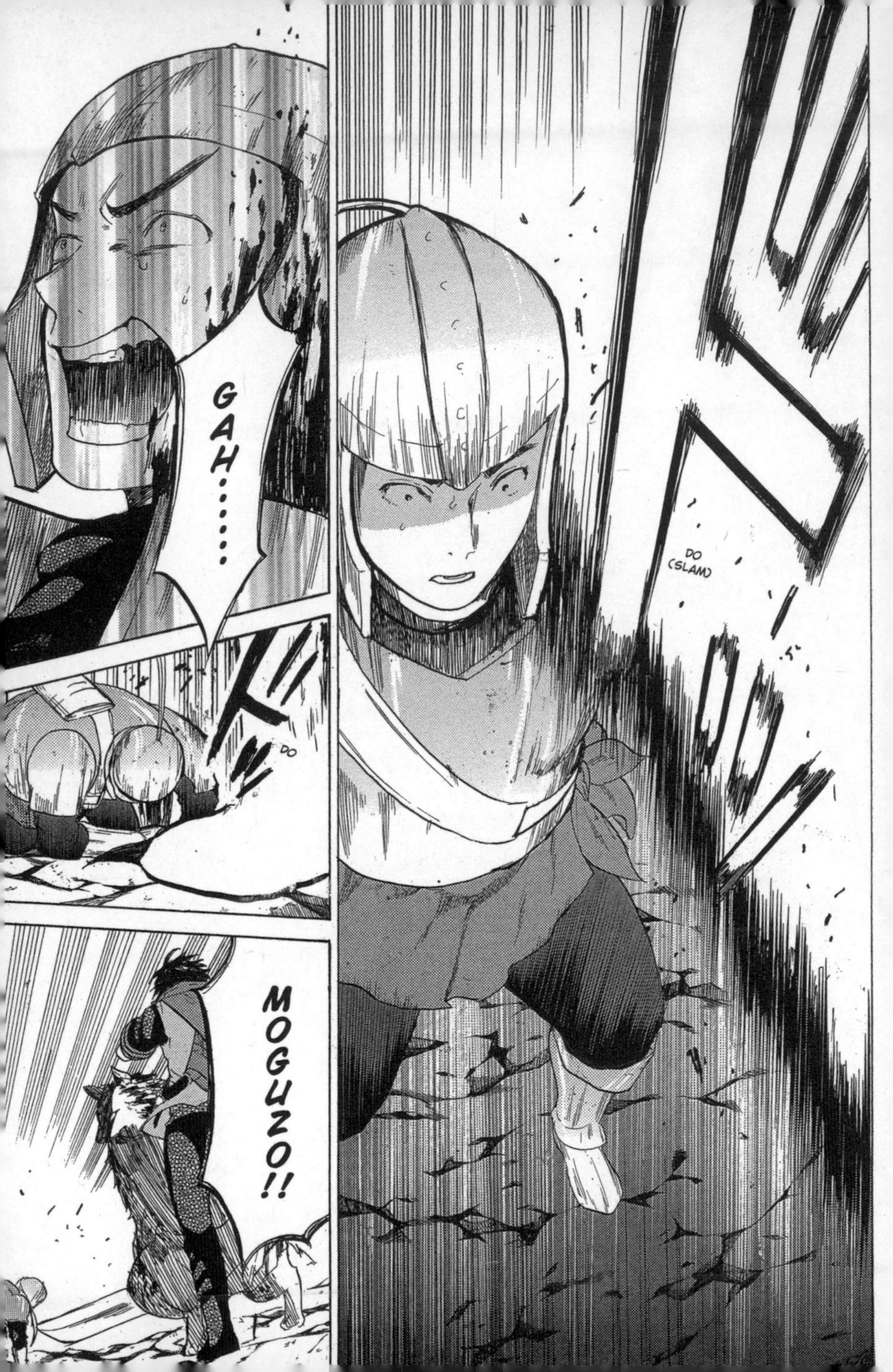
DO
(SLAM)
GAH......
DO
MOGUZO!!

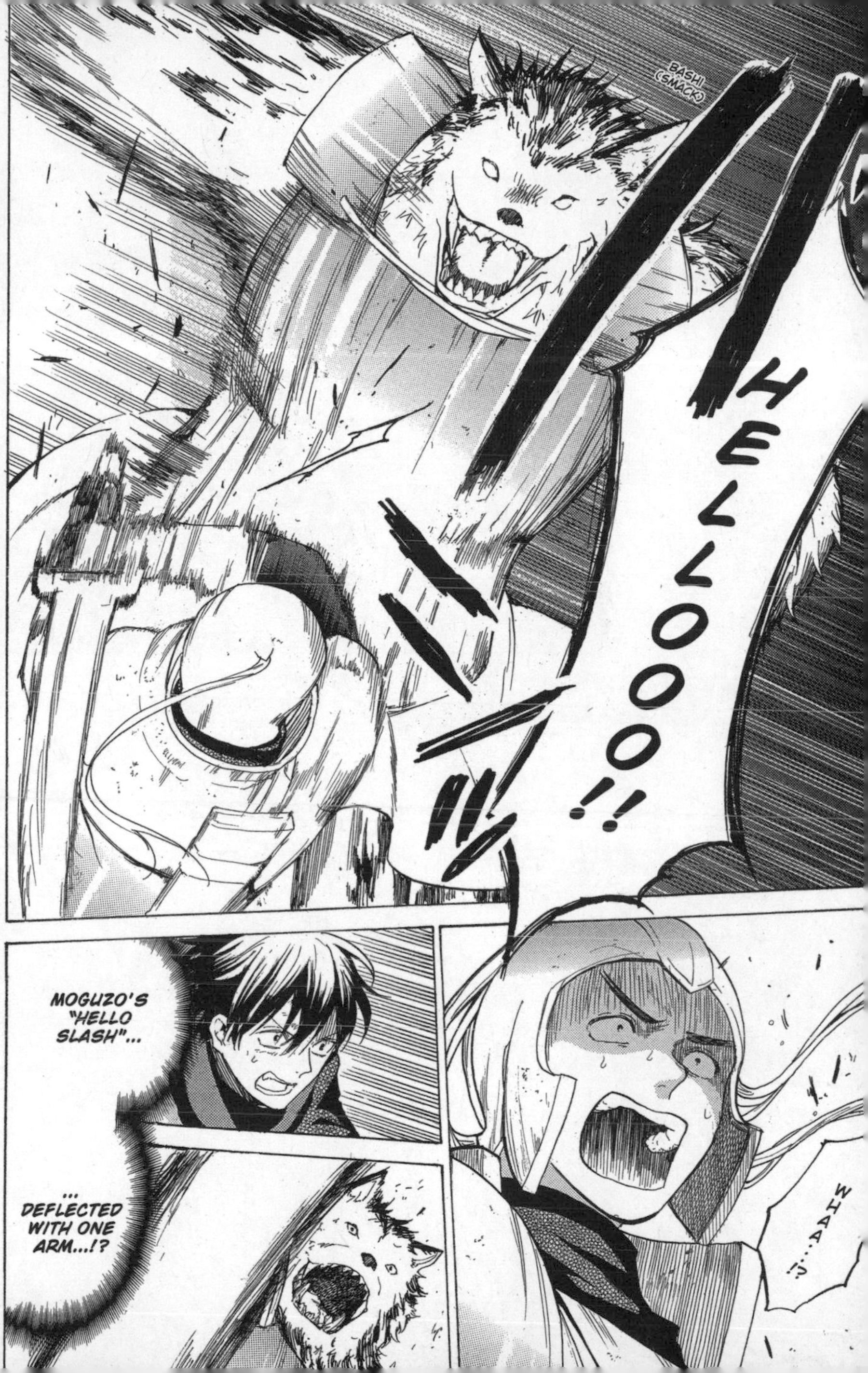
BASHI (SMACK)
HELLOOOO!!
WHAA...!?
MOGUZO'S "HELLO SLASH"...
... DEFLECTED WITH ONE ARM...!?

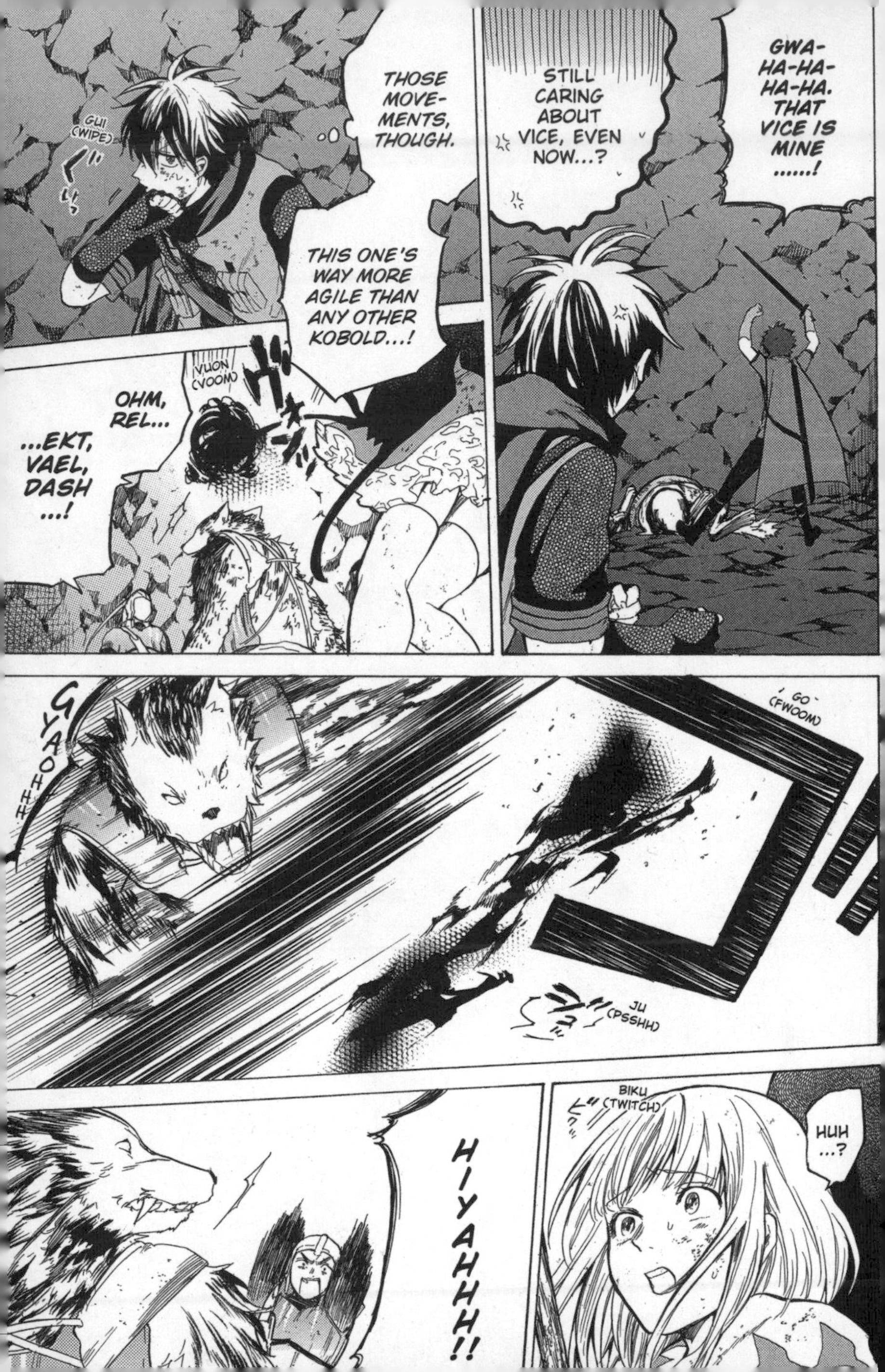
GWA-HA-HA-HA-HA. THAT VICE IS MINE ......!
STILL CARING ABOUT VICE, EVEN NOW...?
THOSE MOVE-MENTS, THOUGH.
GUI (WIPE)
THIS ONE'S WAY MORE AGILE THAN ANY OTHER KOBOLD...!
VUON (VOOM)
OHM, REL...
...EKT, VAEL, DASH ...!
GO (FWOOM)
GYAOHHH
JU (PSSHH)
BIKU (TWITCH)
HUH ...?
HIYAHHH!!

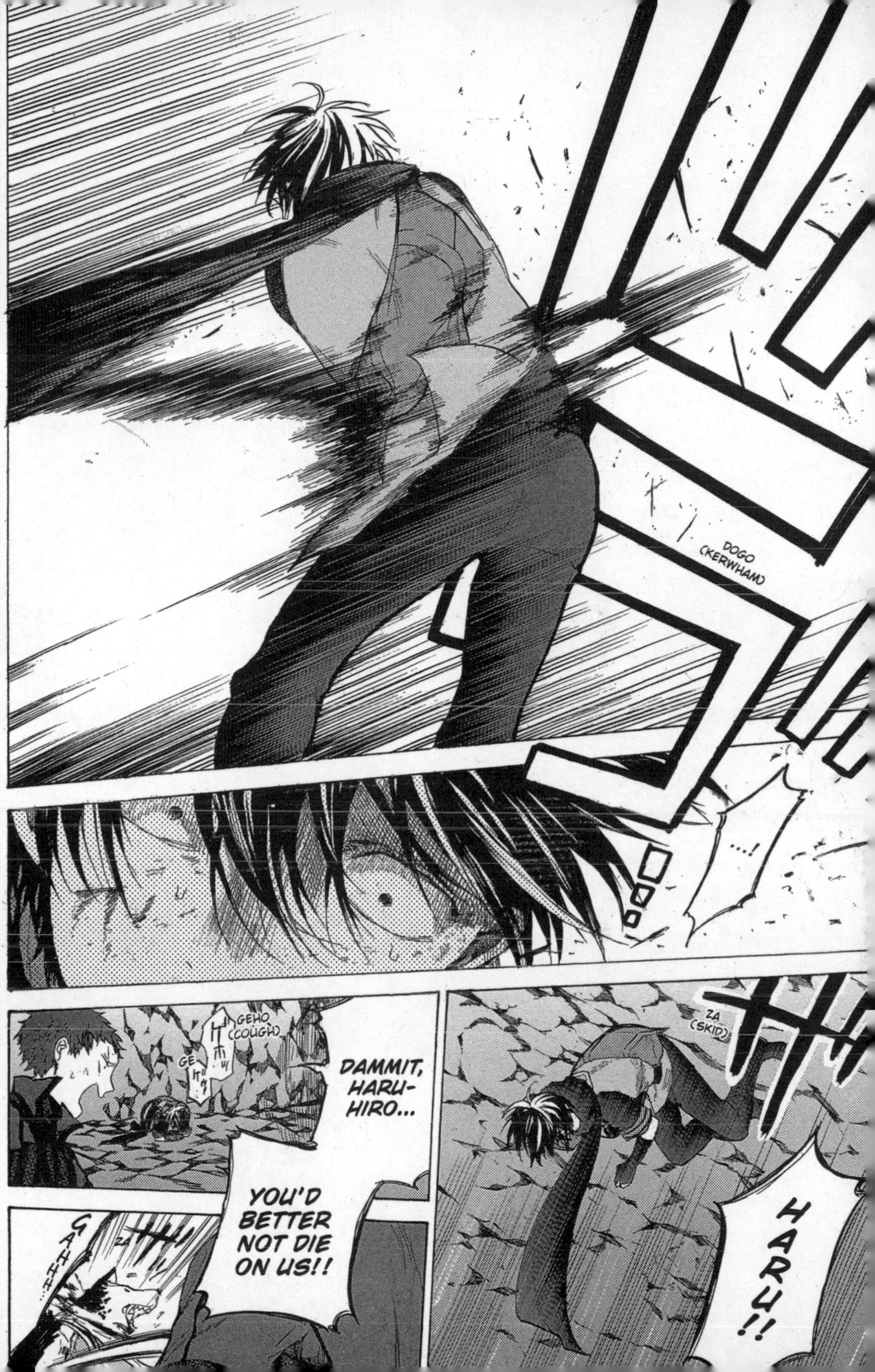
DOGO
(KERWHAM)
...!
ZA
(SKID)
HARU!!
GEHO
(COUGH)
GE
DAMMIT, HARU-HIRO...
YOU'D BETTER NOT DIE ON US!!
ZA
GAHHH...

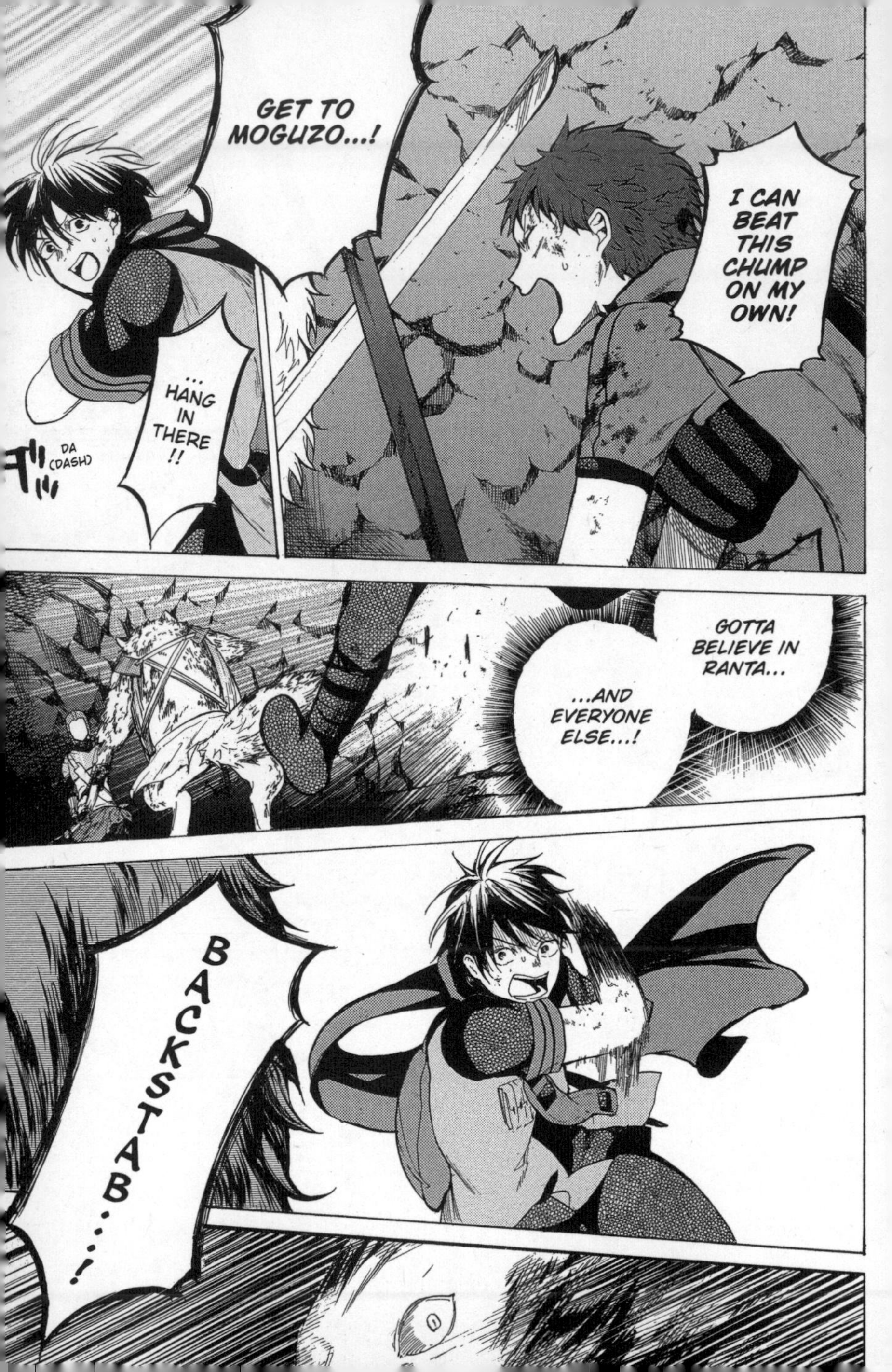
I CAN BEAT THIS CHUMP ON MY OWN!
GET TO MOGUZO...!
...HANG IN THERE!!
DA (DASH)
GOTTA BELIEVE IN RANTA...
...AND EVERYONE ELSE...!
BACKSTAB...!

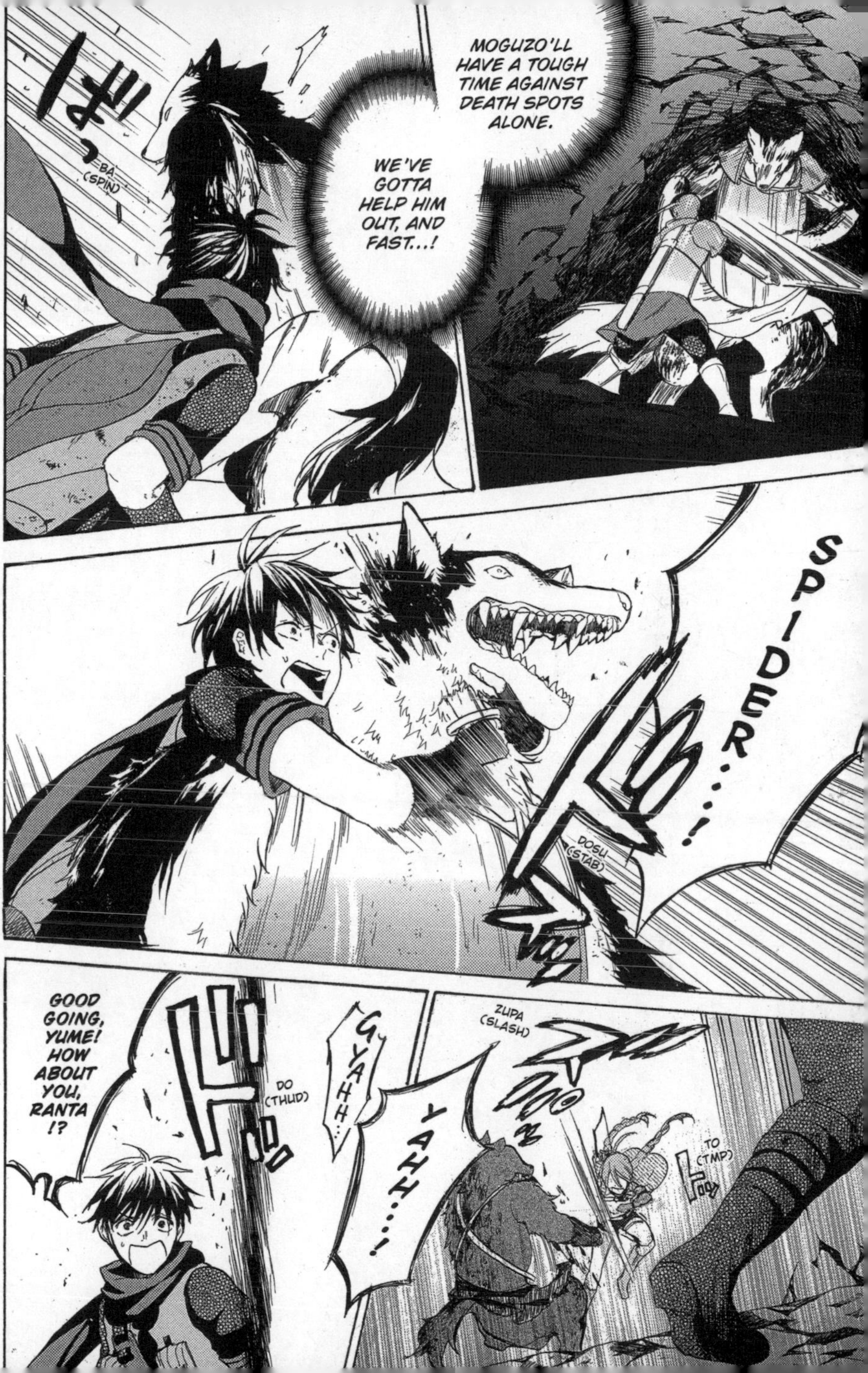
MOGUZO'LL HAVE A TOUGH TIME AGAINST DEATH SPOTS ALONE.
WE'VE GOTTA HELP HIM OUT, AND FAST...!
BA (SPIN)
SPIDER...!
DOSU (STAB)
GOOD GOING, YUME! HOW ABOUT YOU, RANTA!?
DO (THUD)
GYAHH...
YAHH...!
ZUPA (SLASH)
TO (TMP)

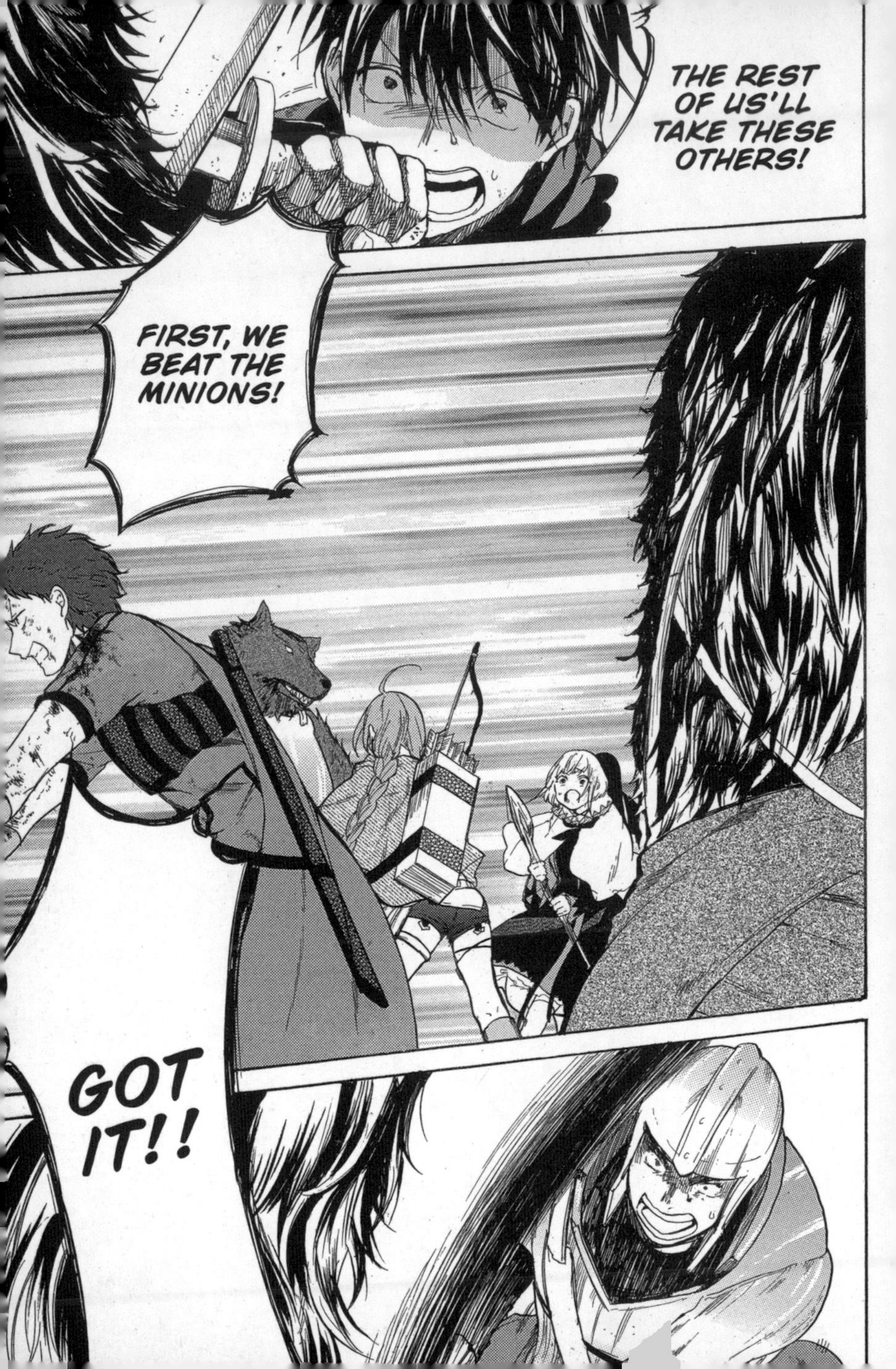
THE REST OF US'LL TAKE THESE OTHERS!
FIRST, WE BEAT THE MINIONS!
GOT IT!!

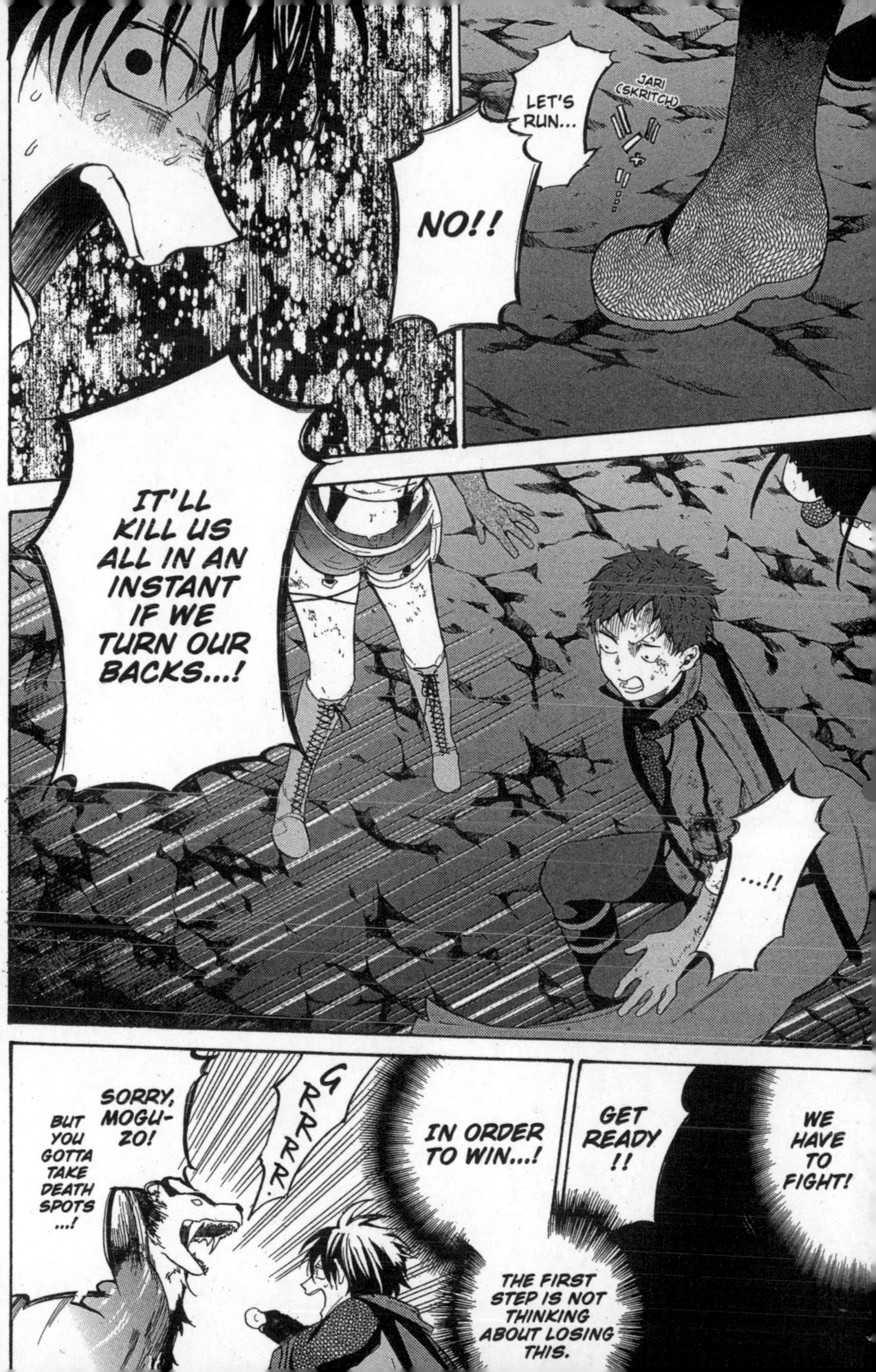

JARI (SKRITCH)
LET'S RUN...
NO!!
IT'LL KILL US ALL IN AN INSTANT IF WE TURN OUR BACKS...!
...!!
WE HAVE TO FIGHT!
GET READY!!
IN ORDER TO WIN...!
THE FIRST STEP IS NOT THINKING ABOUT LOSING THIS.
GRRRR.
SORRY, MOGU-ZO!
BUT YOU GOTTA TAKE DEATH SPOTS...!

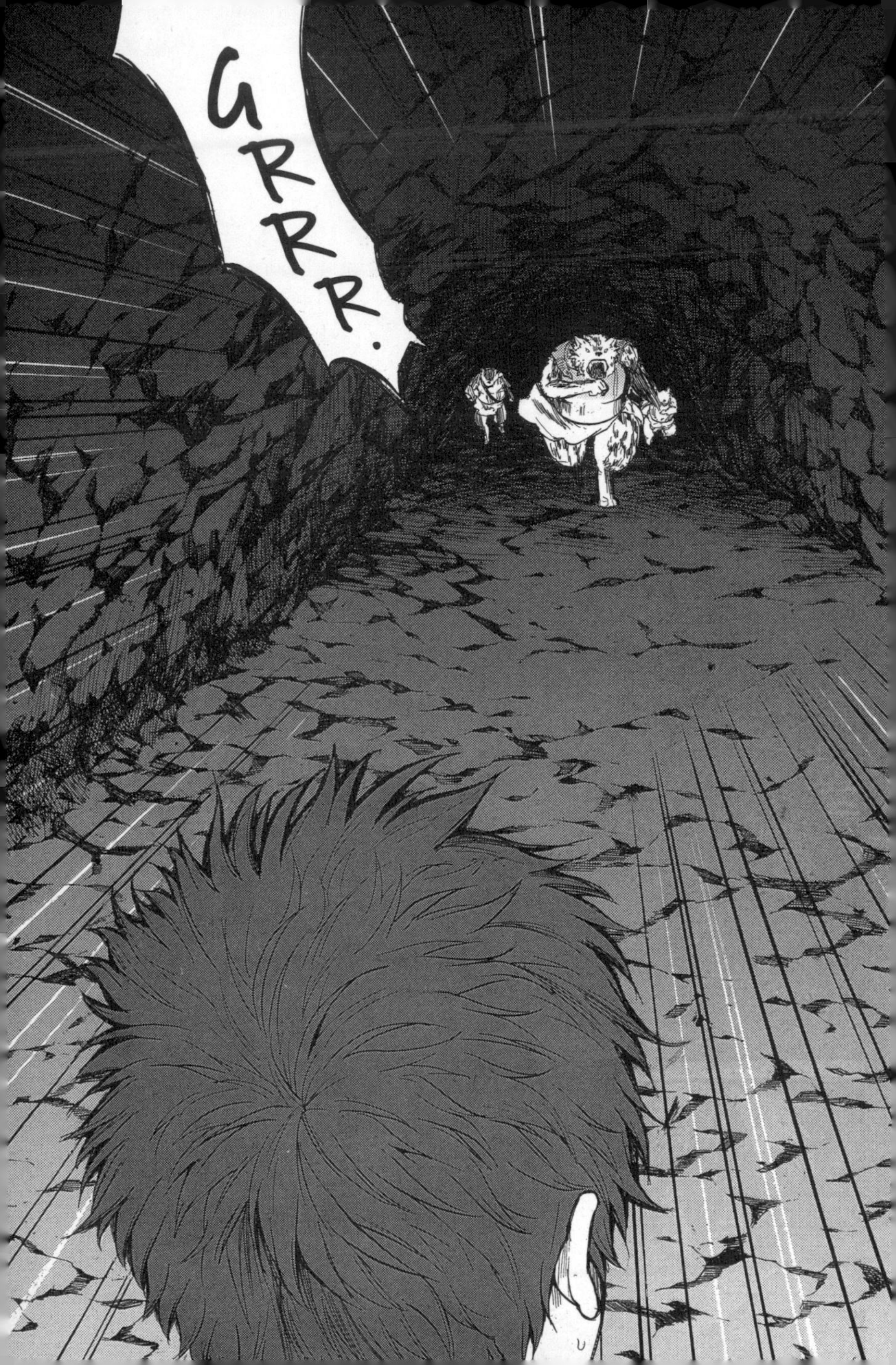
GRRR.

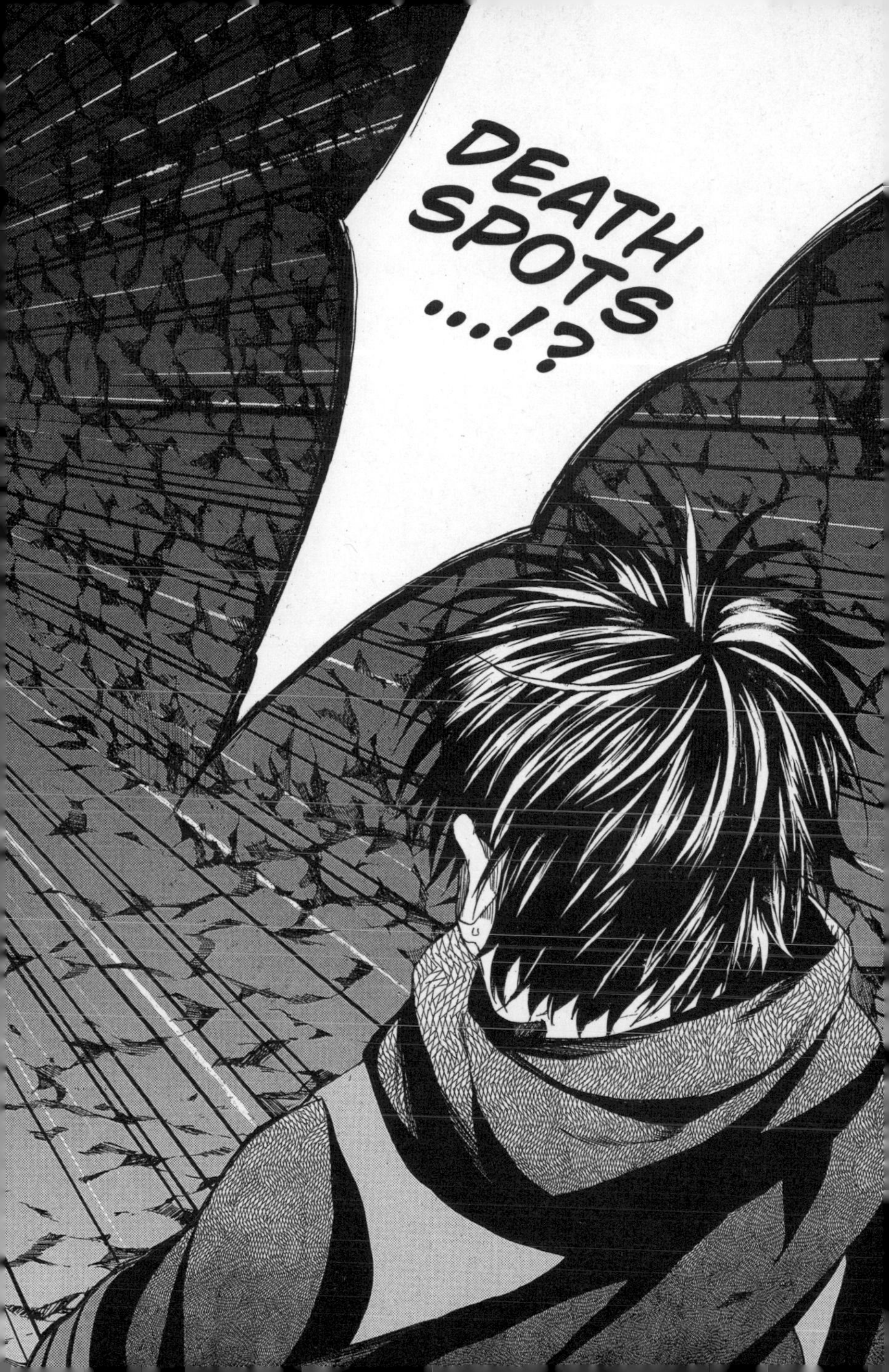
DEATH SPOTS ...!?

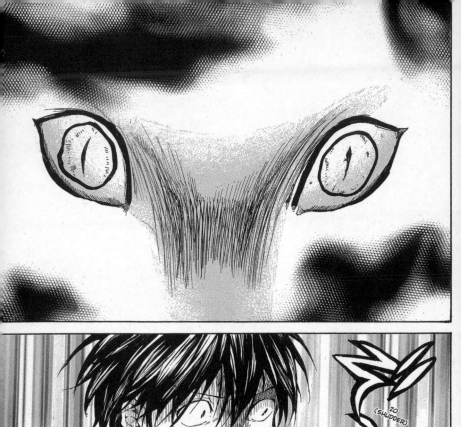

ZO
(SHUDDER)

OH
NO
...

WHY...?

WHY
IS THAT
HERE...!?

......

...
WHOA.

NO
WAY.

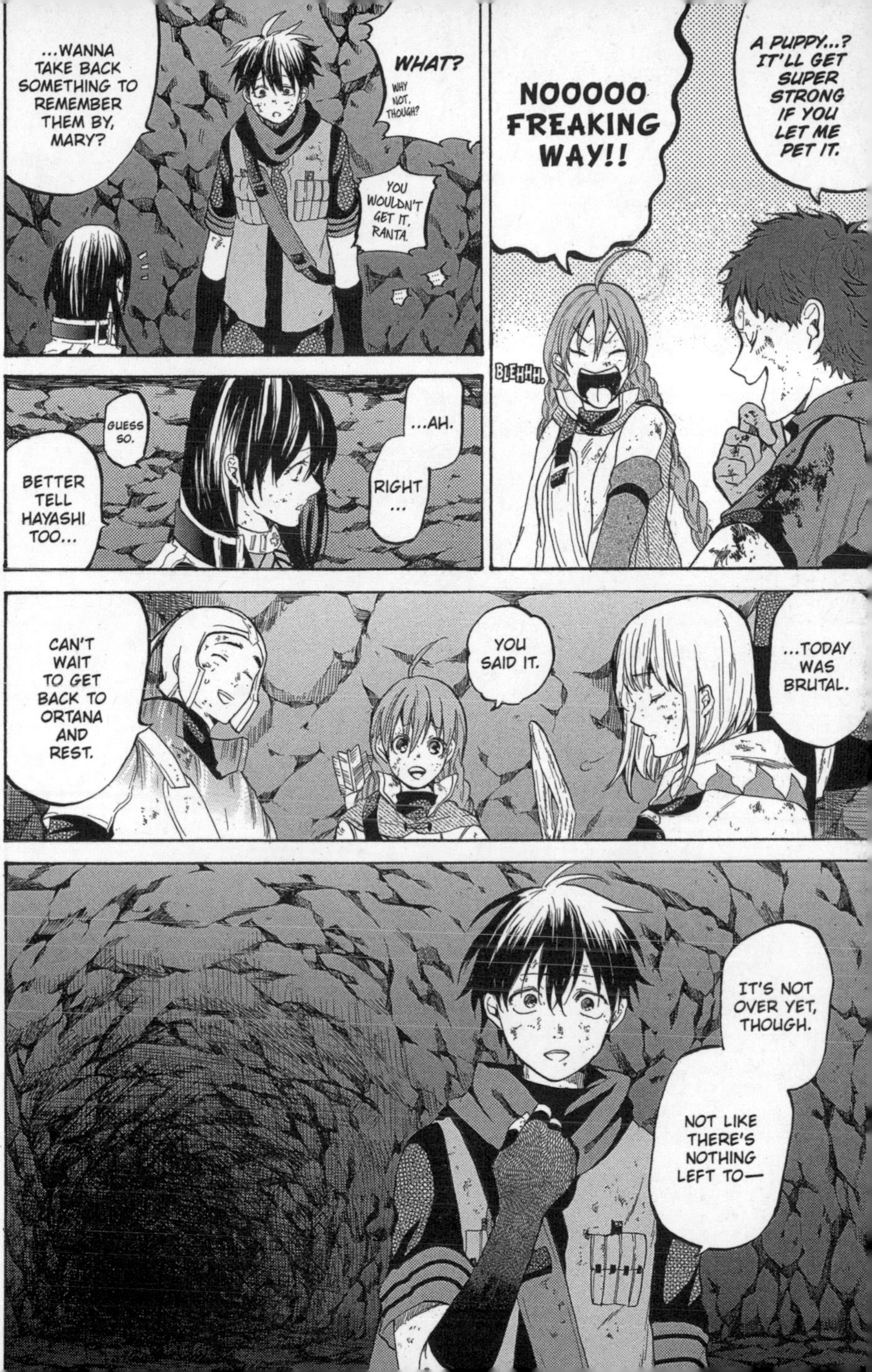
A PUPPY...? IT'LL GET SUPER STRONG IF YOU LET ME PET IT.
NOOOOO FREAKING WAY!!
BLEHHH.
...WANNA TAKE BACK SOMETHING TO REMEMBER THEM BY, MARY?
WHAT?
WHY NOT, THOUGH?
YOU WOULDN'T GET IT, RANTA.
...AH.
RIGHT...
GUESS SO.
BETTER TELL HAYASHI TOO...
...TODAY WAS BRUTAL.
YOU SAID IT.
CAN'T WAIT TO GET BACK TO ORTANA AND REST.
IT'S NOT OVER YET, THOUGH.
NOT LIKE THERE'S NOTHING LEFT TO—

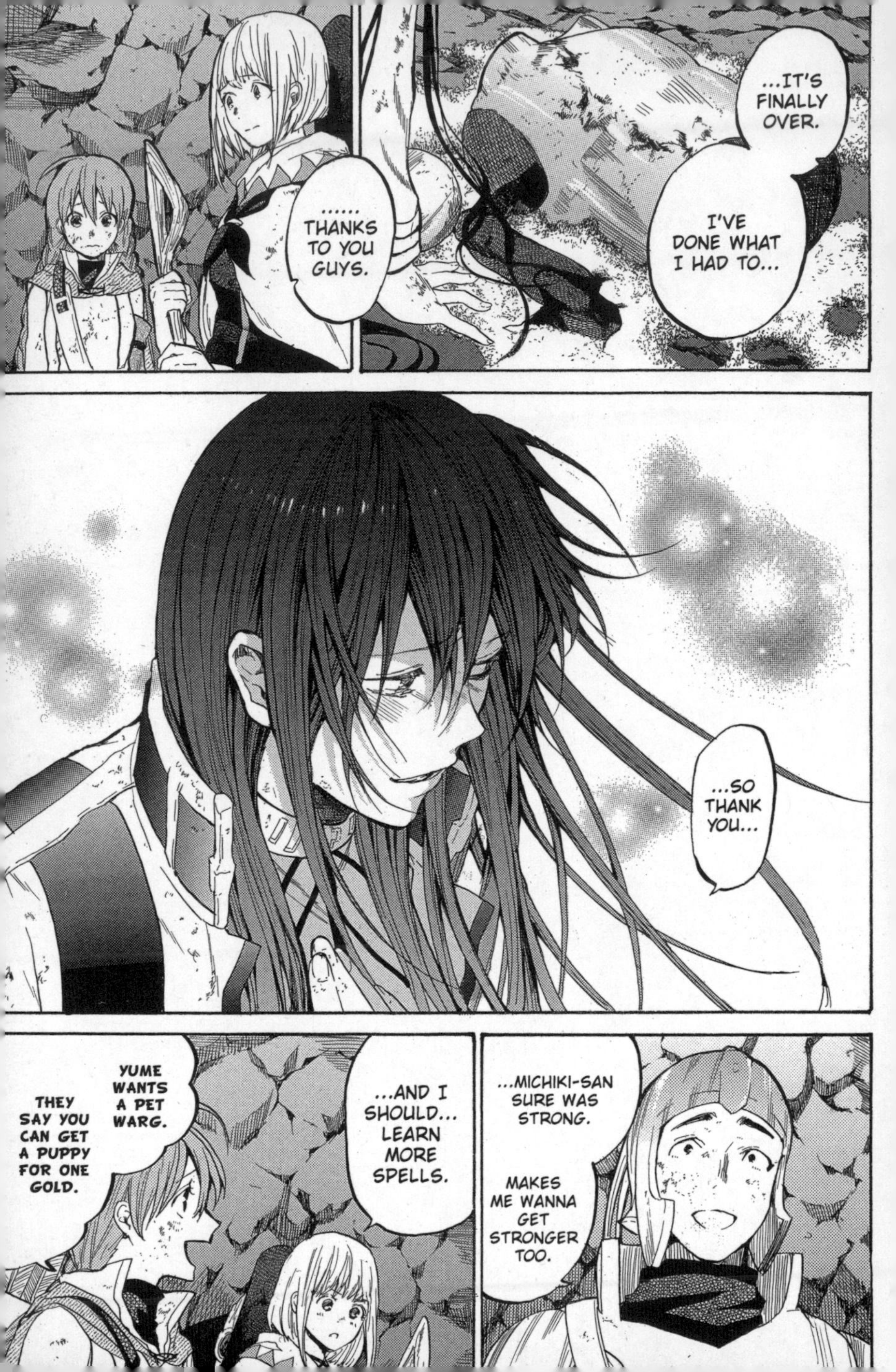
...IT'S FINALLY OVER.
I'VE DONE WHAT I HAD TO...
...... THANKS TO YOU GUYS.
...SO THANK YOU...
...MICHIKI-SAN SURE WAS STRONG.
MAKES ME WANNA GET STRONGER TOO.
...AND I SHOULD... LEARN MORE SPELLS.
YUME WANTS A PET WARG.
THEY SAY YOU CAN GET A PUPPY FOR ONE GOLD.

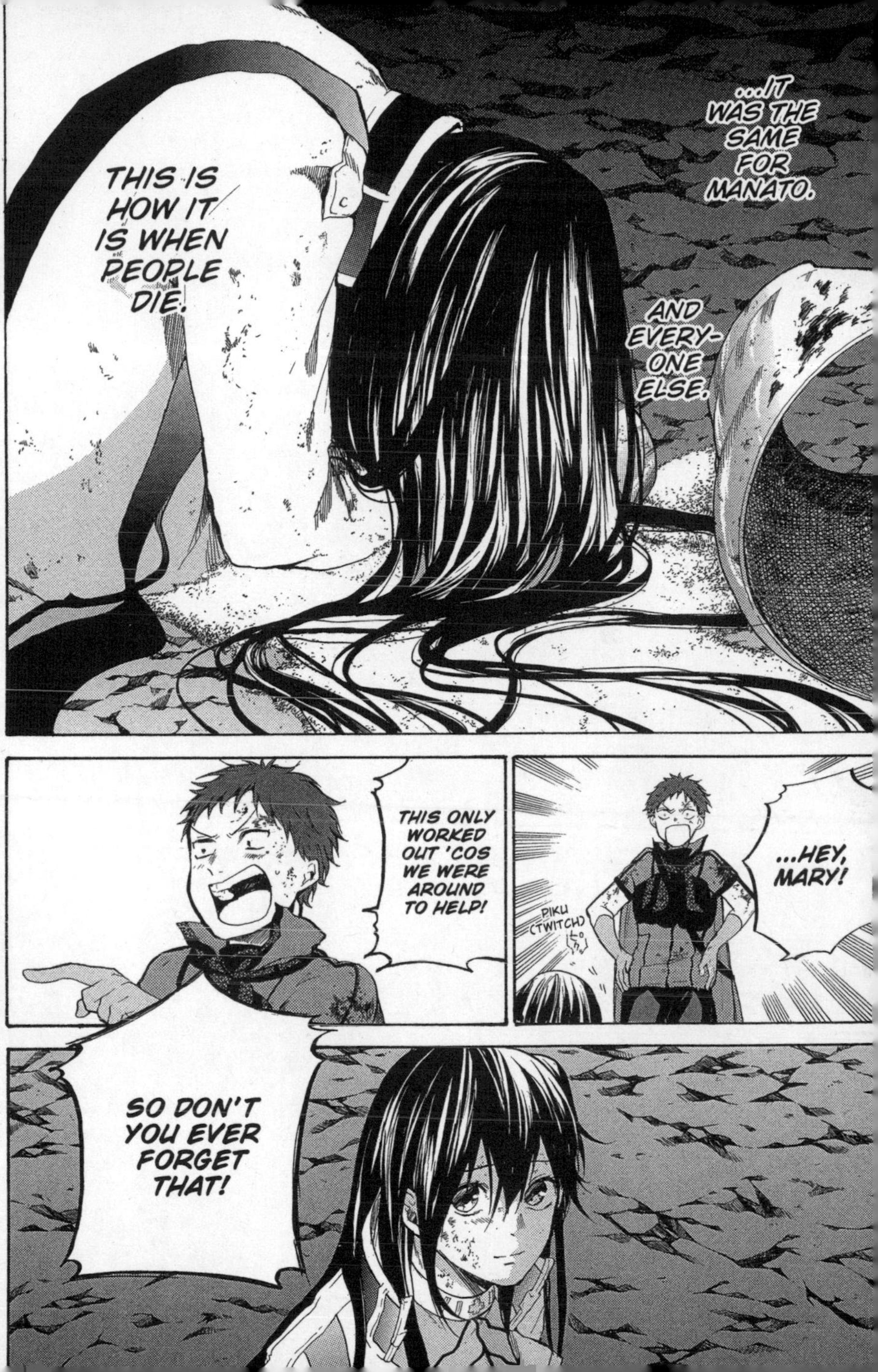
...IT WAS THE SAME FOR MANATO.
AND EVERY-ONE ELSE.
THIS IS HOW IT IS WHEN PEOPLE DIE.
...HEY, MARY!
PIKU (TWITCH)
THIS ONLY WORKED OUT 'COS WE WERE AROUND TO HELP!
SO DON'T YOU EVER FORGET THAT!

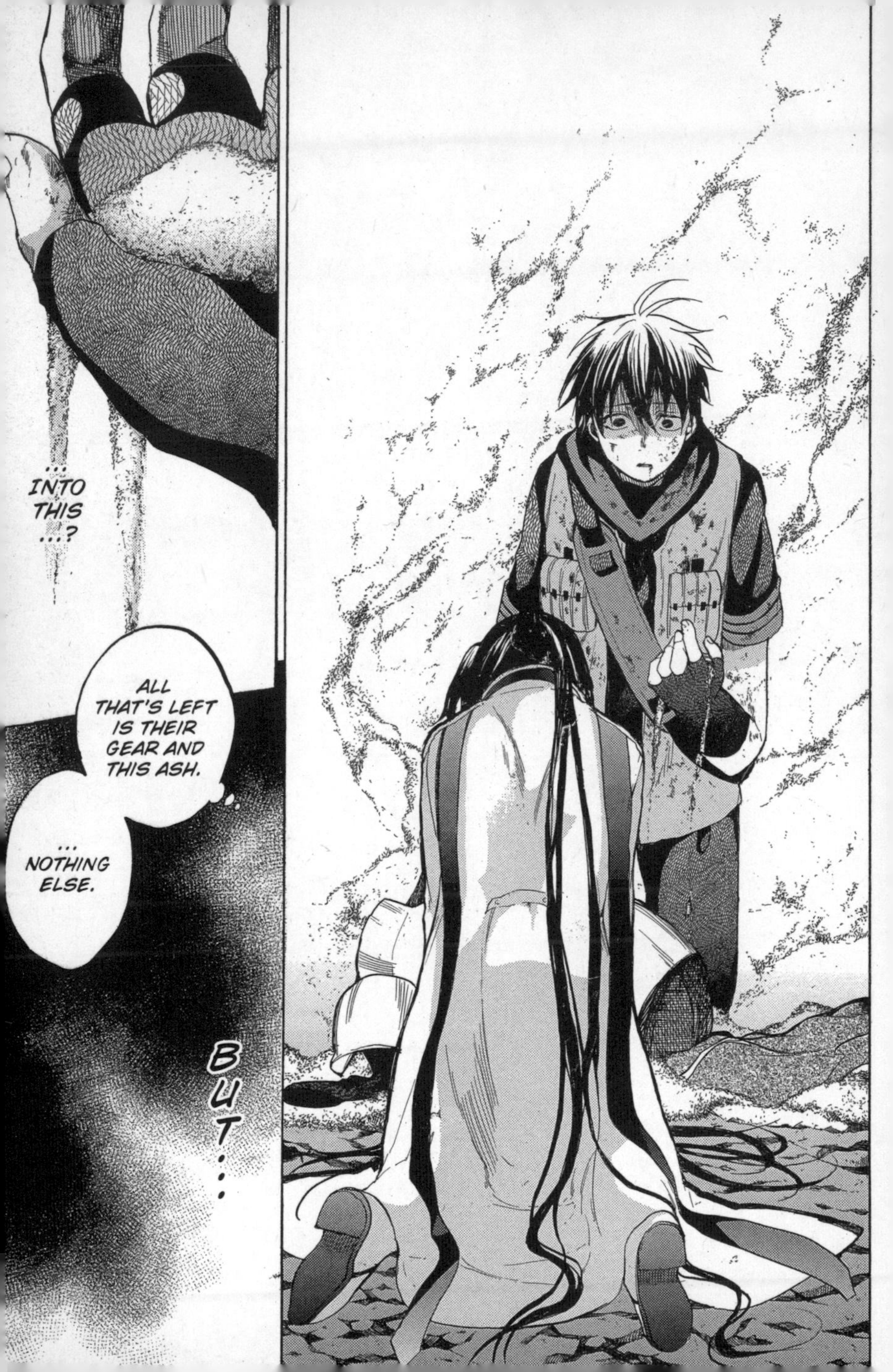

... INTO THIS ...?
ALL THAT'S LEFT IS THEIR GEAR AND THIS ASH.
... NOTHING ELSE.
BUT...

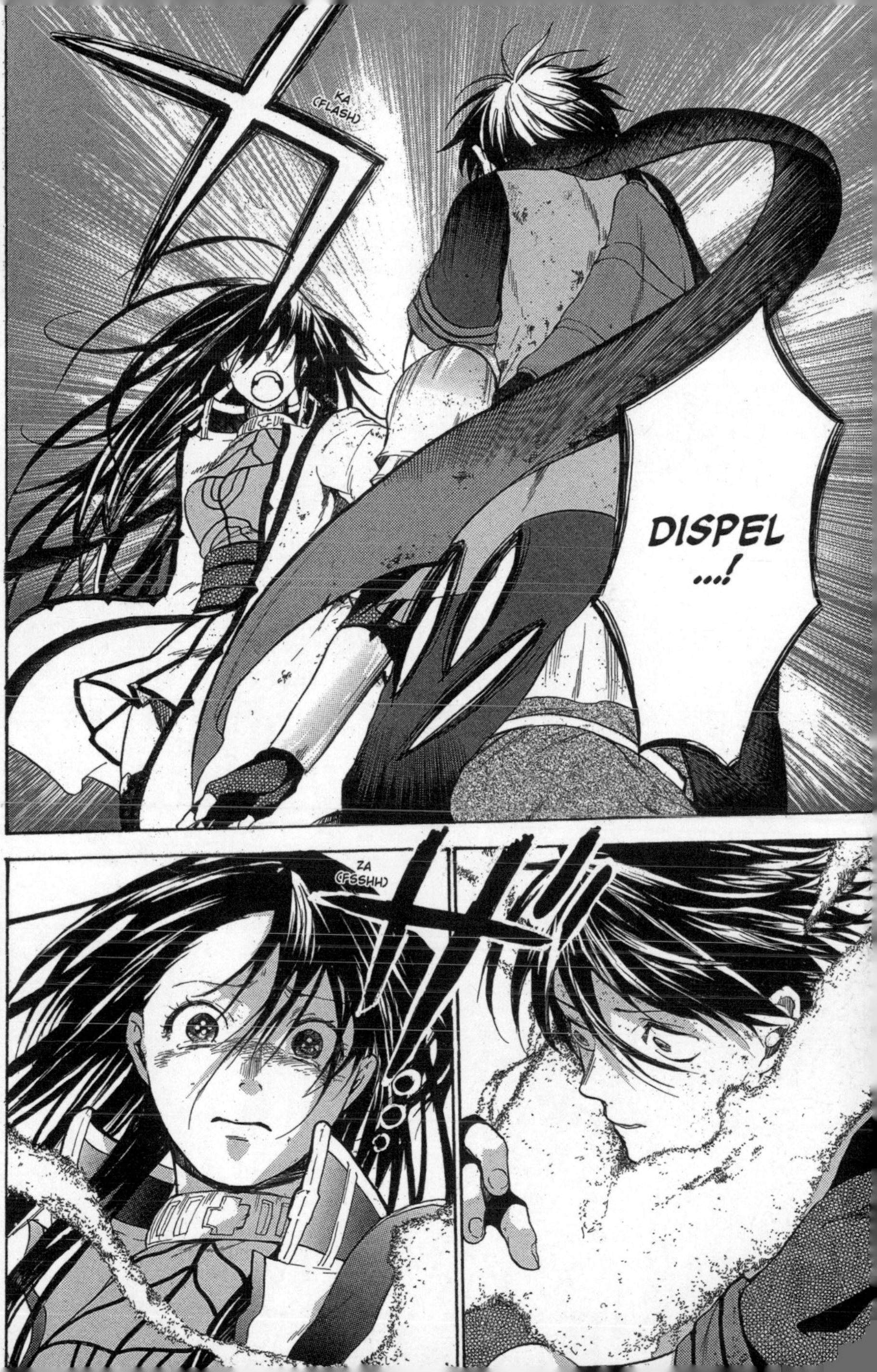
KA
(FLASH)
DISPEL
...!
ZA
(FSSHH)

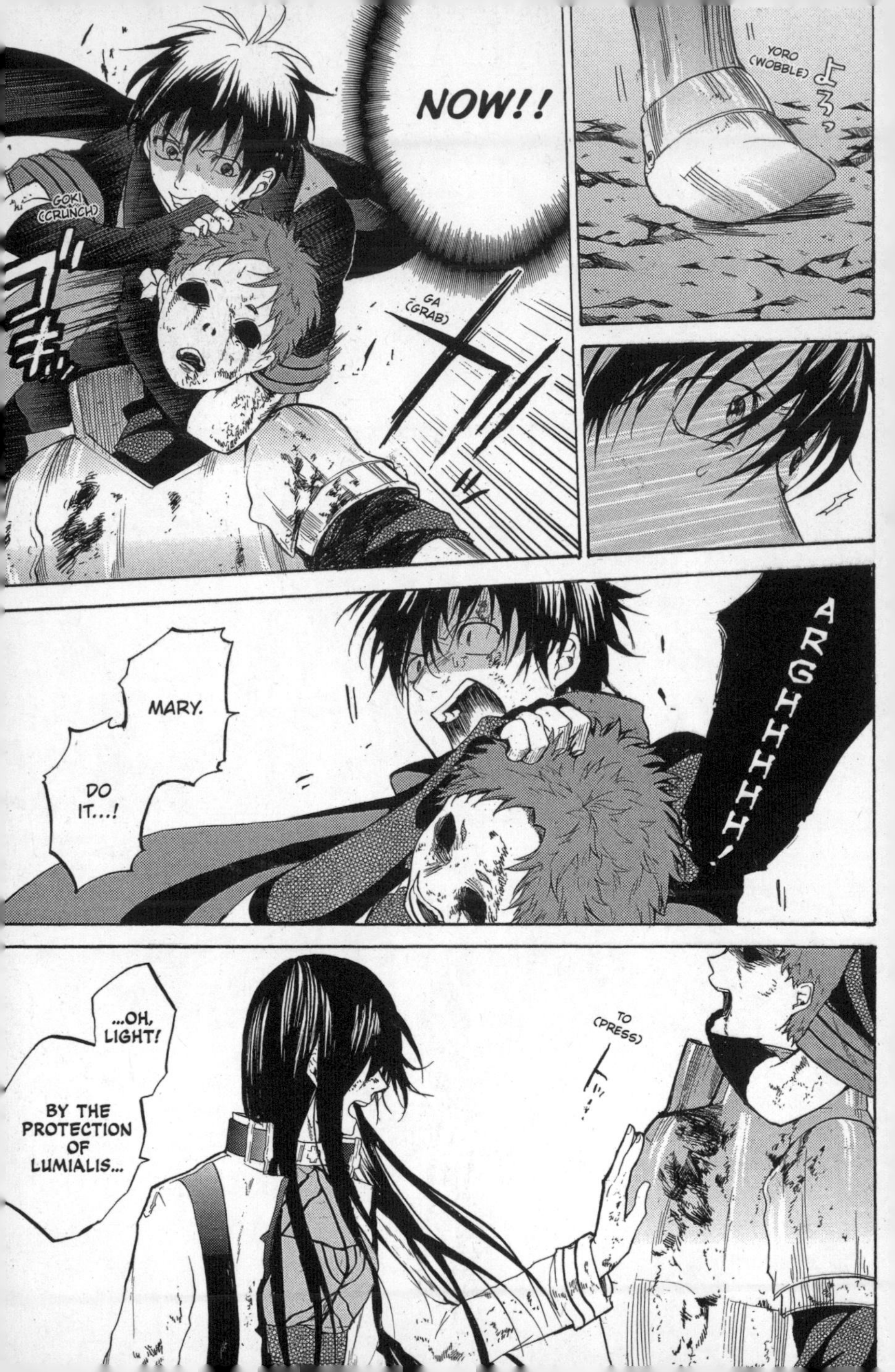
YORO (WOBBLE)
NOW!!
GOKI (CRUNCH)
GA (GRAB)
ARGHHHHH!
MARY.
DO IT...!
TO (PRESS)
...OH, LIGHT!
BY THE PROTECTION OF LUMIALIS...

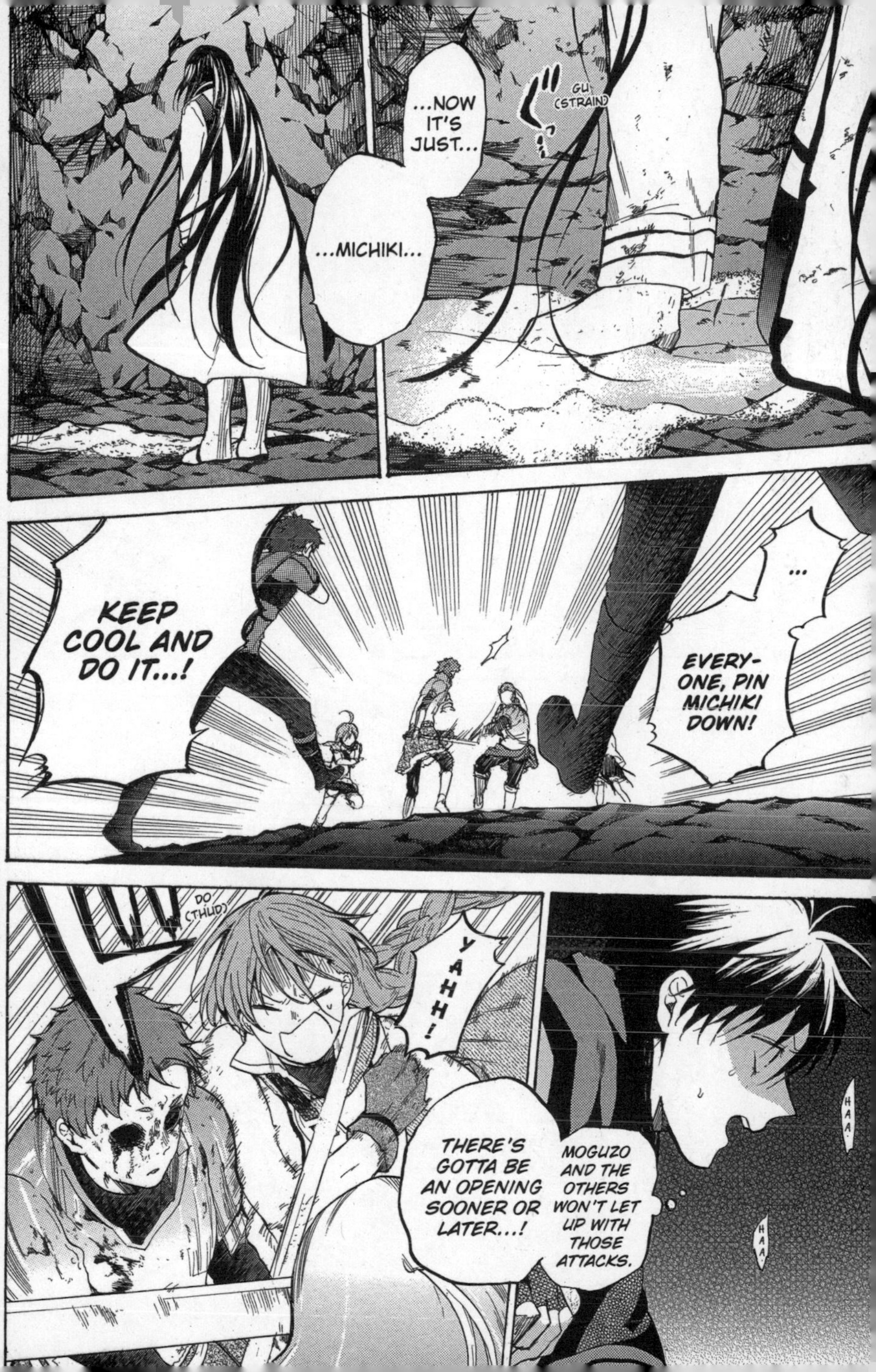
GU (STRAIN)
...NOW IT'S JUST...
...MICHIKI...
...
EVERY-ONE, PIN MICHIKI DOWN!
KEEP COOL AND DO IT...!
HAA.
HAA.
MOGUZO AND THE OTHERS WON'T LET UP WITH THOSE ATTACKS.
THERE'S GOTTA BE AN OPENING SOONER OR LATER...!
YAHH!
DO (THUD)

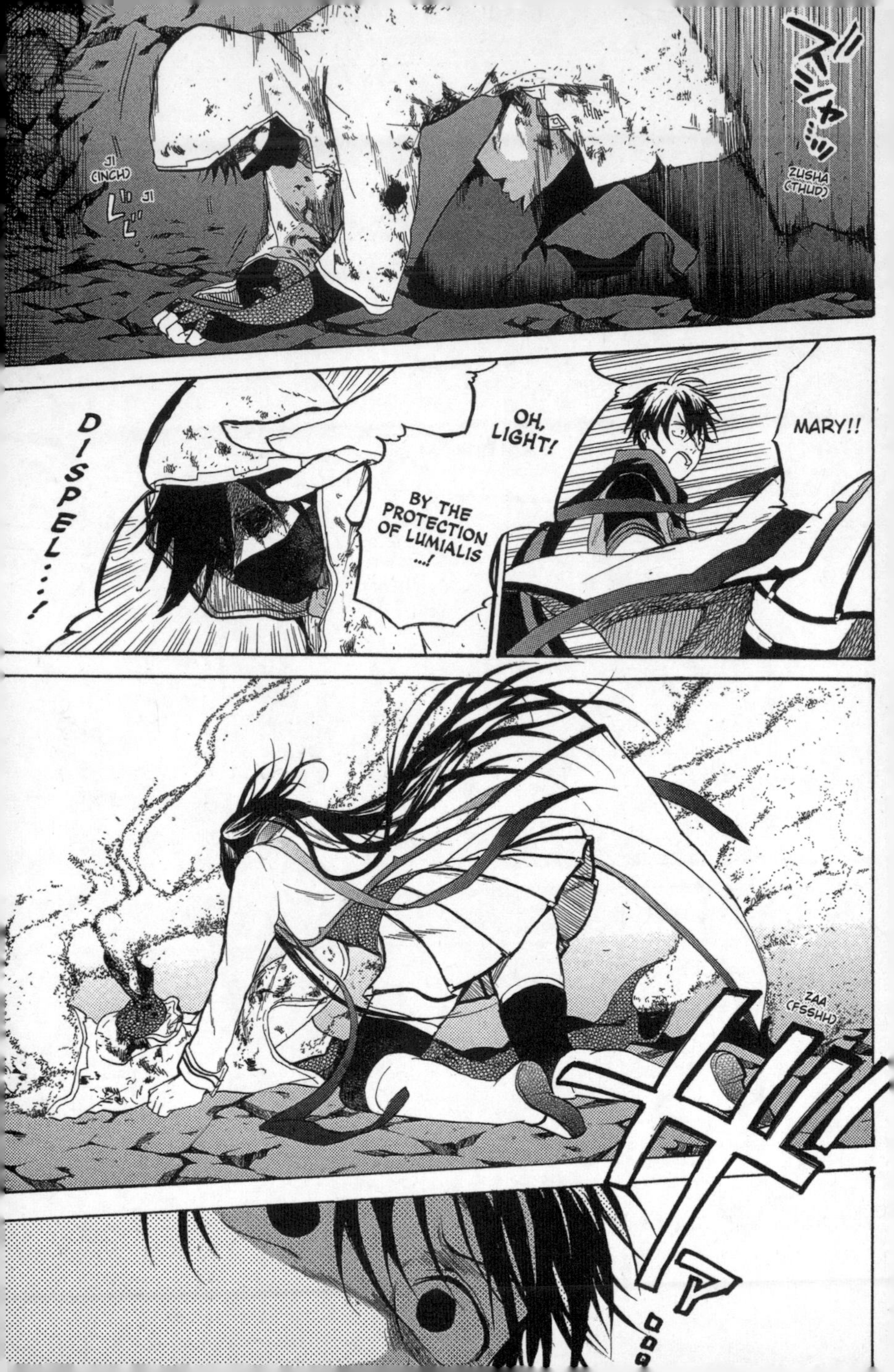
ZUSHA
(THUD)
JI
(INCH)
JI
MARY!!
OH, LIGHT!
BY THE PROTECTION OF LUMIALIS ...!
DISPEL...!
ZAA
(FSSHH)

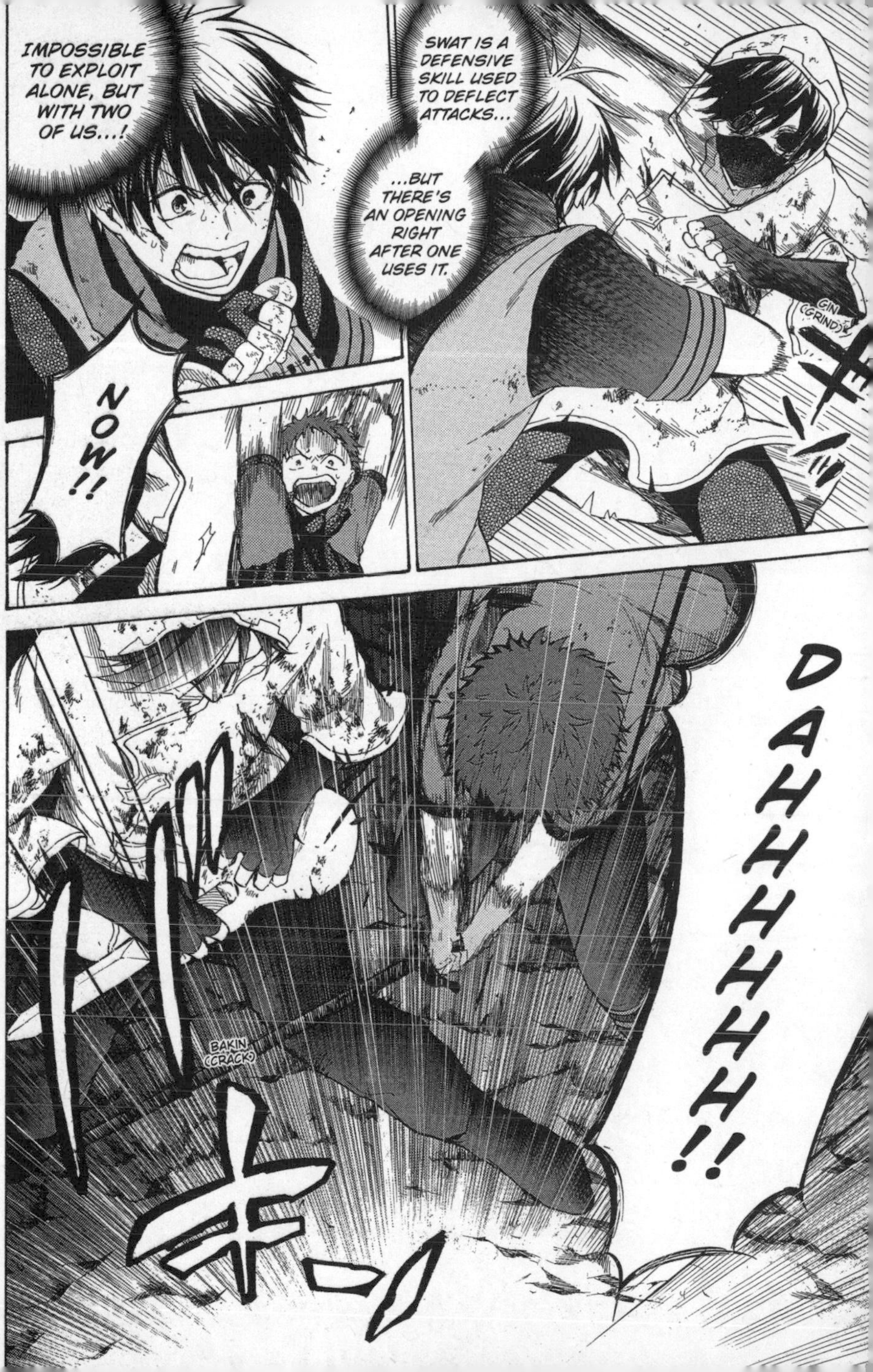
SWAT IS A DEFENSIVE SKILL USED TO DEFLECT ATTACKS...
...BUT THERE'S AN OPENING RIGHT AFTER ONE USES IT.
GIN (GRIND)
IMPOSSIBLE TO EXPLOIT ALONE, BUT WITH TWO OF US...!
NOW!!
DAHHHHHH!!
BAKIN (CRACK)

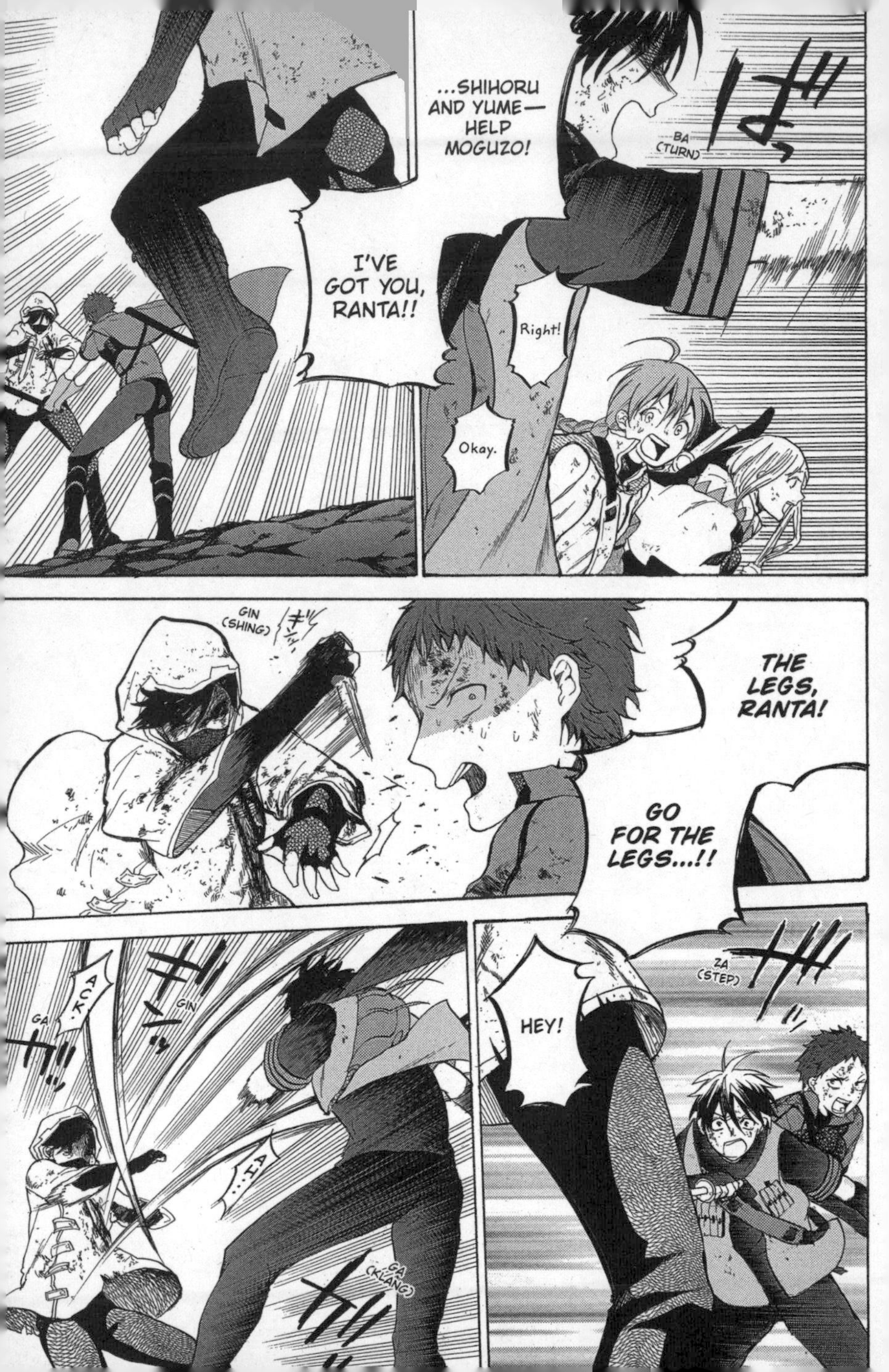
BA (TURN)
...SHIHORU AND YUME—HELP MOGUZO!
Right!
Okay.
I'VE GOT YOU, RANTA!!
THE LEGS, RANTA!
GO FOR THE LEGS...!!
GIN (SHING)
ZA (STEP)
HEY!
GIN
ACK.
GA
...!!
GA (KLANG)

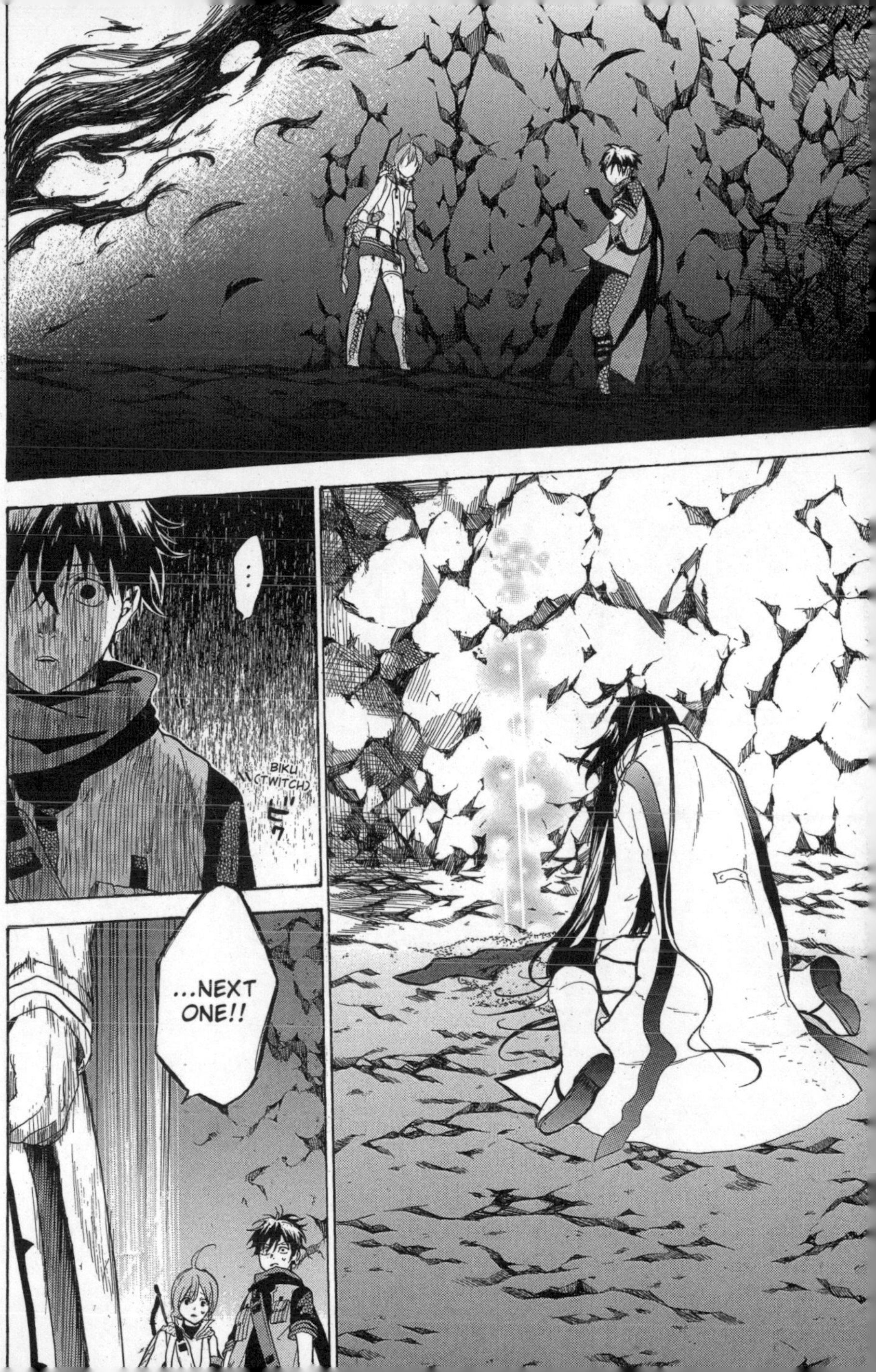
...!
BIKU (TWITCH)
ビクッ
...NEXT ONE!!

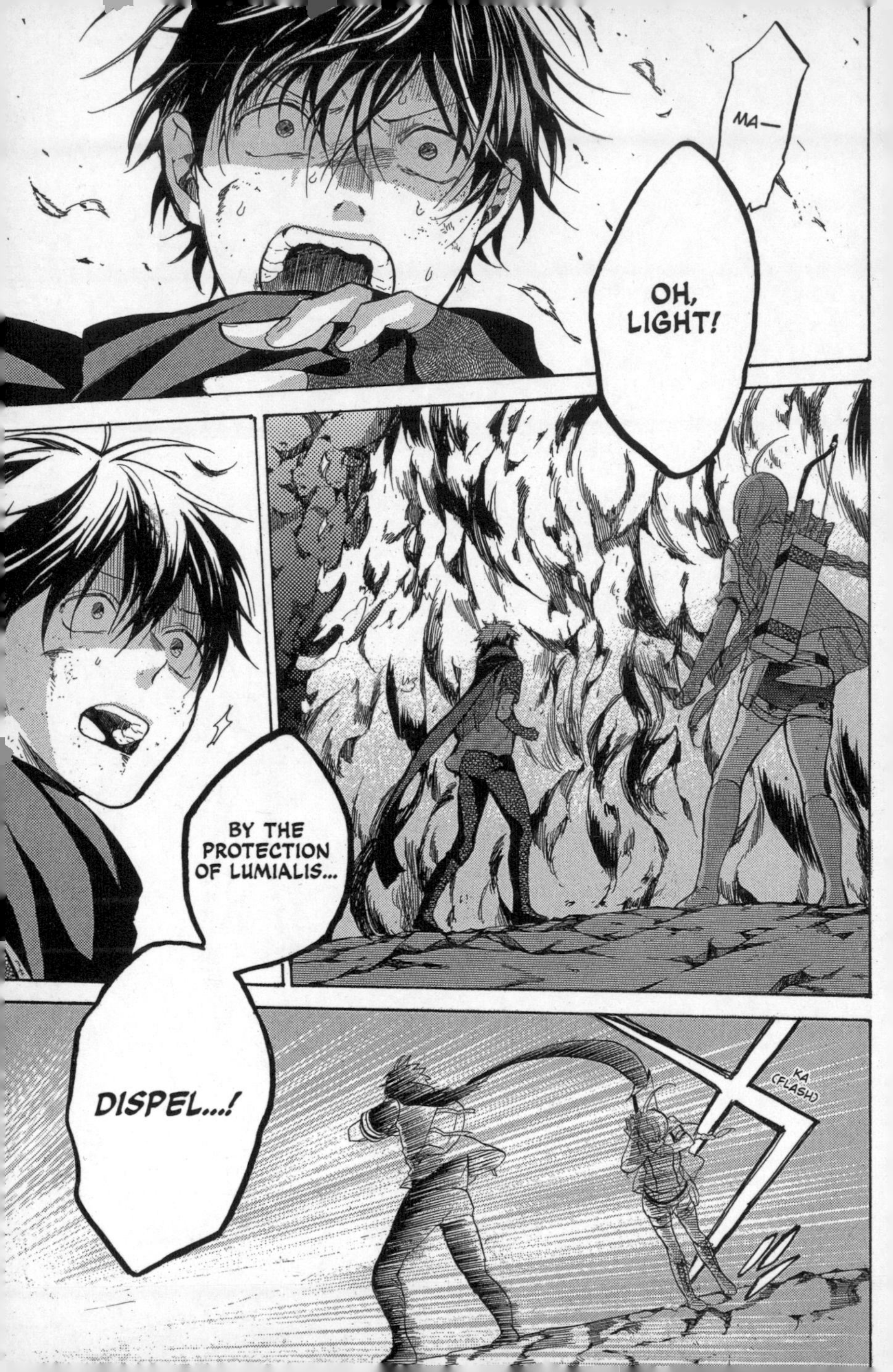

MA—
OH, LIGHT!
BY THE PROTECTION OF LUMIALIS...
DISPEL...!
KA (FLASH)

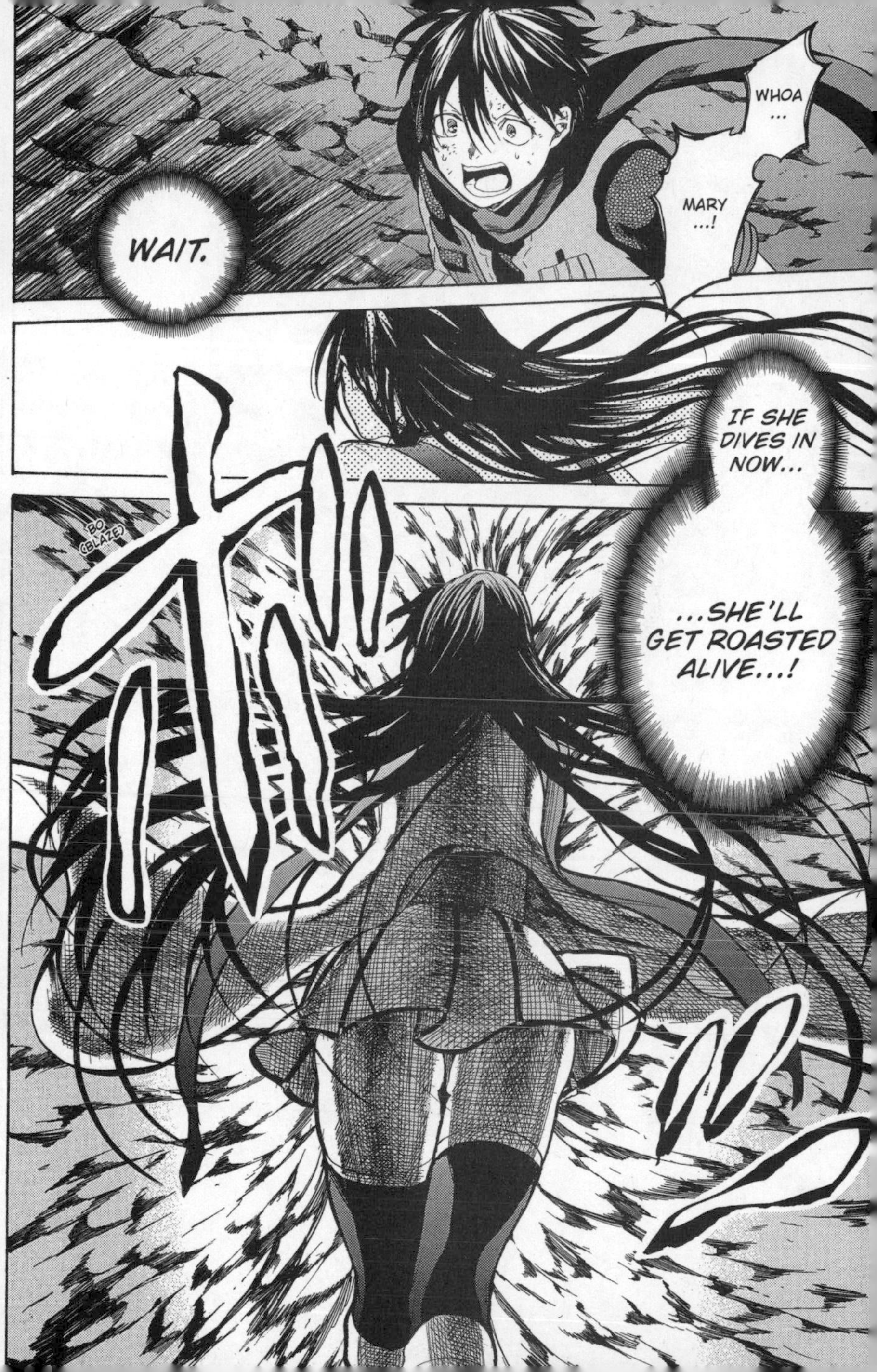
WHOA ...
MARY ...!
WAIT.
IF SHE DIVES IN NOW...
...SHE'LL GET ROASTED ALIVE...!
BO (BLAZE)

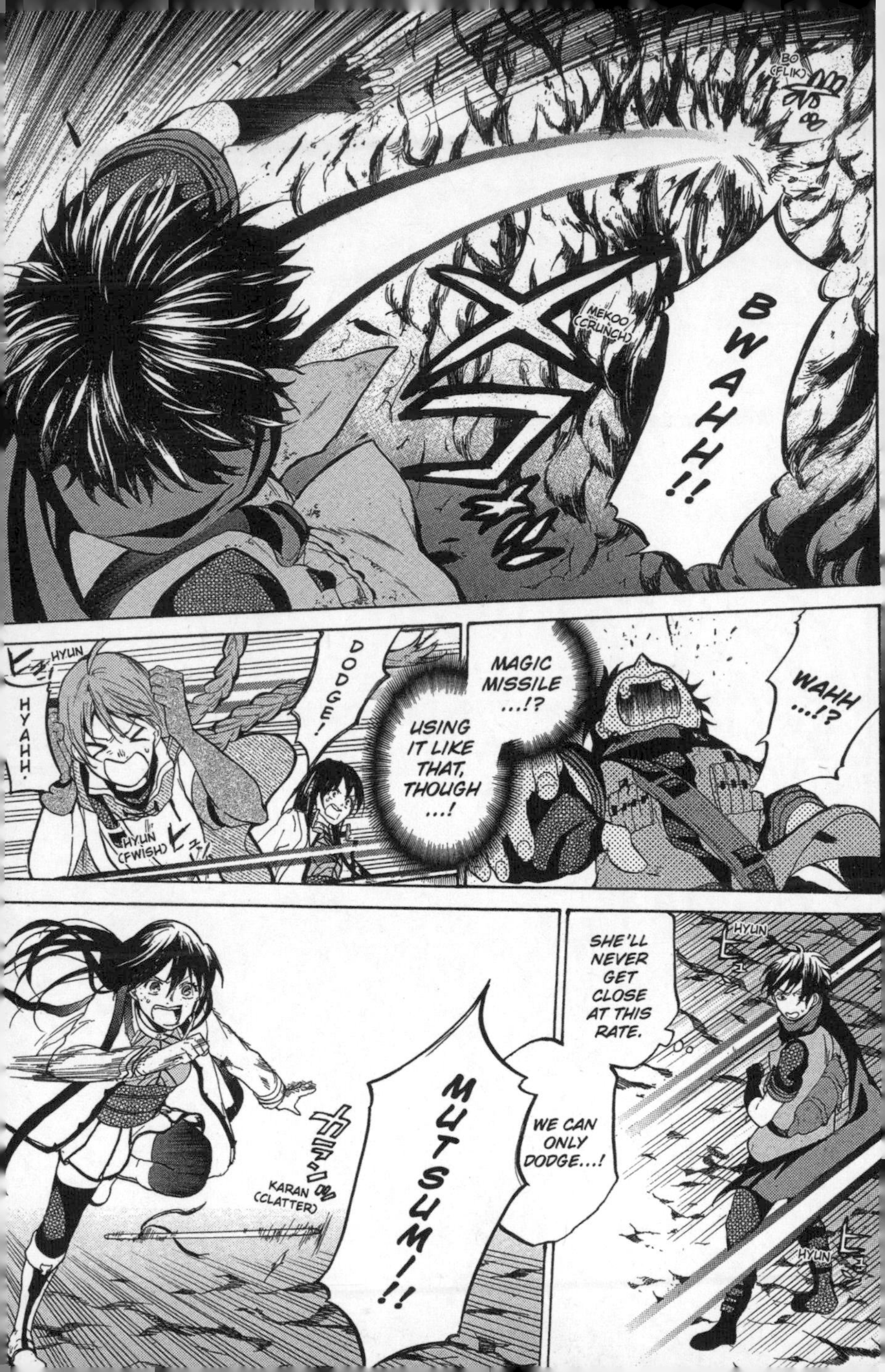
BO (FLIK)
MEKOO (CRUNCH)
BWAHH!!
WAHH ...!?
MAGIC MISSILE ...!?
USING IT LIKE THAT, THOUGH ...!
DODGE!
HYUN
HYAHH.
HYUN (FWISH)
HYUN
SHE'LL NEVER GET CLOSE AT THIS RATE.
WE CAN ONLY DODGE...!
HYUN
MUTSUMI!!
KARAN (CLATTER)

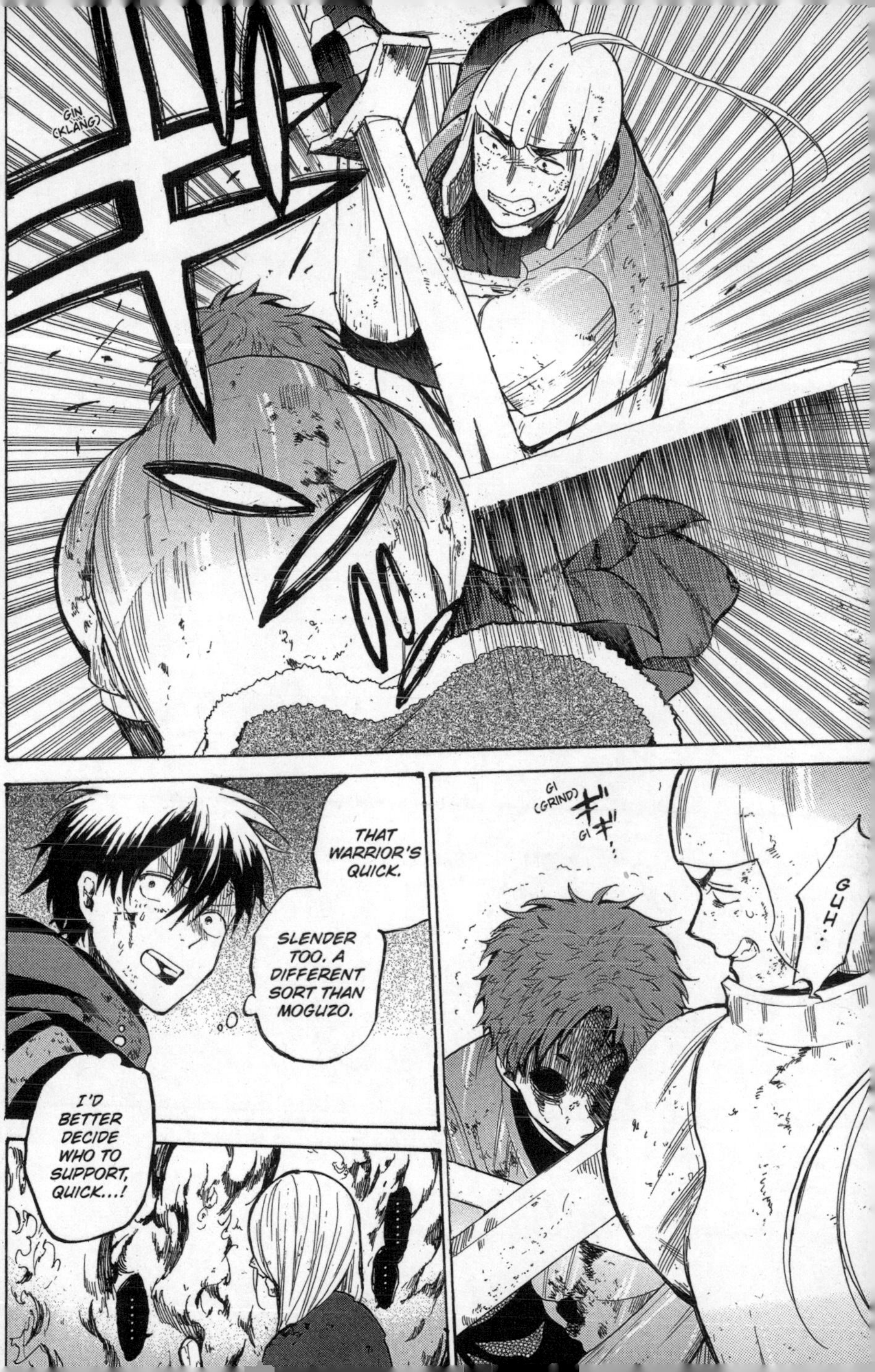
GIN (KLANG)
GI (GRIND) GI
GUH...
THAT WARRIOR'S QUICK.
SLENDER TOO. A DIFFERENT SORT THAN MOGUZO.
I'D BETTER DECIDE WHO TO SUPPORT, QUICK...!
......
......

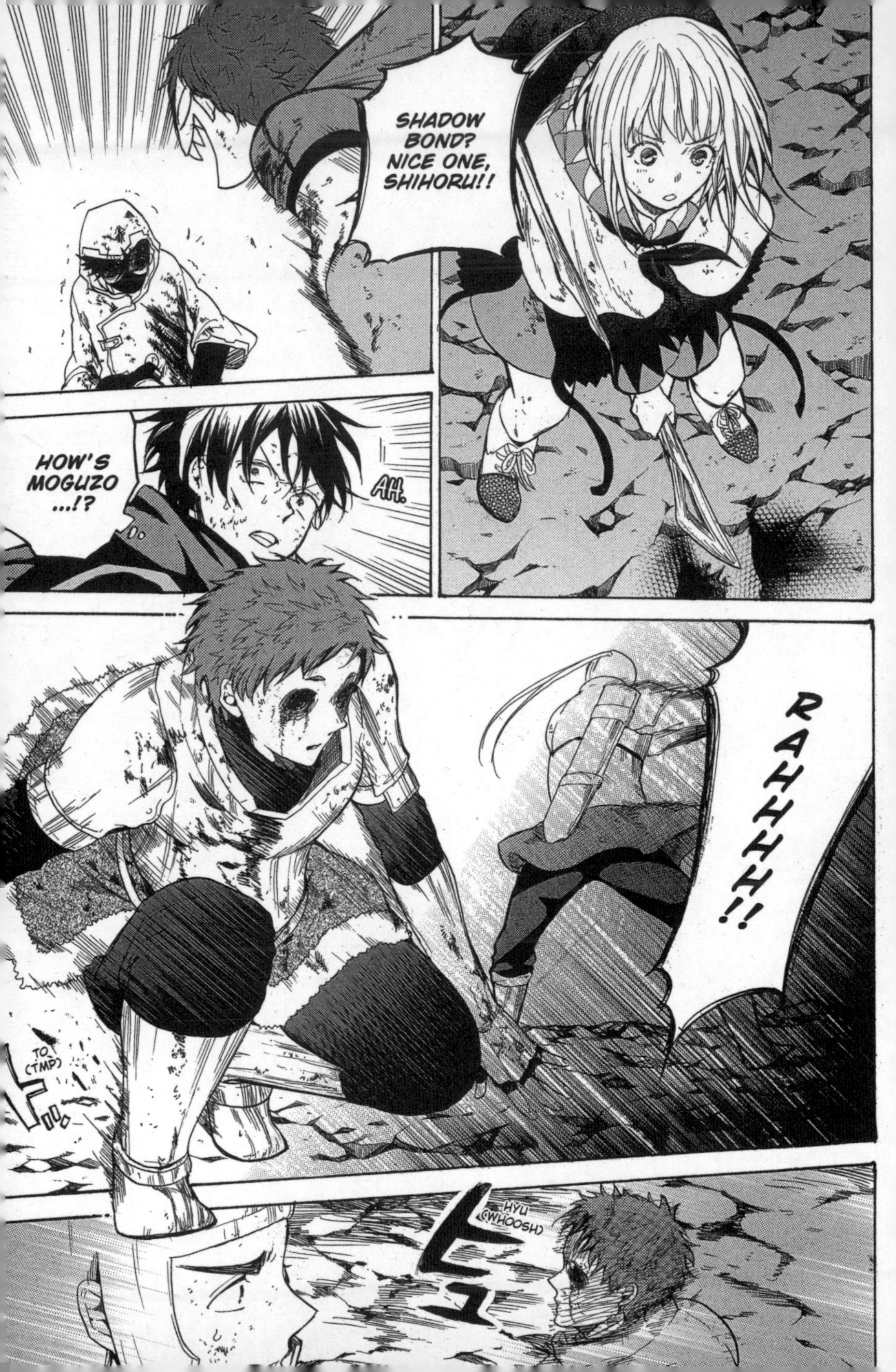
SHADOW BOND? NICE ONE, SHIHORU!!
AH.
HOW'S MOGUZO ...!?
RAHHHH!!
TO (TMP)
HYU (WHOOSH)

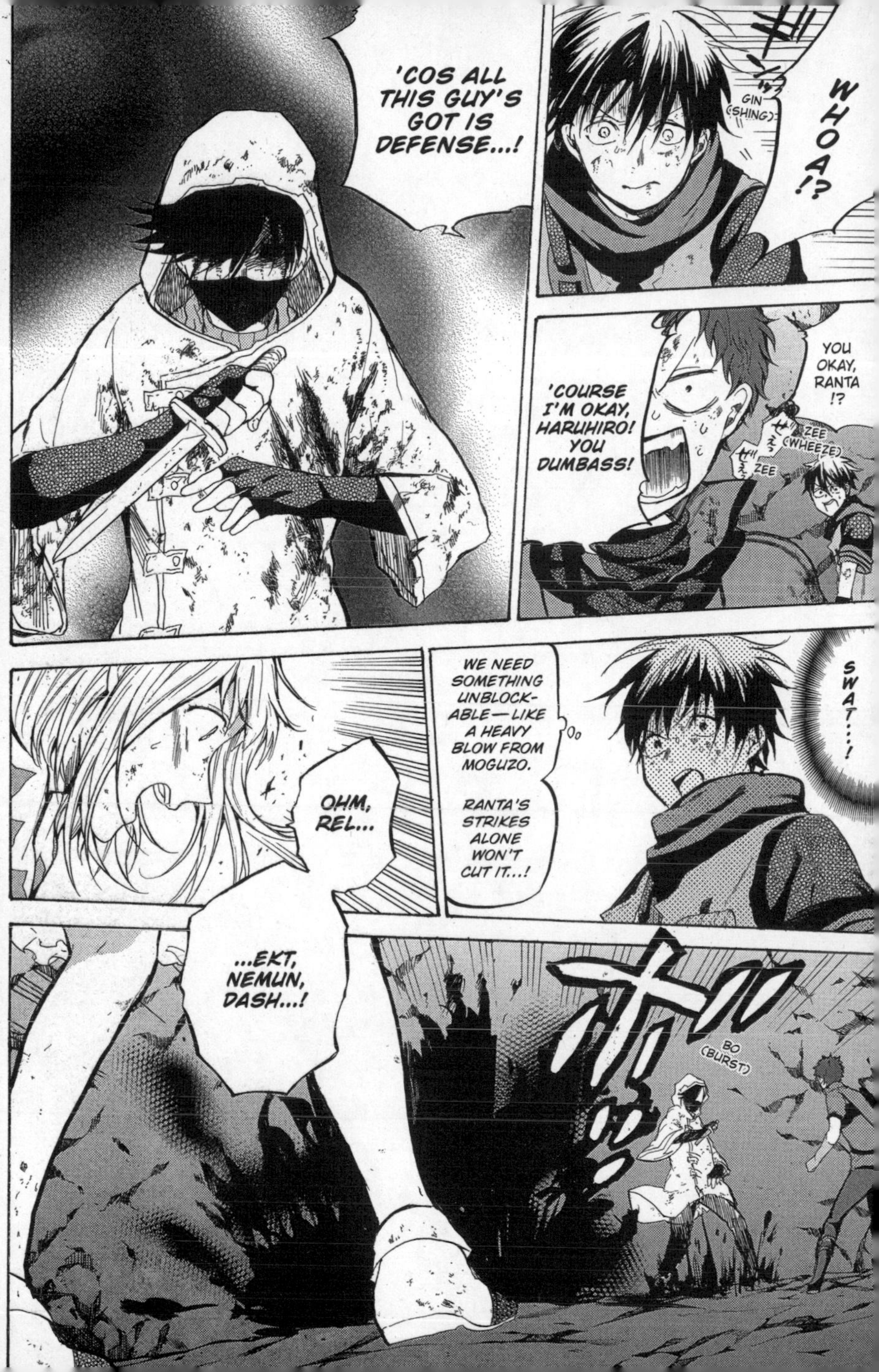
GIN (SHING)
WHOA!?
YOU OKAY, RANTA!?
ZEE (WHEEZE) ZEE
'COURSE I'M OKAY, HARUHIRO! YOU DUMBASS!
'COS ALL THIS GUY'S GOT IS DEFENSE...!
SWAT...!
WE NEED SOMETHING UNBLOCK-ABLE—LIKE A HEAVY BLOW FROM MOGUZO.
RANTA'S STRIKES ALONE WON'T CUT IT...!
OHM, REL...
...EKT, NEMUN, DASH...!
BO (BURST)

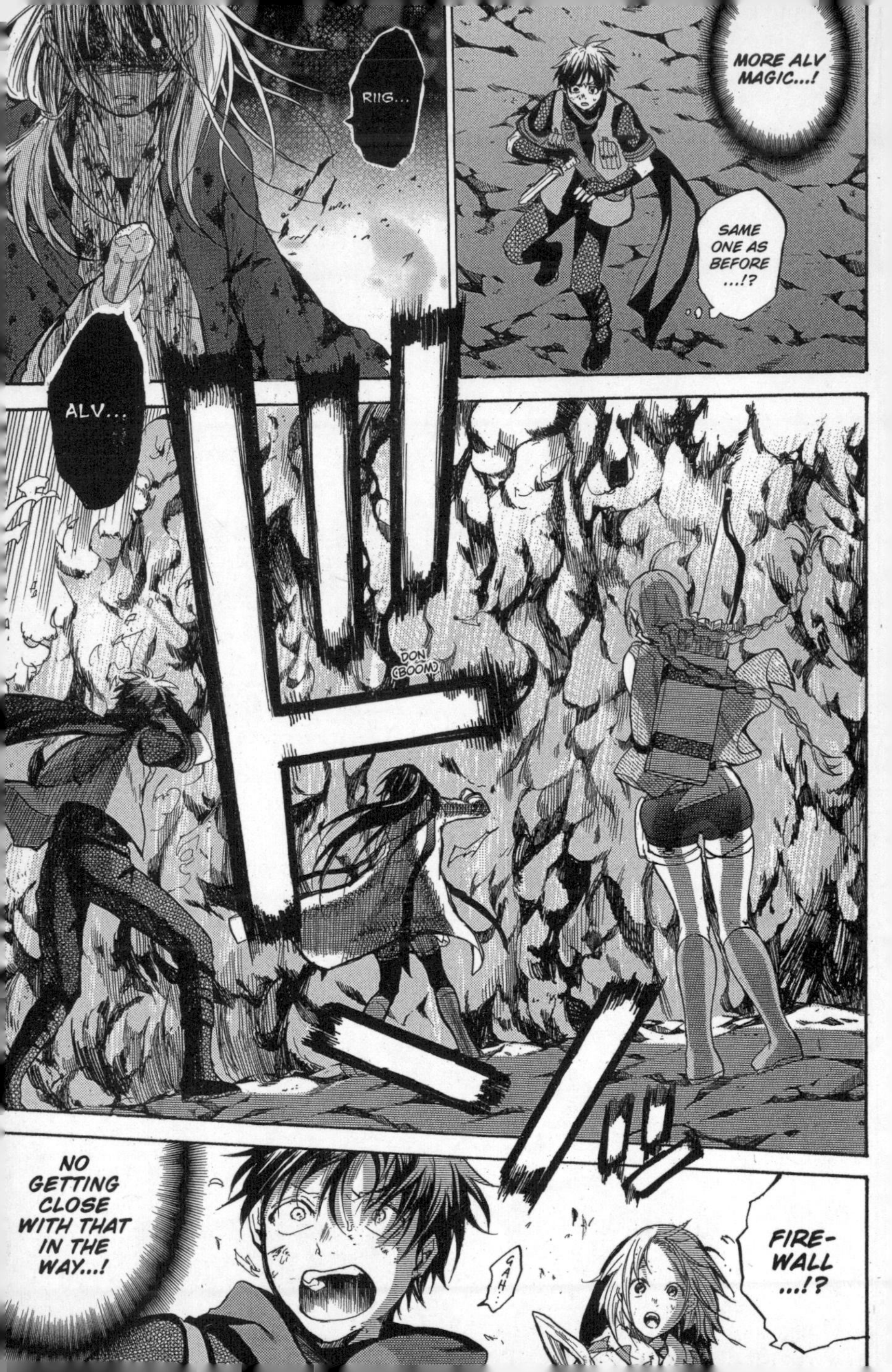
MORE ALV MAGIC...!
SAME ONE AS BEFORE ...!?
RIIG...
ALV...
DON (BOOM)
FIRE-WALL ...!?
GAH...
NO GETTING CLOSE WITH THAT IN THE WAY...!

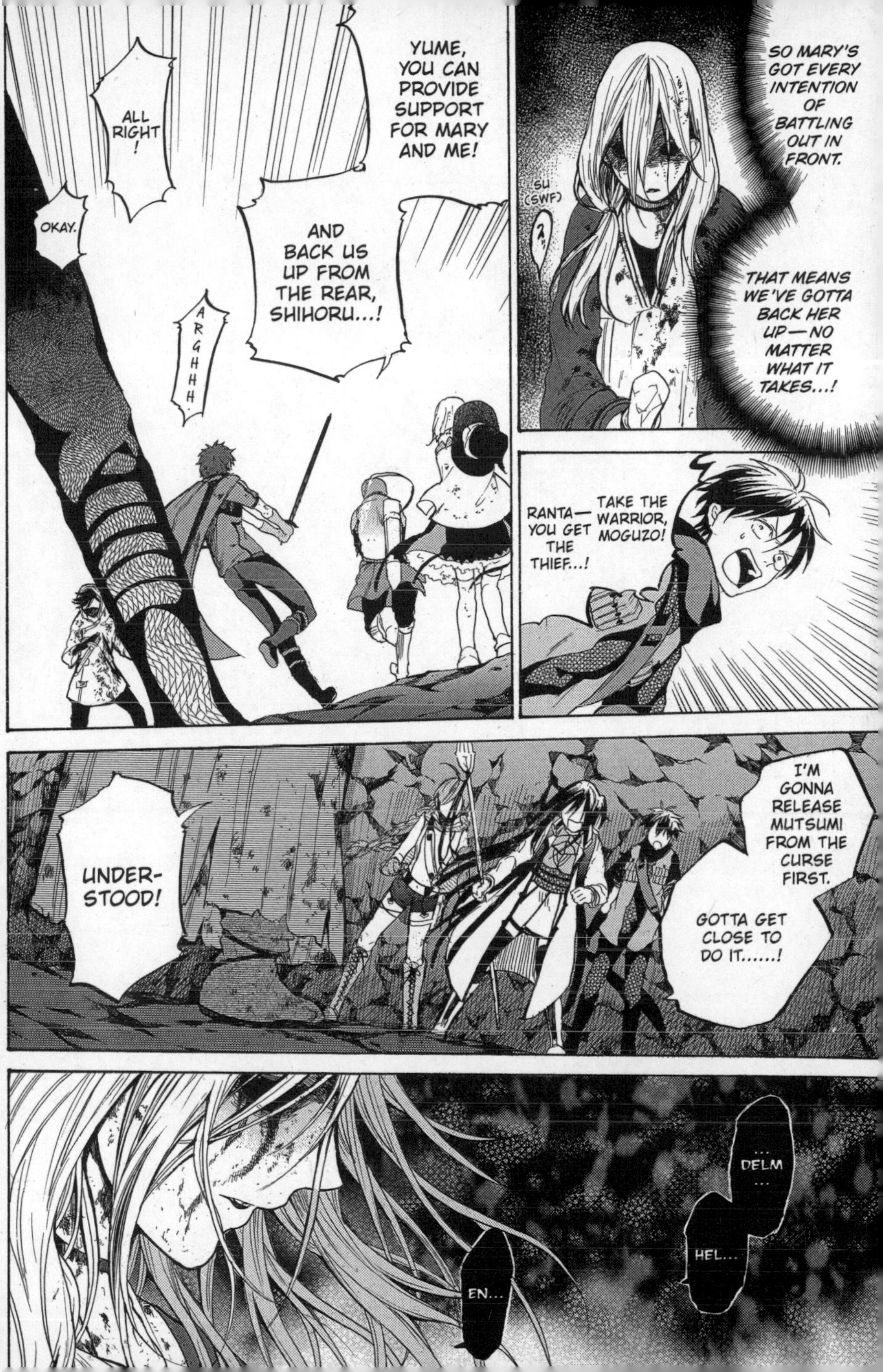
SO MARY'S GOT EVERY INTENTION OF BATTLING OUT IN FRONT.
SU (SWF)
THAT MEANS WE'VE GOTTA BACK HER UP—NO MATTER WHAT IT TAKES...!
TAKE THE WARRIOR, MOGUZO!
RANTA—YOU GET THE THIEF...!
YUME, YOU CAN PROVIDE SUPPORT FOR MARY AND ME!
AND BACK US UP FROM THE REAR, SHIHORU...!
ALL RIGHT!
OKAY.
ARGHHH.
I'M GONNA RELEASE MUTSUMI FROM THE CURSE FIRST.
GOTTA GET CLOSE TO DO IT......!
UNDER-STOOD!
...DELM...
HEL...
EN...

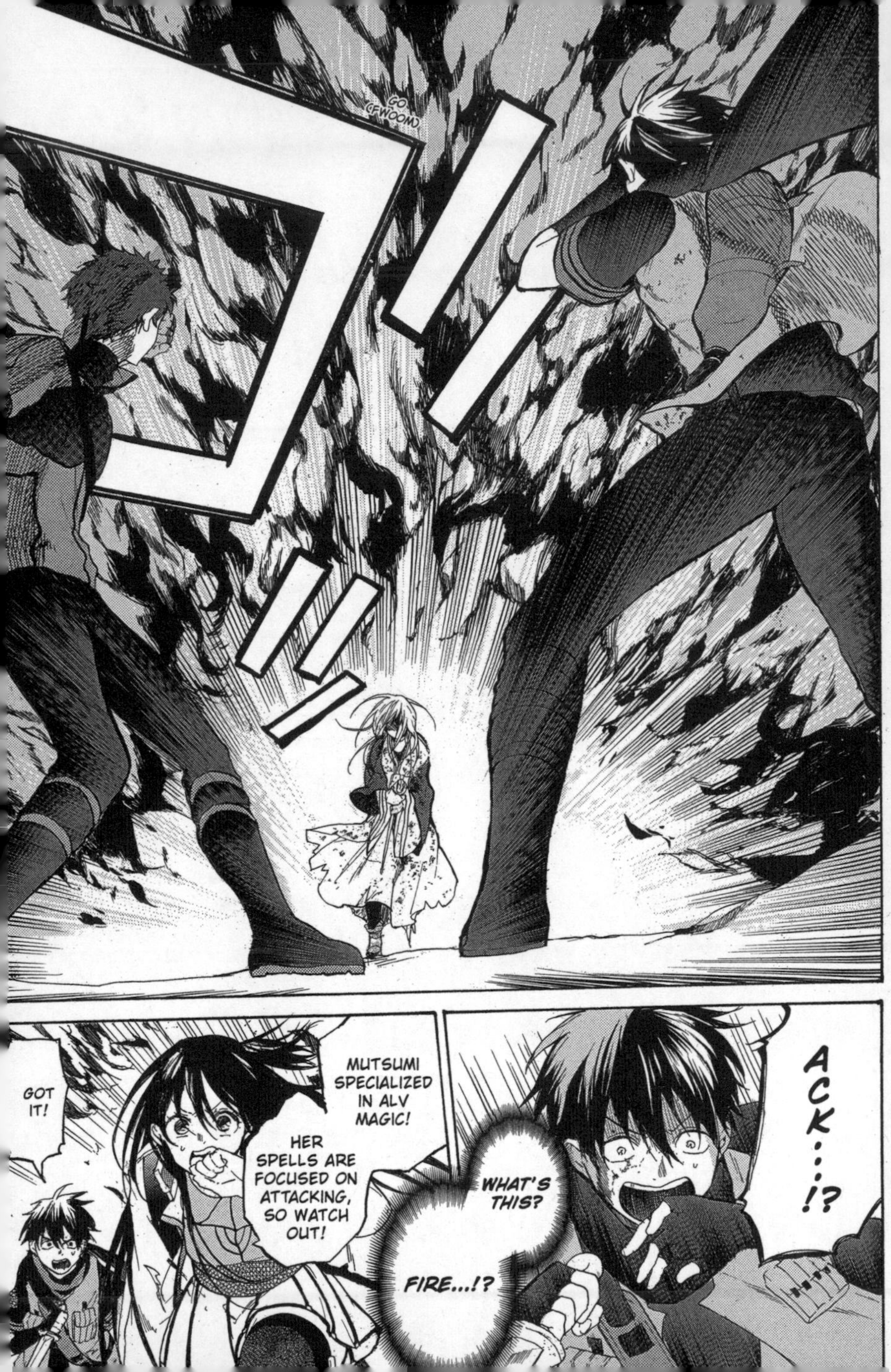
GO (FWOOM)
ACK...!?
WHAT'S THIS?
FIRE...!?
MUTSUMI SPECIALIZED IN ALV MAGIC!
HER SPELLS ARE FOCUSED ON ATTACKING, SO WATCH OUT!
GOT IT!

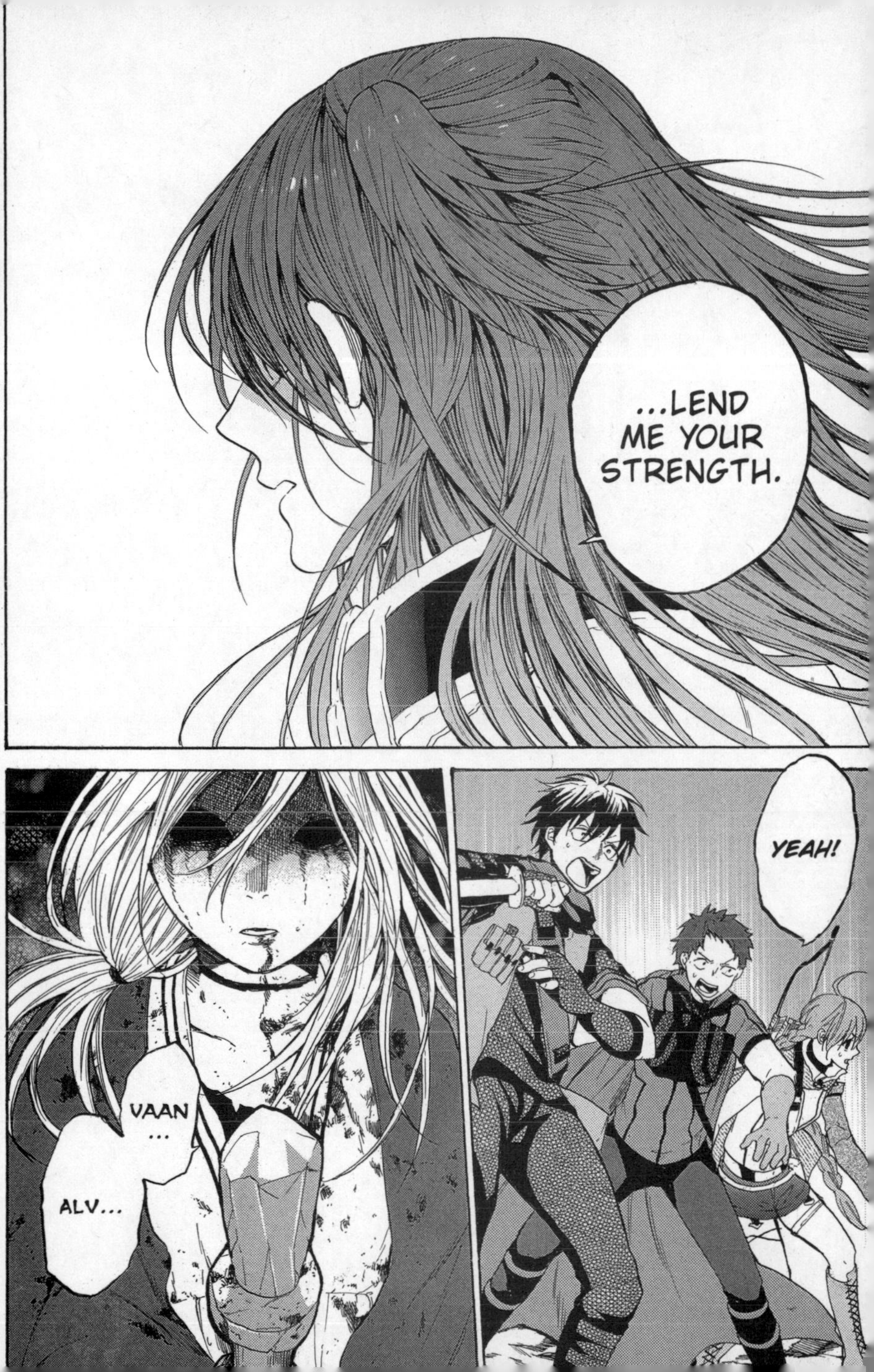
...LEND ME YOUR STRENGTH.
YEAH!
VAAN ...
ALV...

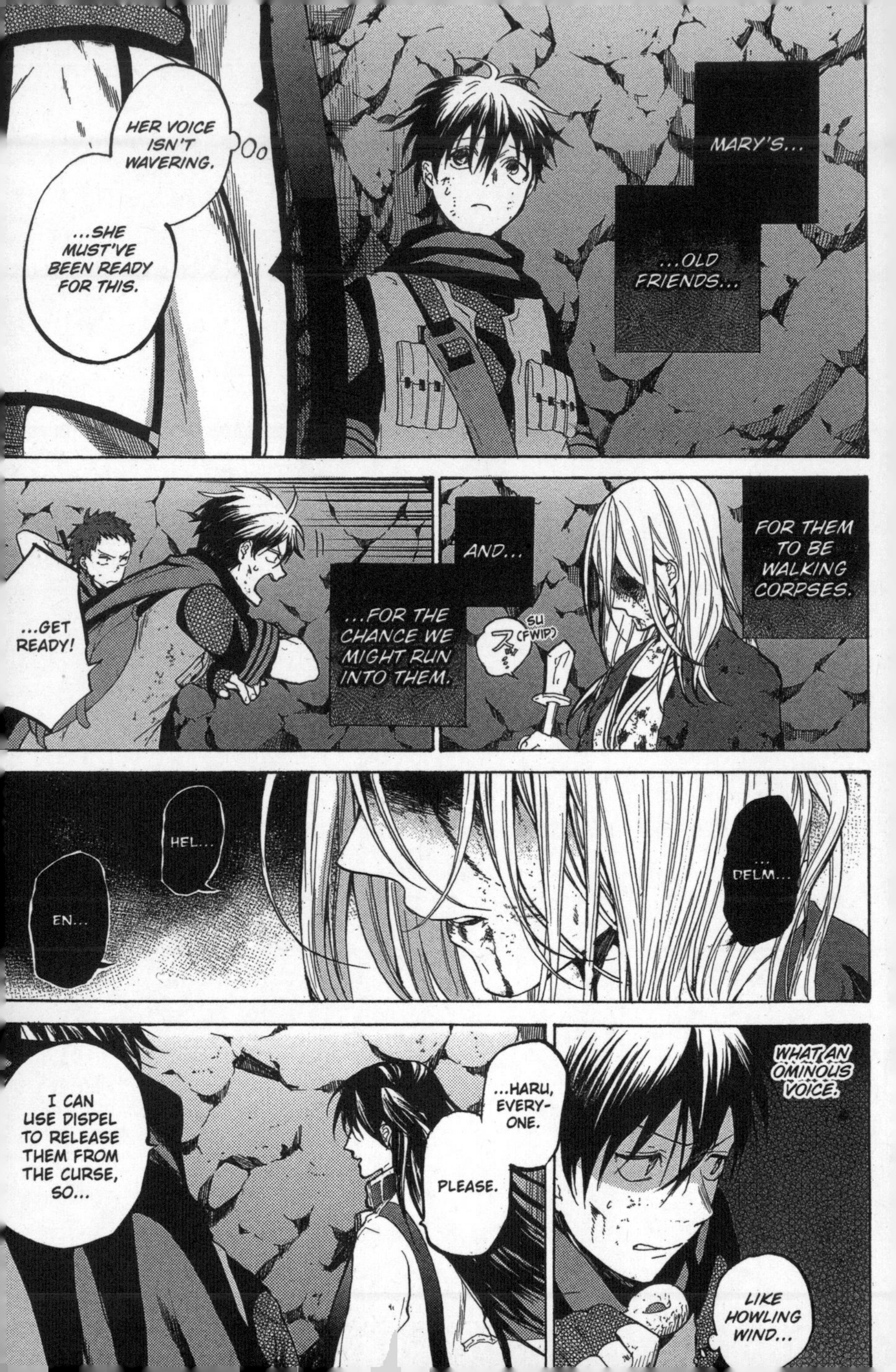
MARY'S...
...OLD FRIENDS...
HER VOICE ISN'T WAVERING.
...SHE MUST'VE BEEN READY FOR THIS.
FOR THEM TO BE WALKING CORPSES.
ス
SU (FWIP)
AND...
...FOR THE CHANCE WE MIGHT RUN INTO THEM.
...GET READY!
... DELM...
HEL...
EN...
WHAT AN OMINOUS VOICE.
LIKE HOWLING WIND...
...HARU, EVERY-ONE.
PLEASE.
I CAN USE DISPEL TO RELEASE THEM FROM THE CURSE, SO...

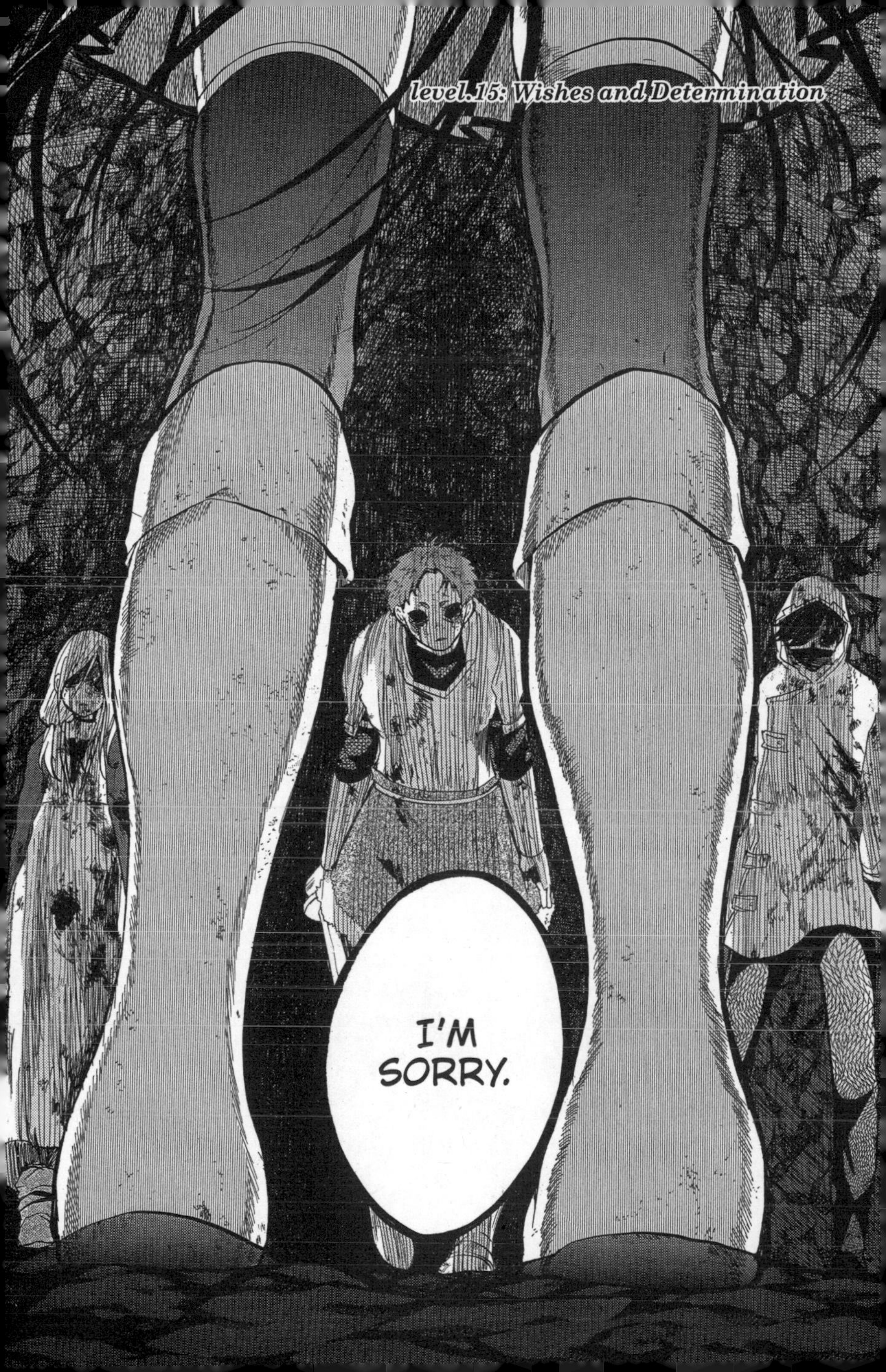
level.15: Wishes and Determination
I'M SORRY.

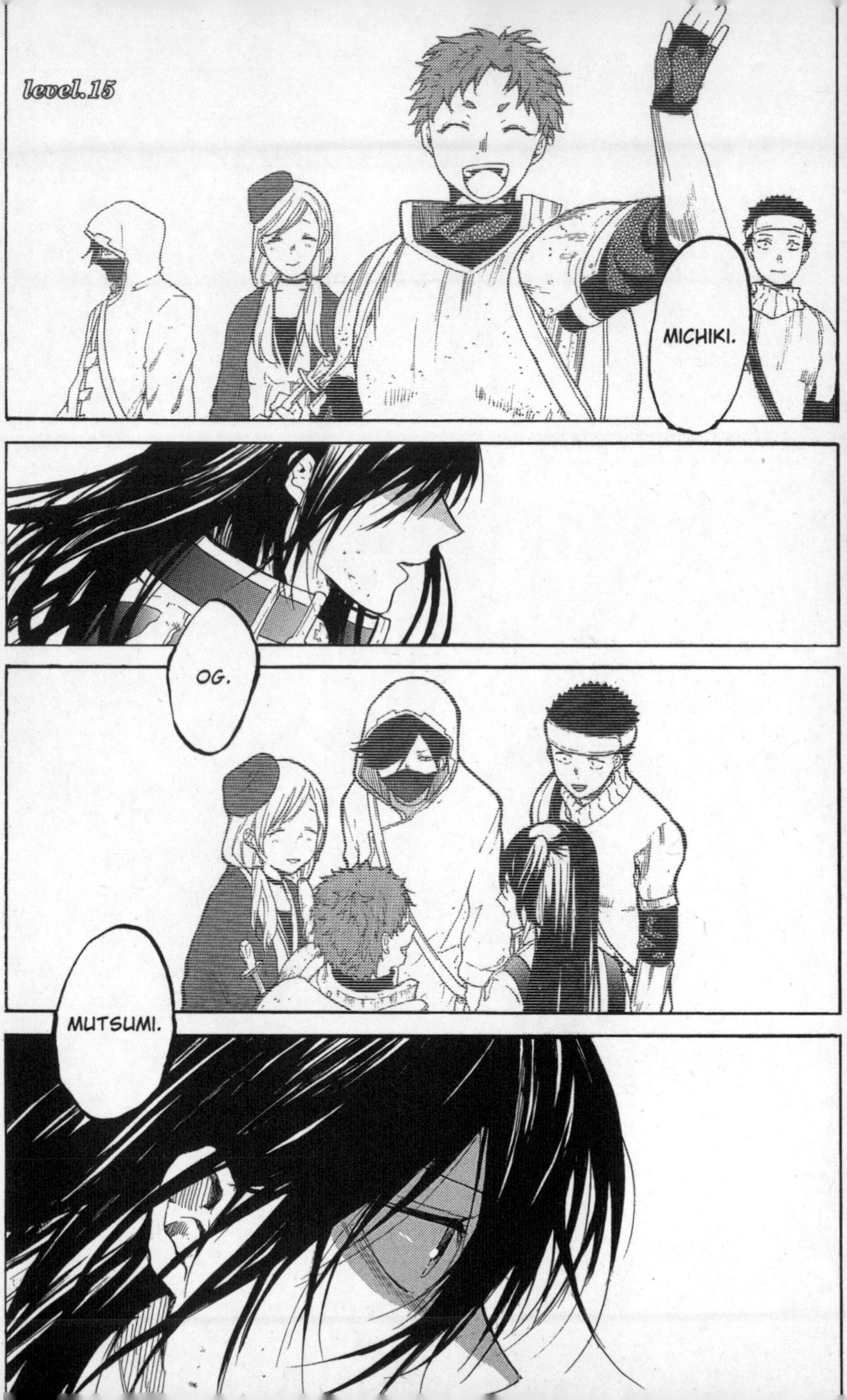
level.15
MICHIKI.
OG.
MUTSUMI.

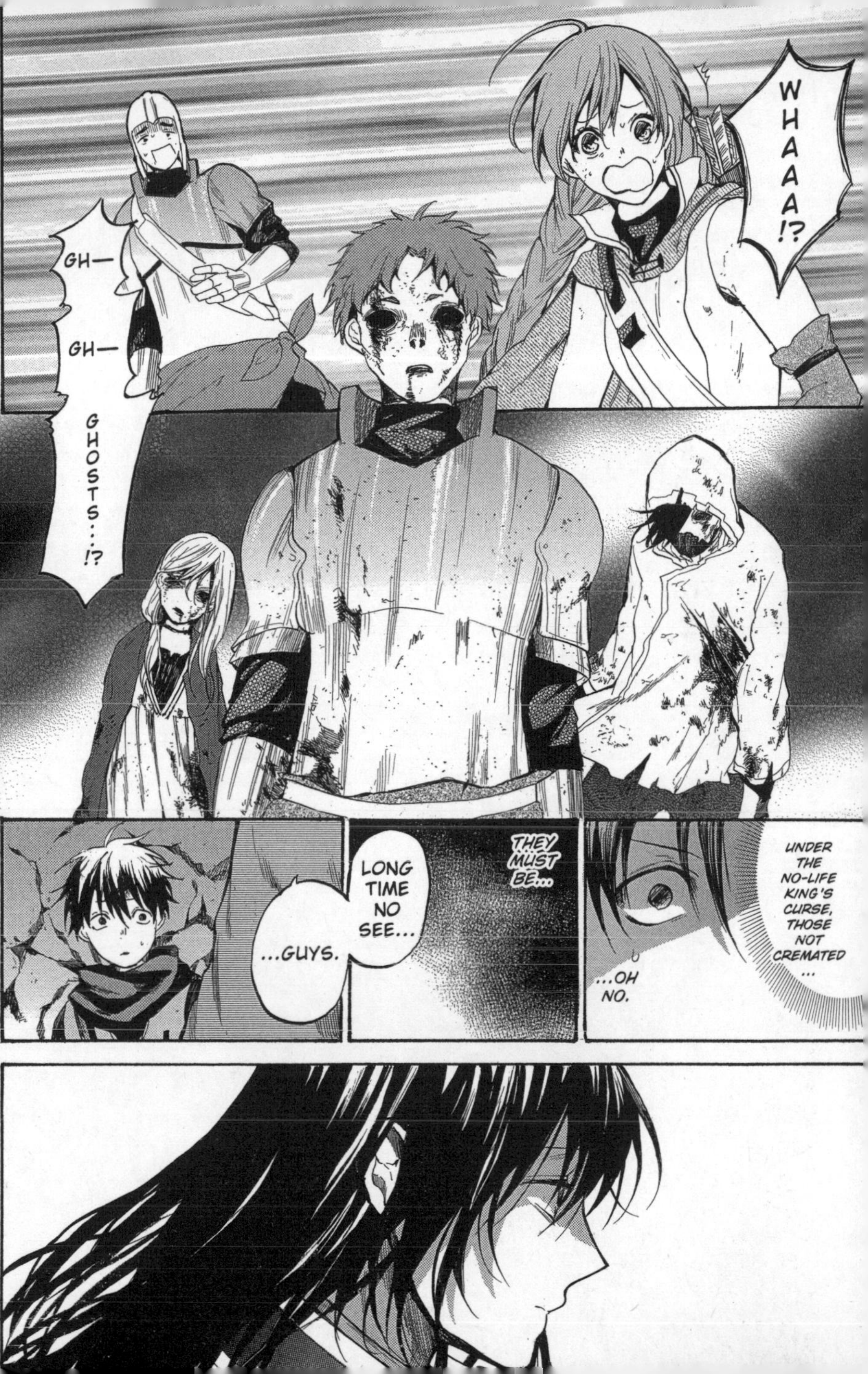
WHAAAA!?
GH— GH—
GHOSTS...!?
UNDER THE NO-LIFE KING'S CURSE, THOSE NOT CREMATED ...
...OH NO.
THEY MUST BE...
LONG TIME NO SEE...
...GUYS.

OKAY.

?

GOT-CHA.

LET'S MAKE OUR WAY UP, THEN...

ZARI (SKRITCH)

ZARI

ZARI

ZARI

...HOLD UP.

......

ZARI

ZARI

ZARI

ZARI

ZARI

ZARI

ZARI

ZARI

ZARI

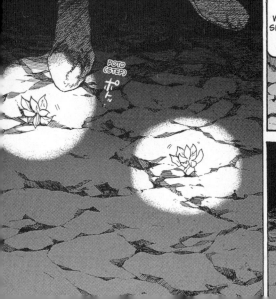

POTO (STEP)

WAIT A SECOND.

BUCHI (RIP)

WHAT'S THAT SOUND...?

HYU (FLING)

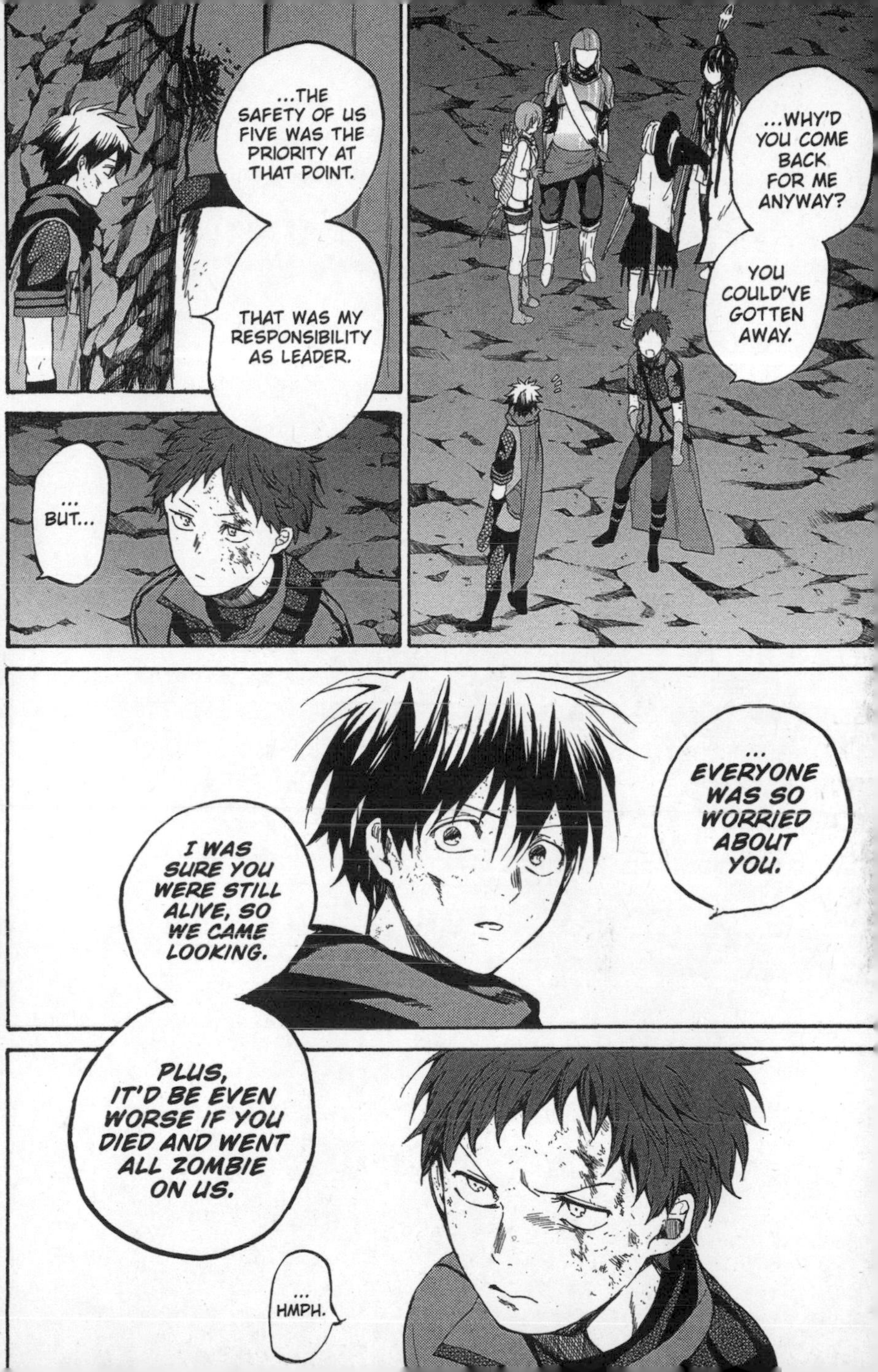
...WHY'D YOU COME BACK FOR ME ANYWAY?
YOU COULD'VE GOTTEN AWAY.
...THE SAFETY OF US FIVE WAS THE PRIORITY AT THAT POINT.
THAT WAS MY RESPONSIBILITY AS LEADER.
... BUT...
... EVERYONE WAS SO WORRIED ABOUT YOU.
I WAS SURE YOU WERE STILL ALIVE, SO WE CAME LOOKING.
PLUS, IT'D BE EVEN WORSE IF YOU DIED AND WENT ALL ZOMBIE ON US.
... HMPH.

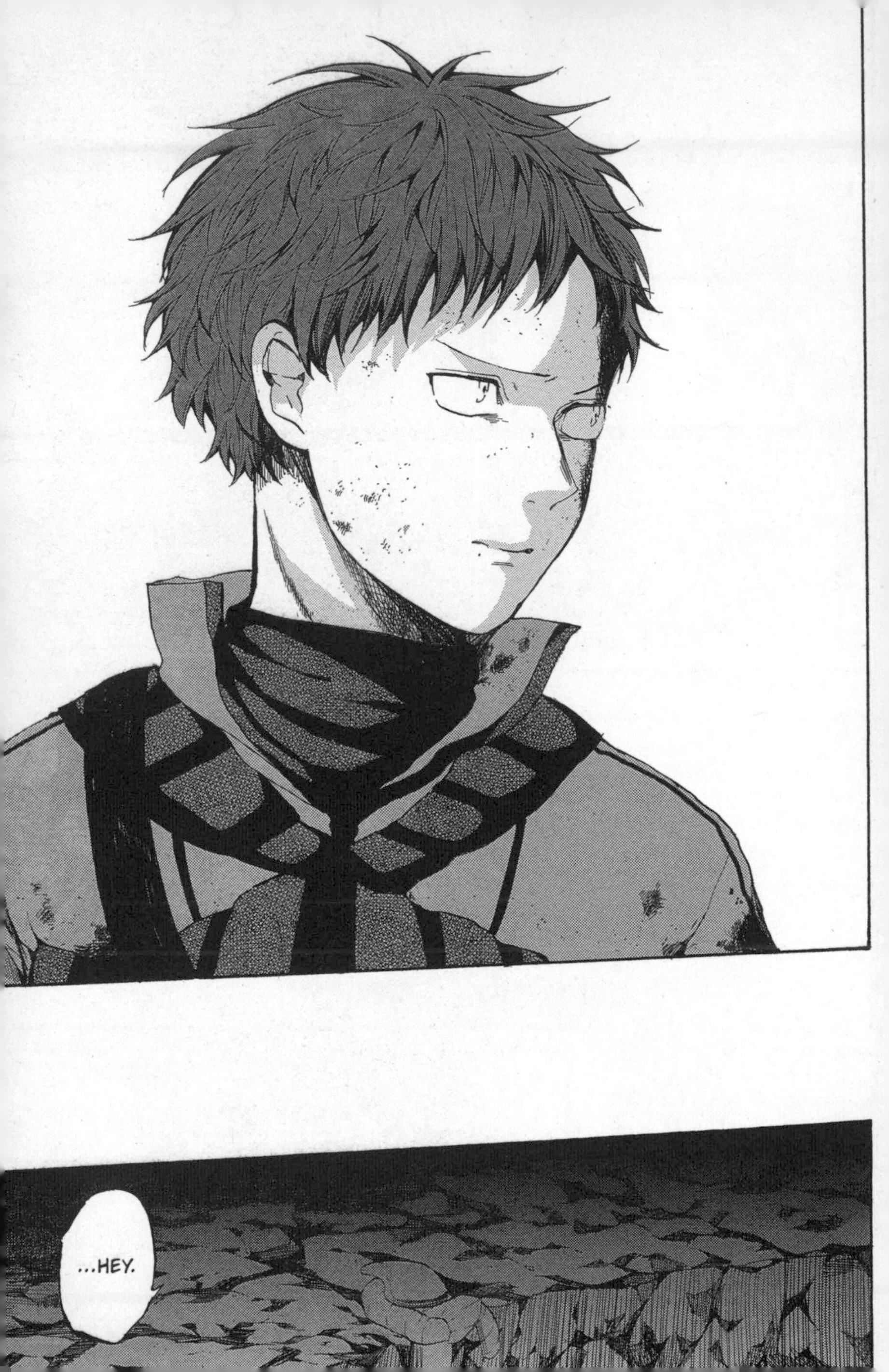
...HEY.

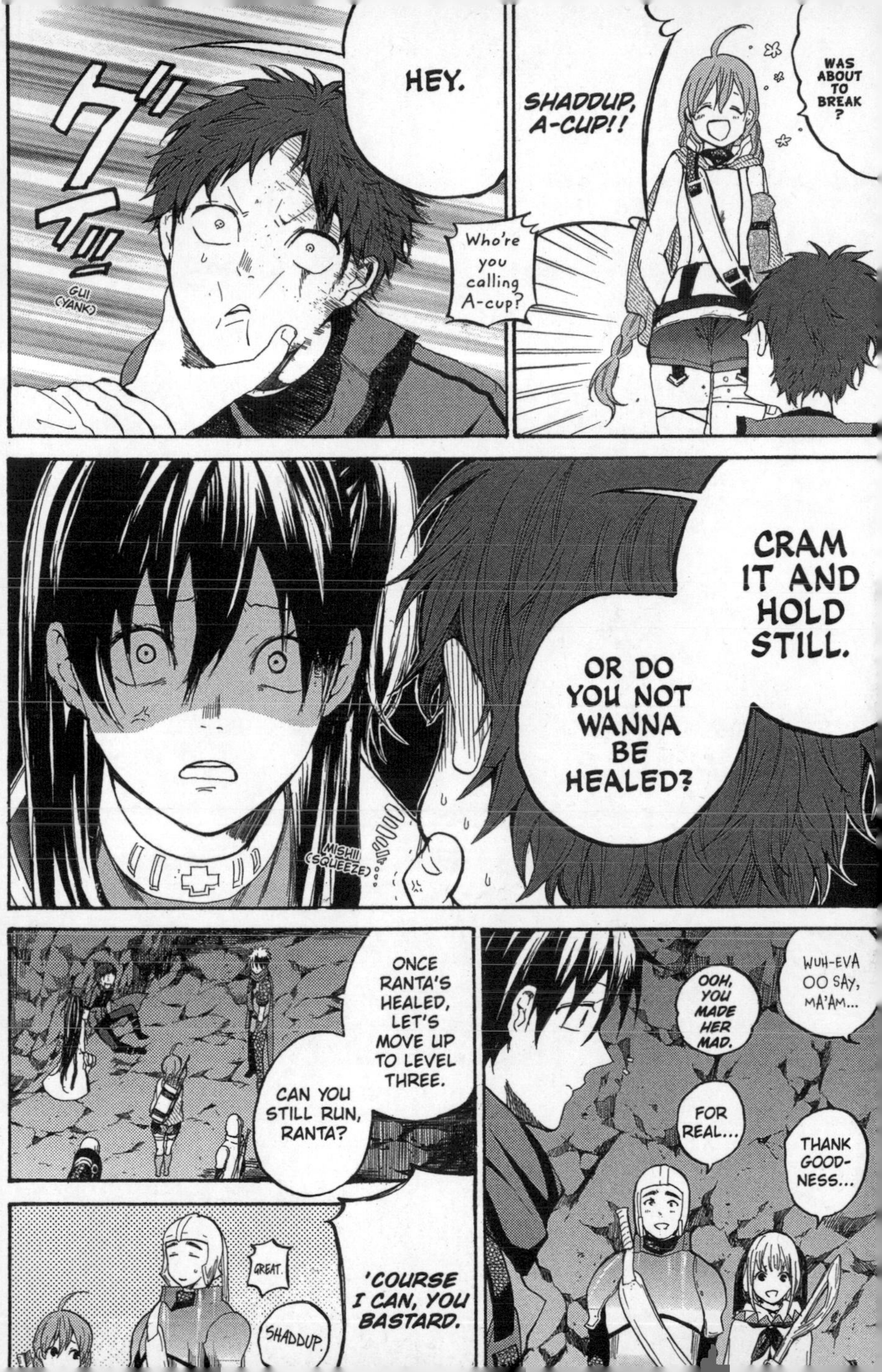
WAS ABOUT TO BREAK?
SHADDUP, A-CUP!!
Who're you calling A-cup?
HEY.
GUI (YANK)
CRAM IT AND HOLD STILL.
OR DO YOU NOT WANNA BE HEALED?
MISHII (SQUEEZE)
WUH-EVA OO SAY, MA'AM...
OOH, YOU MADE HER MAD.
FOR REAL...
THANK GOODNESS...
ONCE RANTA'S HEALED, LET'S MOVE UP TO LEVEL THREE.
CAN YOU STILL RUN, RANTA?
'COURSE I CAN, YOU BASTARD.
GREAT.
SHADDUP.

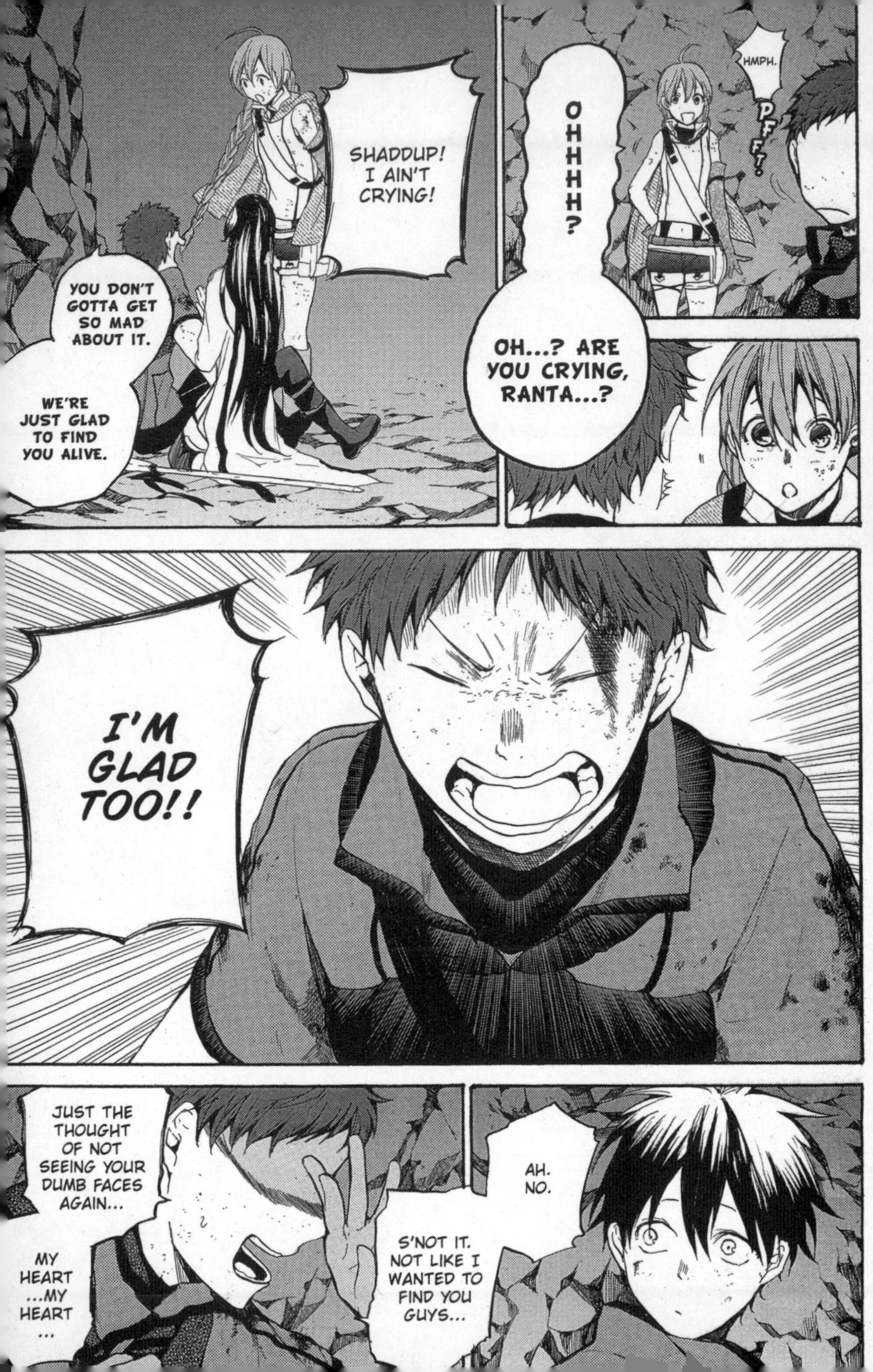
HMPH.
PFFT!
OHHHHH?
OH...? ARE YOU CRYING, RANTA...?
SHADDUP! I AIN'T CRYING!
YOU DON'T GOTTA GET SO MAD ABOUT IT.
WE'RE JUST GLAD TO FIND YOU ALIVE.
I'M GLAD TOO!!
AH. NO.
S'NOT IT. NOT LIKE I WANTED TO FIND YOU GUYS...
JUST THE THOUGHT OF NOT SEEING YOUR DUMB FACES AGAIN...
MY HEART ...MY HEART ...

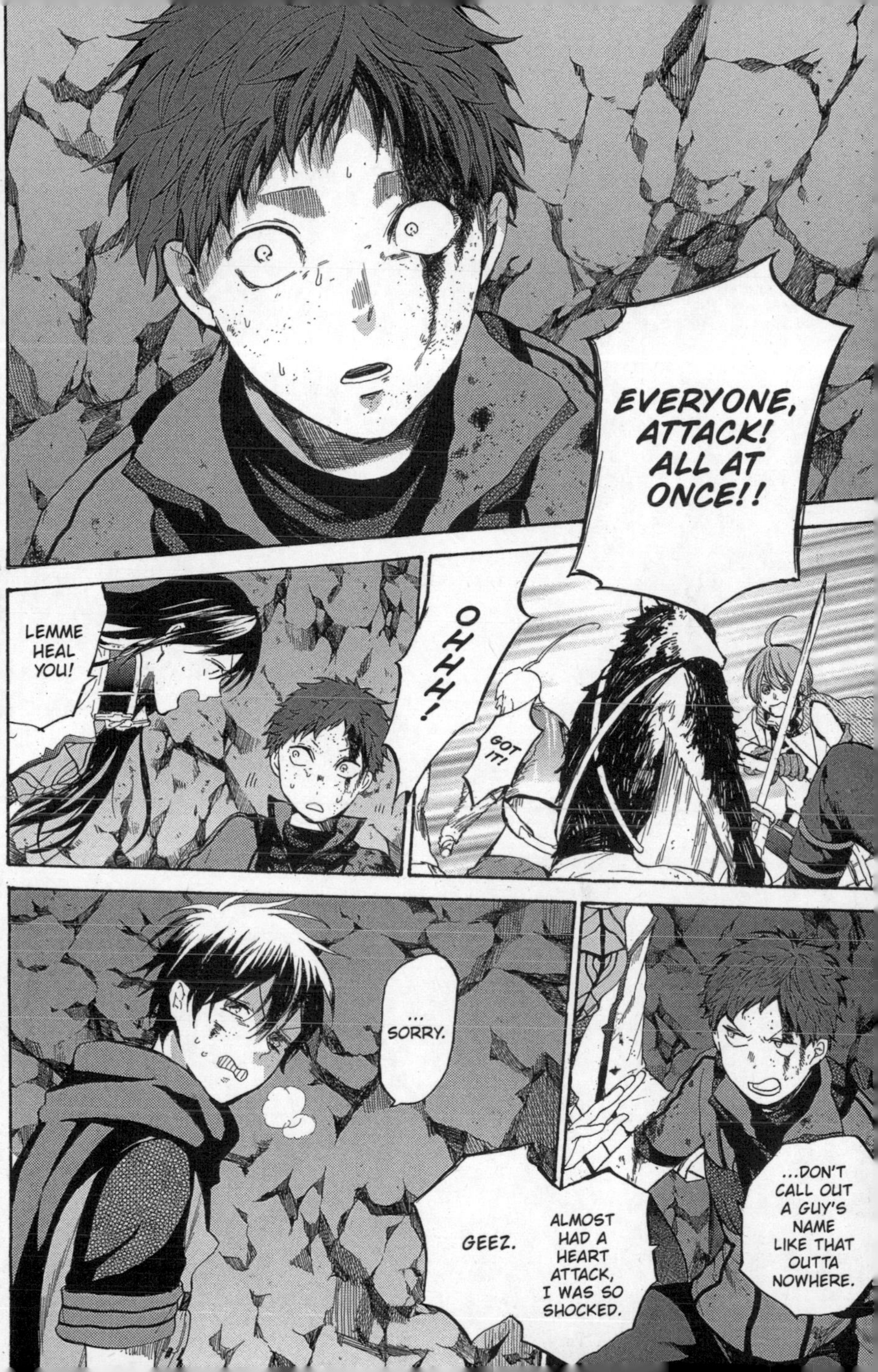
EVERYONE, ATTACK! ALL AT ONCE!!
OHHHH!
GOT IT!
LEMME HEAL YOU!
...DON'T CALL OUT A GUY'S NAME LIKE THAT OUTTA NOWHERE.
ALMOST HAD A HEART ATTACK, I WAS SO SHOCKED.
GEEZ.
... SORRY.

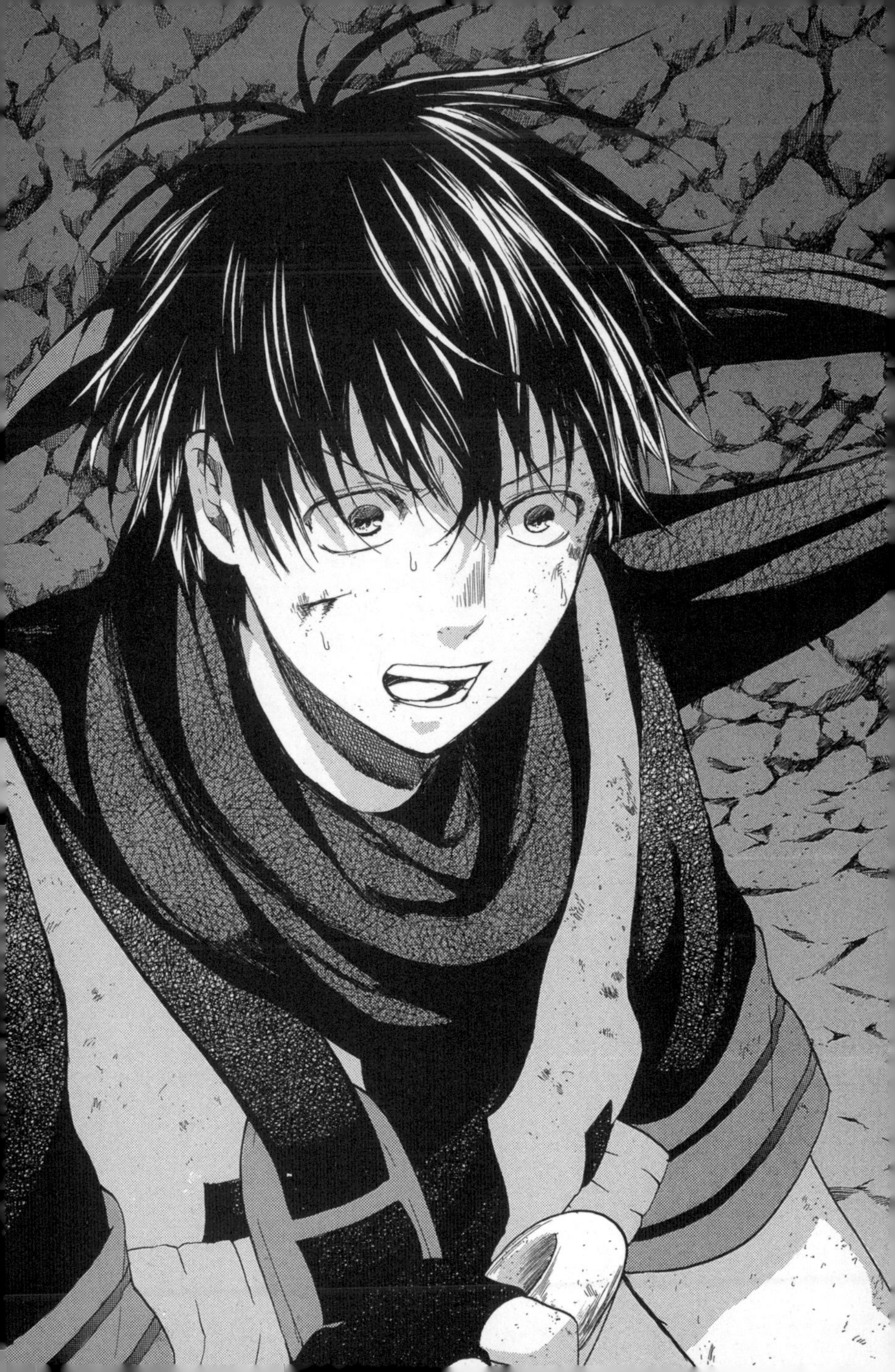

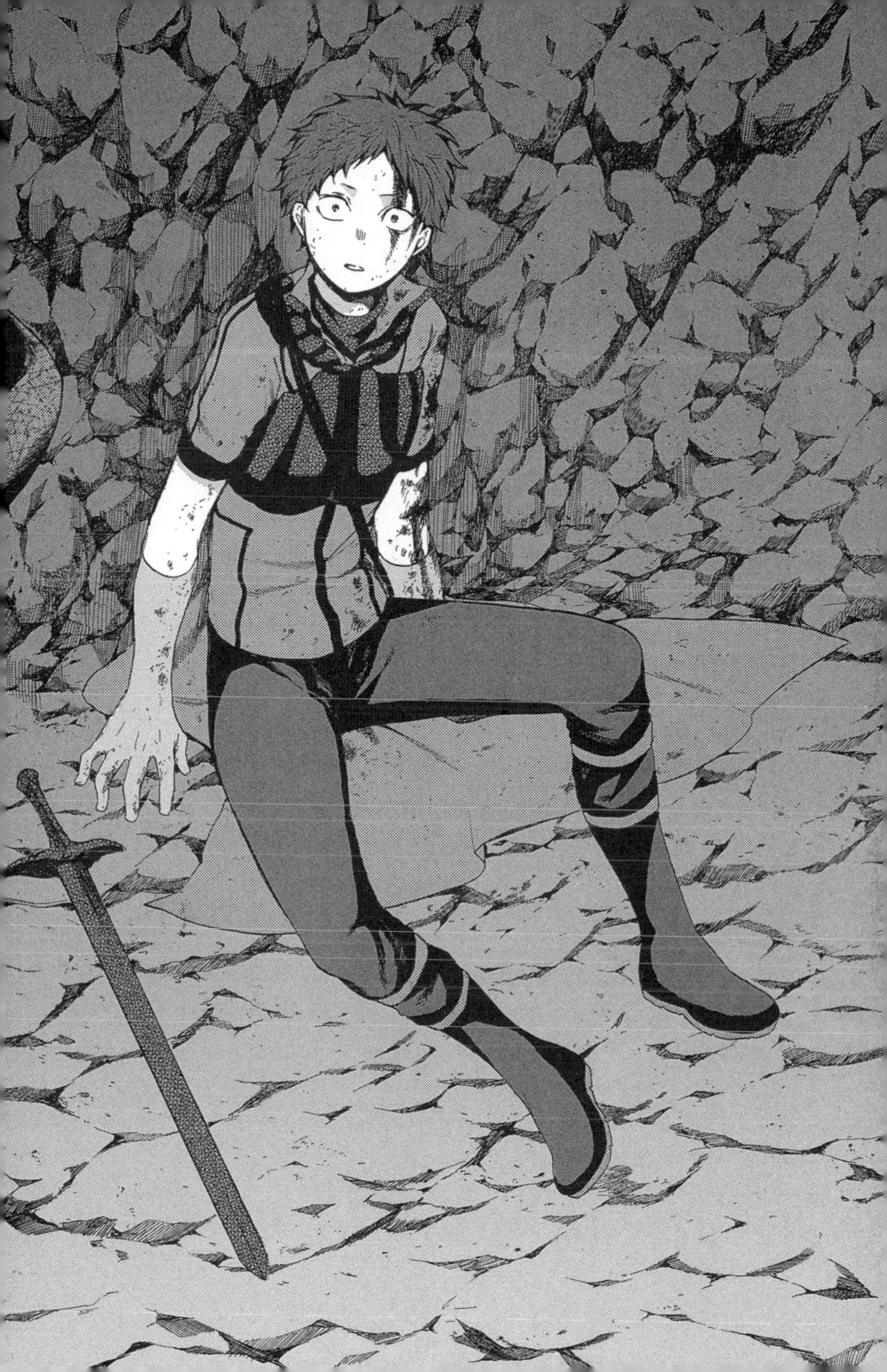

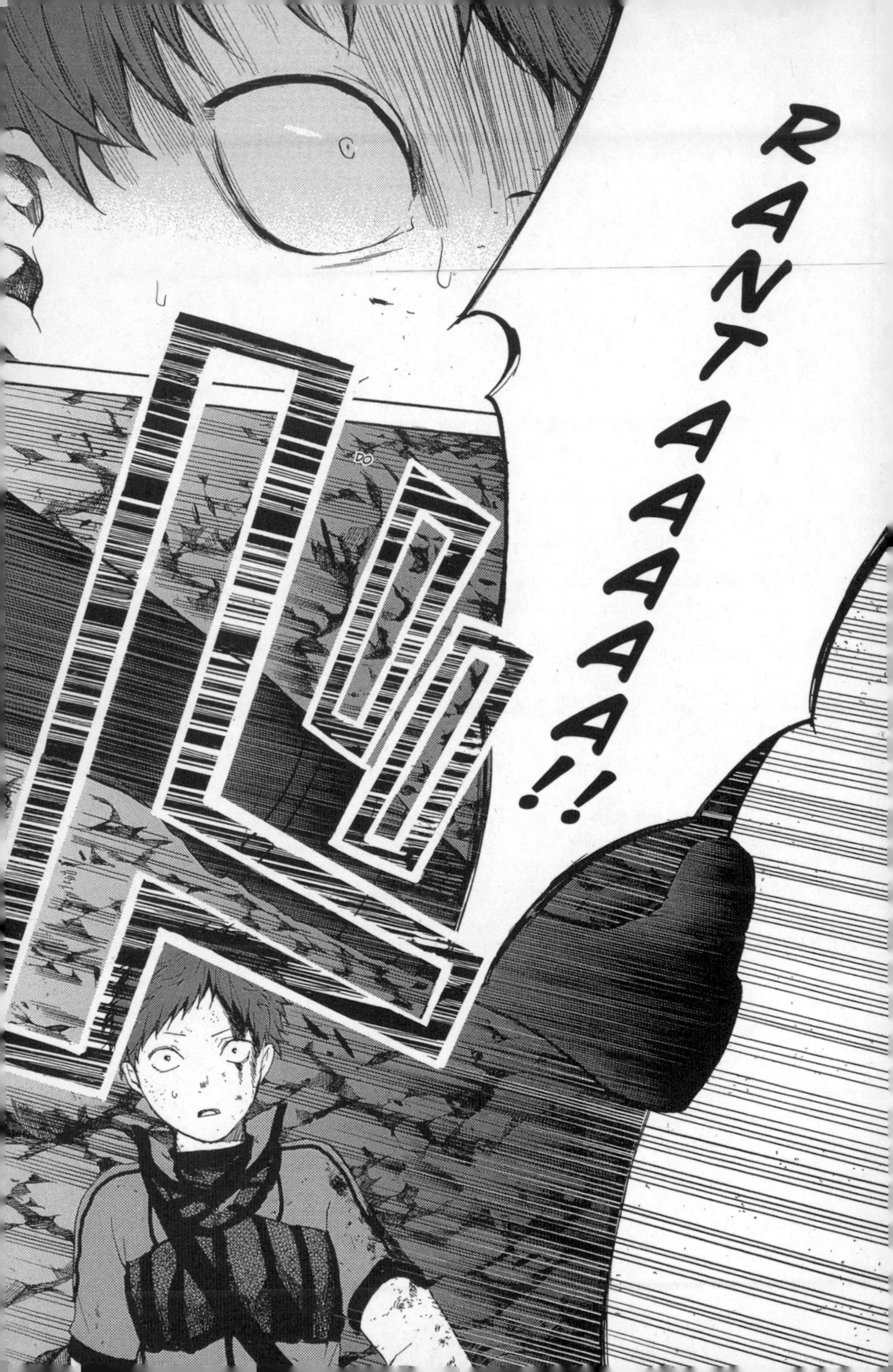
RANTAAAAAA!!
DO

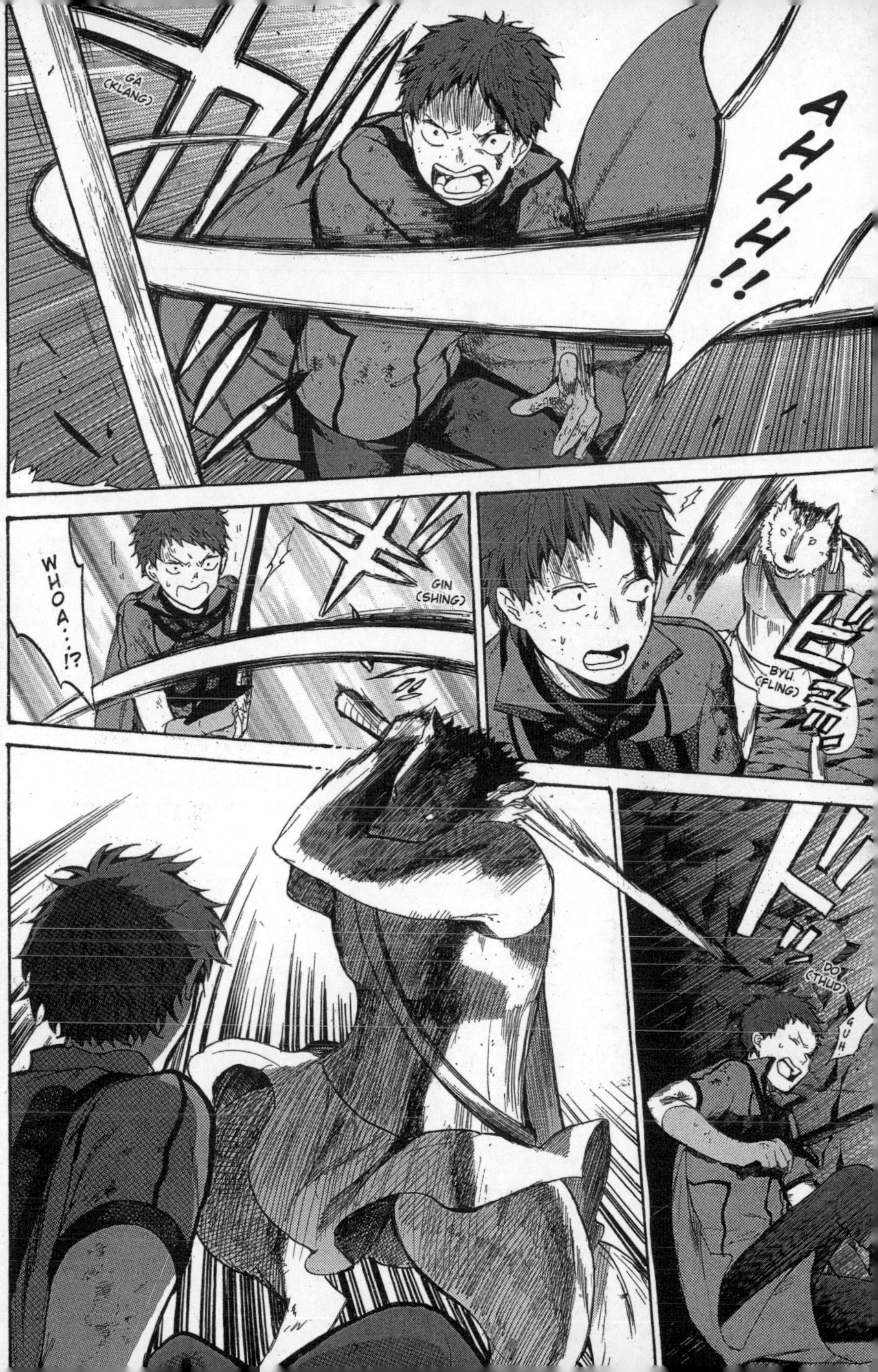

AHHHH!!
GA (KLANG)
GIN (SHING)
WHOA...!?
BYU (FLING)
DO (THUD)
GUH

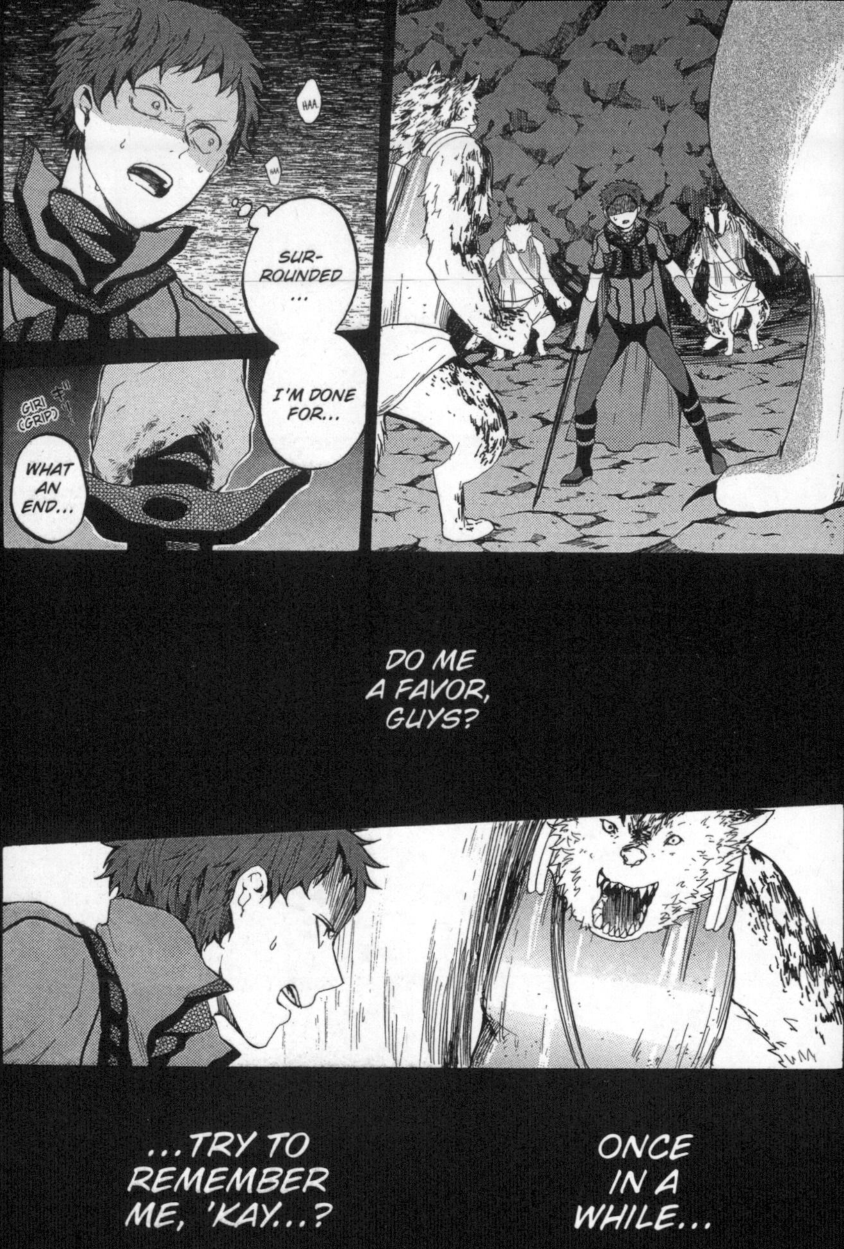
HAA.
HAA.
SUR-ROUNDED...
I'M DONE FOR...
GIRI (GRIP)
WHAT AN END...
DO ME A FAVOR, GUYS?
ONCE IN A WHILE...
...TRY TO REMEMBER ME, 'KAY...?

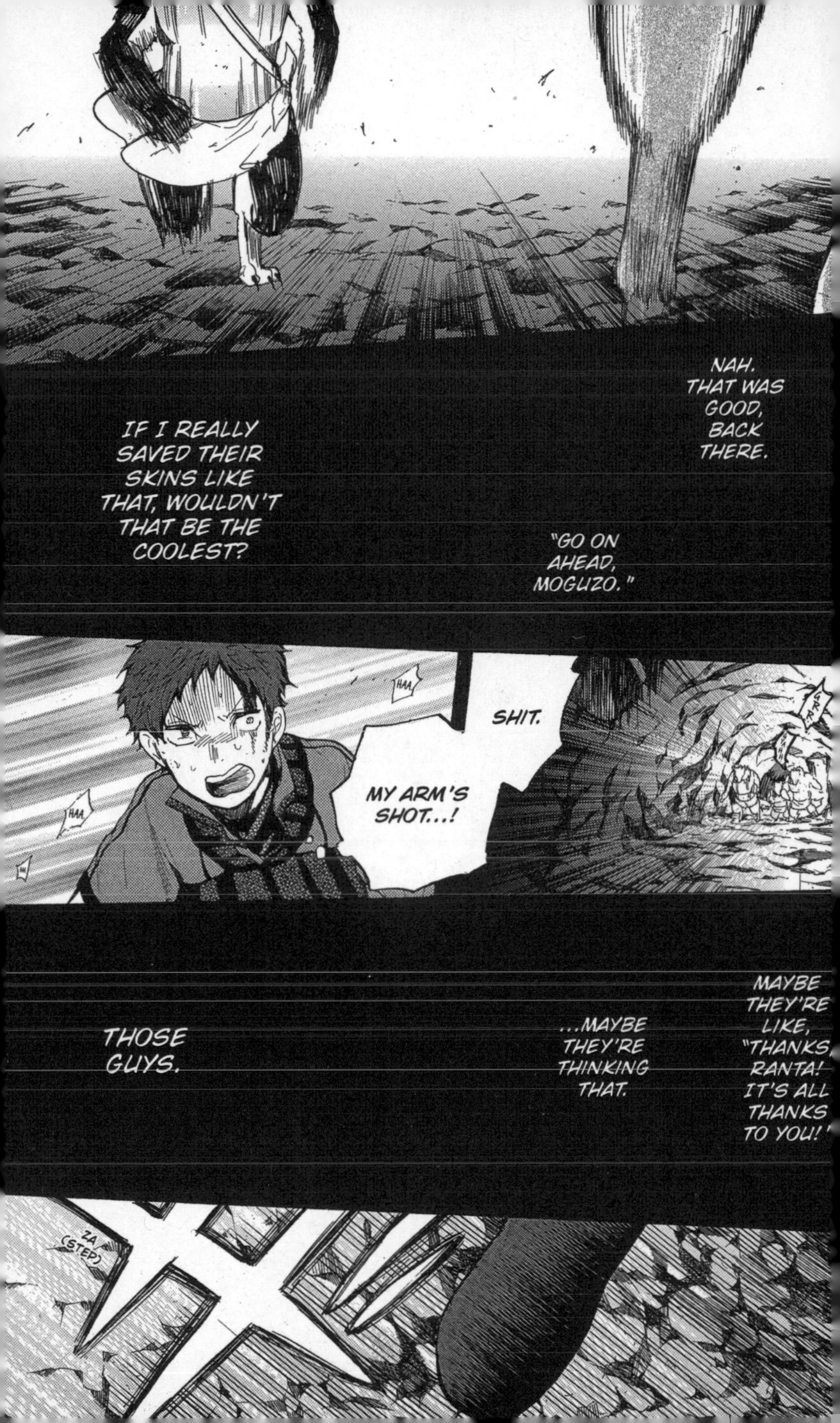
NAH. THAT WAS GOOD, BACK THERE.
"GO ON AHEAD, MOGUZO."
IF I REALLY SAVED THEIR SKINS LIKE THAT, WOULDN'T THAT BE THE COOLEST?
HAA
SHIT.
MY ARM'S SHOT...!
HAA
MAYBE THEY'RE LIKE, "THANKS, RANTA! IT'S ALL THANKS TO YOU!"
...MAYBE THEY'RE THINKING THAT.
THOSE GUYS.
ZA (STEP)

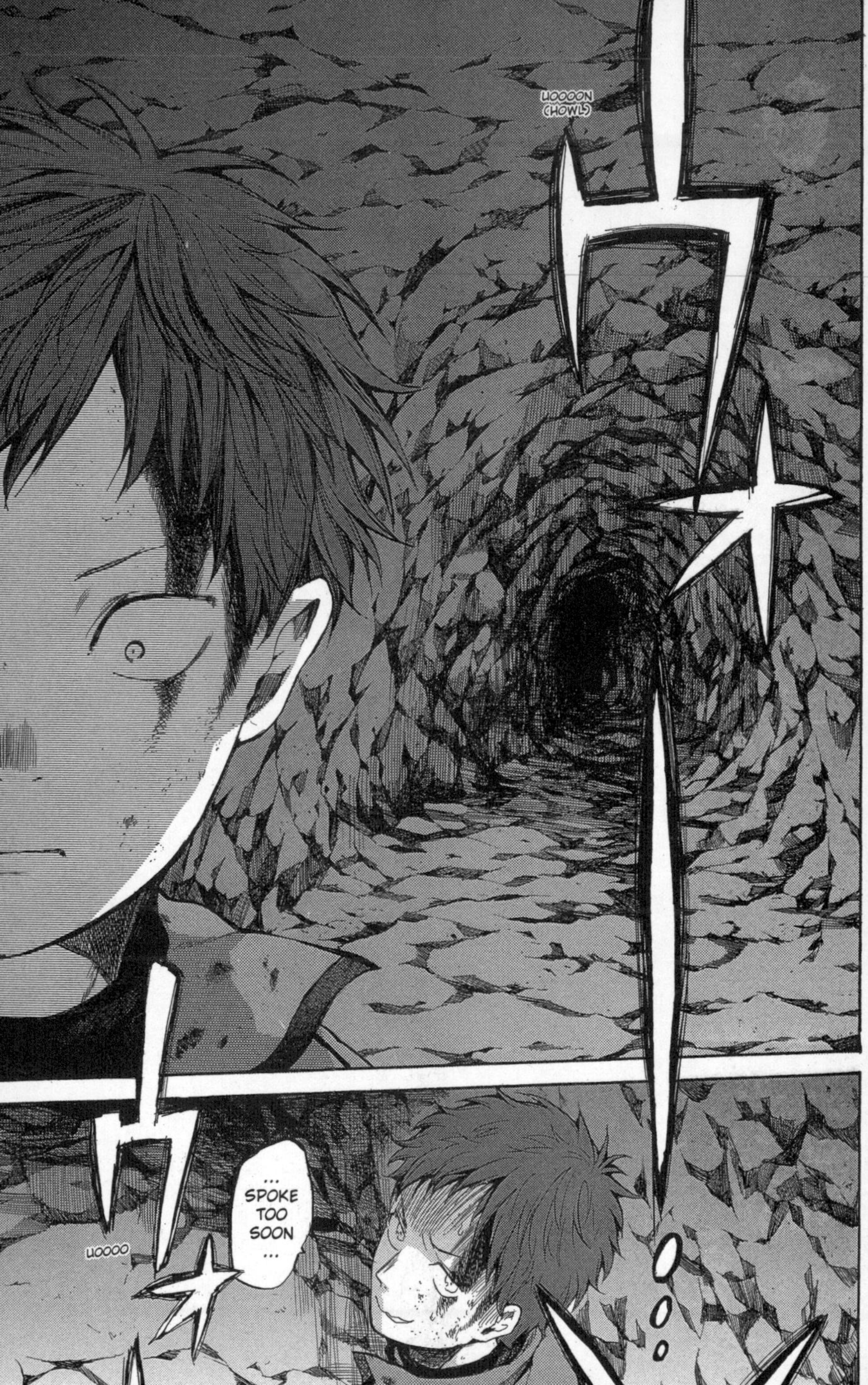
UOOOON
(HOWL)
... SPOKE TOO SOON ...
UOOOO

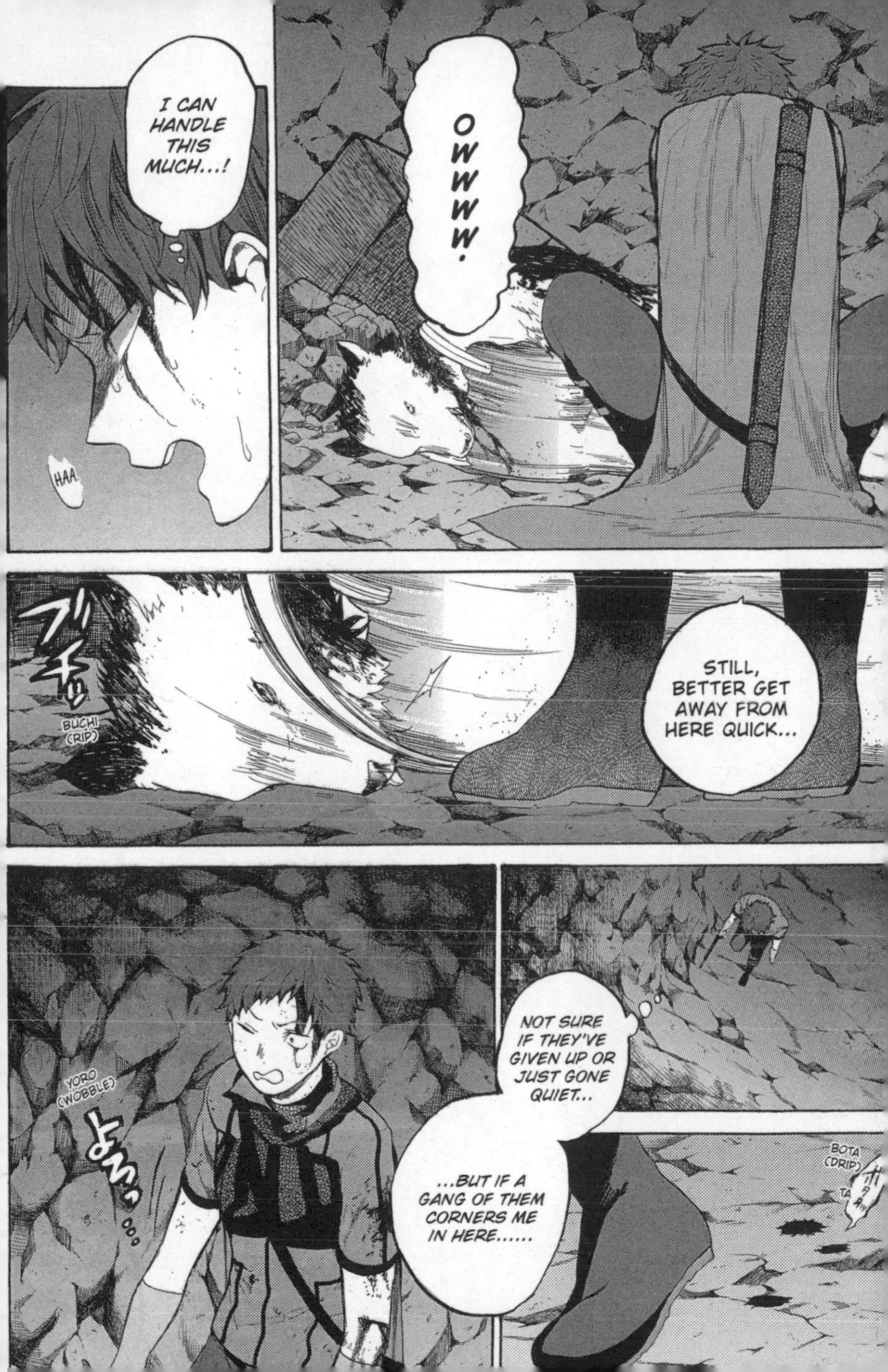
OWWWW!
I CAN HANDLE THIS MUCH...!
HAA.
STILL, BETTER GET AWAY FROM HERE QUICK...
BUCHI (RIP)
NOT SURE IF THEY'VE GIVEN UP OR JUST GONE QUIET...
...BUT IF A GANG OF THEM CORNERS ME IN HERE......
BOTA (DRIP)
YORO (WOBBLE)

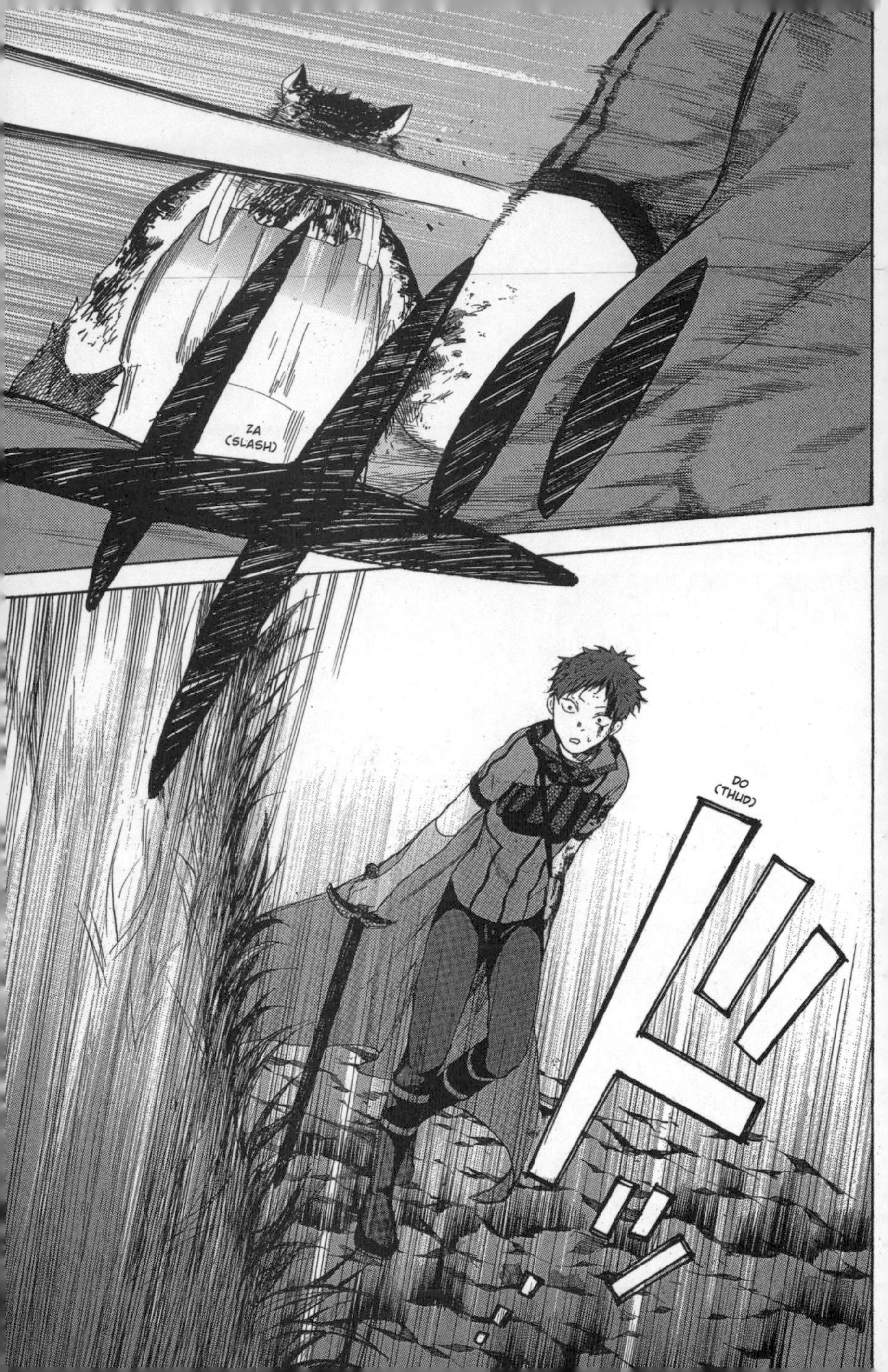
ZA
(SLASH)
DO
(THUD)

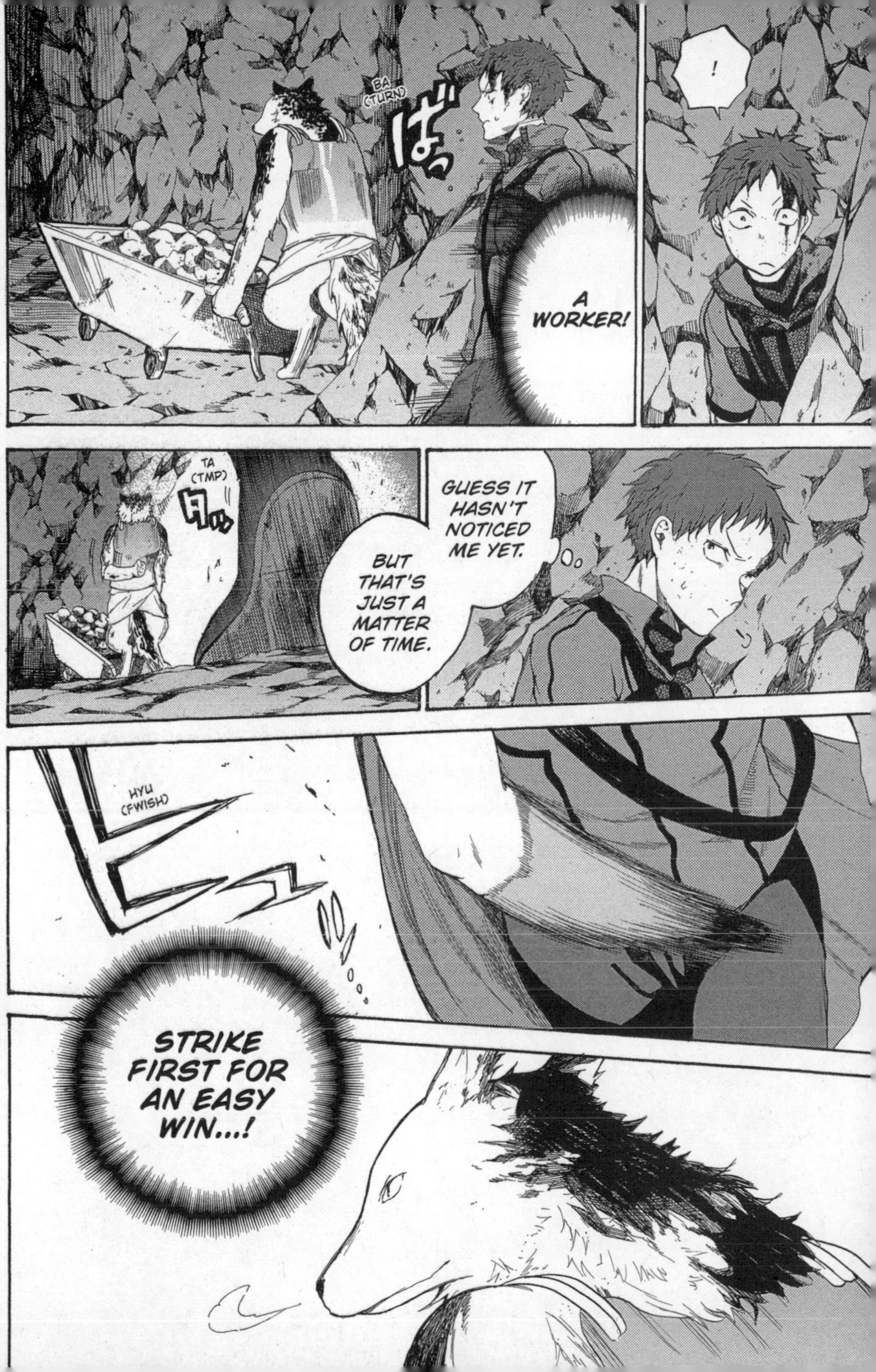
!
BA (TURN)
ばっ
A WORKER!
GUESS IT HASN'T NOTICED ME YET.
BUT THAT'S JUST A MATTER OF TIME.
TA (TMP)
タッ
HYU (FWISH)
STRIKE FIRST FOR AN EASY WIN...!

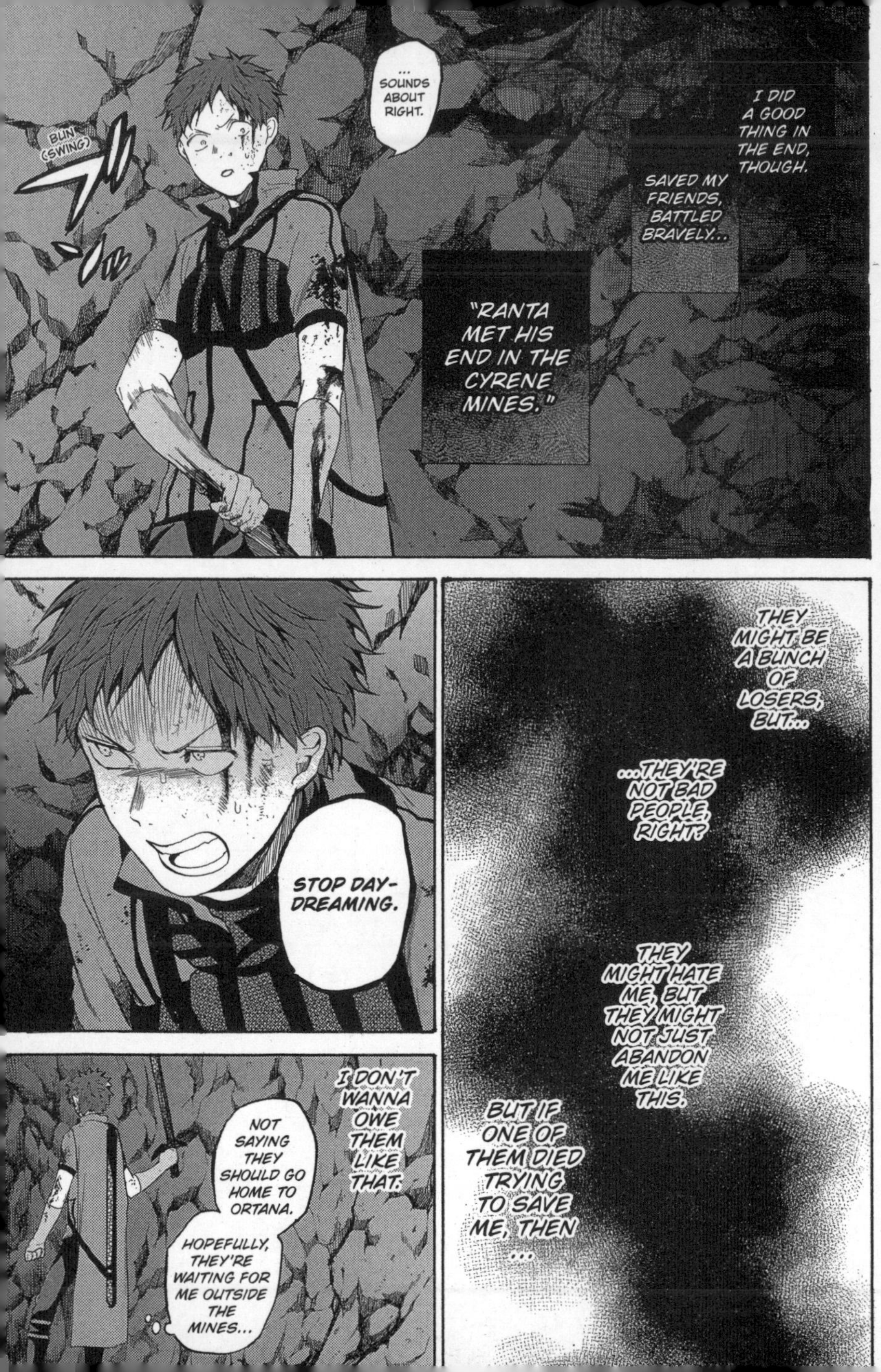
I DID A GOOD THING IN THE END, THOUGH.
SAVED MY FRIENDS, BATTLED BRAVELY...
"RANTA MET HIS END IN THE CYRENE MINES."
...SOUNDS ABOUT RIGHT.
BUN (SWING)
THEY MIGHT BE A BUNCH OF LOSERS, BUT...
...THEY'RE NOT BAD PEOPLE, RIGHT?
THEY MIGHT HATE ME, BUT THEY MIGHT NOT JUST ABANDON ME LIKE THIS.
BUT IF ONE OF THEM DIED TRYING TO SAVE ME, THEN ...
STOP DAY-DREAMING.
I DON'T WANNA OWE THEM LIKE THAT.
NOT SAYING THEY SHOULD GO HOME TO ORTANA.
HOPEFULLY, THEY'RE WAITING FOR ME OUTSIDE THE MINES...

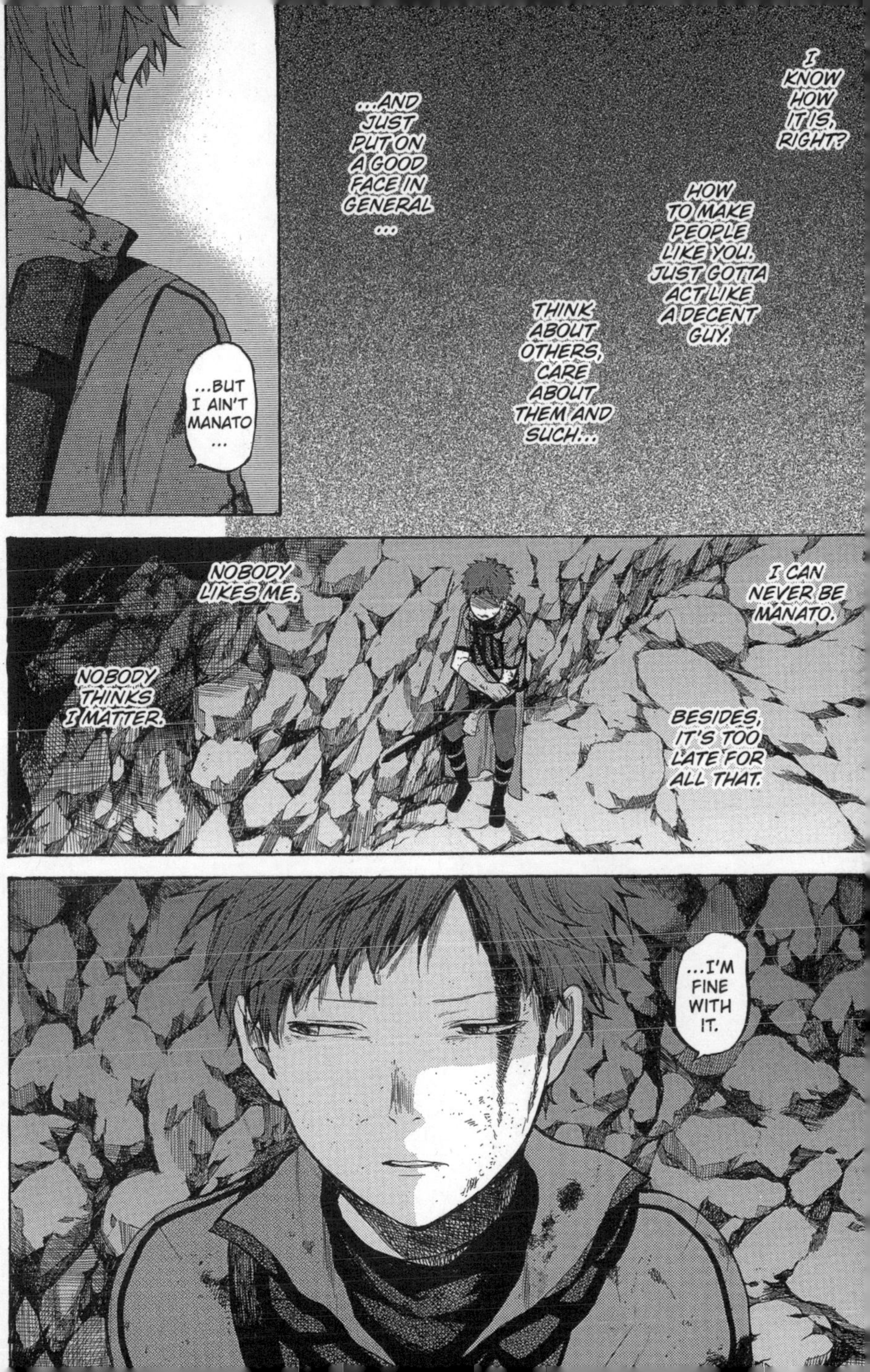
I KNOW HOW IT IS, RIGHT?
HOW TO MAKE PEOPLE LIKE YOU. JUST GOTTA ACT LIKE A DECENT GUY.
THINK ABOUT OTHERS, CARE ABOUT THEM AND SUCH...
...AND JUST PUT ON A GOOD FACE IN GENERAL...
...BUT I AIN'T MANATO...
I CAN NEVER BE MANATO.
BESIDES, IT'S TOO LATE FOR ALL THAT.
NOBODY LIKES ME.
NOBODY THINKS I MATTER.
...I'M FINE WITH IT.

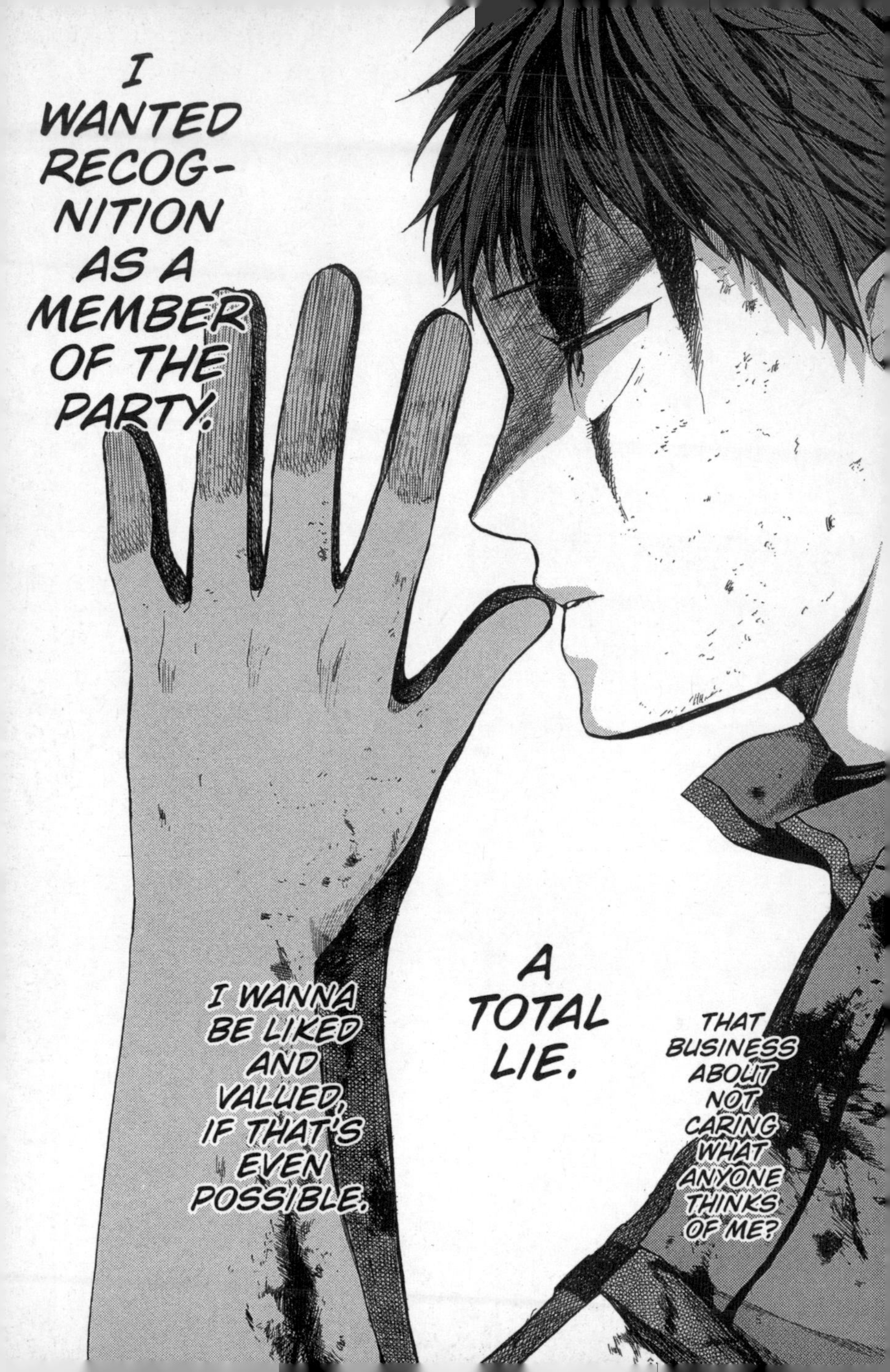
I WANTED RECOG-NITION AS A MEMBER OF THE PARTY.
THAT BUSINESS ABOUT NOT CARING WHAT ANYONE THINKS OF ME?
A TOTAL LIE.
I WANNA BE LIKED AND VALUED, IF THAT'S EVEN POSSIBLE.

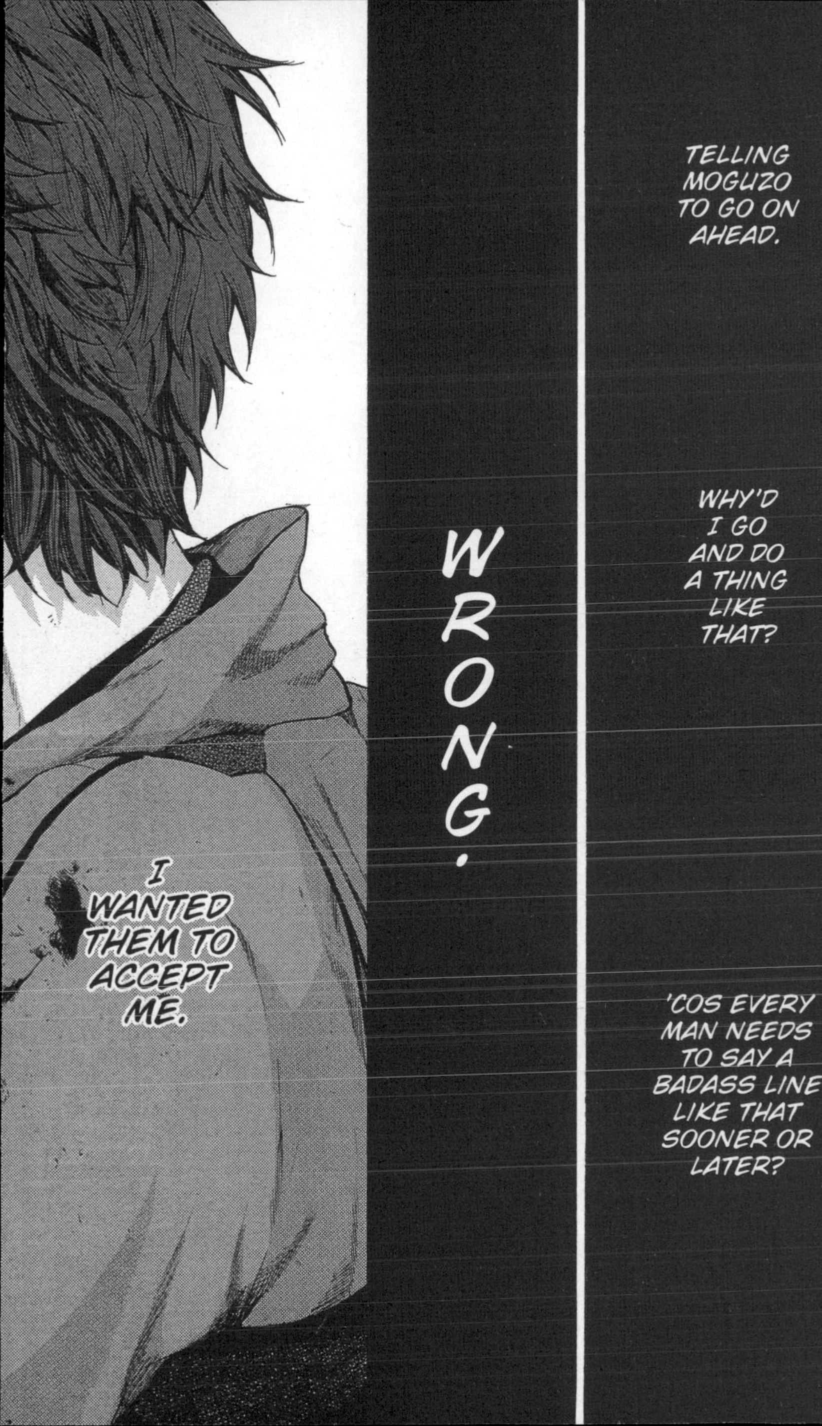
TELLING MOGUZO TO GO ON AHEAD.
WHY'D I GO AND DO A THING LIKE THAT?
'COS EVERY MAN NEEDS TO SAY A BADASS LINE LIKE THAT SOONER OR LATER?
WRONG.
I WANTED THEM TO ACCEPT ME.

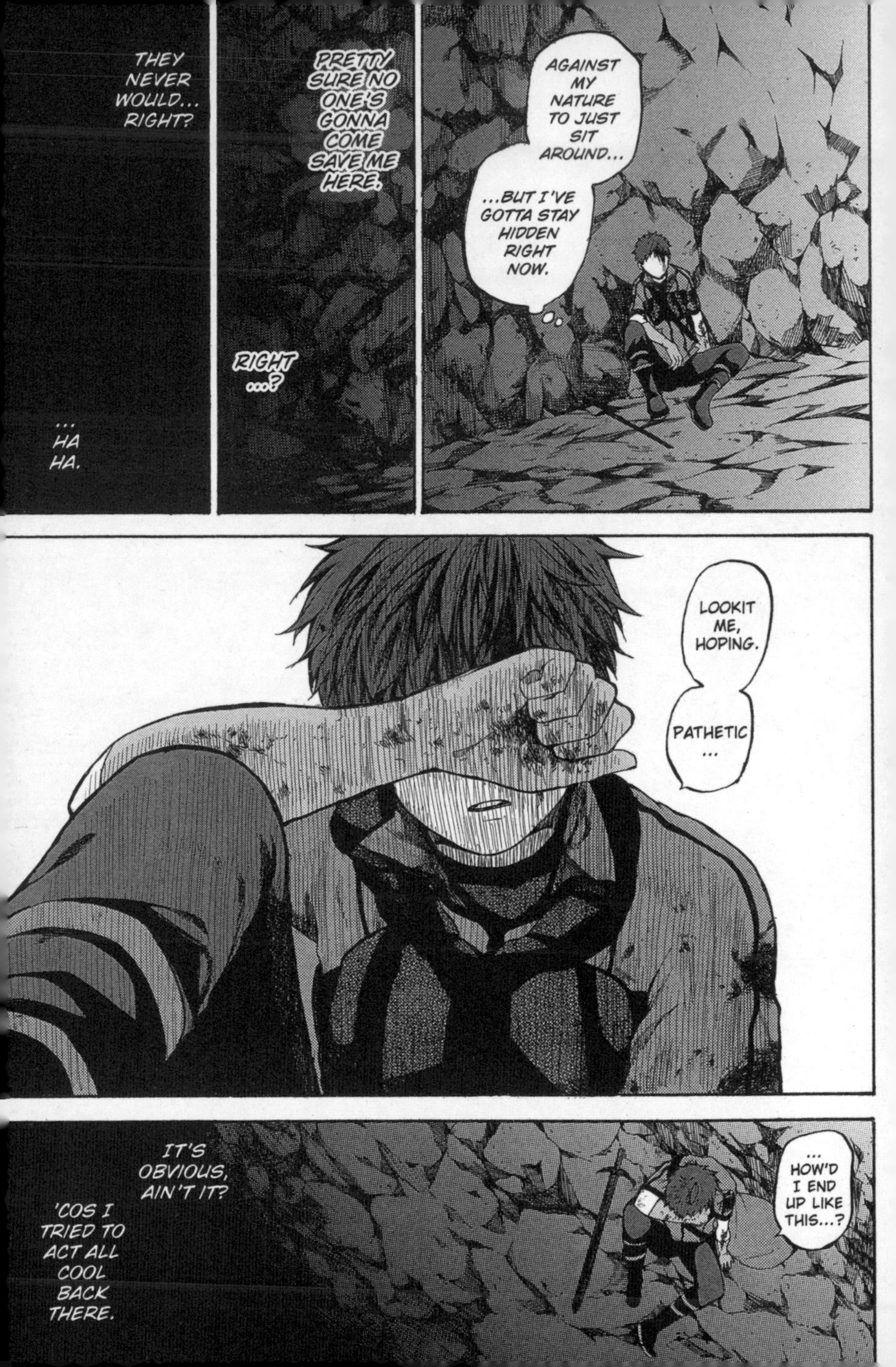
AGAINST MY NATURE TO JUST SIT AROUND...
...BUT I'VE GOTTA STAY HIDDEN RIGHT NOW.
PRETTY SURE NO ONE'S GONNA COME SAVE ME HERE.
RIGHT ...?
THEY NEVER WOULD... RIGHT?
... HA HA.
LOOKIT ME, HOPING.
PATHETIC ...
... HOW'D I END UP LIKE THIS...?
IT'S OBVIOUS, AIN'T IT?
'COS I TRIED TO ACT ALL COOL BACK THERE.

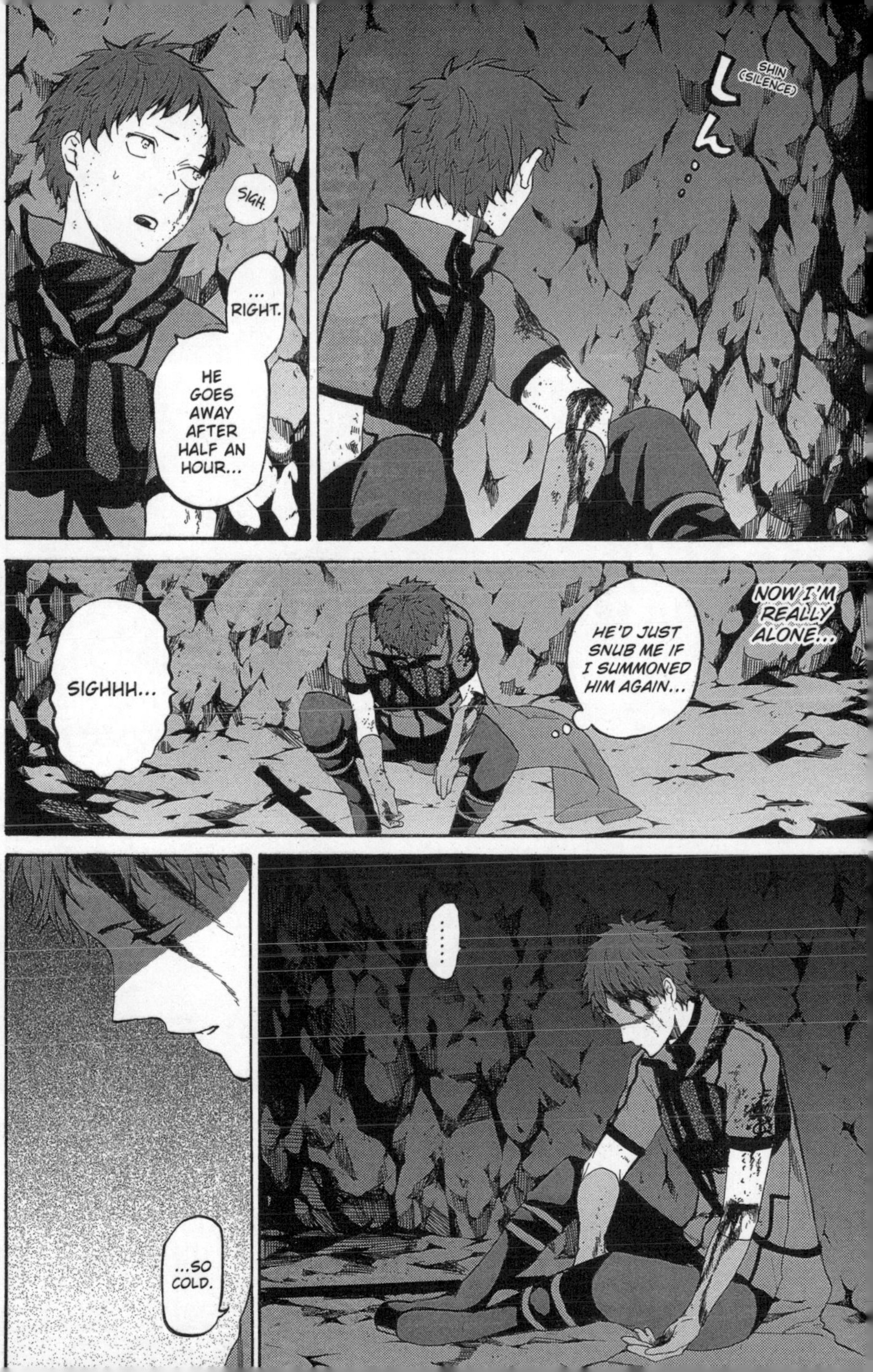

しん
SHIN (SILENCE)
SIGH.
...RIGHT.
HE GOES AWAY AFTER HALF AN HOUR...
NOW I'M REALLY ALONE...
HE'D JUST SNUB ME IF I SUMMONED HIM AGAIN...
SIGHHH...
......
...SO COLD.

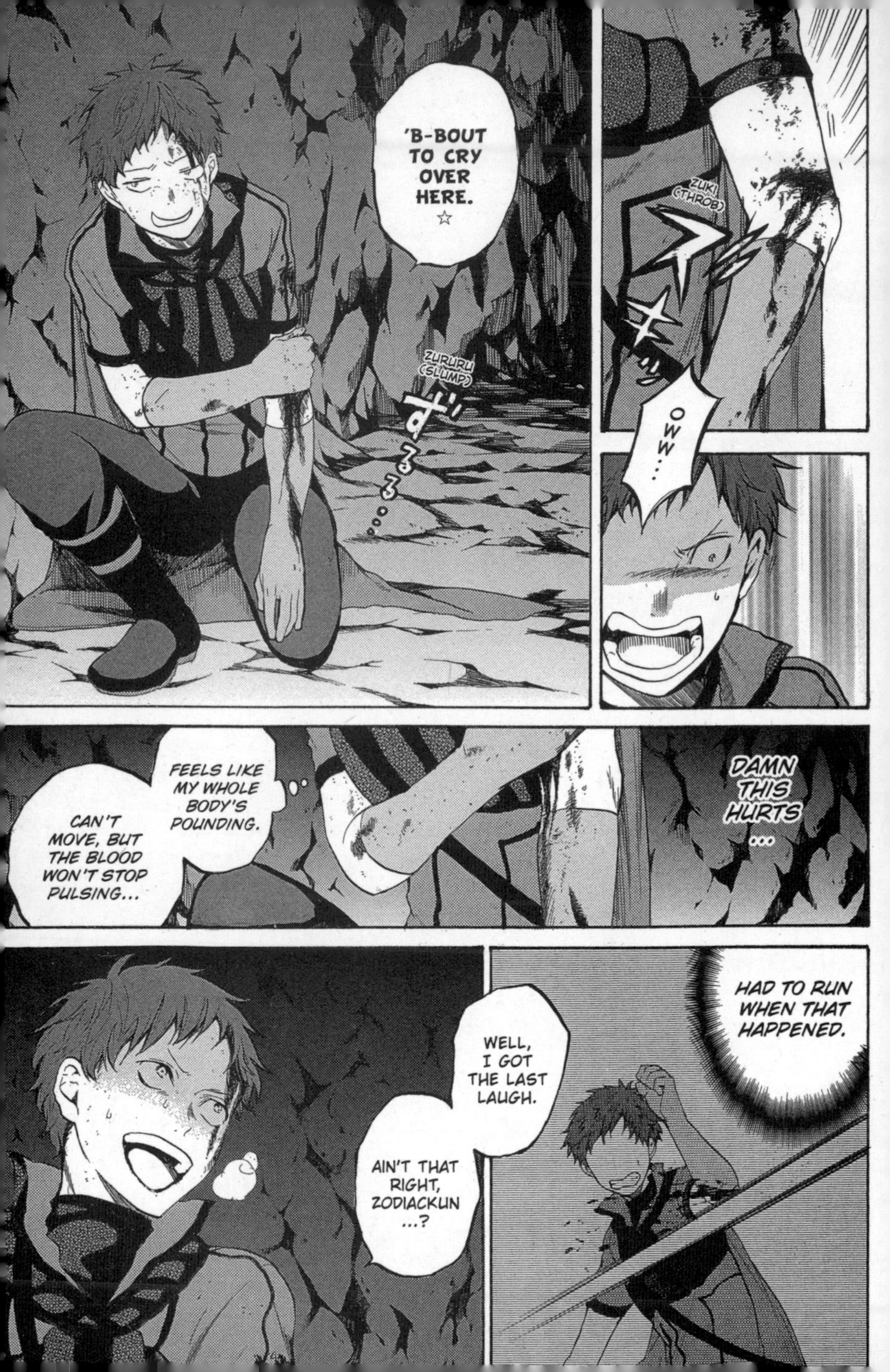
ZUKI (THROB)
OWW...
'B-BOUT TO CRY OVER HERE. ☆
ZURURU (SLUMP)
DAMN THIS HURTS...
FEELS LIKE MY WHOLE BODY'S POUNDING.
CAN'T MOVE, BUT THE BLOOD WON'T STOP PULSING...
HAD TO RUN WHEN THAT HAPPENED.
WELL, I GOT THE LAST LAUGH.
AIN'T THAT RIGHT, ZODIACKUN...?

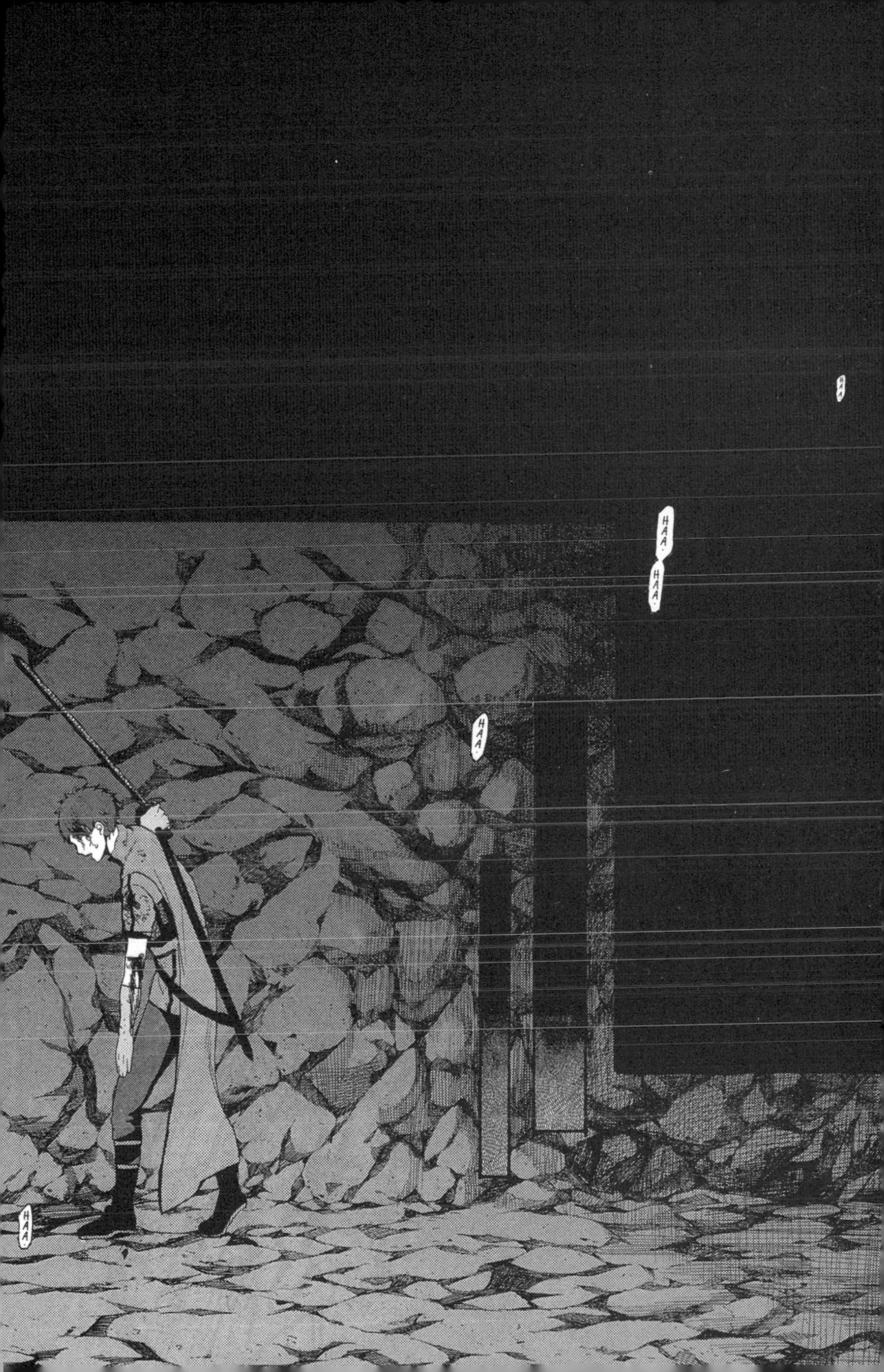
HAA
HAA.
HAA.
HAA.
HAA.

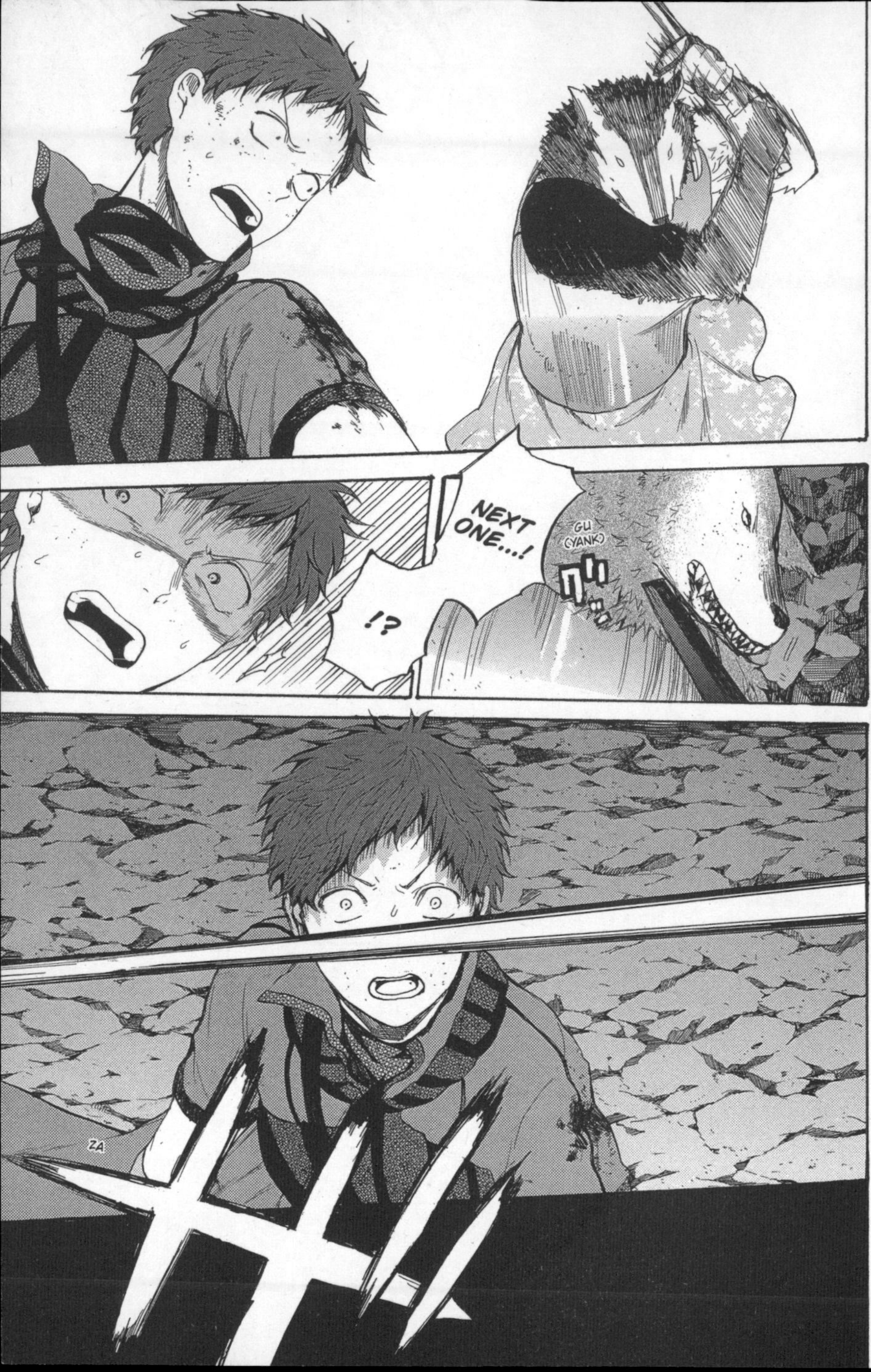
NEXT ONE...!
GU (YANK)
!?
ZA

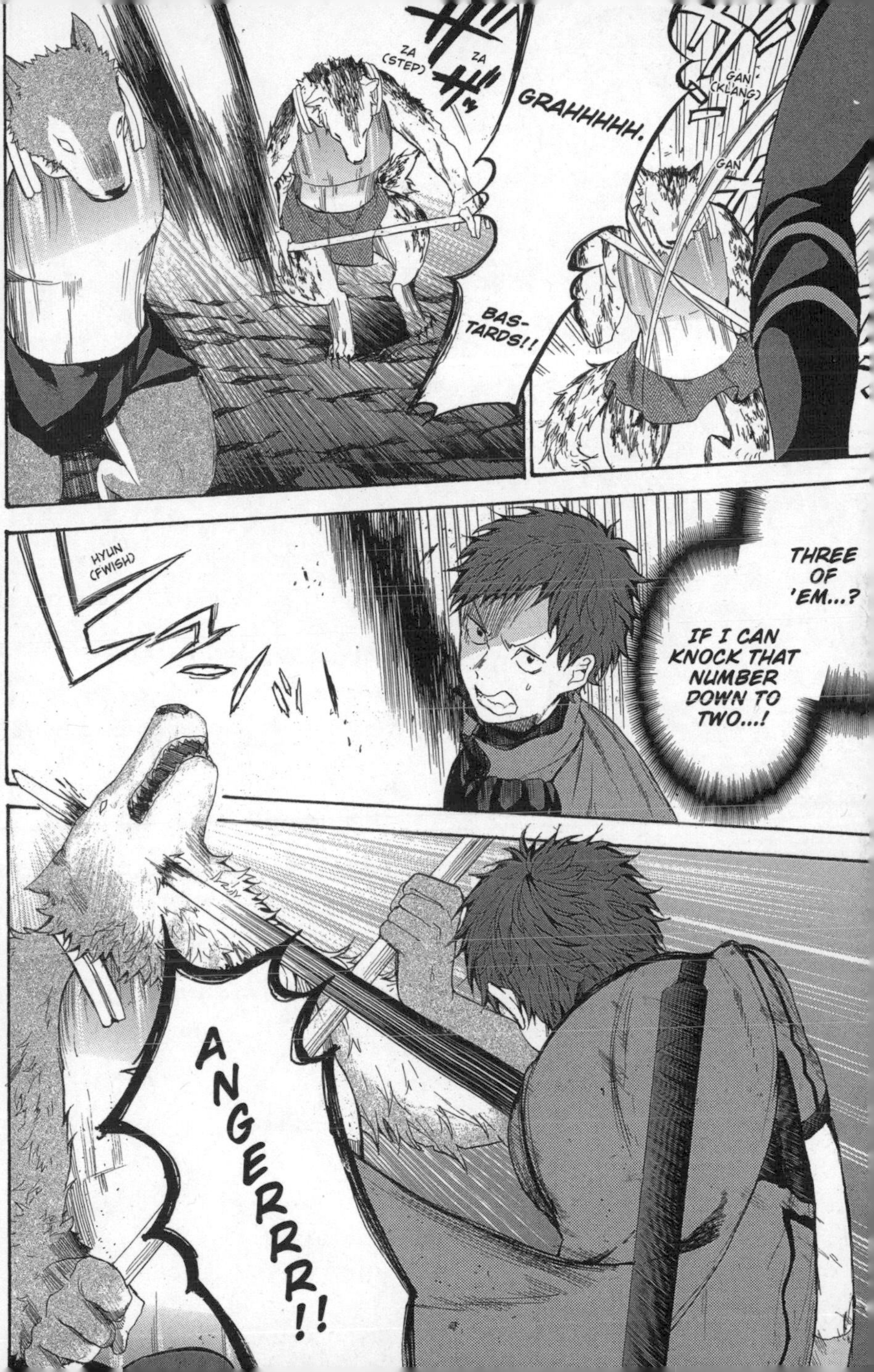

ZA (STEP)
ZA
GRAHHHHH.
GAN (KLANG)
GAN
BAS-TARDS!!
HYUN (FWISH)
THREE OF 'EM...?
IF I CAN KNOCK THAT NUMBER DOWN TO TWO...!
ANGERRRR!!

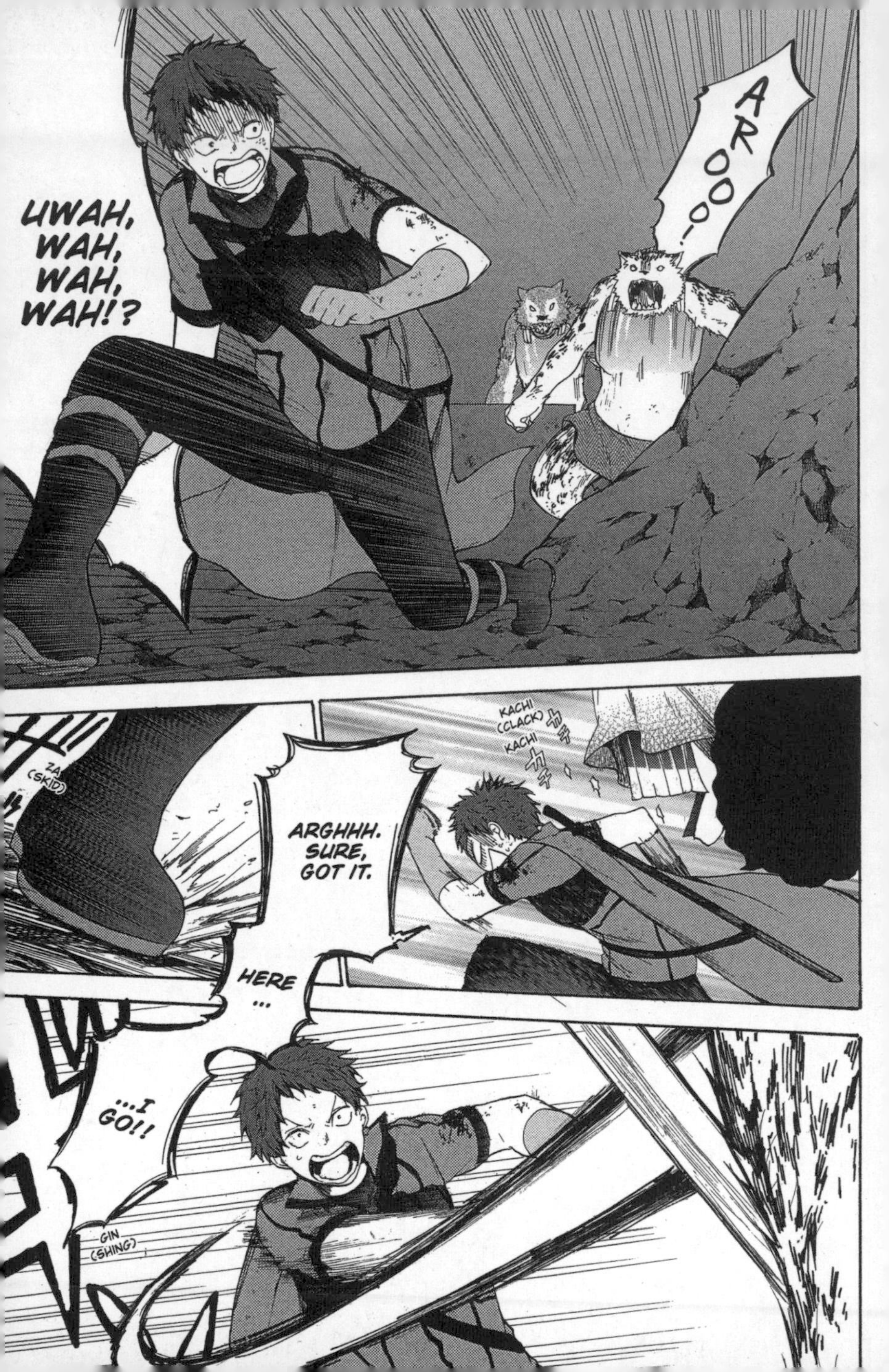
AROOOO-!
UWAH, WAH, WAH, WAH!?
KACHI (CLACK) KACHI
ZA (SKID)
ARGHHH. SURE, GOT IT.
HERE...
...I GO!!
GIN (SHING)

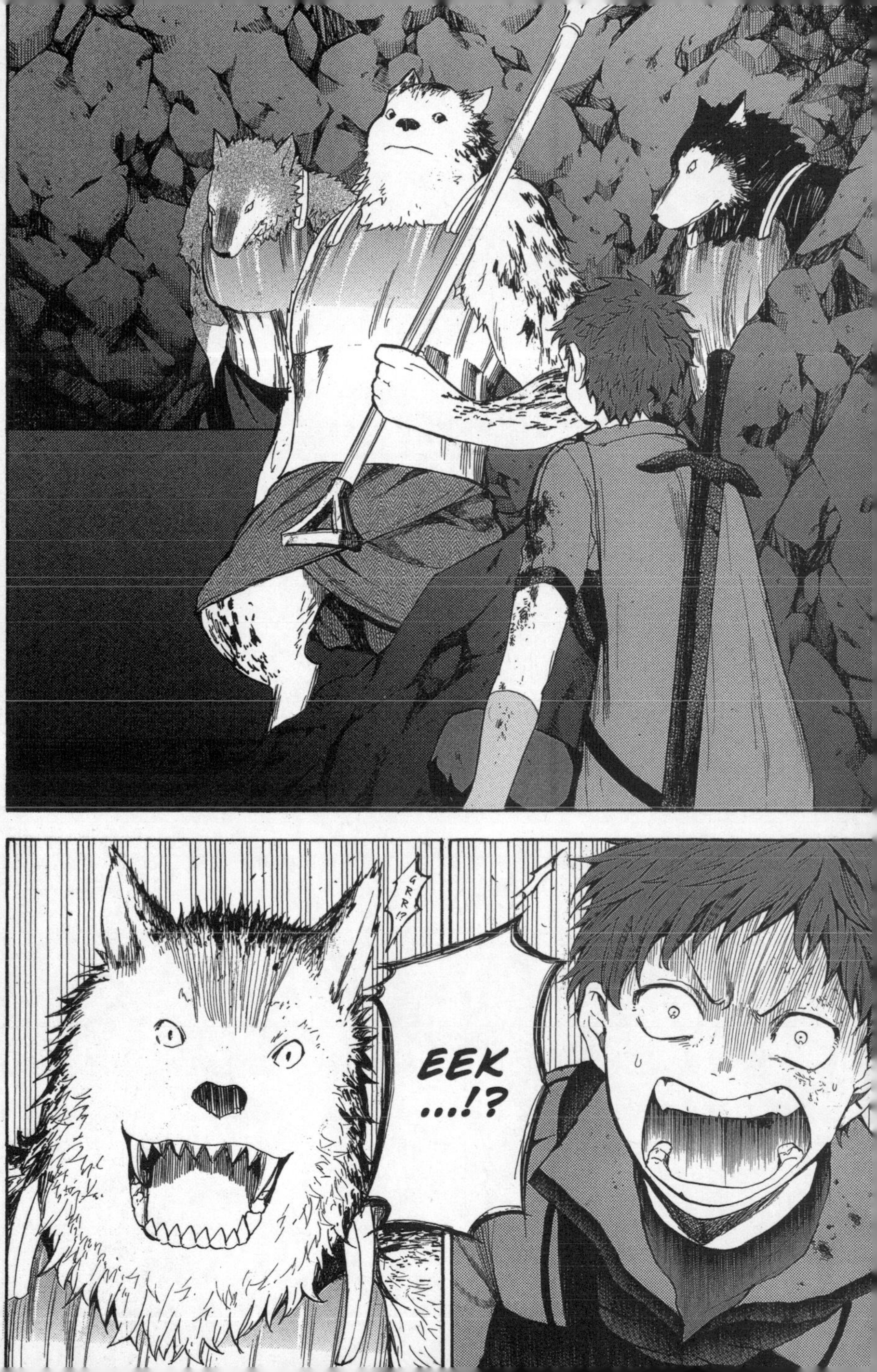
EEK ...!?
GRR!?

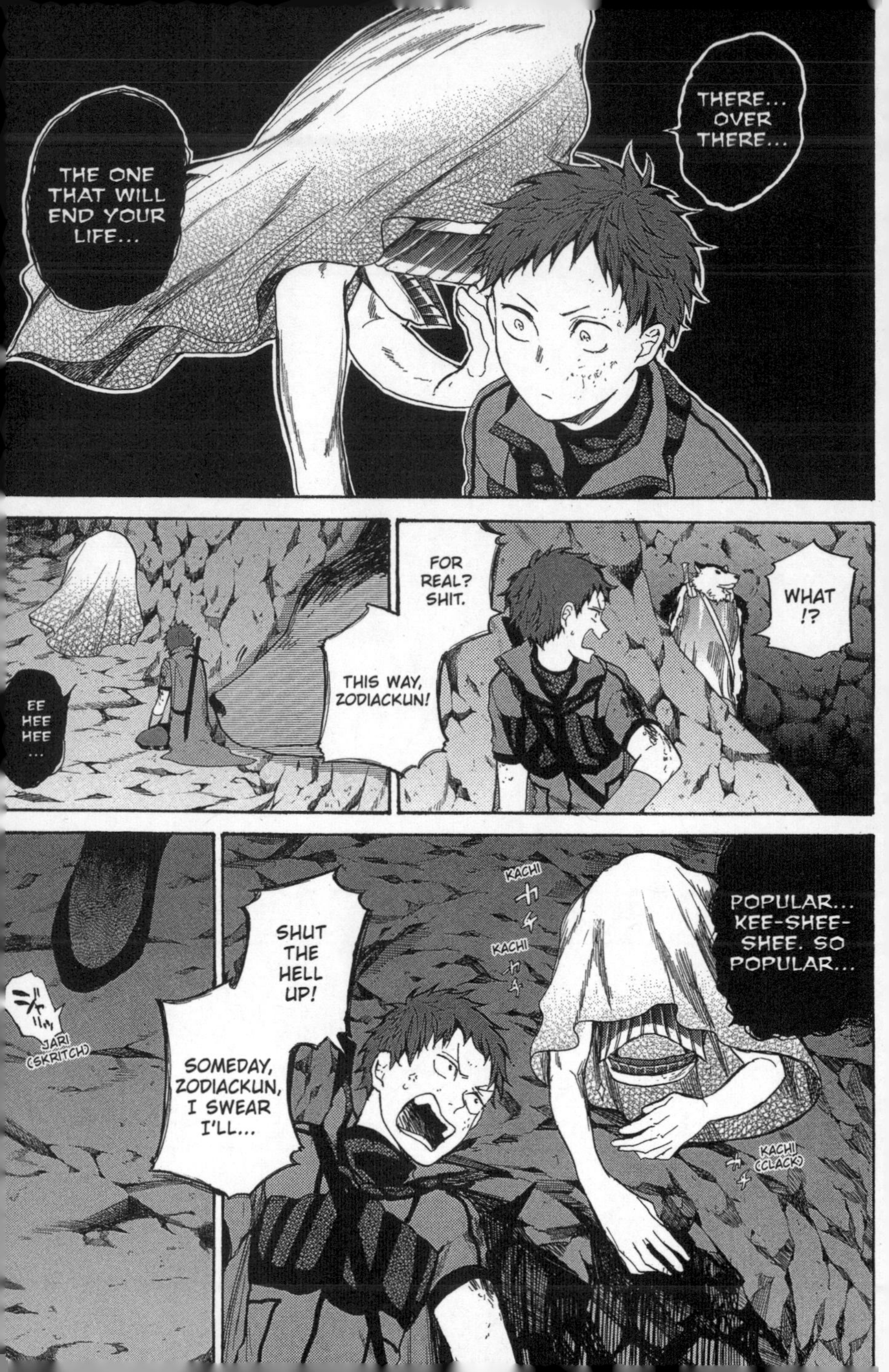
THERE... OVER THERE...
THE ONE THAT WILL END YOUR LIFE...
WHAT!?
FOR REAL? SHIT.
THIS WAY, ZODIACKUN!
EE HEE HEE ...
POPULAR... KEE-SHEE-SHEE. SO POPULAR...
KACHI
KACHI
KACHI (CLACK)
SHUT THE HELL UP!
SOMEDAY, ZODIACKUN, I SWEAR I'LL...
JARI (SKRITCH)

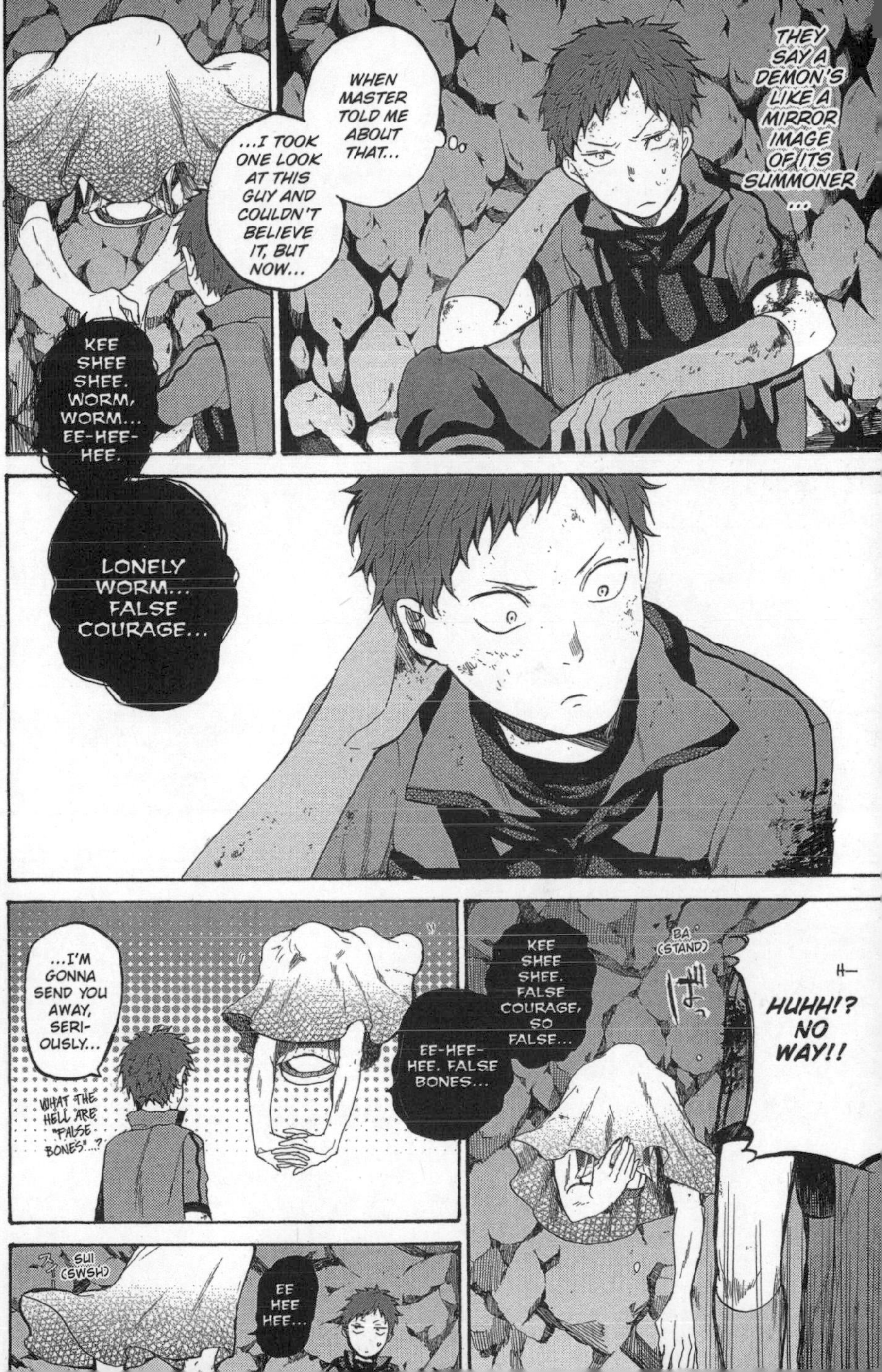
THEY SAY A DEMON'S LIKE A MIRROR IMAGE OF ITS SUMMONER...
WHEN MASTER TOLD ME ABOUT THAT...
...I TOOK ONE LOOK AT THIS GUY AND COULDN'T BELIEVE IT, BUT NOW...
KEE SHEE SHEE. WORM, WORM... EE-HEE-HEE.
LONELY WORM... FALSE COURAGE...
HUHH!? NO WAY!!
BA (STAND)
KEE SHEE SHEE. FALSE COURAGE, SO FALSE...
EE-HEE-HEE. FALSE BONES...
...I'M GONNA SEND YOU AWAY, SERIOUSLY...
WHAT THE HELL ARE "FALSE BONES"...?
EE HEE HEE...
SUI (SWSH)

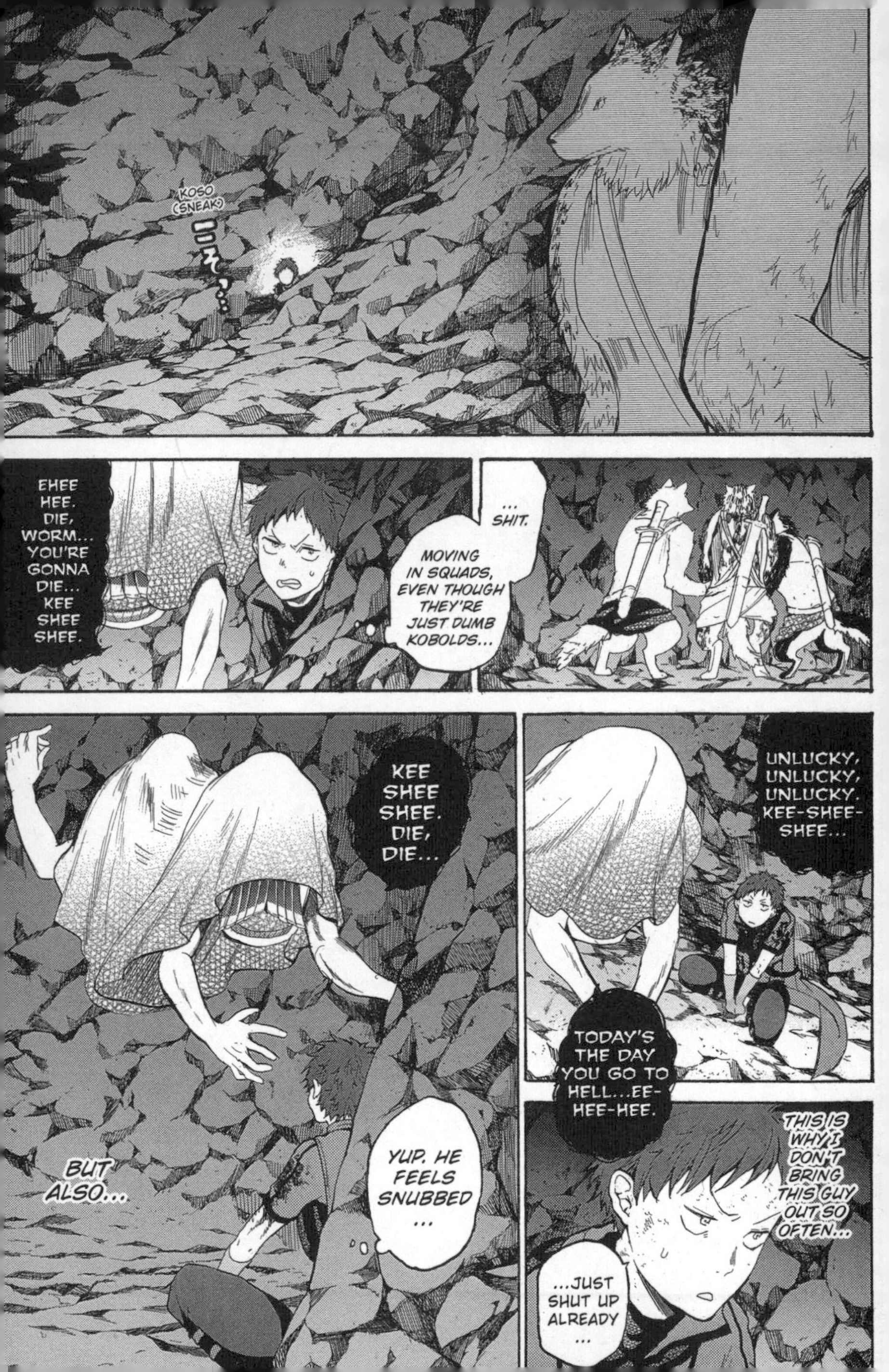
KOSO (SNEAK)
こそっ…
... SHIT.
MOVING IN SQUADS, EVEN THOUGH THEY'RE JUST DUMB KOBOLDS...
EHEE HEE. DIE, WORM... YOU'RE GONNA DIE... KEE SHEE SHEE.
UNLUCKY, UNLUCKY, UNLUCKY. KEE-SHEE-SHEE...
TODAY'S THE DAY YOU GO TO HELL...EE-HEE-HEE.
KEE SHEE SHEE. DIE, DIE...
THIS IS WHY I DON'T BRING THIS GUY OUT SO OFTEN...
...JUST SHUT UP ALREADY ...
YUP. HE FEELS SNUBBED ...
BUT ALSO...

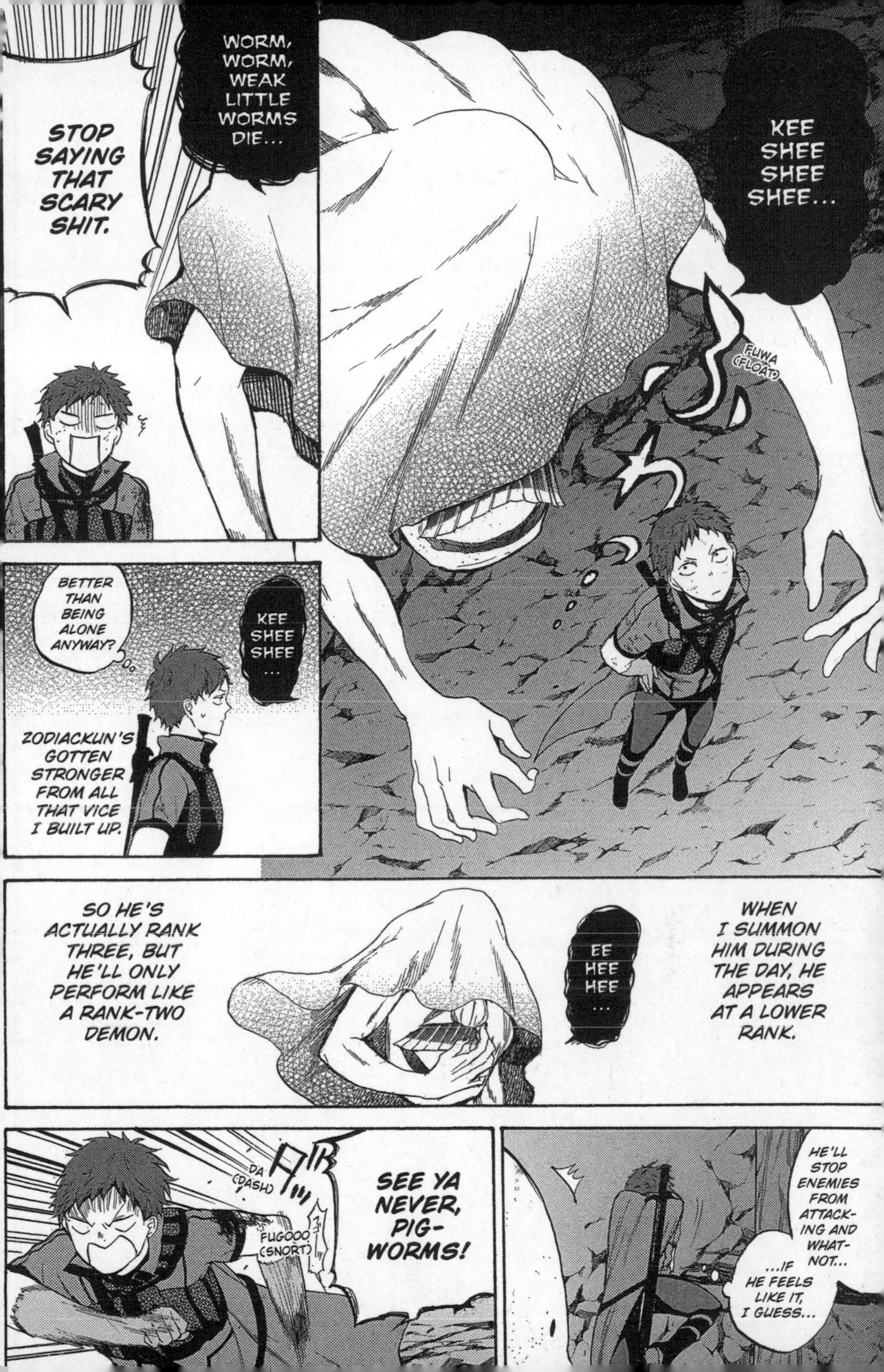
WORM, WORM, WEAK LITTLE WORMS DIE...
KEE SHEE SHEE SHEE...
FUWA (FLOAT)
STOP SAYING THAT SCARY SHIT.
KEE SHEE SHEE...
BETTER THAN BEING ALONE ANYWAY?
ZODIACKUN'S GOTTEN STRONGER FROM ALL THAT VICE I BUILT UP.
WHEN I SUMMON HIM DURING THE DAY, HE APPEARS AT A LOWER RANK.
EE HEE HEE...
SO HE'S ACTUALLY RANK THREE, BUT HE'LL ONLY PERFORM LIKE A RANK-TWO DEMON.
HE'LL STOP ENEMIES FROM ATTACKING AND WHAT-NOT...
...IF HE FEELS LIKE IT, I GUESS...
SEE YA NEVER, PIG-WORMS!
DA (DASH)
FUGOOO (SNORT)

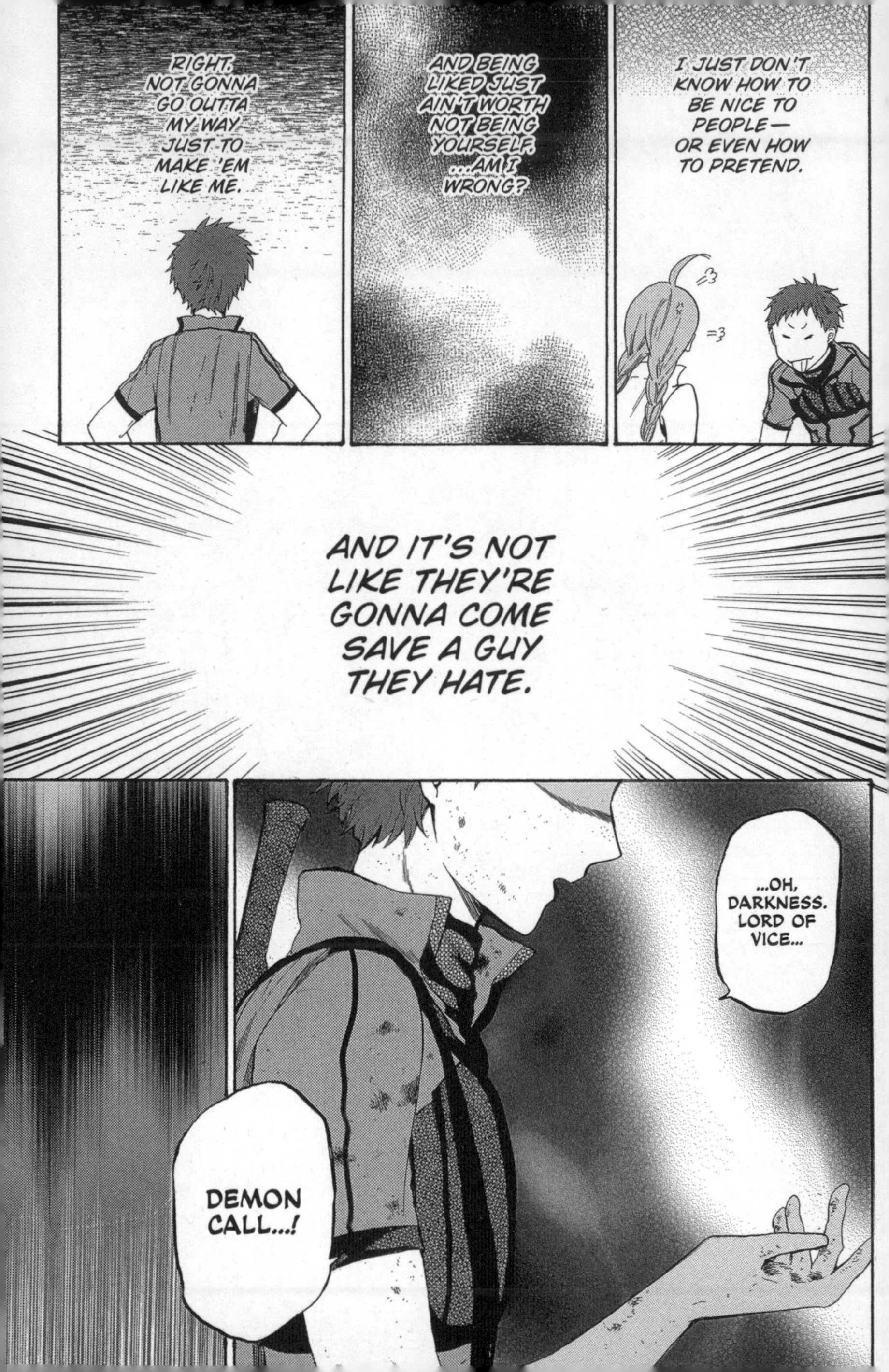
RIGHT. NOT GONNA GO OUTTA MY WAY JUST TO MAKE 'EM LIKE ME.
AND BEING LIKED JUST AIN'T WORTH NOT BEING YOURSELF. ...AM I WRONG?
I JUST DON'T KNOW HOW TO BE NICE TO PEOPLE— OR EVEN HOW TO PRETEND.
AND IT'S NOT LIKE THEY'RE GONNA COME SAVE A GUY THEY HATE.
...OH, DARKNESS. LORD OF VICE...
DEMON CALL...!

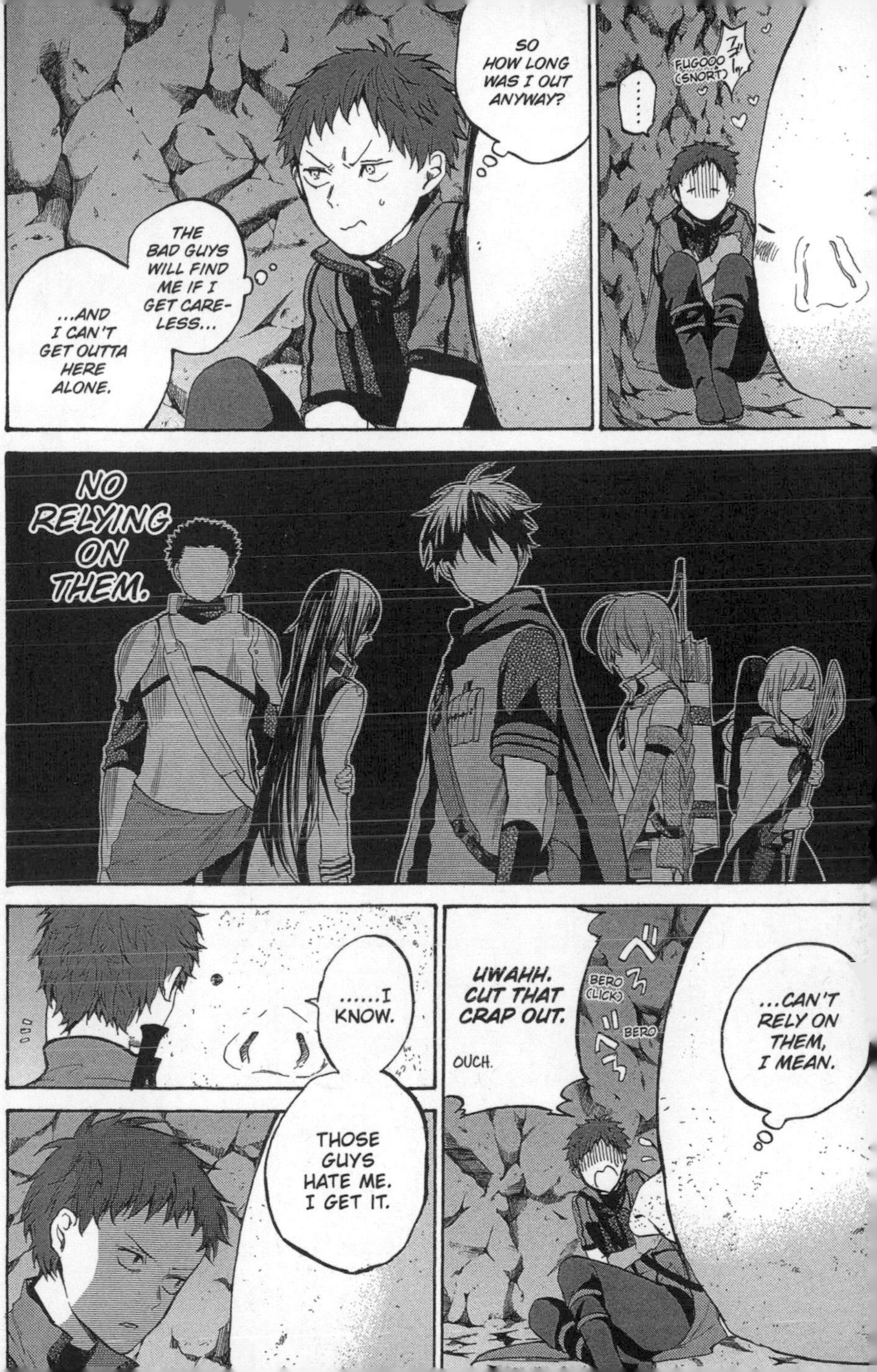
FUGOOO (SNORT)
.....
SO HOW LONG WAS I OUT ANYWAY?
THE BAD GUYS WILL FIND ME IF I GET CARE-LESS...
...AND I CAN'T GET OUTTA HERE ALONE.
NO RELYING ON THEM.
...CAN'T RELY ON THEM, I MEAN.
BERO (LICK)
BERO
UWAHH. CUT THAT CRAP OUT.
OUCH.
......I KNOW.
THOSE GUYS HATE ME. I GET IT.

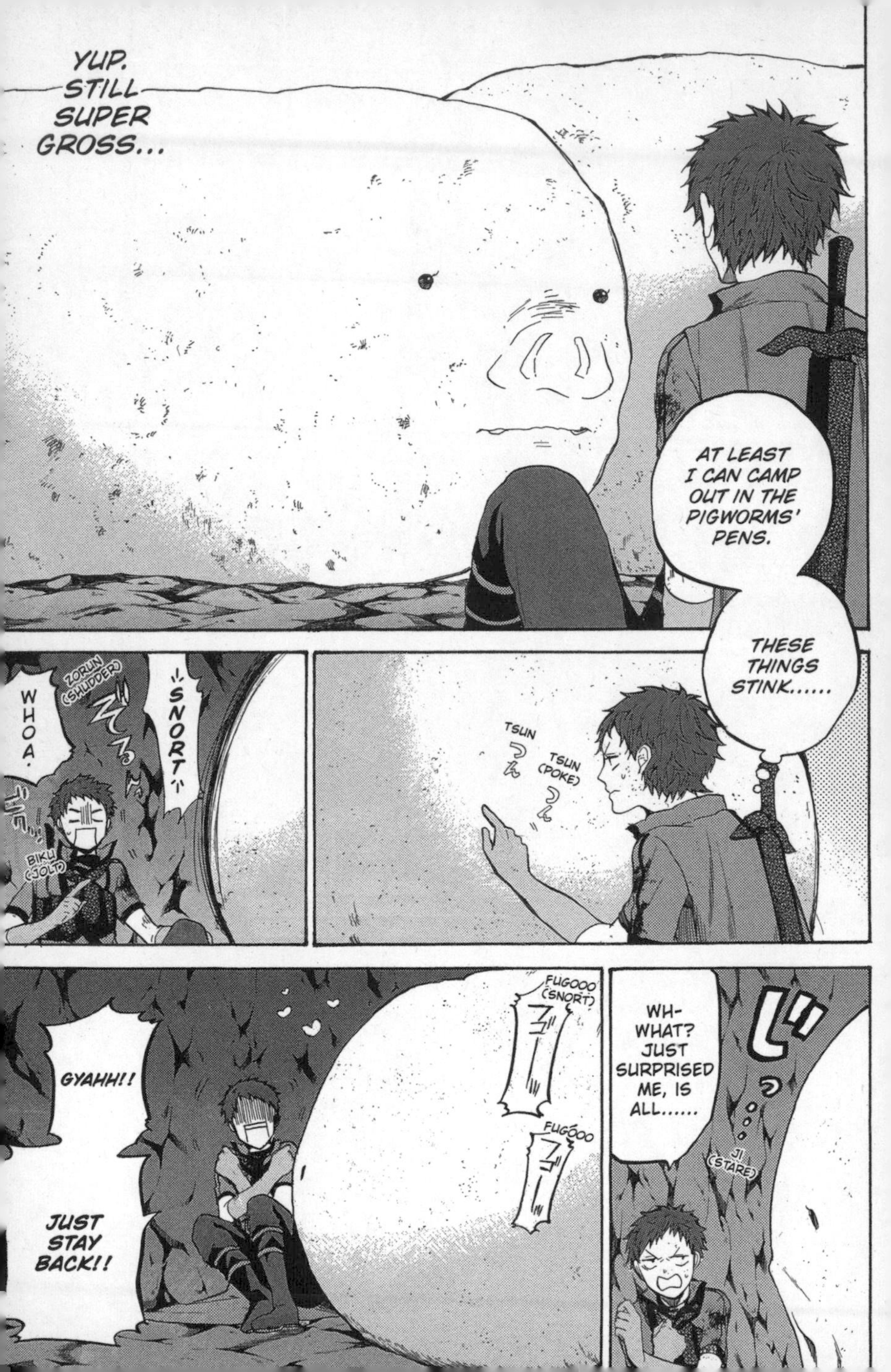
YUP. STILL SUPER GROSS...
AT LEAST I CAN CAMP OUT IN THE PIGWORMS' PENS.
THESE THINGS STINK......
TSUN TSUN (POKE)
SNORT
ZORUN (SHUDDER)
WHOA.
BIKU (JOLT)
WH-WHAT? JUST SURPRISED ME, IS ALL......
JI (STARE)
FUGOOO (SNORT)
FUGOOO
GYAHH!!
JUST STAY BACK!!

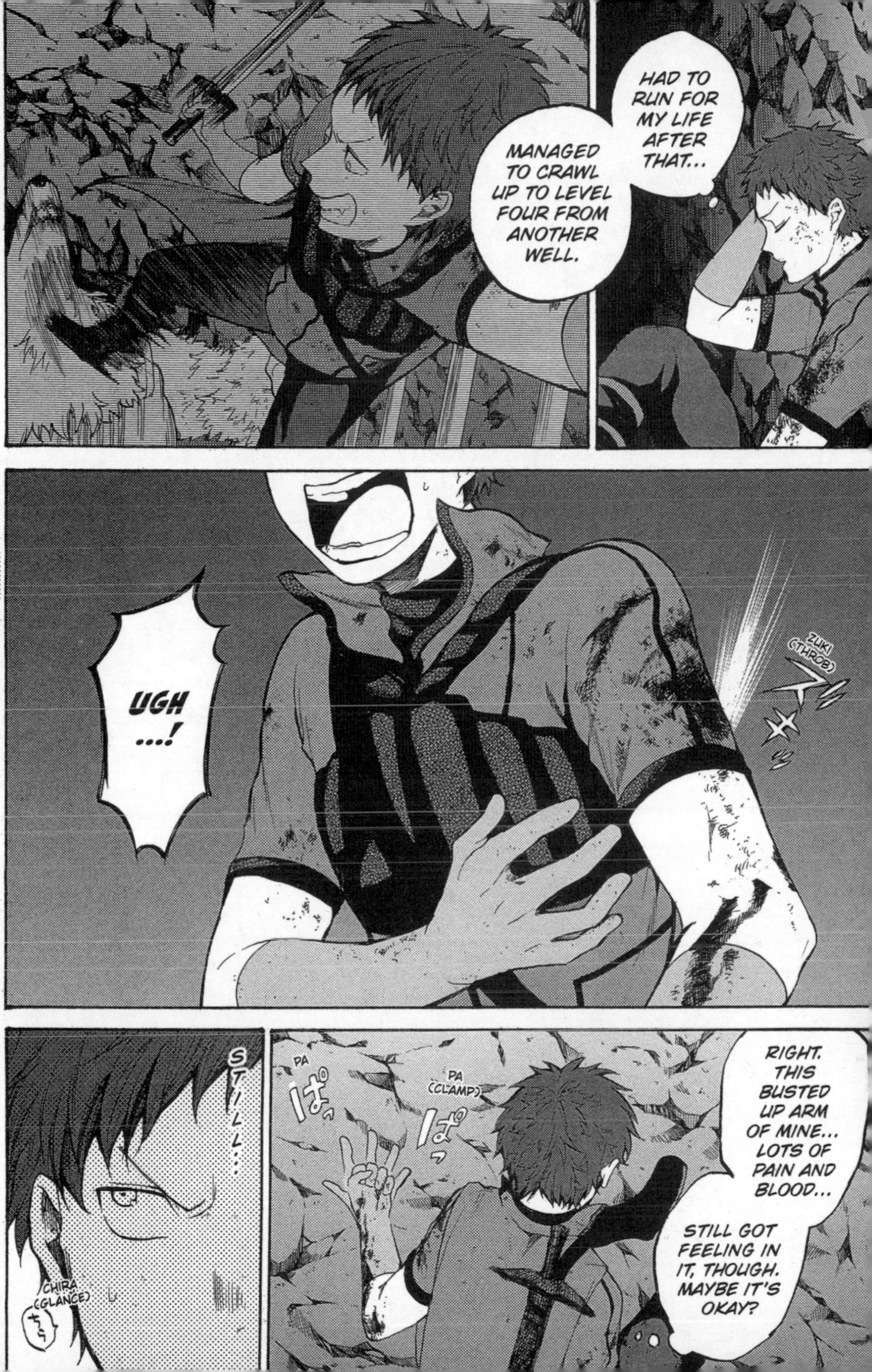
HAD TO RUN FOR MY LIFE AFTER THAT...
MANAGED TO CRAWL UP TO LEVEL FOUR FROM ANOTHER WELL.
ZUKI (THROB)
UGH ...!
RIGHT. THIS BUSTED UP ARM OF MINE... LOTS OF PAIN AND BLOOD...
STILL GOT FEELING IN IT, THOUGH. MAYBE IT'S OKAY?
PA (CLAMP)
ぱっ
PA
ぱっ
STILL...
CHIRA (GLANCE)
ちら

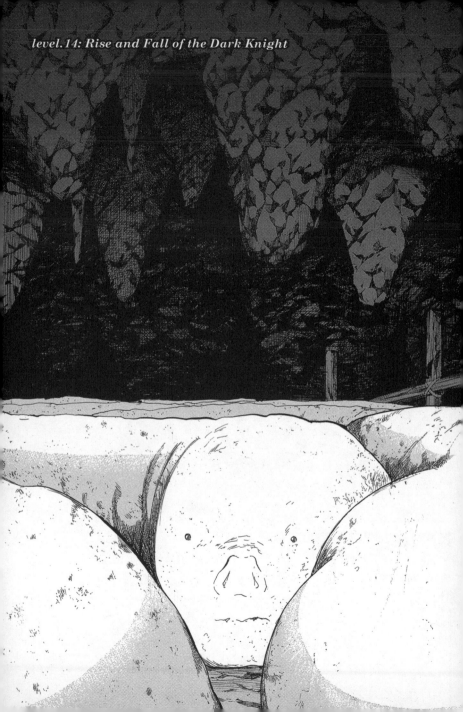

level.14: Rise and Fall of the Dark Knight

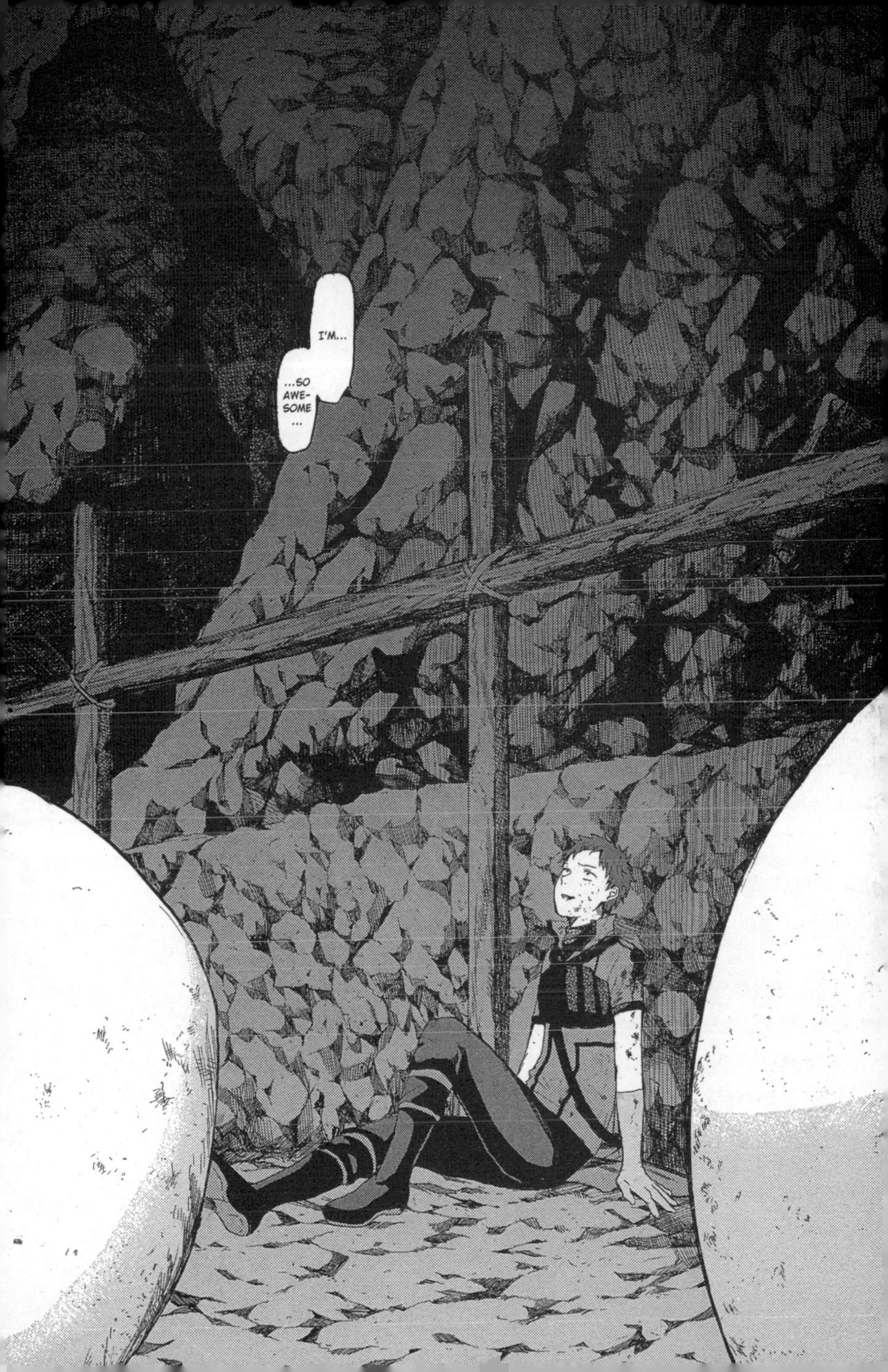
I'M...
...SO AWESOME...

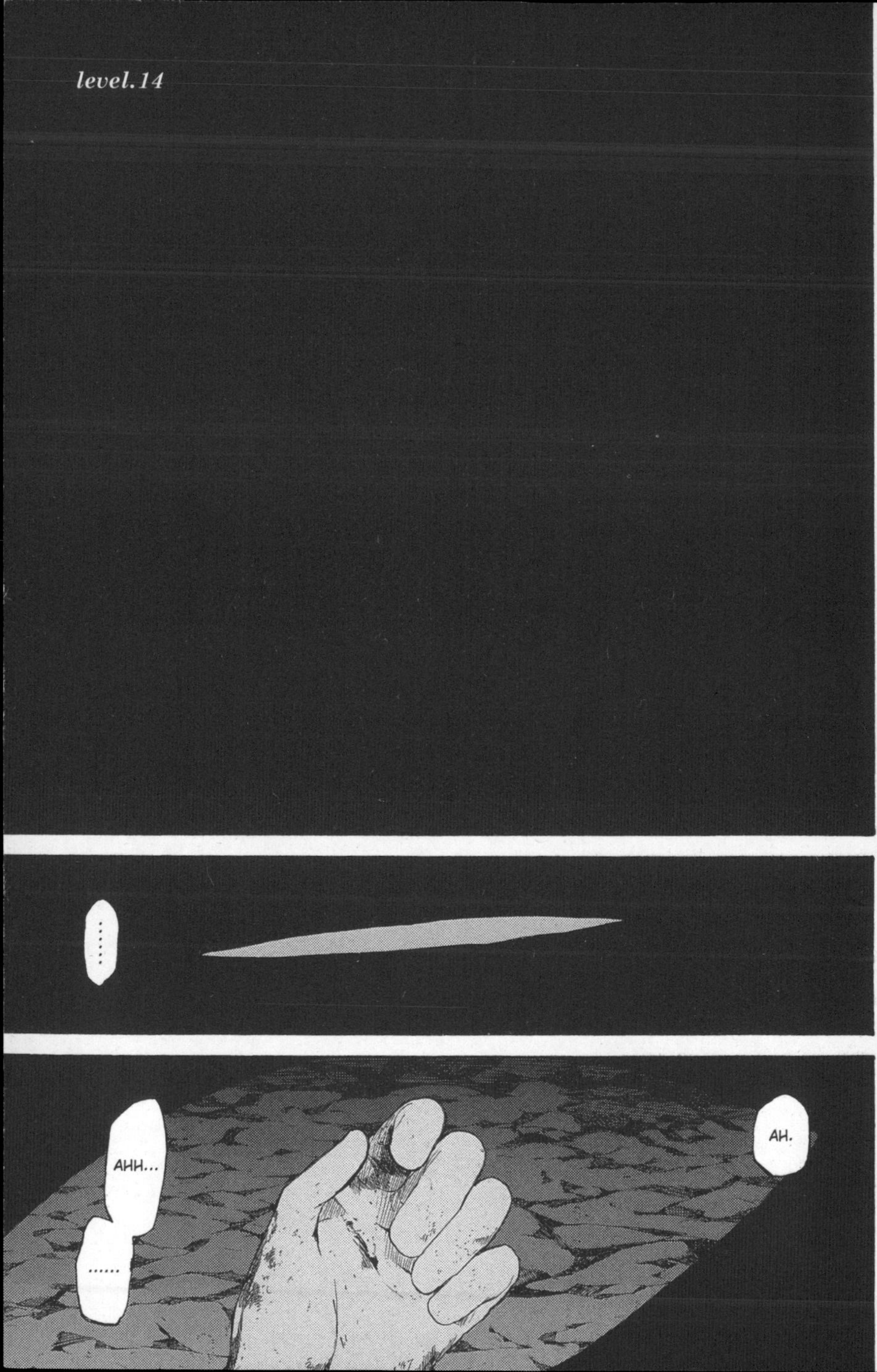
level.14
……
AH.
AHH…
……

Grimgar
of Fantasy and Ash

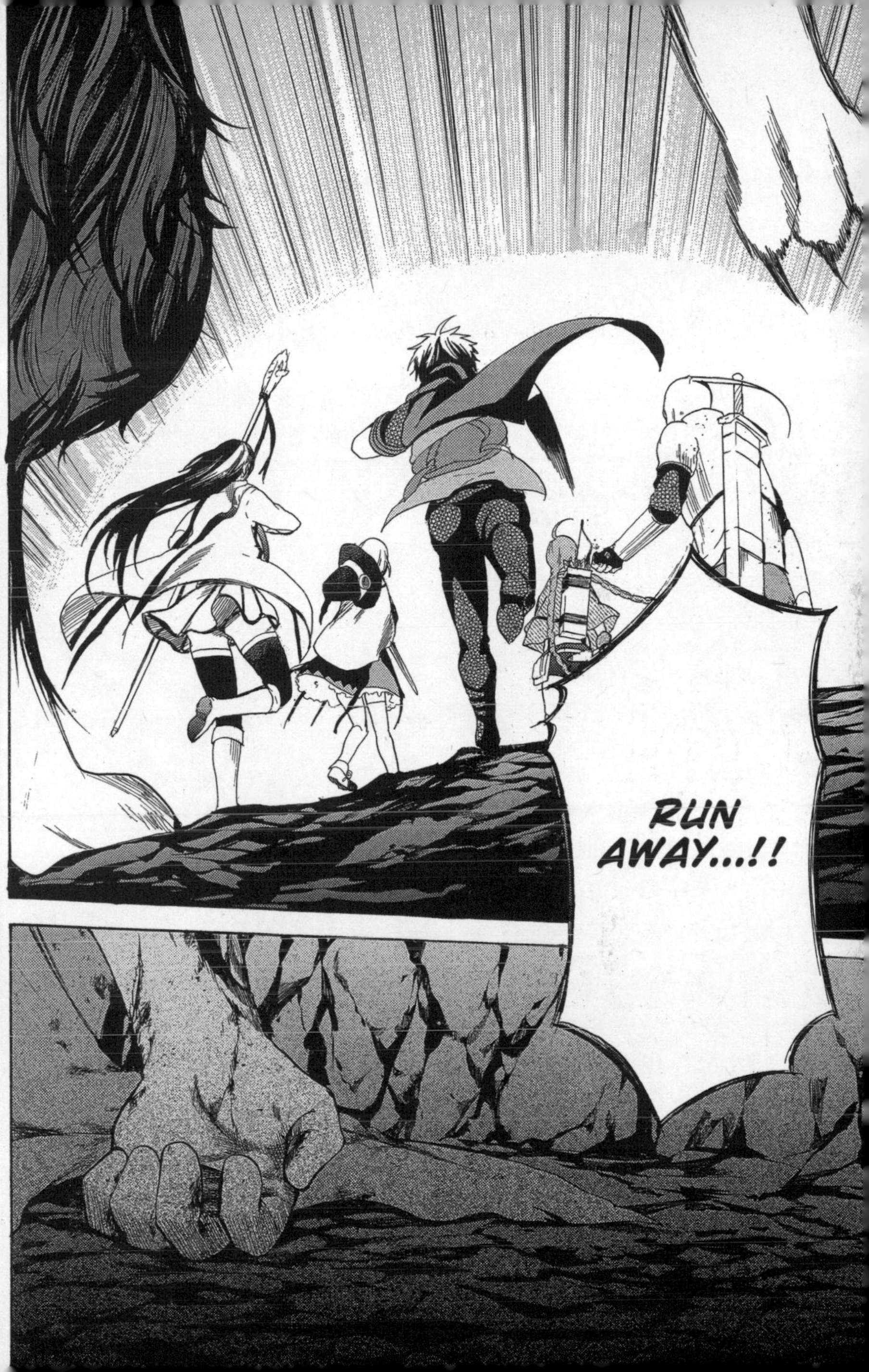
RUN AWAY...!!

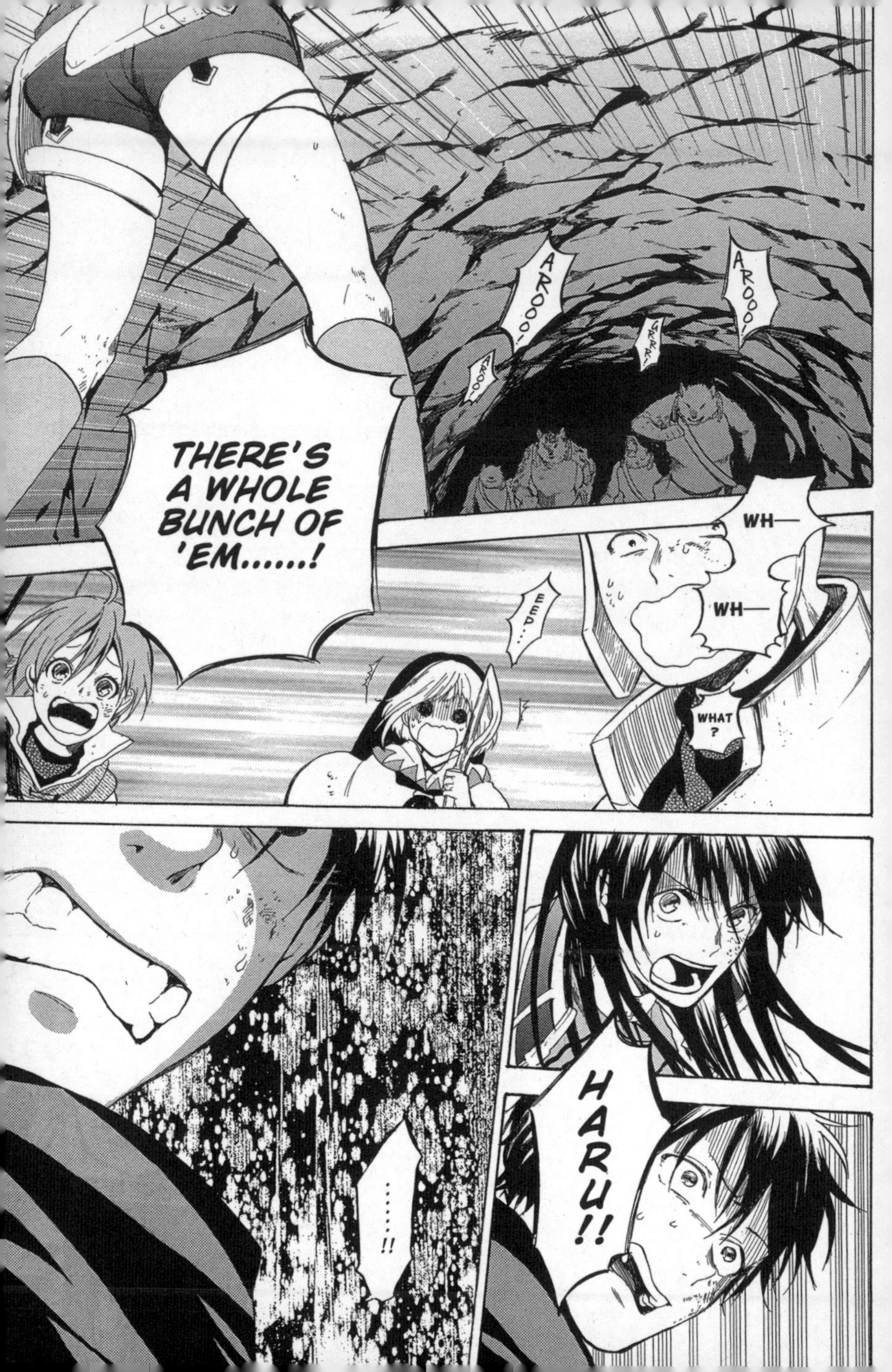
AROOO!
GRRR!
AROOO!
AROO!
THERE'S A WHOLE BUNCH OF 'EM......!
WH—
WH—
WHAT?
EEP...
HARU!!
......!!

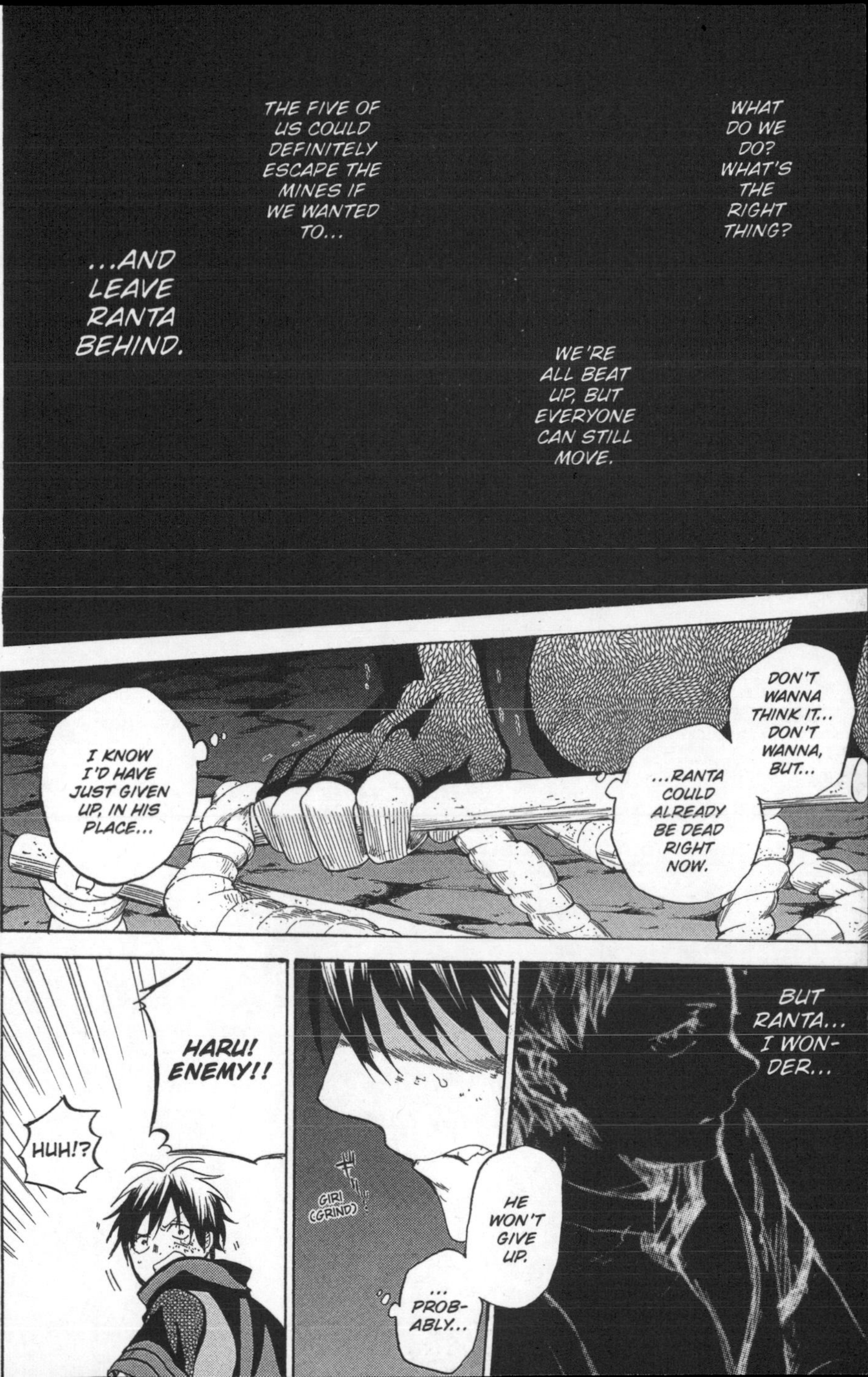
WHAT DO WE DO? WHAT'S THE RIGHT THING?
WE'RE ALL BEAT UP, BUT EVERYONE CAN STILL MOVE.
THE FIVE OF US COULD DEFINITELY ESCAPE THE MINES IF WE WANTED TO...
...AND LEAVE RANTA BEHIND.
DON'T WANNA THINK IT... DON'T WANNA, BUT...
...RANTA COULD ALREADY BE DEAD RIGHT NOW.
I KNOW I'D HAVE JUST GIVEN UP, IN HIS PLACE...
BUT RANTA... I WONDER...
HE WON'T GIVE UP.
...PROBABLY...
GIRI (GRIND)
HARU! ENEMY!!
HUH!?

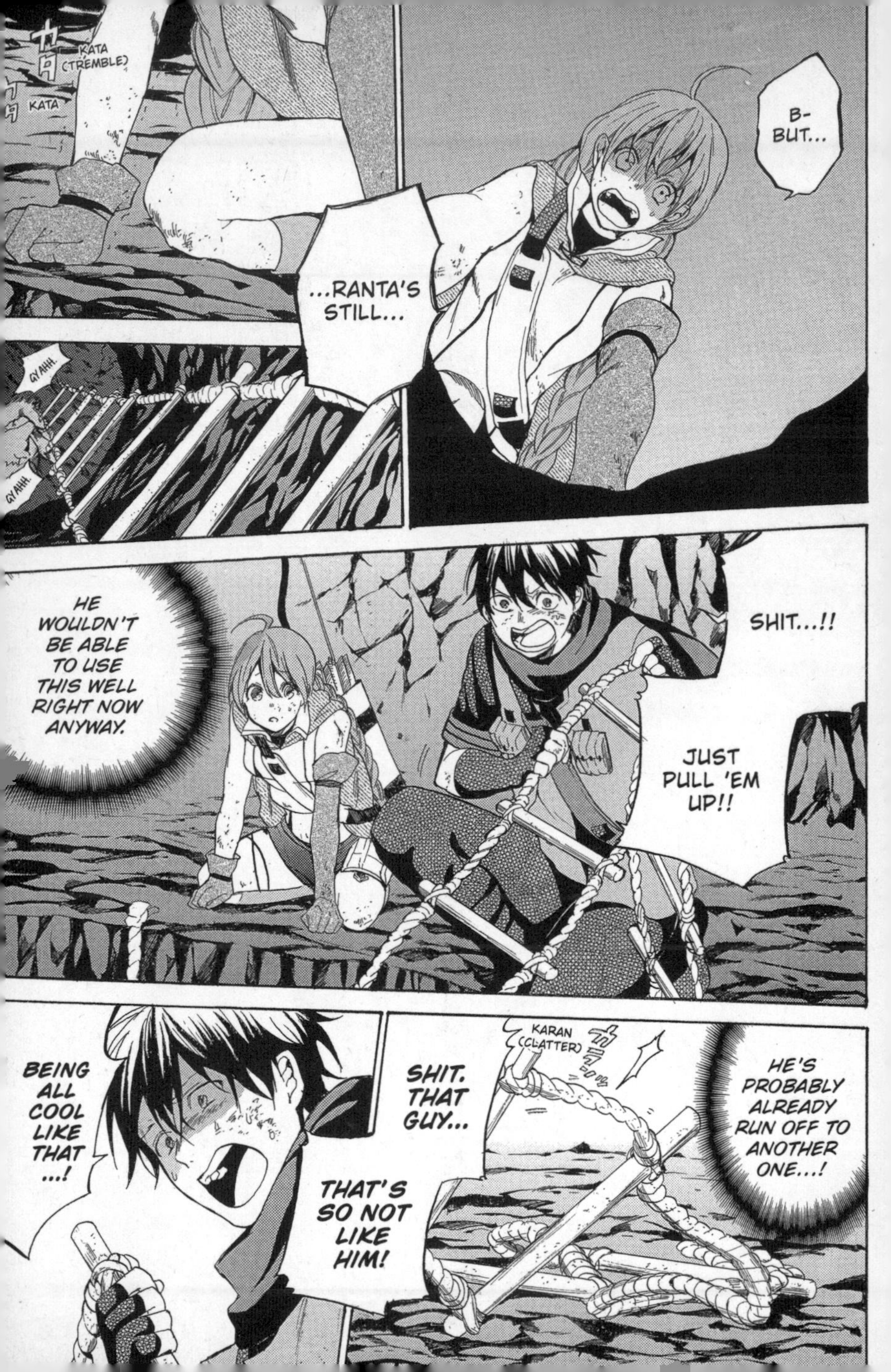
KATA (TREMBLE)
KATA
B-BUT...
...RANTA'S STILL...
GYAHH.
GYAHH.
SHIT...!!
JUST PULL 'EM UP!!
HE WOULDN'T BE ABLE TO USE THIS WELL RIGHT NOW ANYWAY.
HE'S PROBABLY ALREADY RUN OFF TO ANOTHER ONE...!
KARAN (CLATTER)
SHIT. THAT GUY...
THAT'S SO NOT LIKE HIM!
BEING ALL COOL LIKE THAT...!

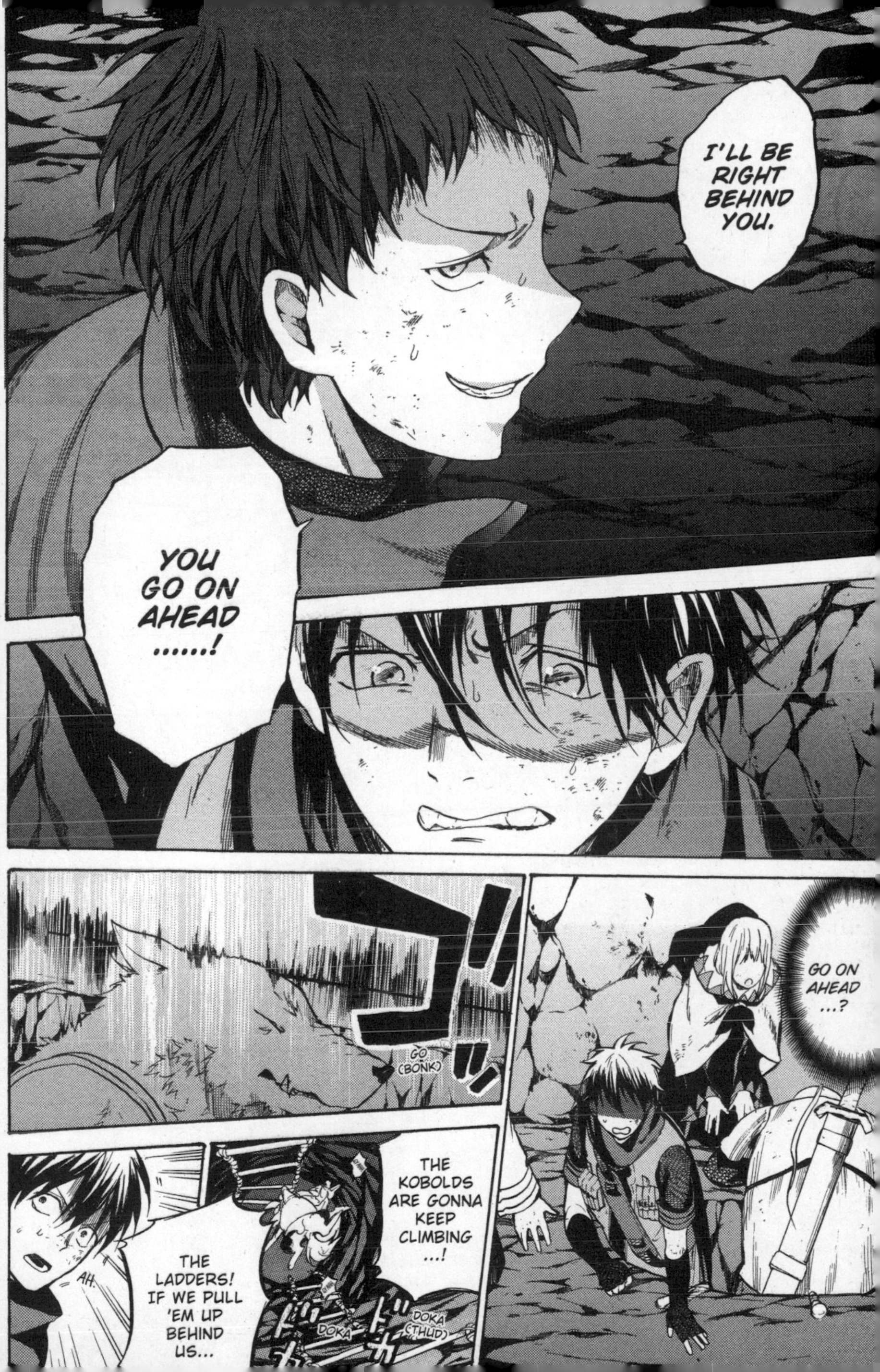
I'LL BE RIGHT BEHIND YOU.
YOU GO ON AHEAD ......!
GO (BONK)
GO ON AHEAD ...?
THE KOBOLDS ARE GONNA KEEP CLIMBING ...!
DOKA (THUD)
DOKA
AH.
THE LADDERS! IF WE PULL 'EM UP BEHIND US...

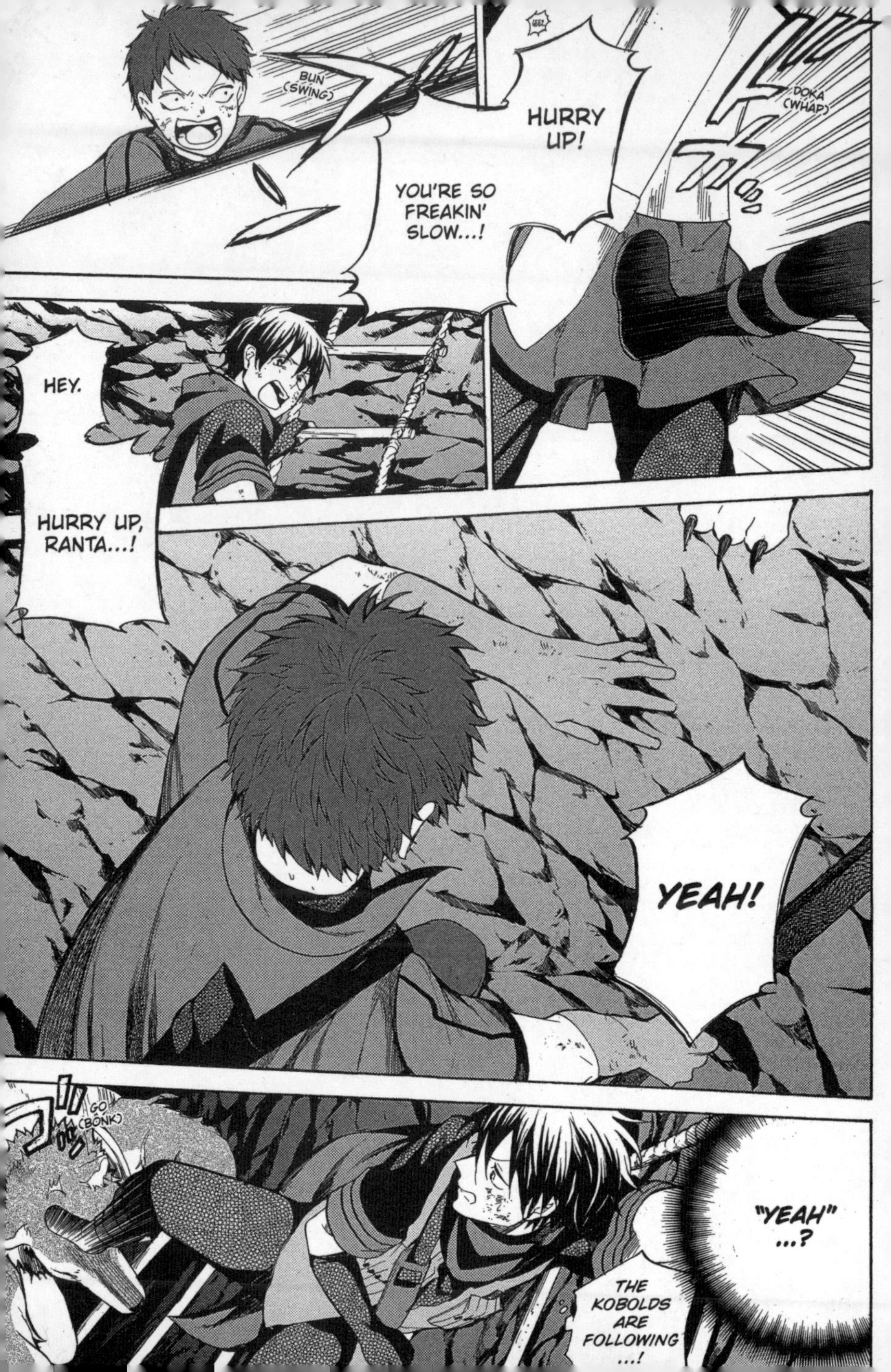
DOKA (WHAP)
GEEZ
HURRY UP!
YOU'RE SO FREAKIN' SLOW...!
BUN (SWING)
HEY.
HURRY UP, RANTA...!
YEAH!
"YEAH" ...?
THE KOBOLDS ARE FOLLOWING ...!
GO (BONK)

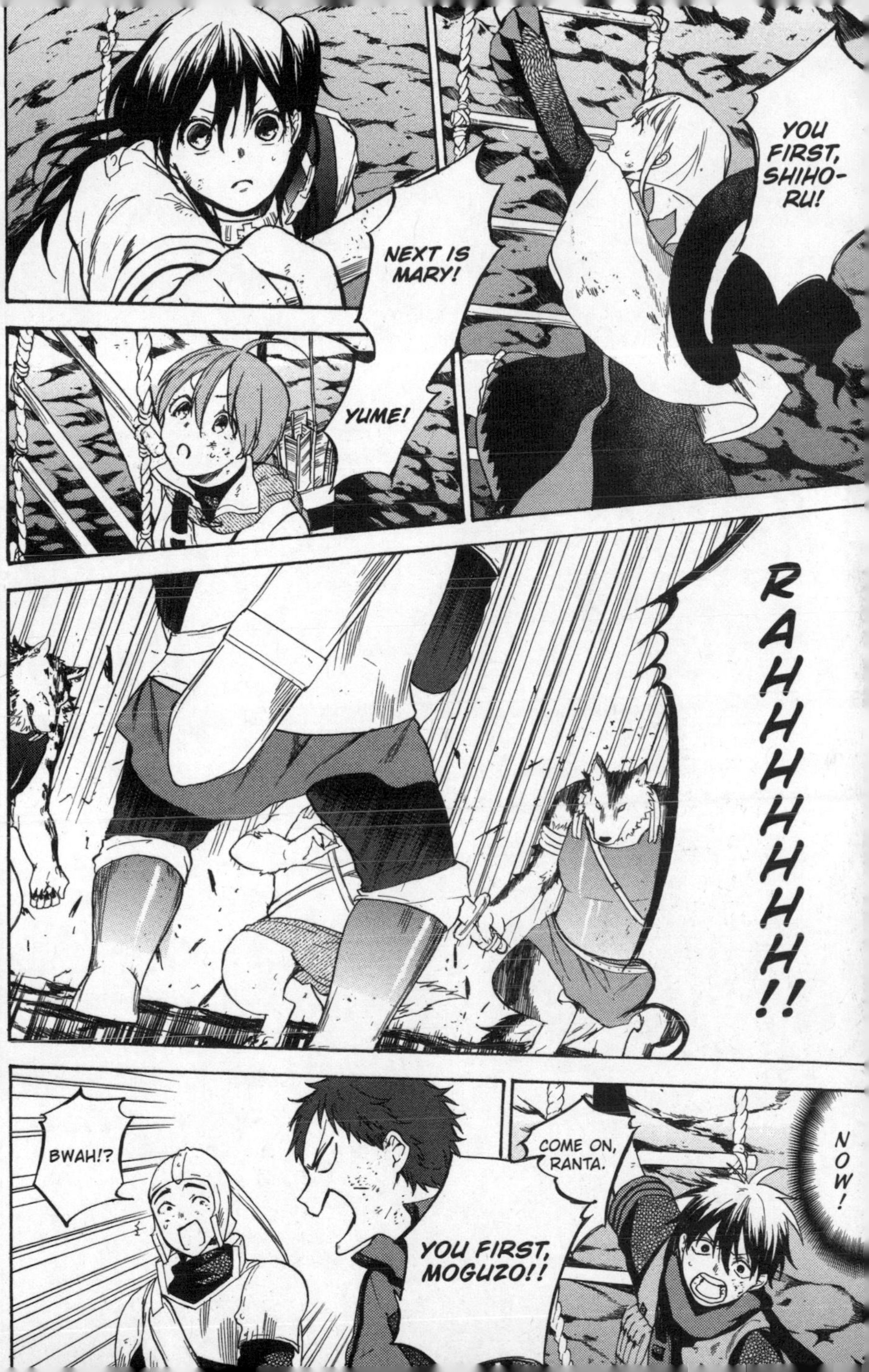
YOU FIRST, SHIHO-RU!
NEXT IS MARY!
YUME!
RAHHHHHHH!!
NOW!
COME ON, RANTA.
YOU FIRST, MOGUZO!!
BWAH!?

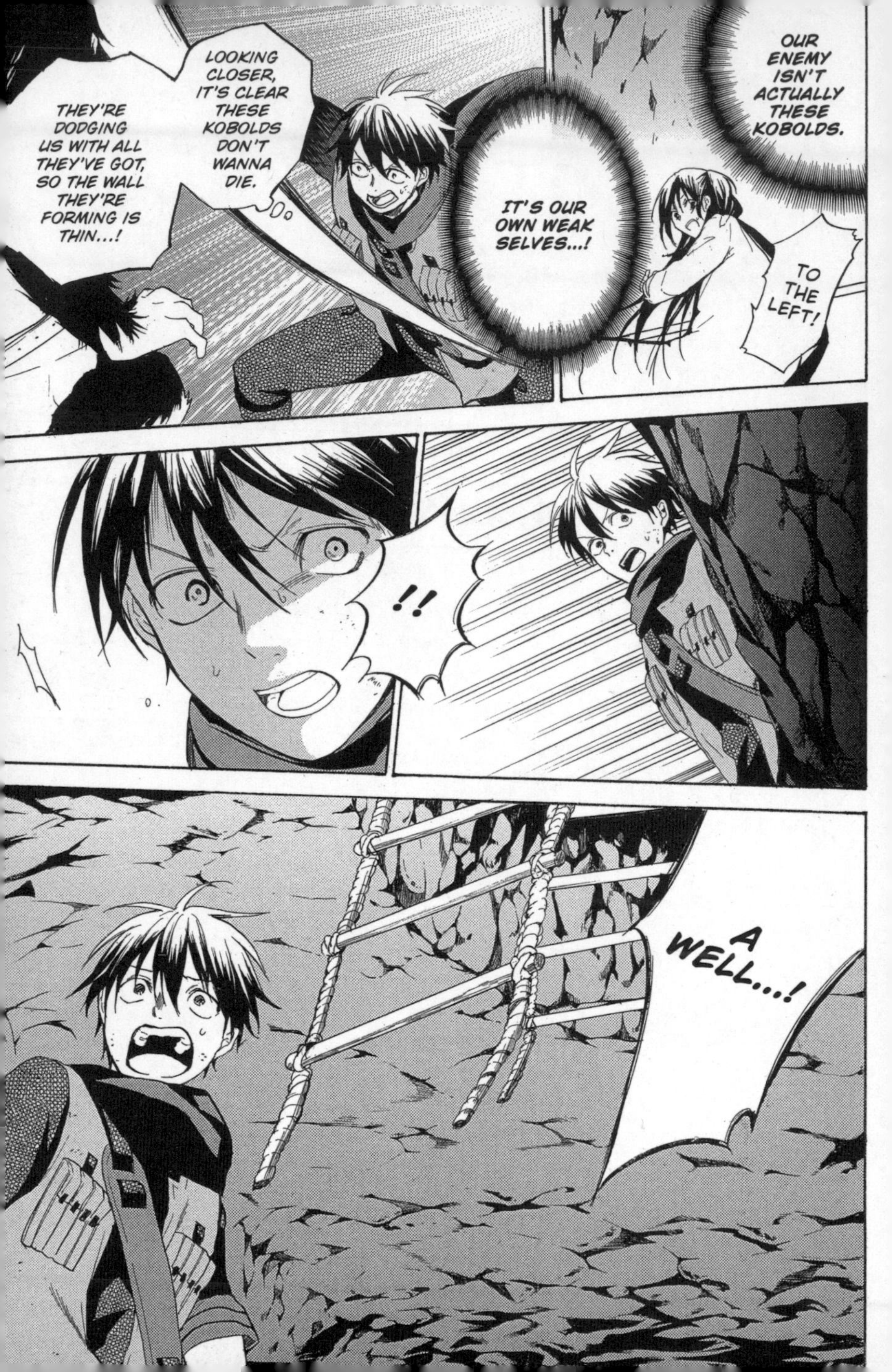
OUR ENEMY ISN'T ACTUALLY THESE KOBOLDS.
IT'S OUR OWN WEAK SELVES...!
TO THE LEFT!
LOOKING CLOSER, IT'S CLEAR THESE KOBOLDS DON'T WANNA DIE.
THEY'RE DODGING US WITH ALL THEY'VE GOT, SO THE WALL THEY'RE FORMING IS THIN...!
!!
A WELL...!

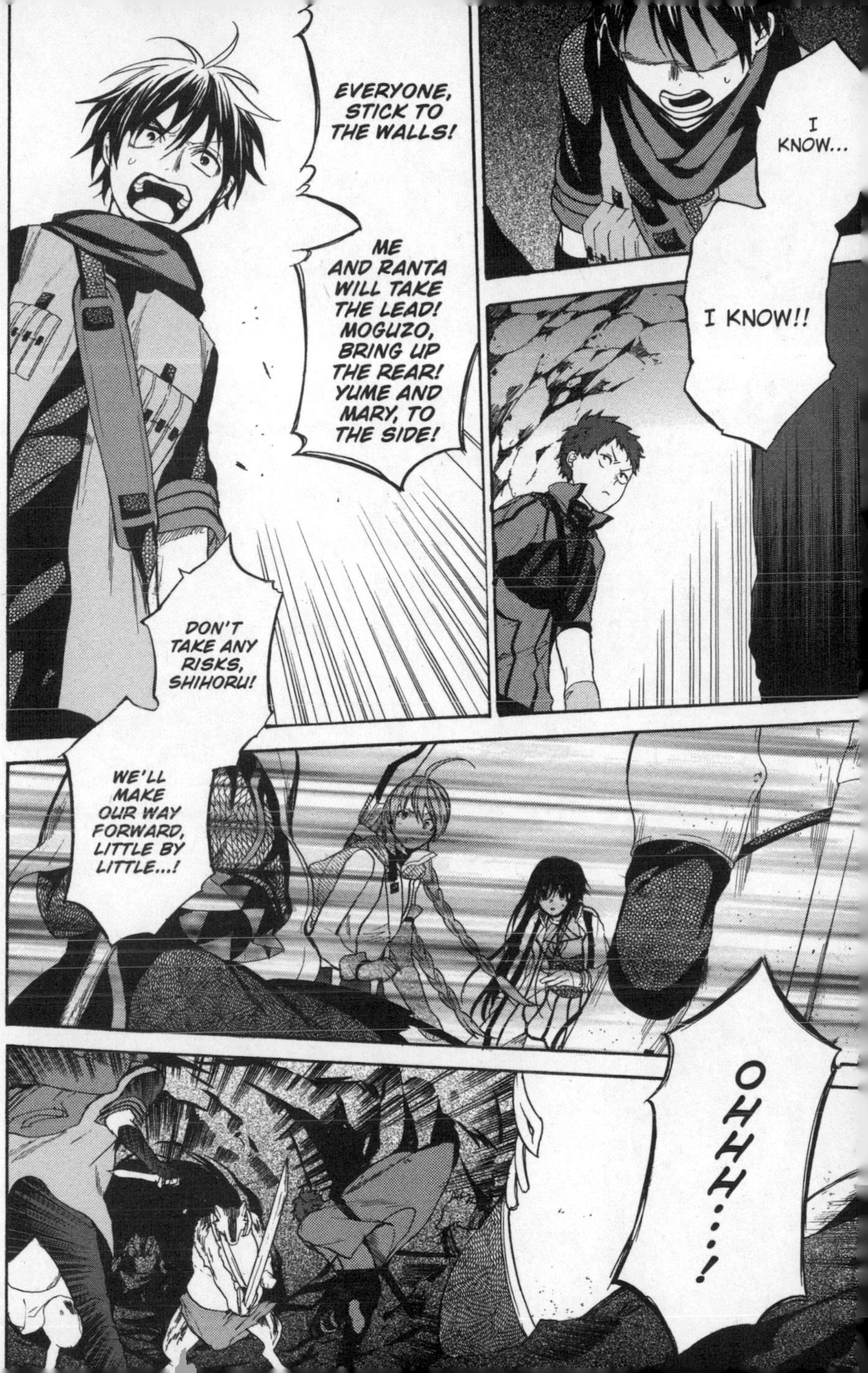
I KNOW...
I KNOW!!
EVERYONE, STICK TO THE WALLS!
ME AND RANTA WILL TAKE THE LEAD! MOGUZO, BRING UP THE REAR! YUME AND MARY, TO THE SIDE!
DON'T TAKE ANY RISKS, SHIHORU!
WE'LL MAKE OUR WAY FORWARD, LITTLE BY LITTLE...!
OHHH...!

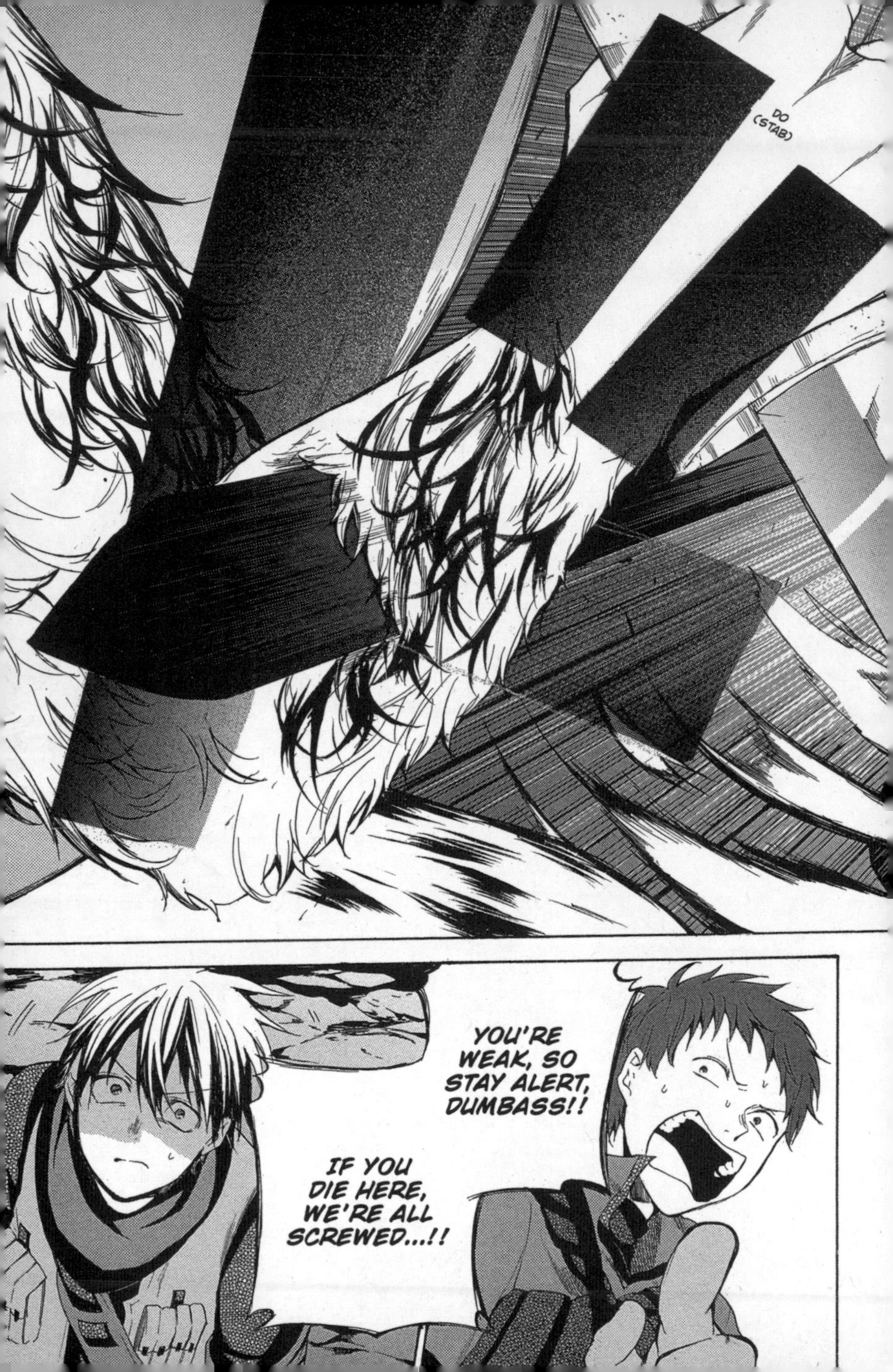
DO (STAB)
YOU'RE WEAK, SO STAY ALERT, DUMBASS!!
IF YOU DIE HERE, WE'RE ALL SCREWED...!!

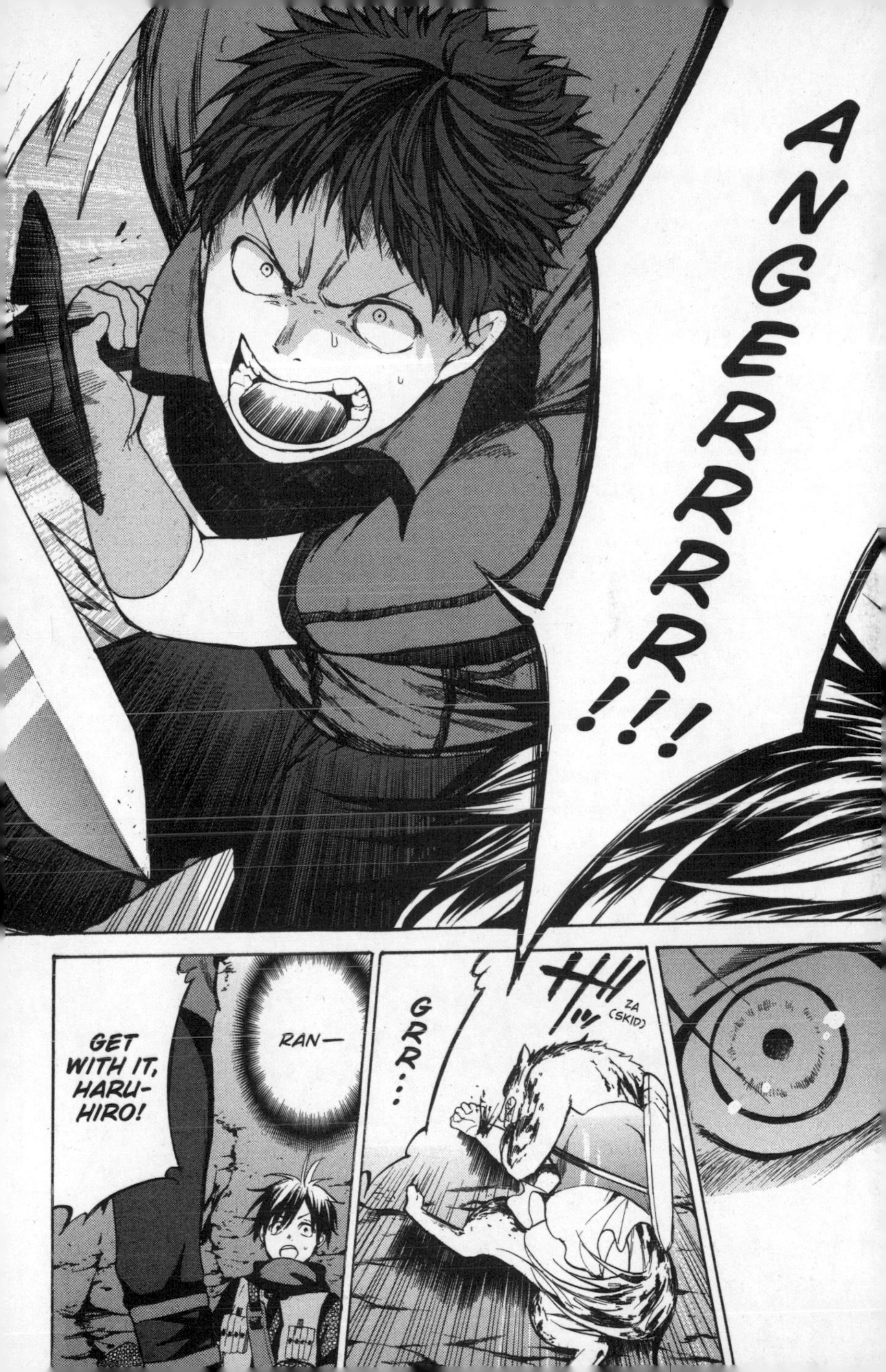
ANGERRRRR!!!
ZA (SKID)
GRR...
RAN—
GET WITH IT, HARU-HIRO!

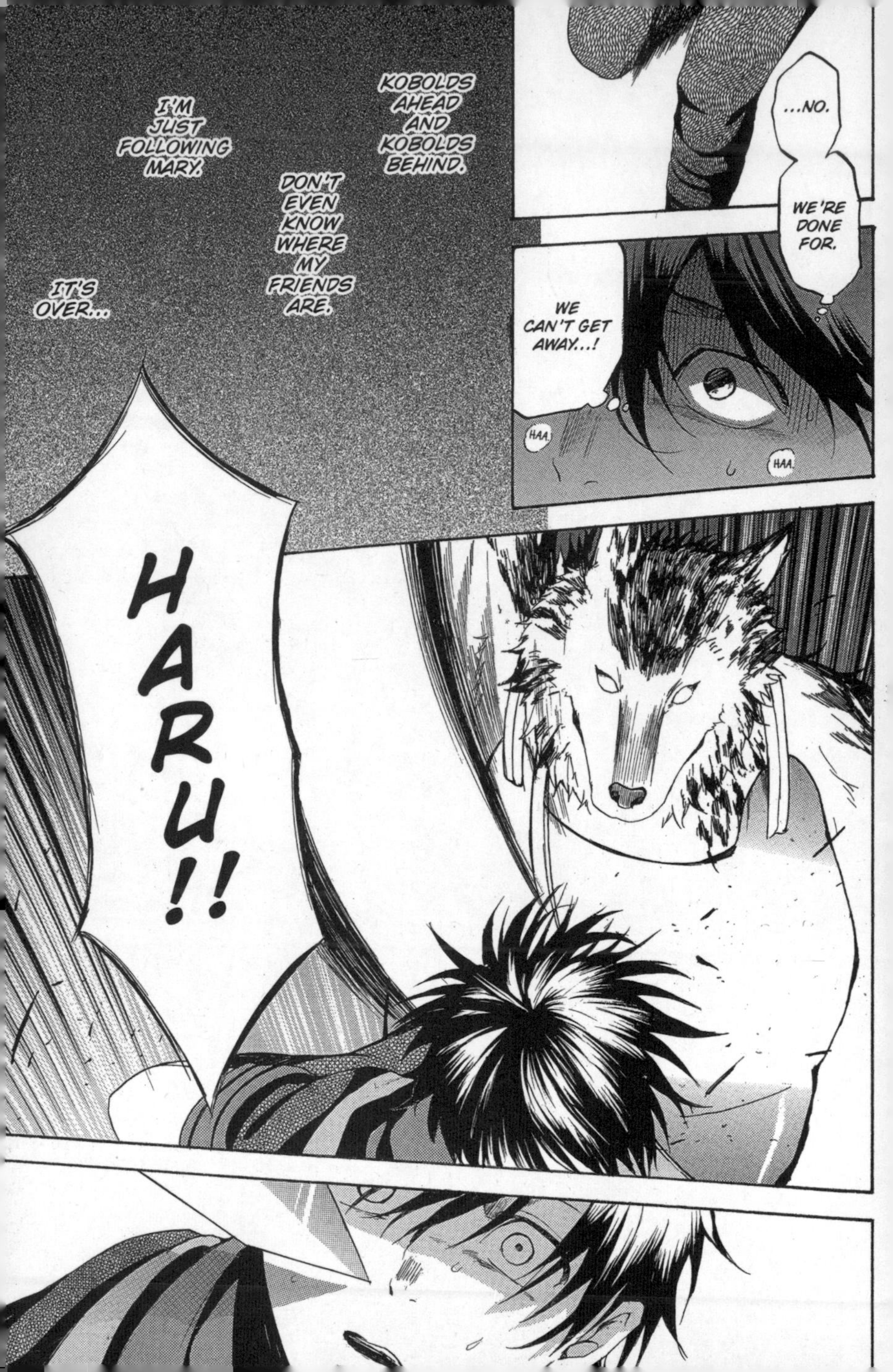
...NO.
WE'RE DONE FOR.
WE CAN'T GET AWAY...!
HAA
HAA
KOBOLDS AHEAD AND KOBOLDS BEHIND.
DON'T EVEN KNOW WHERE MY FRIENDS ARE.
I'M JUST FOLLOWING MARY.
IT'S OVER...
HARU!!

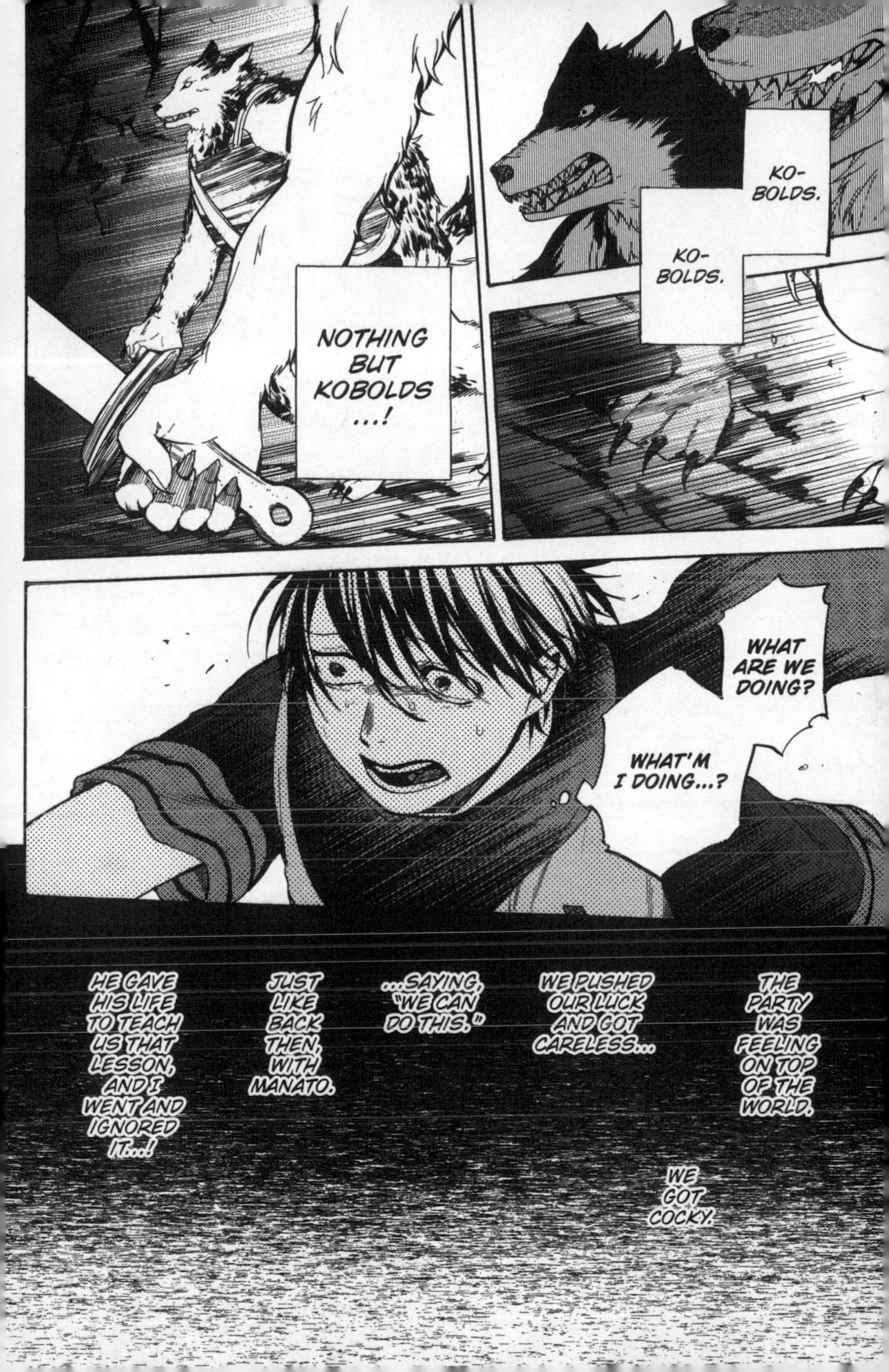
KO-BOLDS.
KO-BOLDS.
NOTHING BUT KOBOLDS ...!
WHAT ARE WE DOING?
WHAT'M I DOING...?
THE PARTY WAS FEELING ON TOP OF THE WORLD.
WE GOT COCKY.
WE PUSHED OUR LUCK AND GOT CARELESS...
...SAYING, "WE CAN DO THIS."
JUST LIKE BACK THEN, WITH MANATO.
HE GAVE HIS LIFE TO TEACH US THAT LESSON, AND I WENT AND IGNORED IT...!

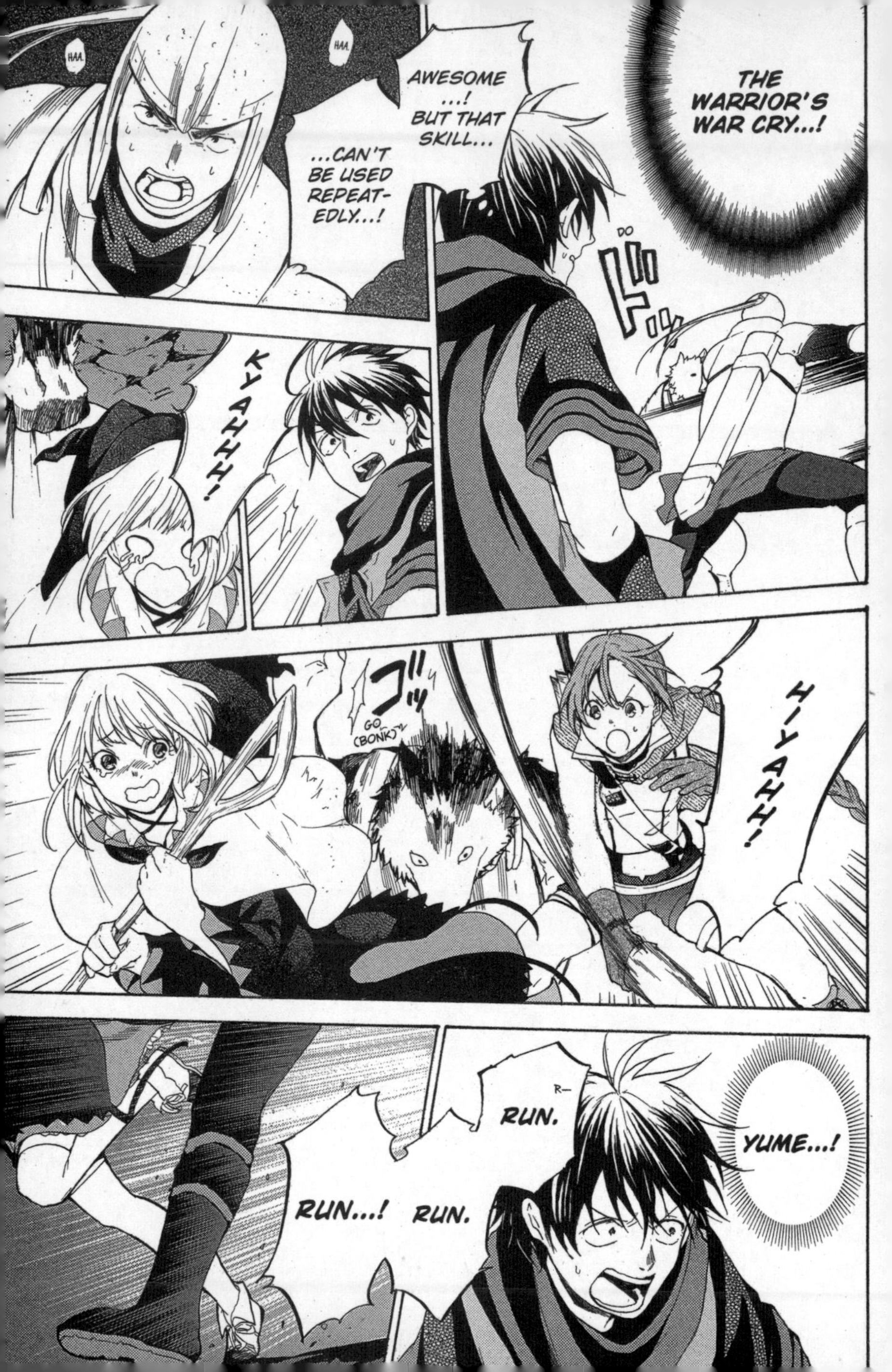
THE WARRIOR'S WAR CRY...!
AWESOME ...! BUT THAT SKILL...
...CAN'T BE USED REPEAT-EDLY...!
HAA.
HAA.
DO
KYAHHH!
HIYAHH!
GO (BONK)
YUME...!
R—
RUN.
RUN.
RUN...!

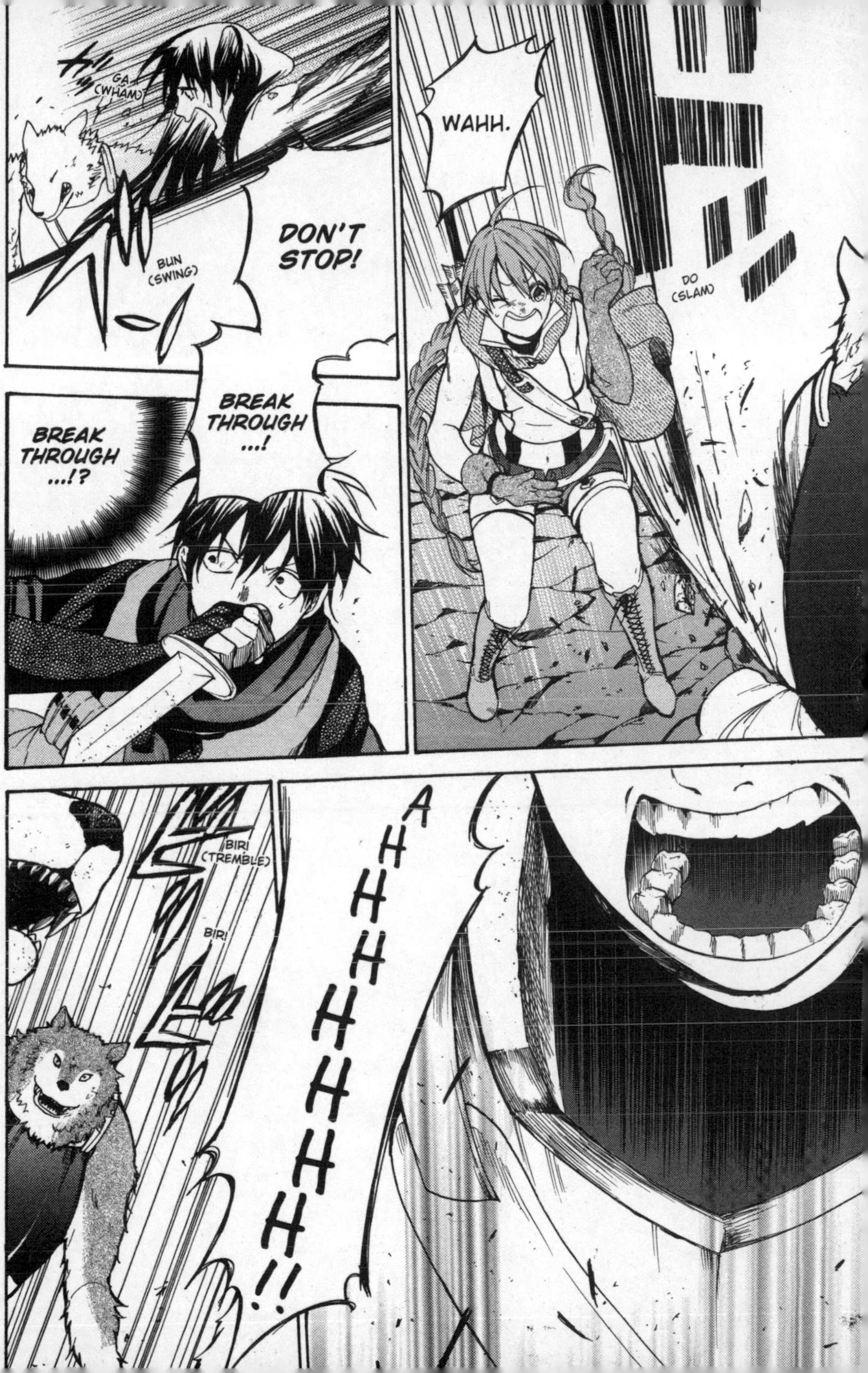
WAHH.
DO (SLAM)
GA (WHAM)
BUN (SWING)
DON'T STOP!
BREAK THROUGH ...!
BREAK THROUGH ...!?
AHHHHHHHHH!!
BIRI (TREMBLE)
BIRI

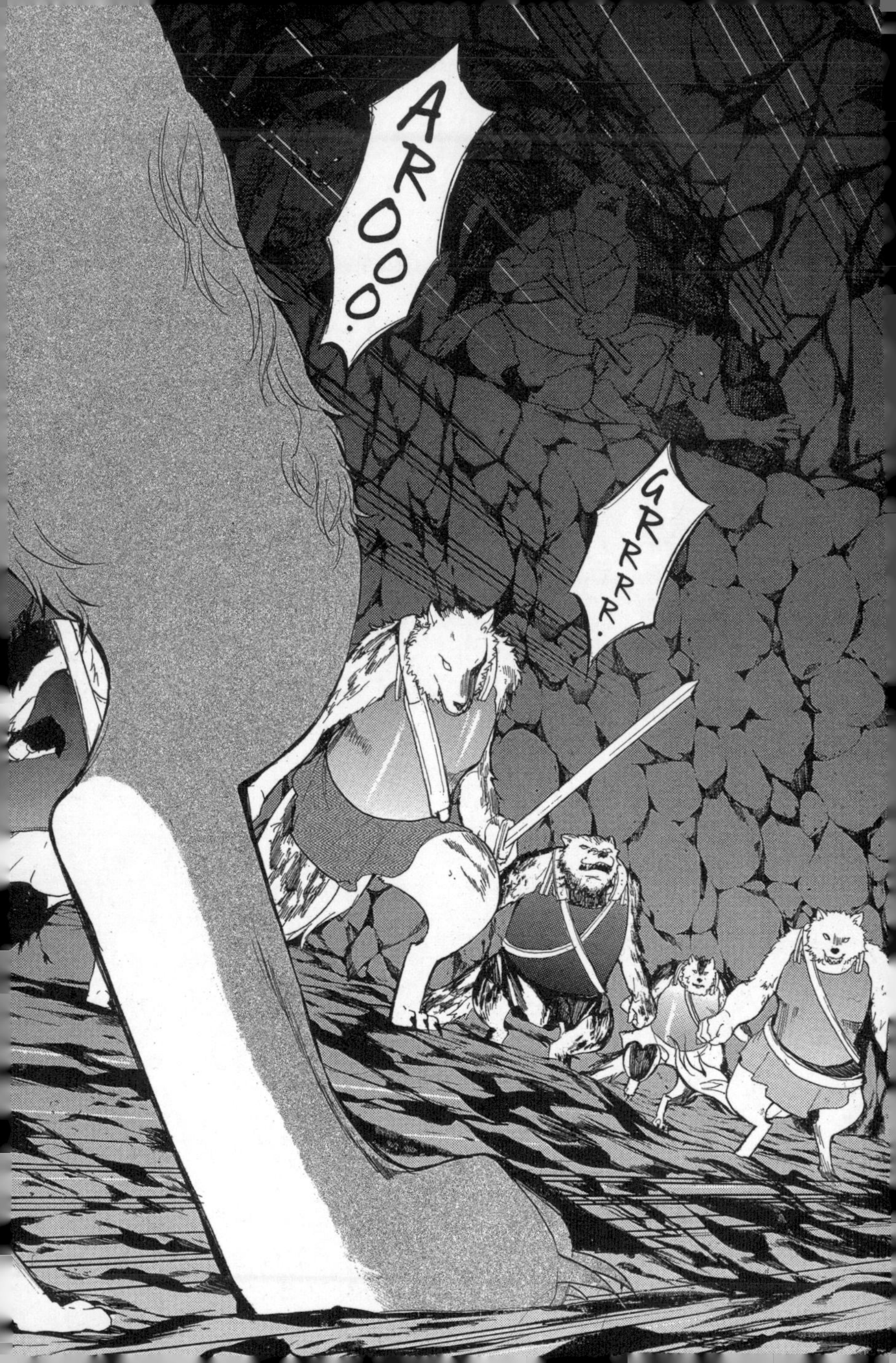
AROOO.
GRRRR.

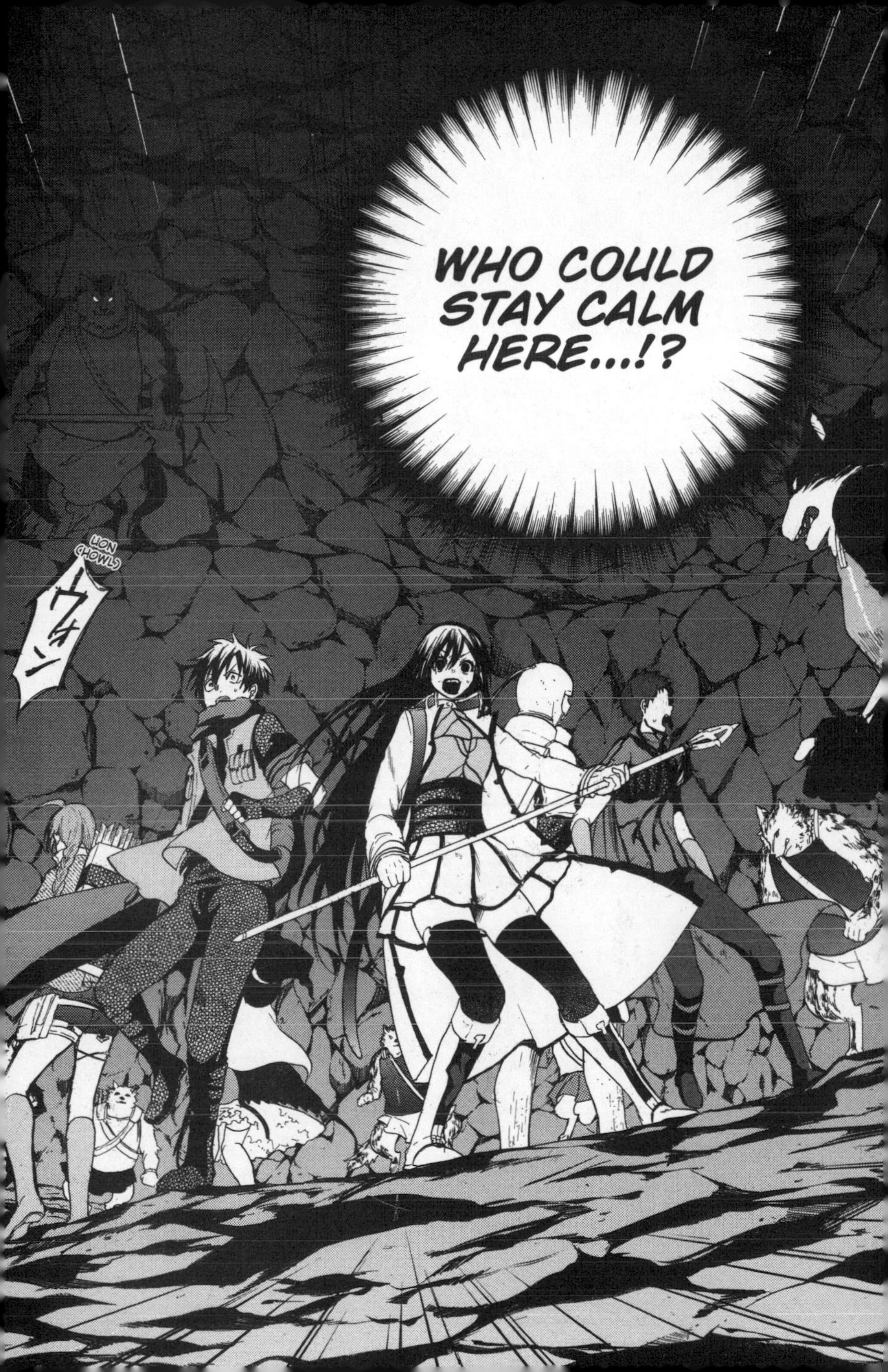
WHO COULD STAY CALM HERE...!?
ウォン
UON (HOWL)

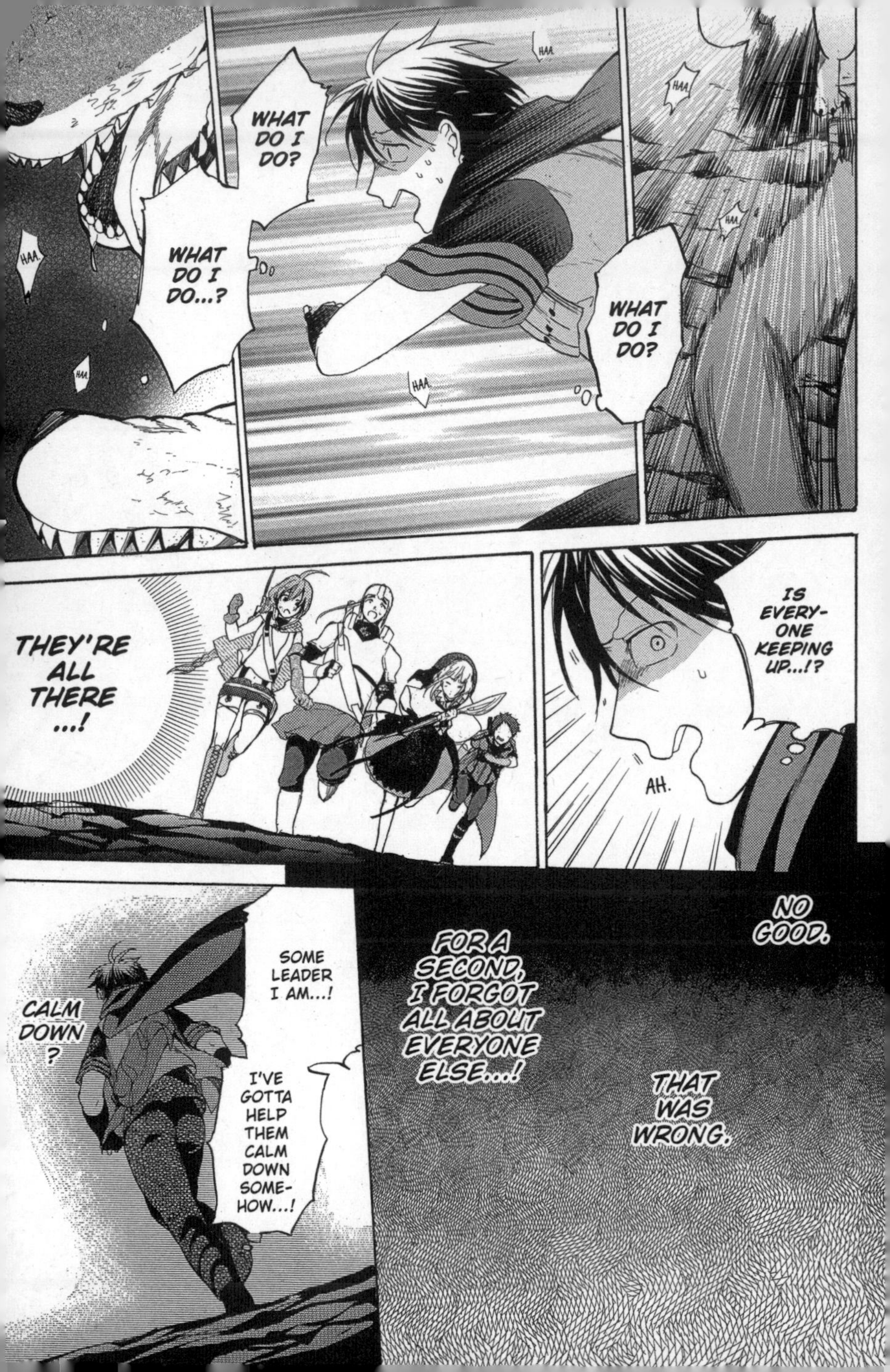
HAA.
HAA.
WHAT DO I DO?
HAA.
WHAT DO I DO?
HAA.
HAA.
WHAT DO I DO...?
HAA.
IS EVERY-ONE KEEPING UP...!?
AH.
THEY'RE ALL THERE...!
NO GOOD.
FOR A SECOND, I FORGOT ALL ABOUT EVERYONE ELSE...!
THAT WAS WRONG.
SOME LEADER I AM...!
I'VE GOTTA HELP THEM CALM DOWN SOMEHOW...!
CALM DOWN?

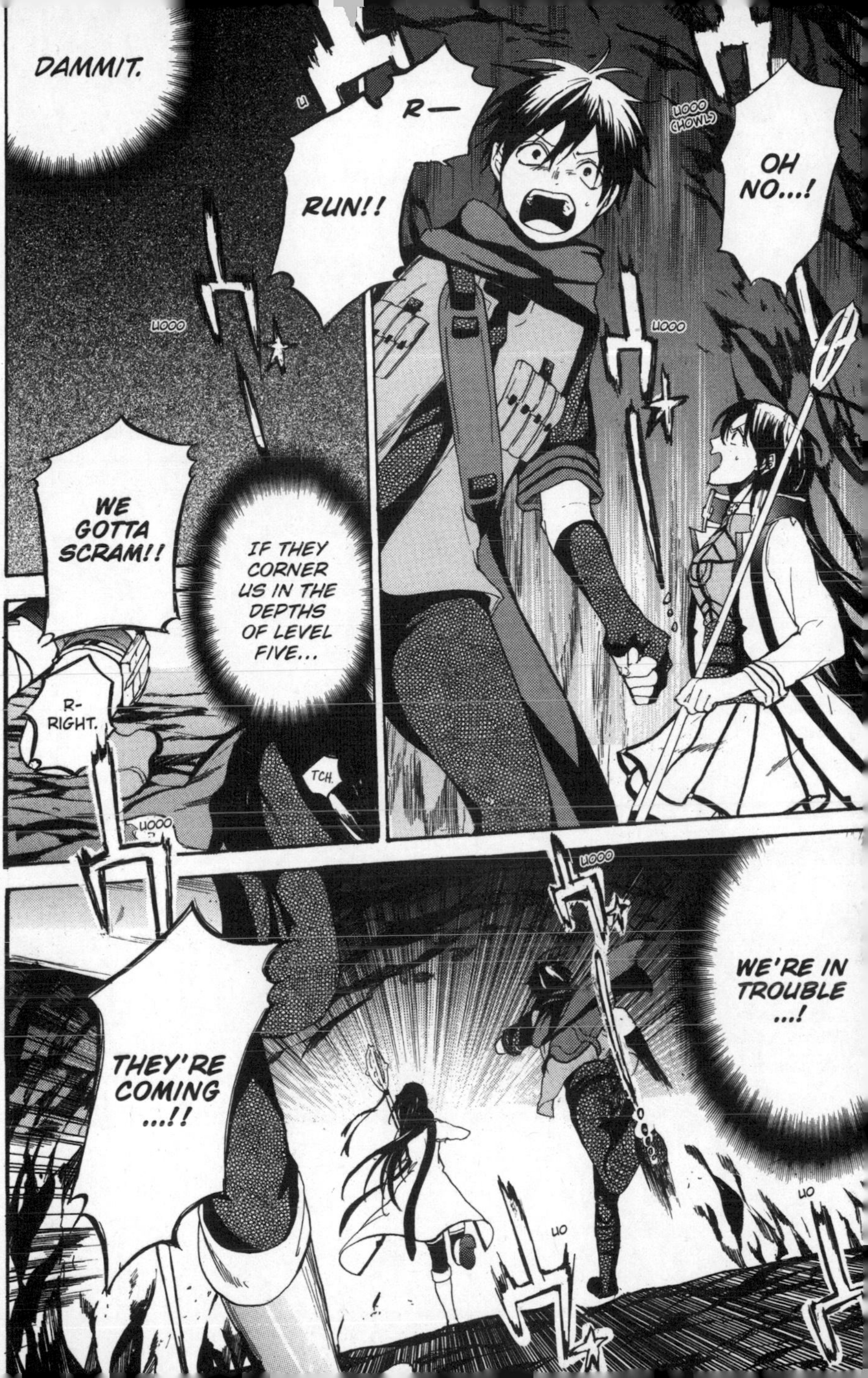

UOOO (HOWL)
OH NO...!
R—
U
DAMMIT.
RUN!!
UOOO
UOOO
IF THEY CORNER US IN THE DEPTHS OF LEVEL FIVE...
WE GOTTA SCRAM!!
R- RIGHT.
TCH.
UOOO
UOOO
WE'RE IN TROUBLE ...!
UO
UO
THEY'RE COMING ...!!

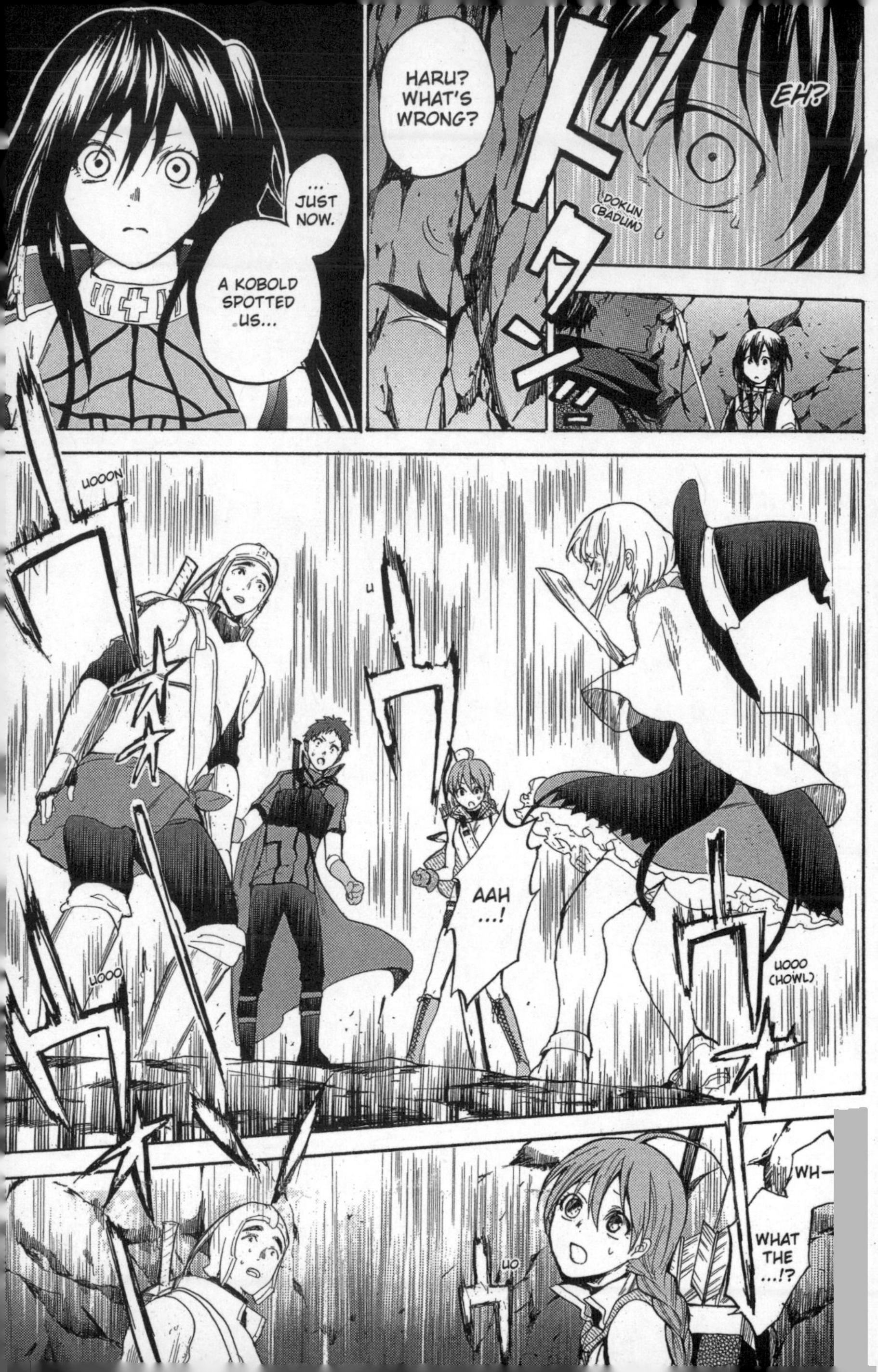
EH?
DOKUN (BADUM)
HARU? WHAT'S WRONG?
... JUST NOW.
A KOBOLD SPOTTED US...
UOOO (HOWL)
AAH ...!
U
UOOON
UOOO
WH—
WHAT THE ...!?
UO

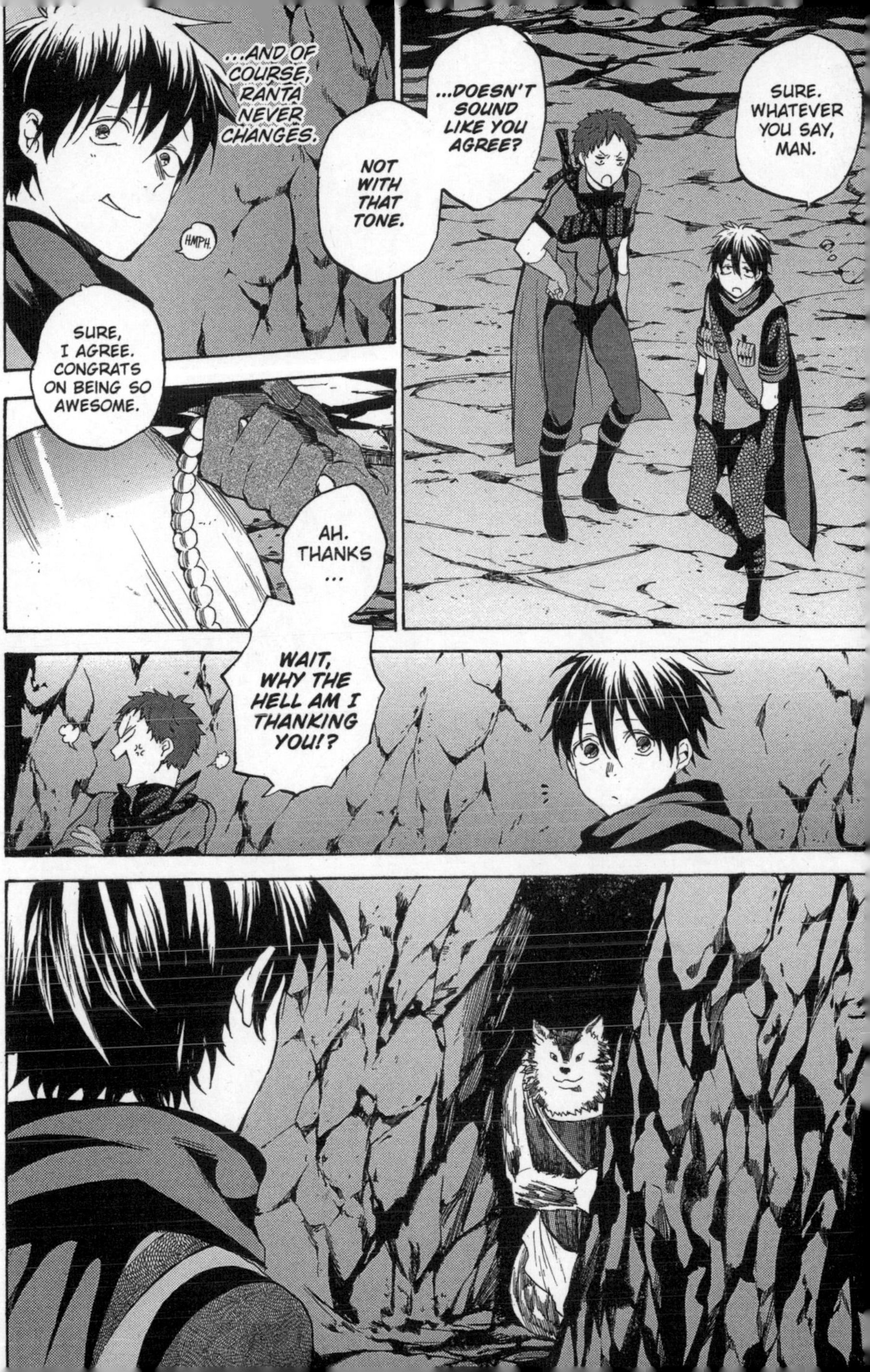
SURE. WHATEVER YOU SAY, MAN.
...DOESN'T SOUND LIKE YOU AGREE?
NOT WITH THAT TONE.
...AND OF COURSE, RANTA NEVER CHANGES.
HMPH.
SURE, I AGREE. CONGRATS ON BEING SO AWESOME.
AH. THANKS ...
WAIT, WHY THE HELL AM I THANKING YOU!?

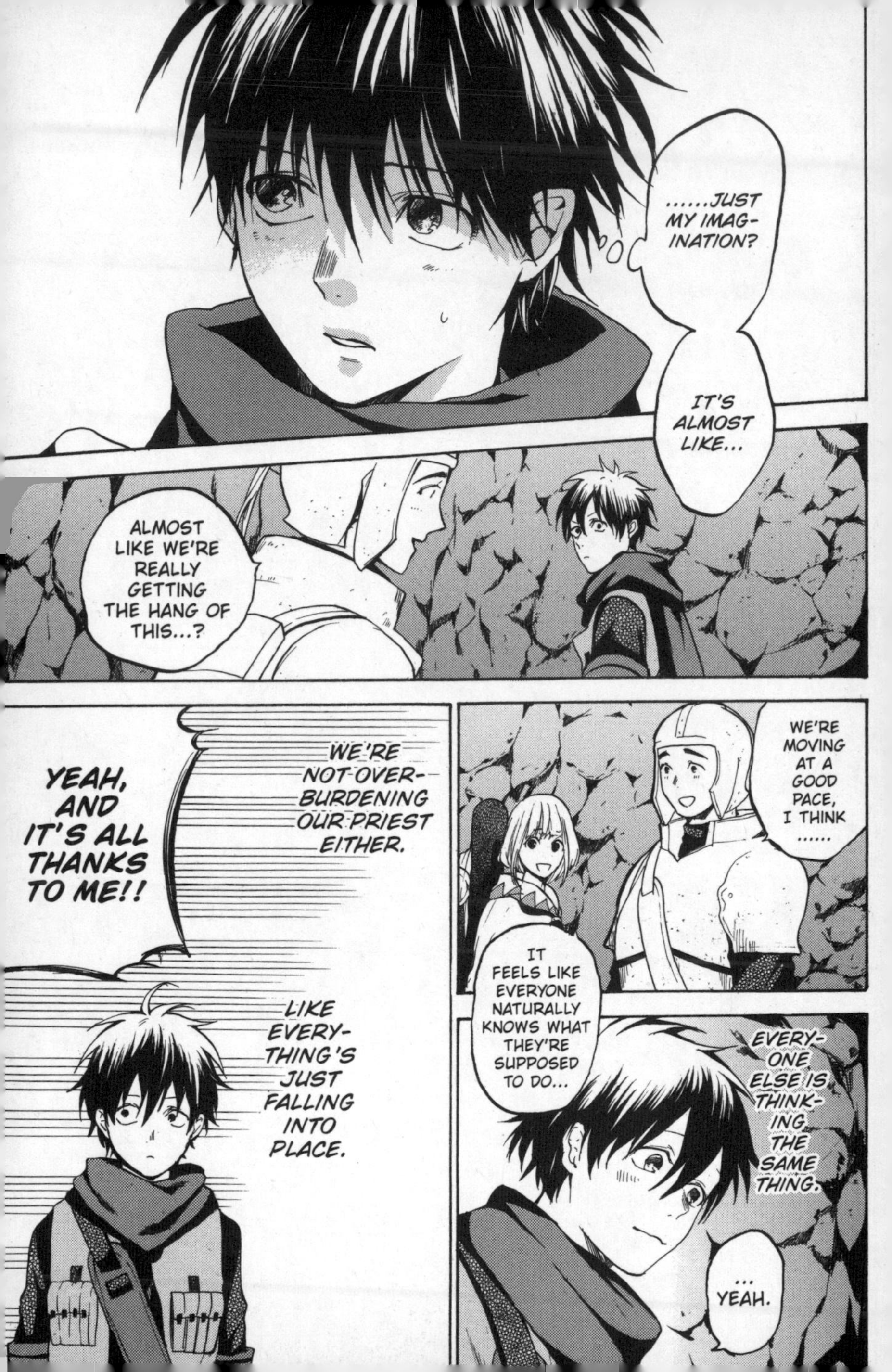
......JUST MY IMAG-INATION?
IT'S ALMOST LIKE...
ALMOST LIKE WE'RE REALLY GETTING THE HANG OF THIS...?
WE'RE MOVING AT A GOOD PACE, I THINK ......
IT FEELS LIKE EVERYONE NATURALLY KNOWS WHAT THEY'RE SUPPOSED TO DO...
EVERY-ONE ELSE IS THINK-ING THE SAME THING.
... YEAH.
WE'RE NOT OVER-BURDENING OUR PRIEST EITHER.
YEAH, AND IT'S ALL THANKS TO ME!!
LIKE EVERY-THING'S JUST FALLING INTO PLACE.

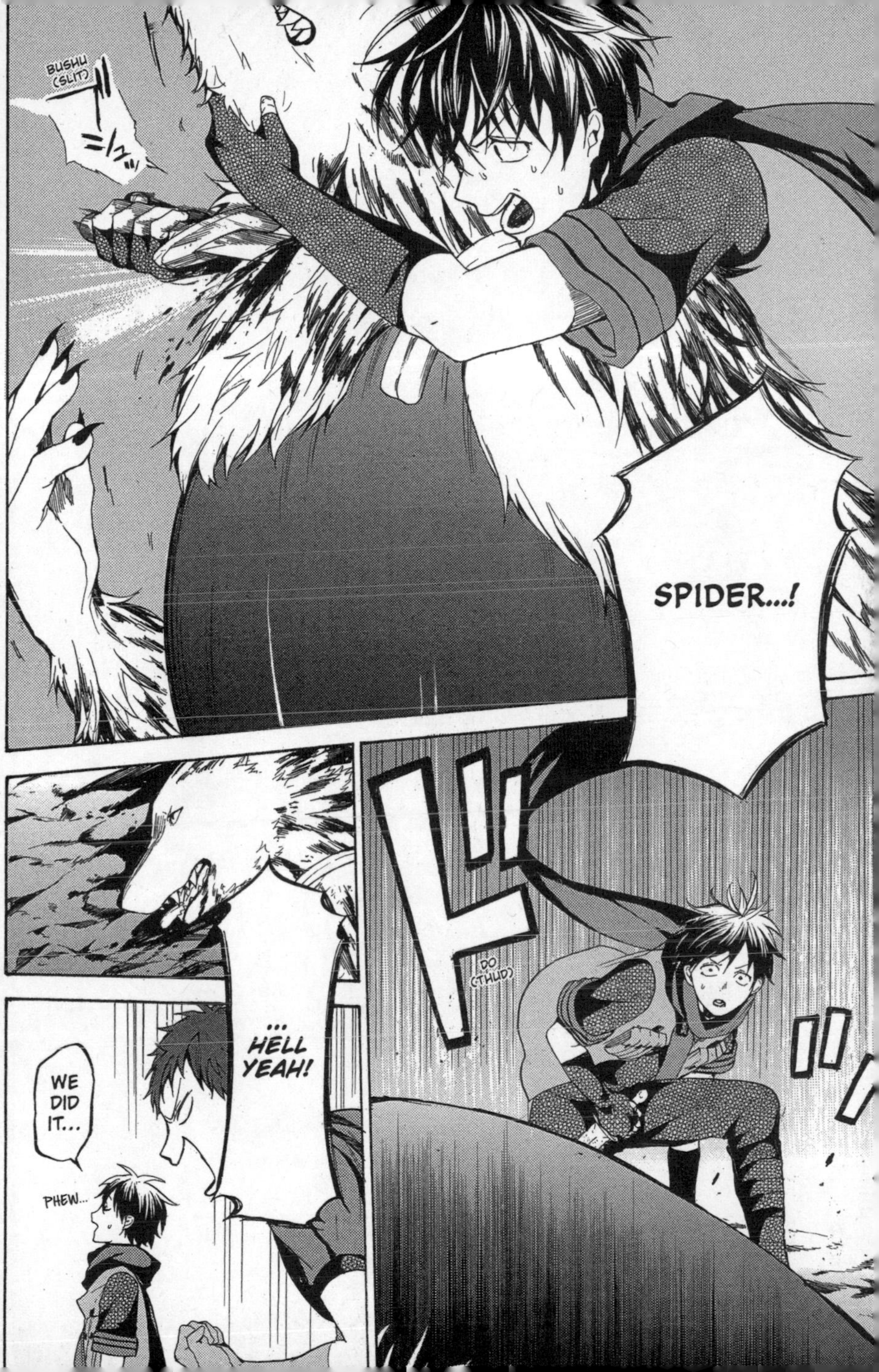
BUSHU (SLIT)
SPIDER...!
DO (THUD)
...HELL YEAH!
WE DID IT...
PHEW...

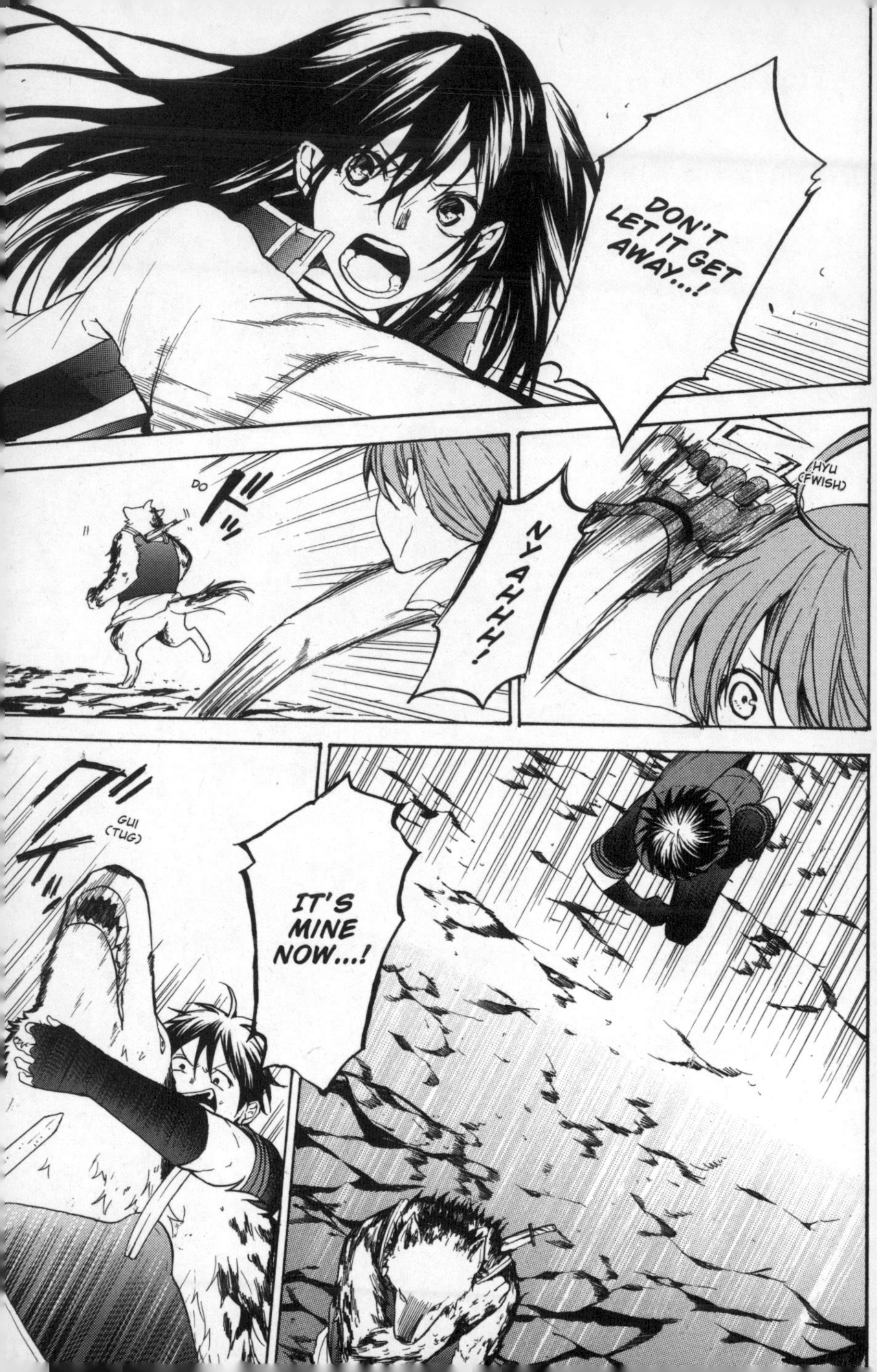
DON'T LET IT GET AWAY...!
HYU (FWISH)
NYAHHH!
DO
IT'S MINE NOW...!
GUI (TUG)

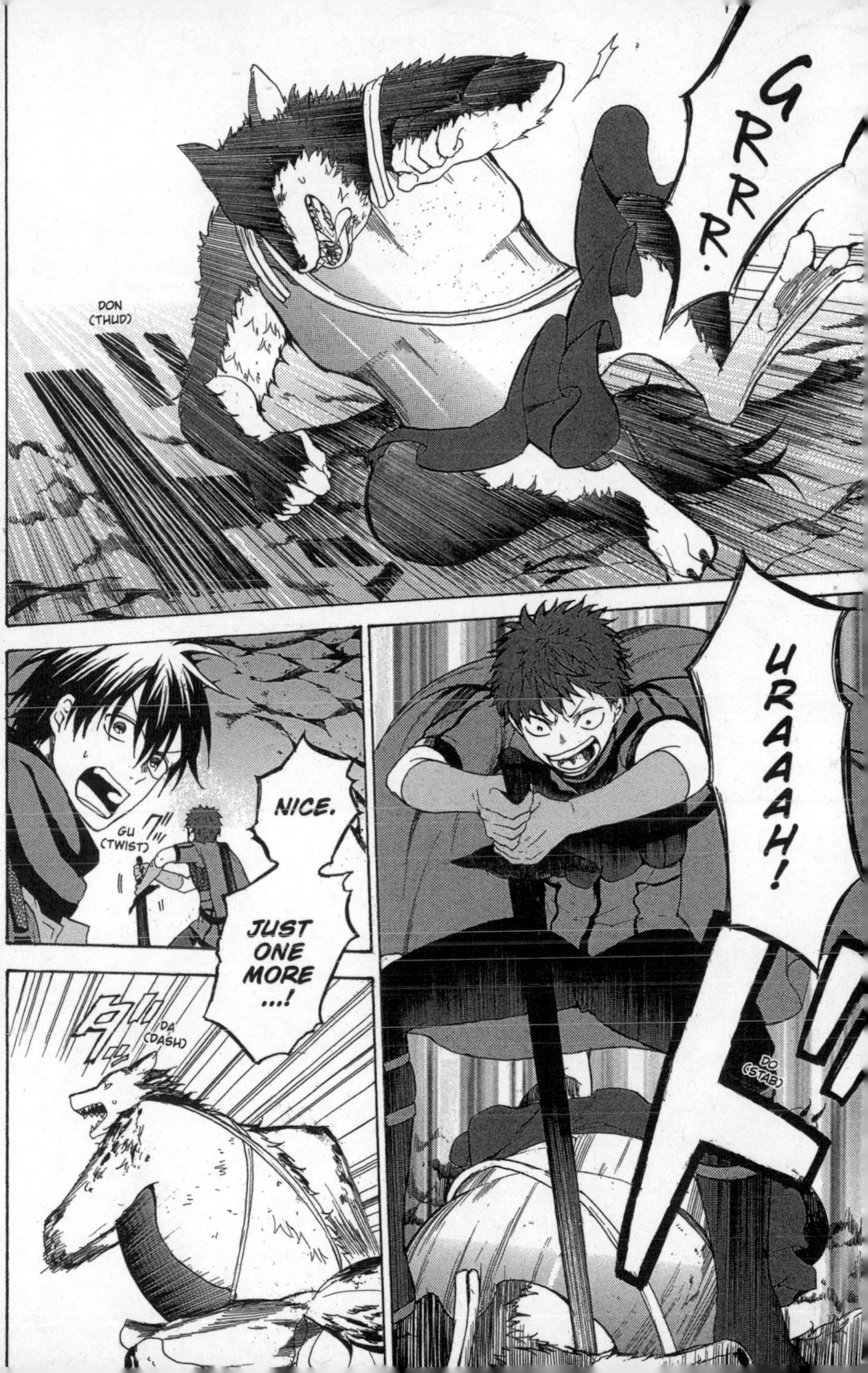
GRRR.
DON (THUD)
URAAAAH!
DO (STAB)
NICE.
GU (TWIST)
JUST ONE MORE ...!
DA (DASH)

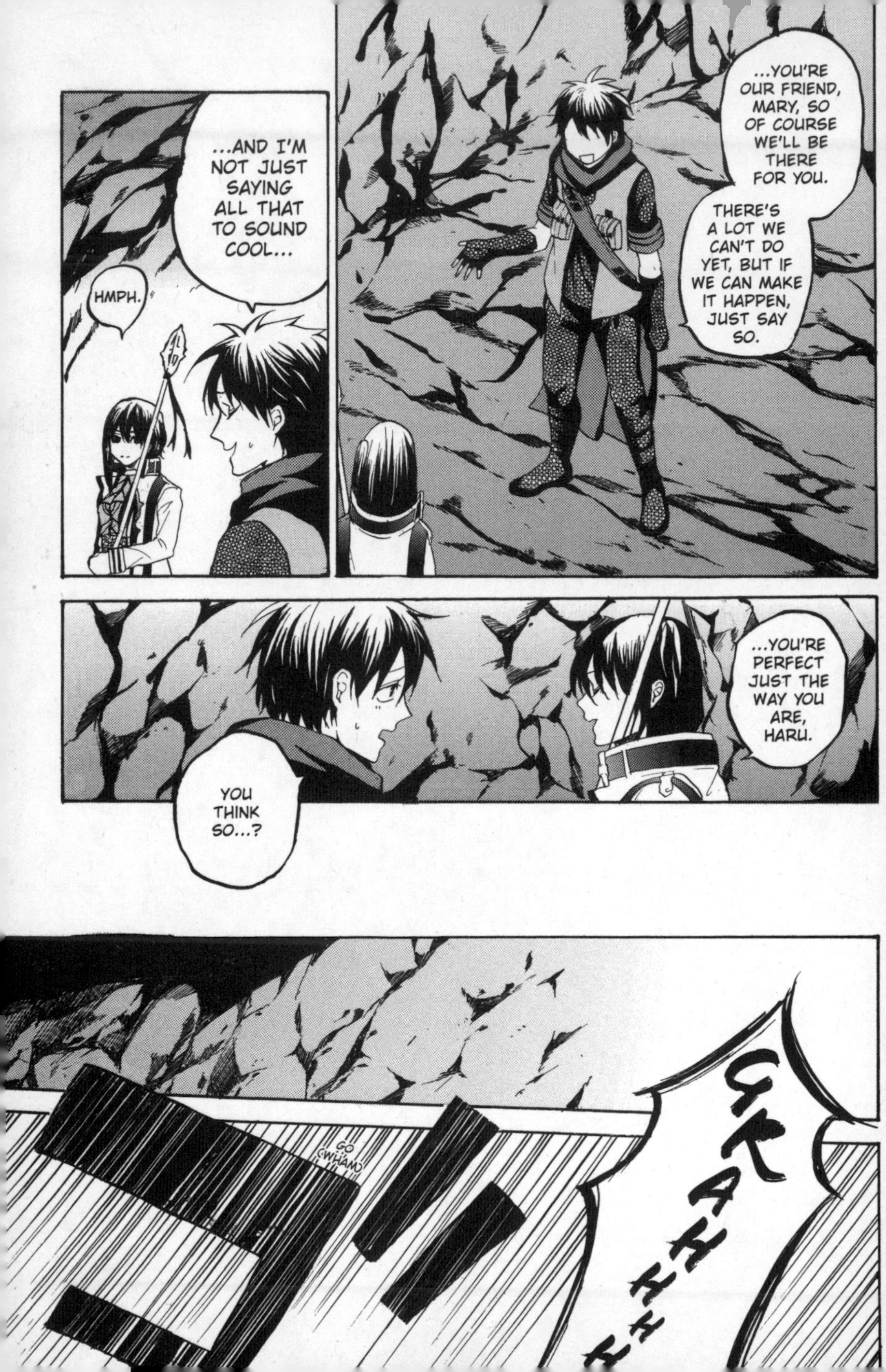
...YOU'RE OUR FRIEND, MARY, SO OF COURSE WE'LL BE THERE FOR YOU.
THERE'S A LOT WE CAN'T DO YET, BUT IF WE CAN MAKE IT HAPPEN, JUST SAY SO.
...AND I'M NOT JUST SAYING ALL THAT TO SOUND COOL...
HMPH.
...YOU'RE PERFECT JUST THE WAY YOU ARE, HARU.
YOU THINK SO...?
GO (WHAM)
GRAHHHH

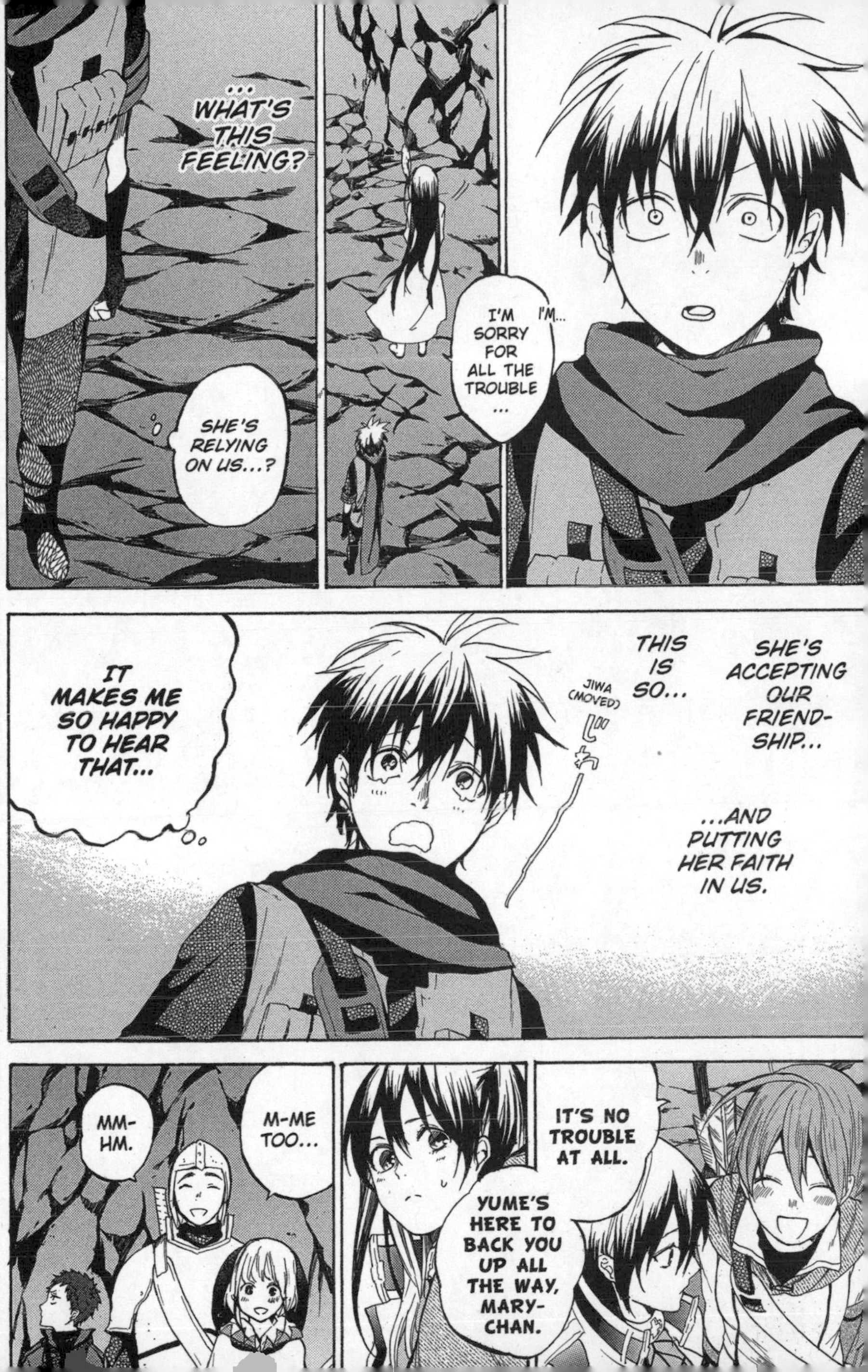
I'M...
I'M SORRY FOR ALL THE TROUBLE...
...WHAT'S THIS FEELING?
SHE'S RELYING ON US...?
SHE'S ACCEPTING OUR FRIENDSHIP...
...AND PUTTING HER FAITH IN US.
THIS IS SO...
JIWA (MOVED)
IT MAKES ME SO HAPPY TO HEAR THAT...
IT'S NO TROUBLE AT ALL.
YUME'S HERE TO BACK YOU UP ALL THE WAY, MARY-CHAN.
M-ME TOO...
MM-HM.

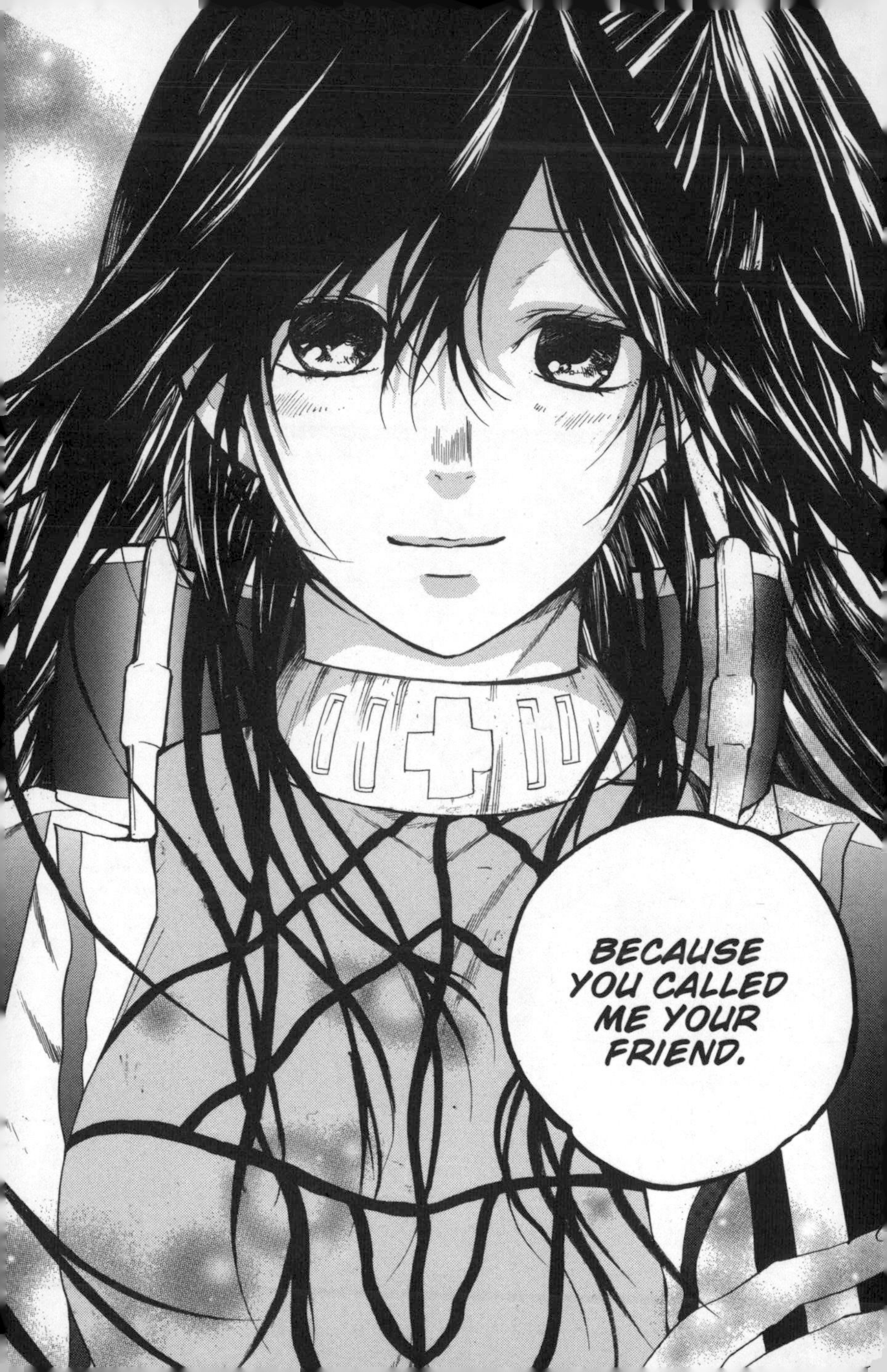
BECAUSE YOU CALLED ME YOUR FRIEND.

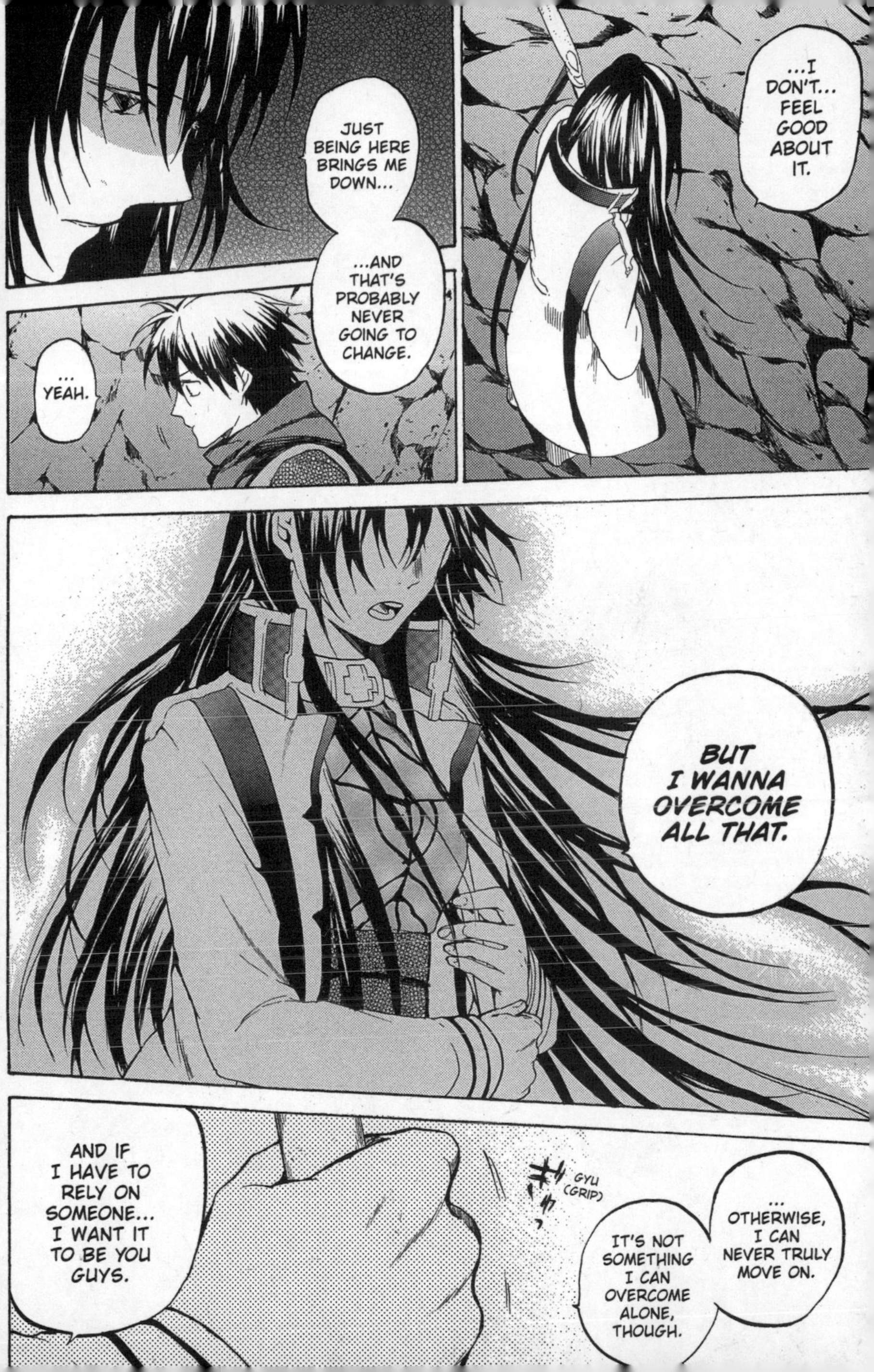
...I DON'T... FEEL GOOD ABOUT IT.
JUST BEING HERE BRINGS ME DOWN...
...AND THAT'S PROBABLY NEVER GOING TO CHANGE.
... YEAH.
BUT I WANNA OVERCOME ALL THAT.
...OTHERWISE, I CAN NEVER TRULY MOVE ON.
IT'S NOT SOMETHING I CAN OVERCOME ALONE, THOUGH.
GYU (GRIP)
AND IF I HAVE TO RELY ON SOMEONE... I WANT IT TO BE YOU GUYS.

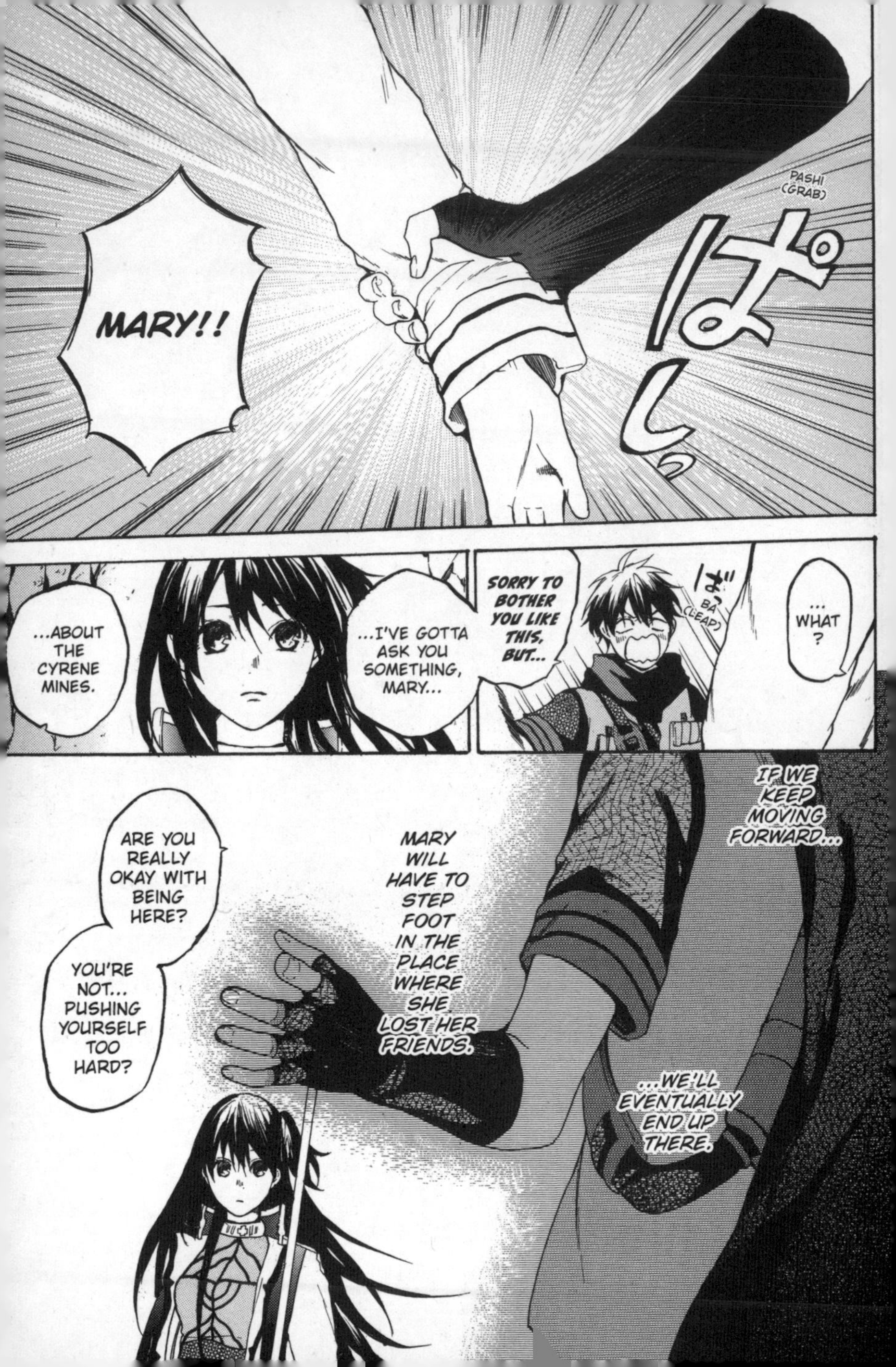
ぱしっ
PASHI (GRAB)
MARY!!
...WHAT?
ばっ
BA (LEAP)
SORRY TO BOTHER YOU LIKE THIS, BUT...
...I'VE GOTTA ASK YOU SOMETHING, MARY...
...ABOUT THE CYRENE MINES.
IF WE KEEP MOVING FORWARD...
MARY WILL HAVE TO STEP FOOT IN THE PLACE WHERE SHE LOST HER FRIENDS.
...WE'LL EVENTUALLY END UP THERE.
ARE YOU REALLY OKAY WITH BEING HERE?
YOU'RE NOT... PUSHING YOURSELF TOO HARD?

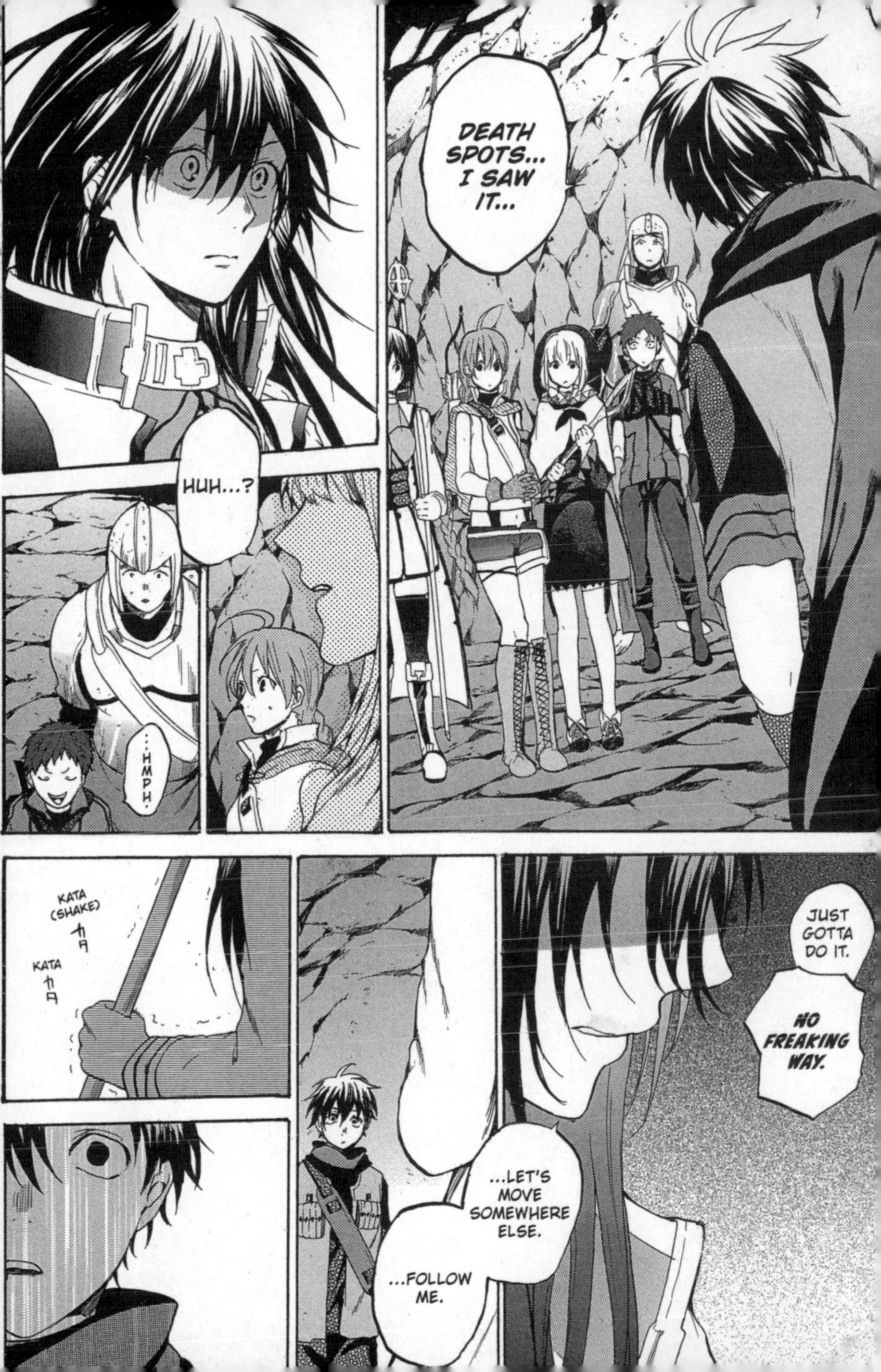
DEATH SPOTS... I SAW IT...
HUH...?
...HMPH.
KATA (SHAKE) カタ
KATA カタ
JUST GOTTA DO IT.
NO FREAKING WAY.
...LET'S MOVE SOMEWHERE ELSE.
...FOLLOW ME.

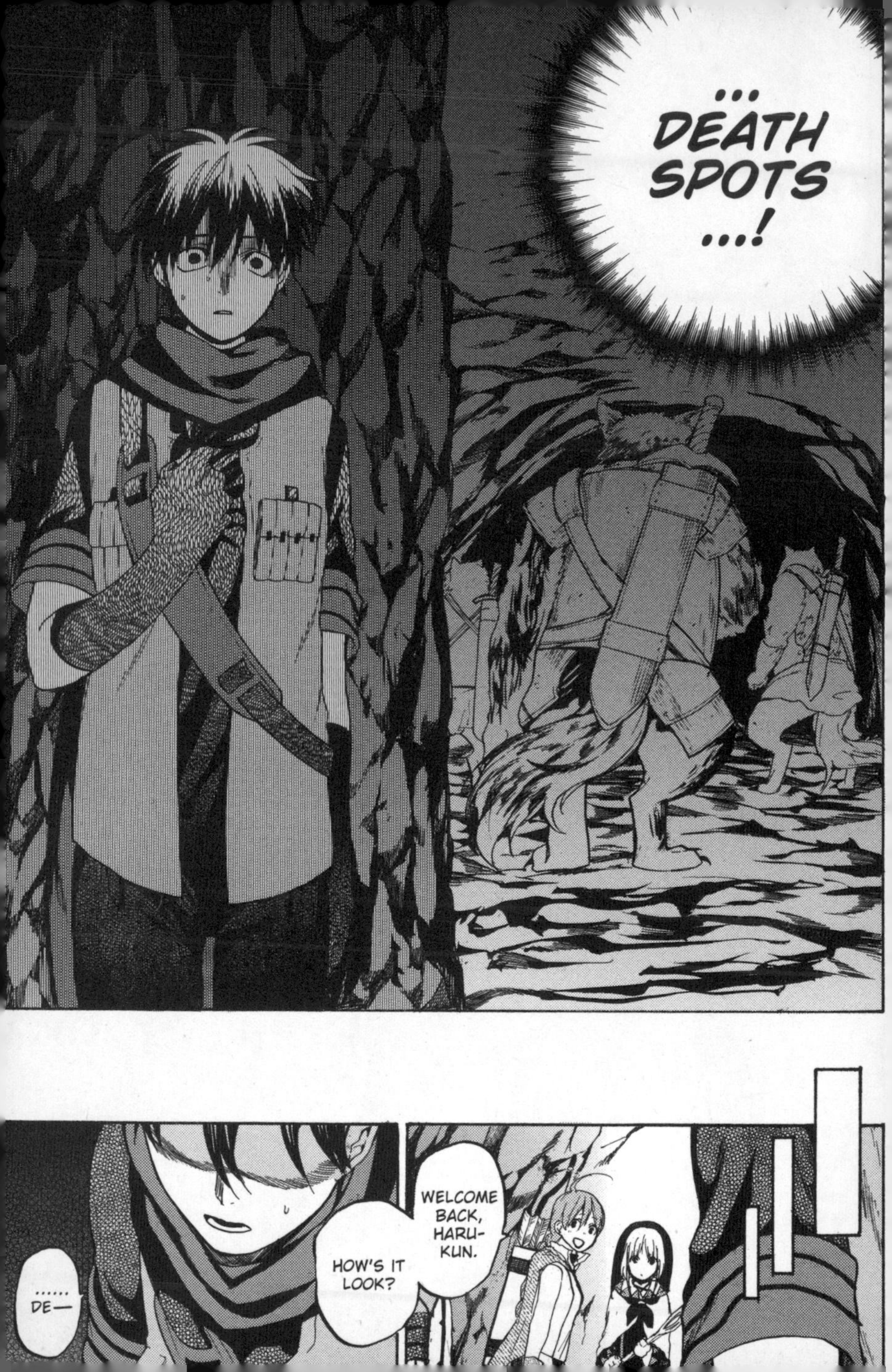
...DEATH SPOTS ...!
WELCOME BACK, HARU-KUN.
HOW'S IT LOOK?
...... DE—

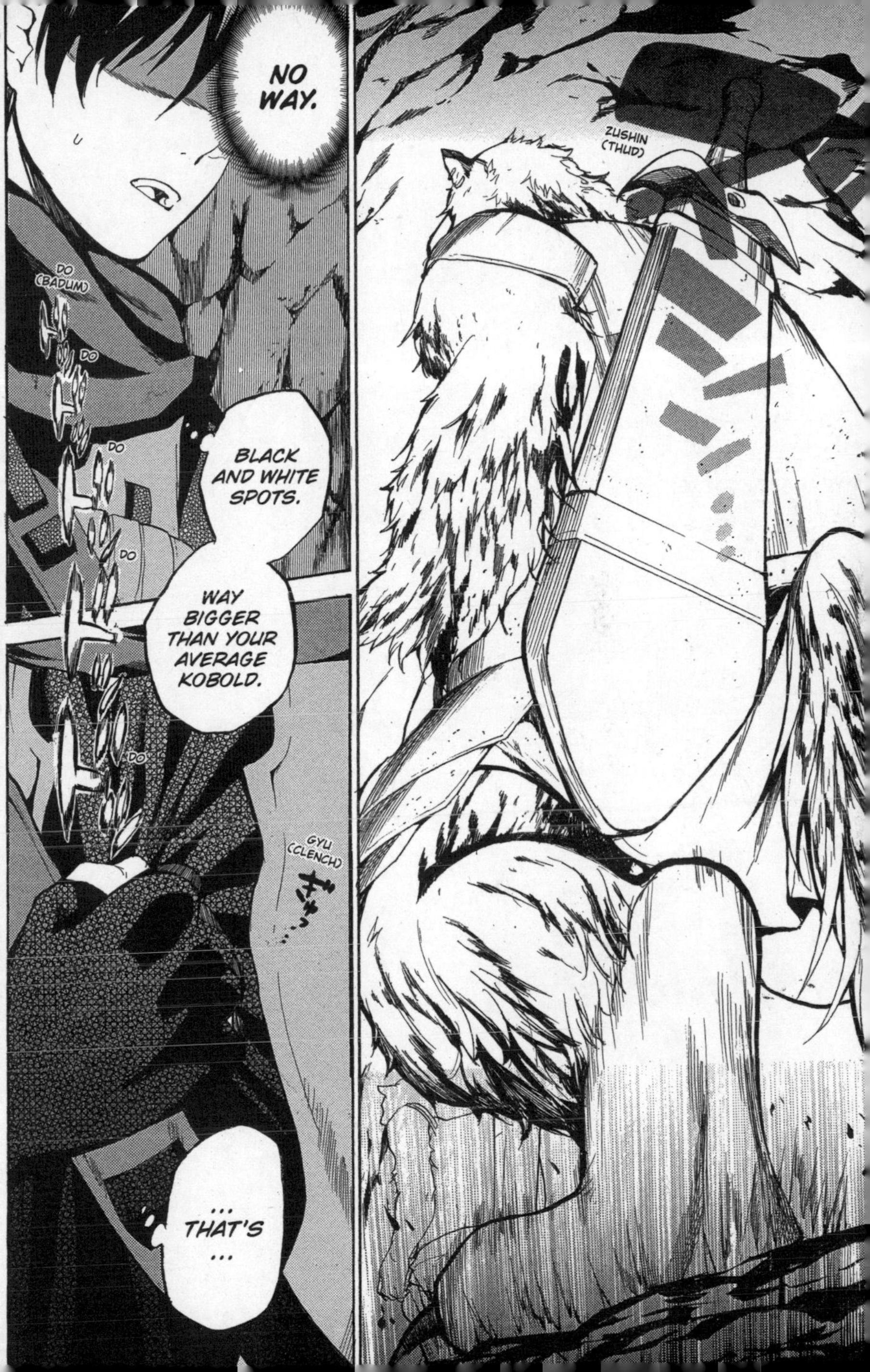
ZUSHIN (THUD)
NO WAY.
DO (BADUM)
DO
DO
DO
DO
BLACK AND WHITE SPOTS.
WAY BIGGER THAN YOUR AVERAGE KOBOLD.
GYU (CLENCH)
... THAT'S ...

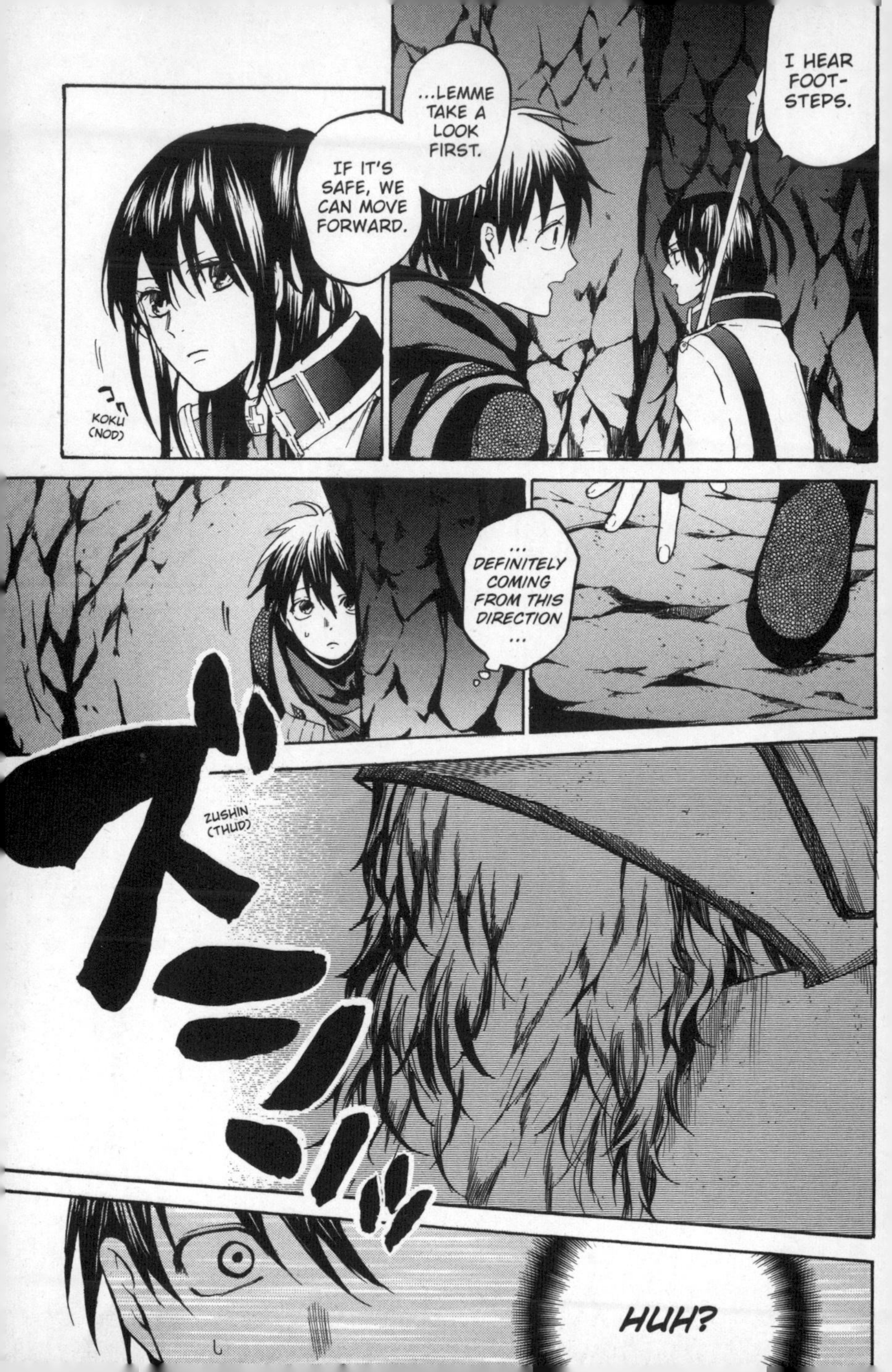

I HEAR FOOT-STEPS.
...LEMME TAKE A LOOK FIRST.
IF IT'S SAFE, WE CAN MOVE FORWARD.
KOKU (NOD)
... DEFINITELY COMING FROM THIS DIRECTION ...
ZUSHIN (THUD)
HUH?

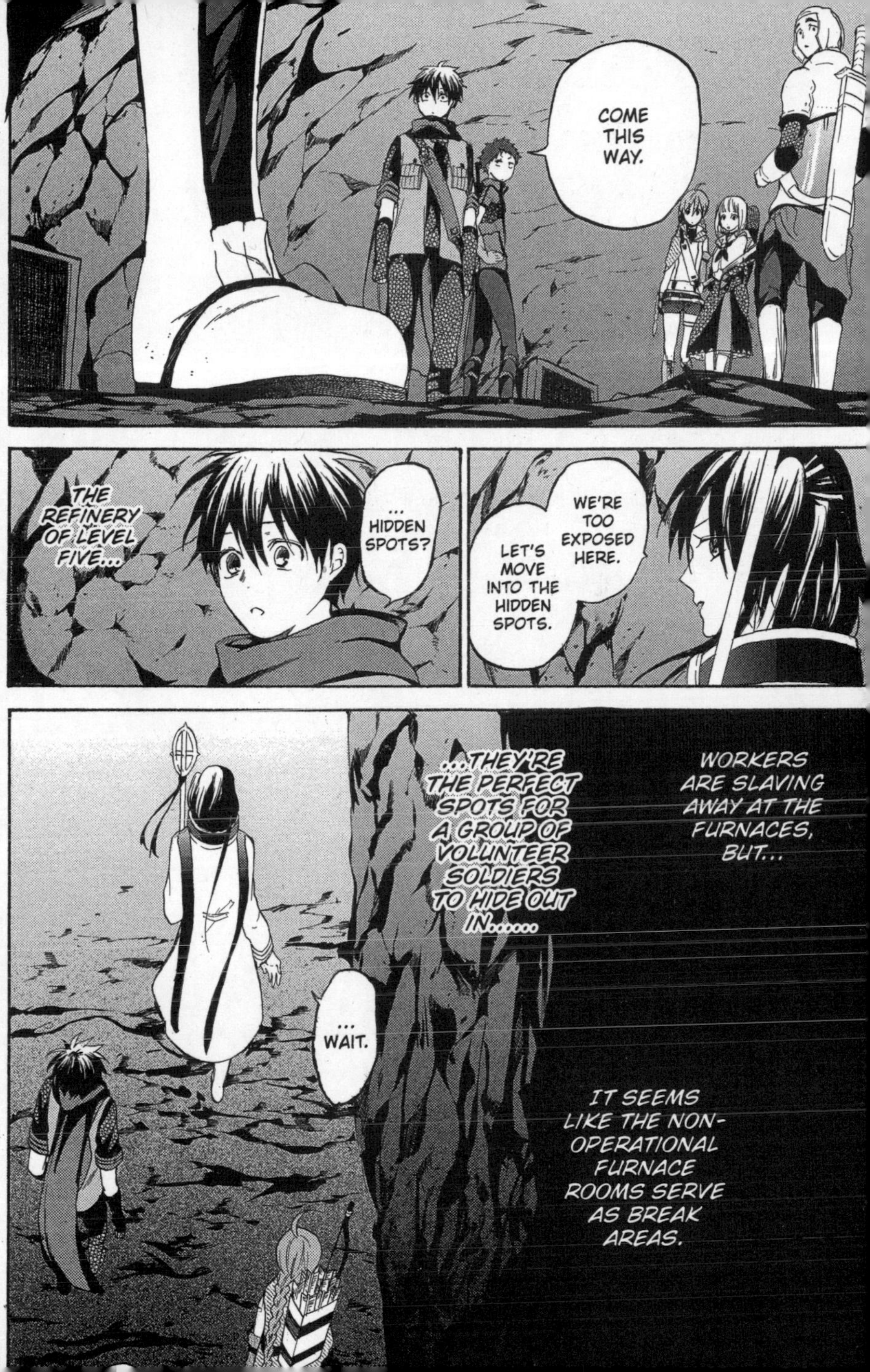
COME THIS WAY.
WE'RE TOO EXPOSED HERE.
LET'S MOVE INTO THE HIDDEN SPOTS.
...HIDDEN SPOTS?
THE REFINERY OF LEVEL FIVE...
WORKERS ARE SLAVING AWAY AT THE FURNACES, BUT...
IT SEEMS LIKE THE NON-OPERATIONAL FURNACE ROOMS SERVE AS BREAK AREAS.
...THEY'RE THE PERFECT SPOTS FOR A GROUP OF VOLUNTEER SOLDIERS TO HIDE OUT IN......
...WAIT.

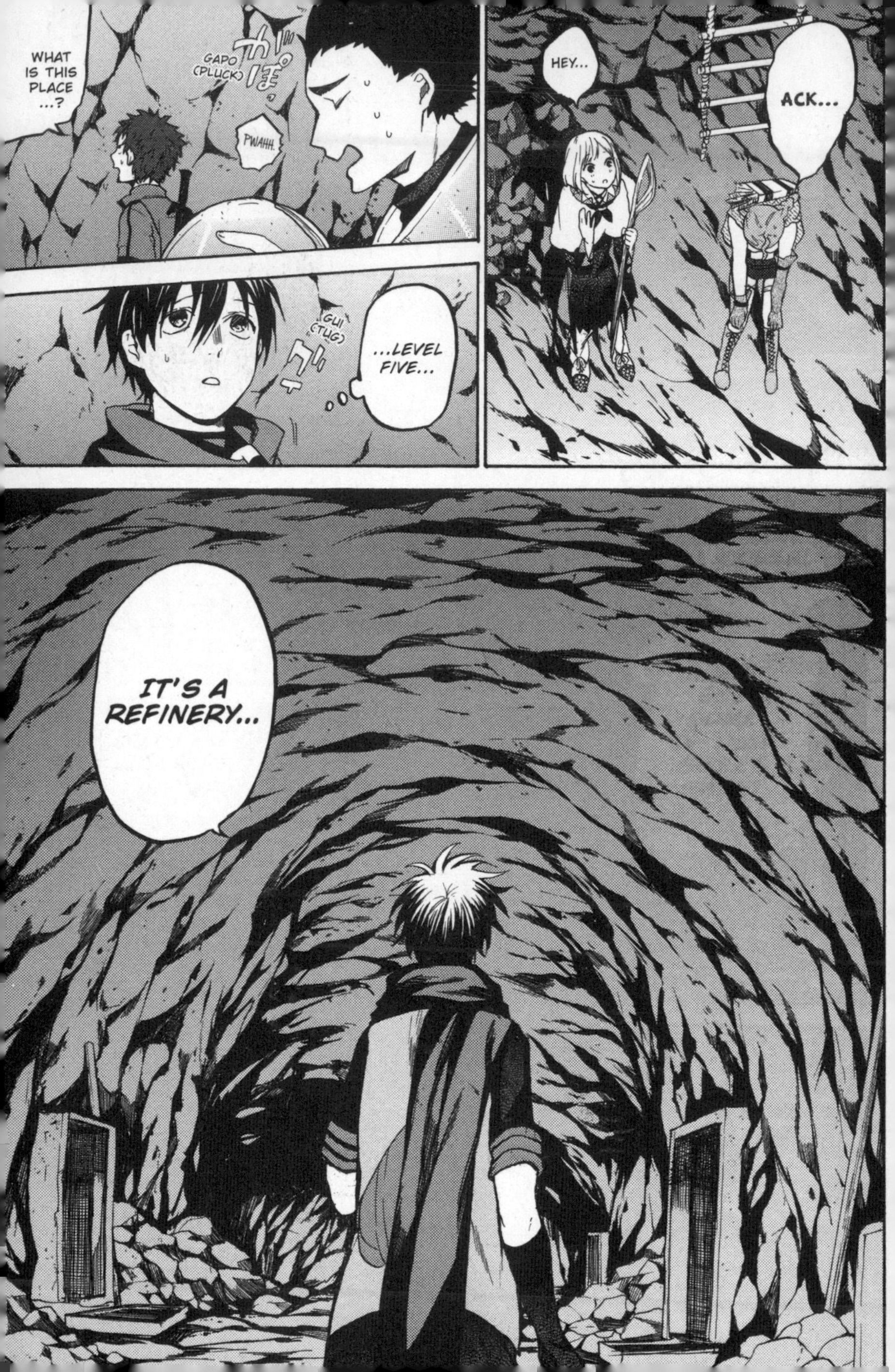
ACK...
HEY...
GAPO (PLUCK)
PWAHH.
WHAT IS THIS PLACE ...?
GUI (TUG)
...LEVEL FIVE...
IT'S A REFINERY...

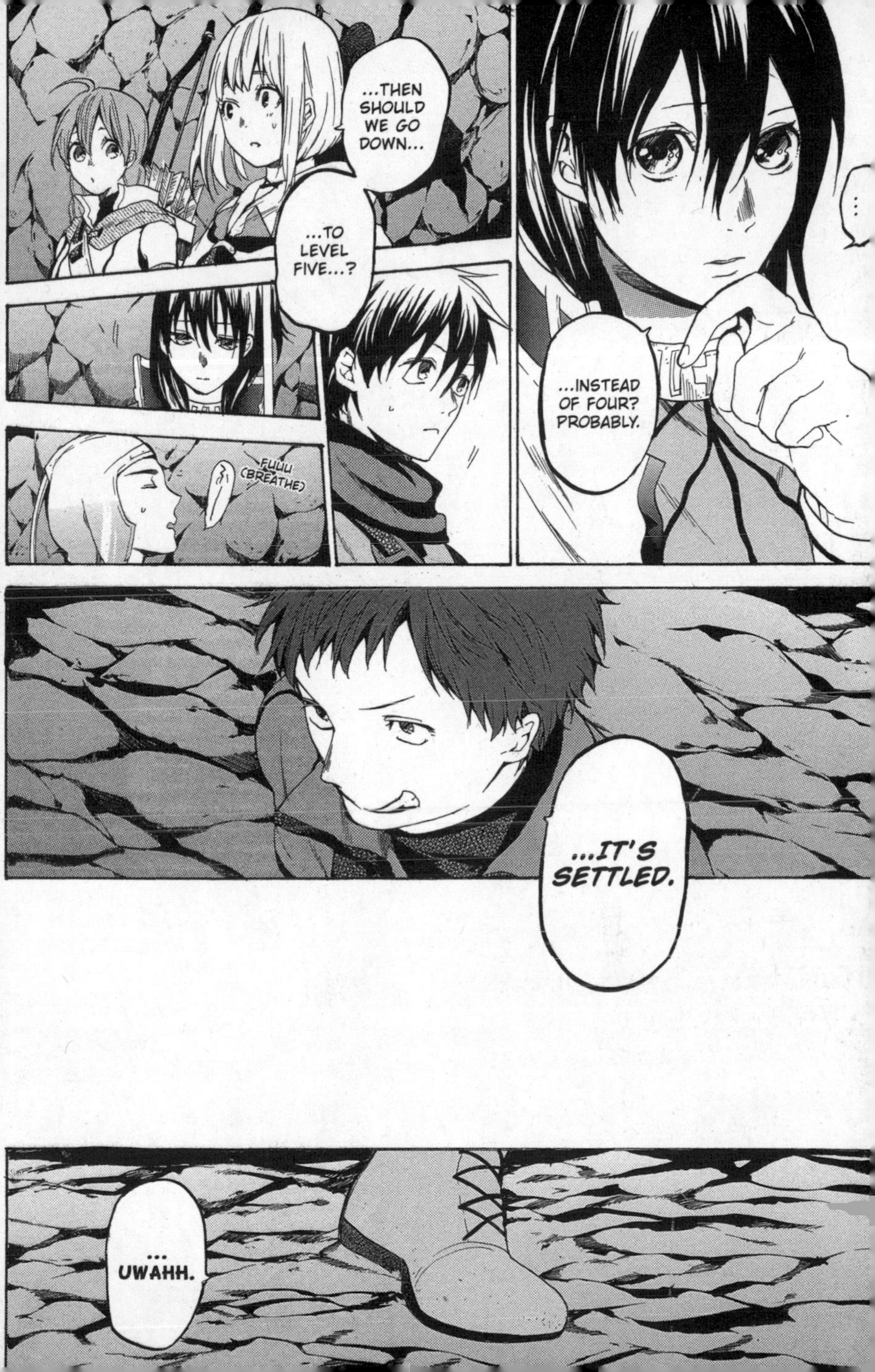
...THEN SHOULD WE GO DOWN...
...TO LEVEL FIVE...?
Fuuu (BREATHE)
...
...INSTEAD OF FOUR? PROBABLY.
...IT'S SETTLED.
... UWAHH.

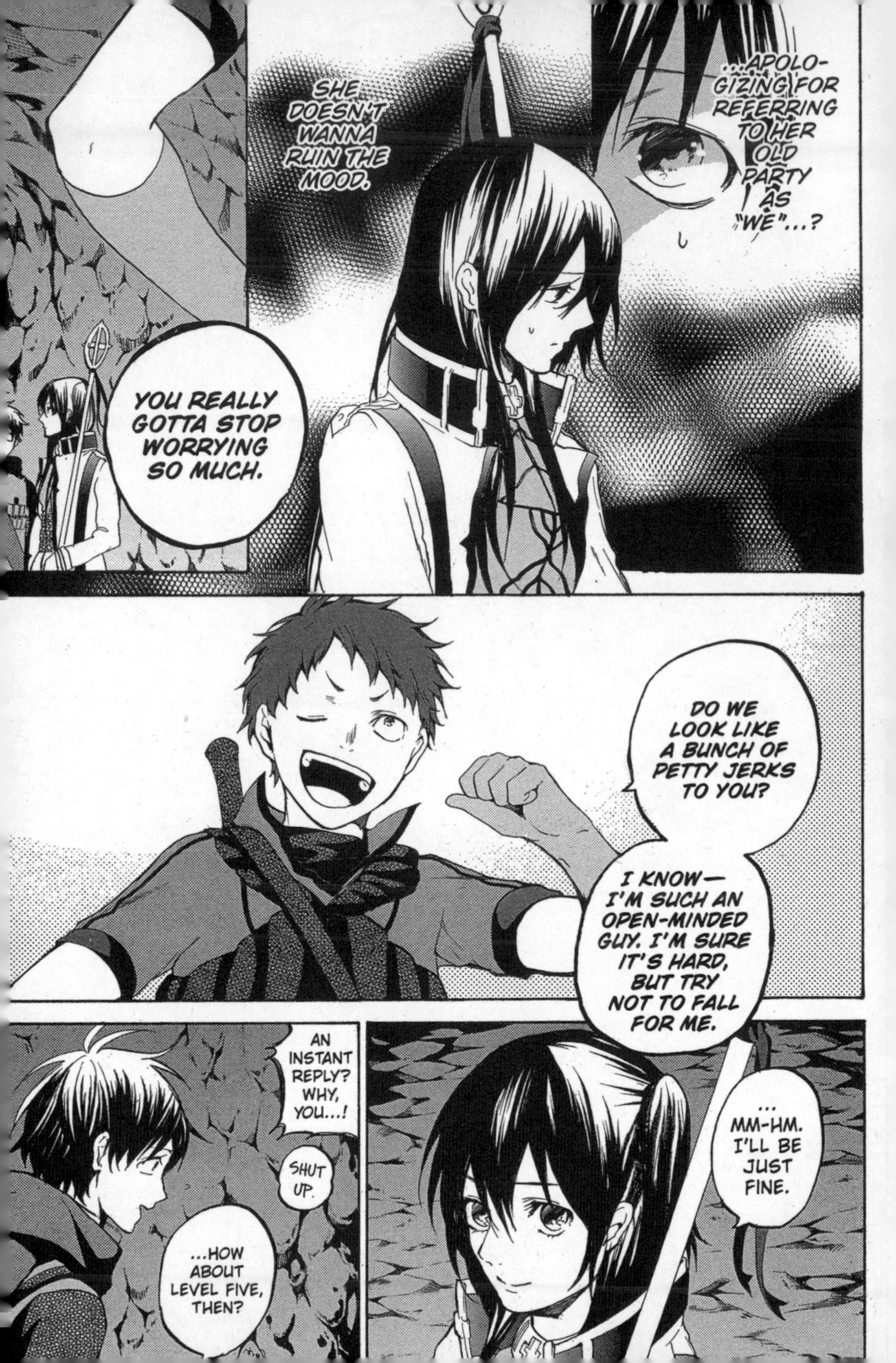
...APOLOGIZING FOR REFERRING TO HER OLD PARTY AS "WE"...?
SHE DOESN'T WANNA RUIN THE MOOD.
YOU REALLY GOTTA STOP WORRYING SO MUCH.
DO WE LOOK LIKE A BUNCH OF PETTY JERKS TO YOU?
I KNOW— I'M SUCH AN OPEN-MINDED GUY. I'M SURE IT'S HARD, BUT TRY NOT TO FALL FOR ME.
... MM-HM. I'LL BE JUST FINE.
AN INSTANT REPLY? WHY, YOU...!
SHUT UP.
...HOW ABOUT LEVEL FIVE, THEN?

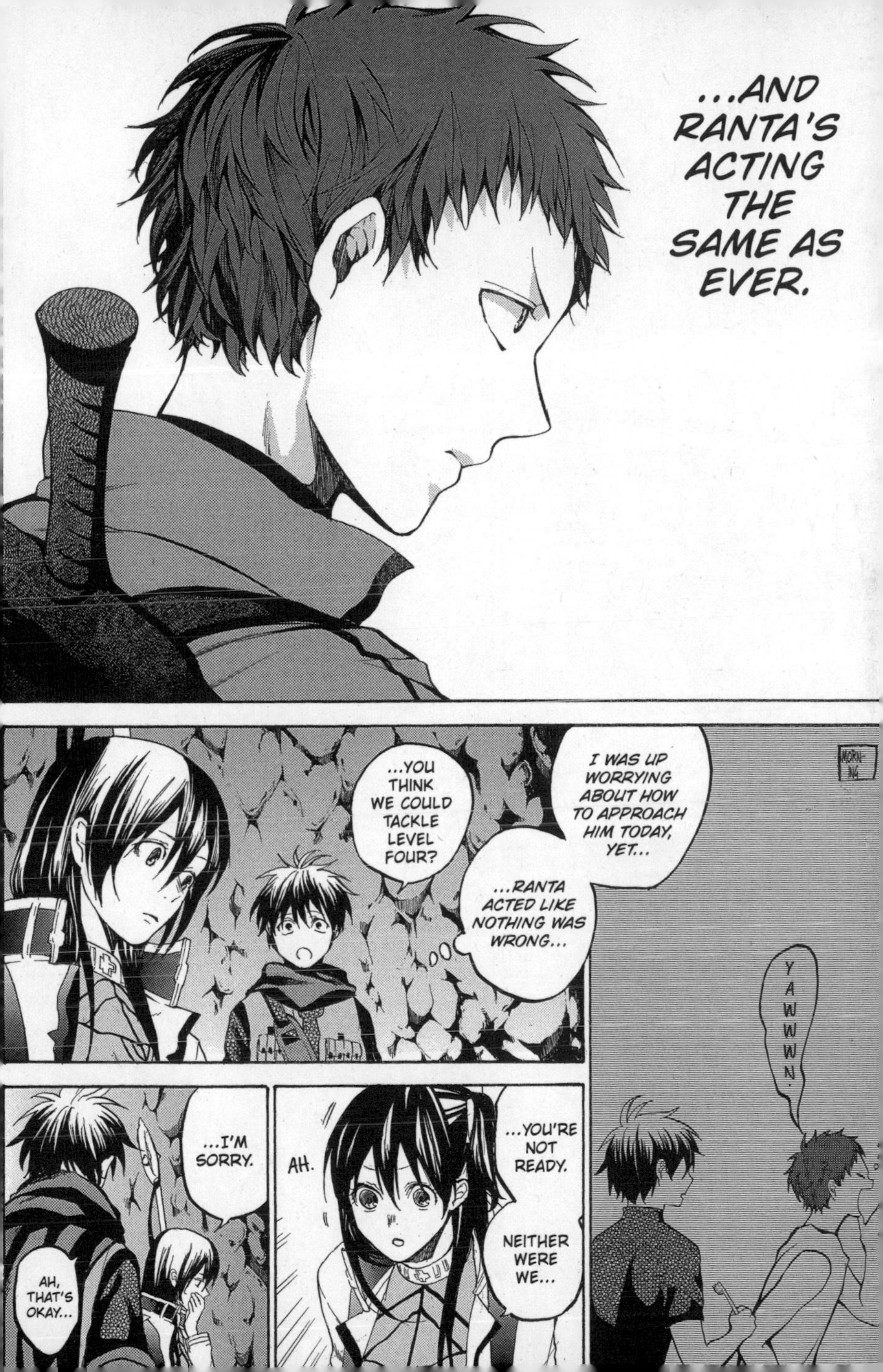

...AND RANTA'S ACTING THE SAME AS EVER.
MORNING
YAWWWN.
I WAS UP WORRYING ABOUT HOW TO APPROACH HIM TODAY, YET...
...RANTA ACTED LIKE NOTHING WAS WRONG...
...YOU THINK WE COULD TACKLE LEVEL FOUR?
...YOU'RE NOT READY.
NEITHER WERE WE...
AH.
...I'M SORRY.
AH, THAT'S OKAY...

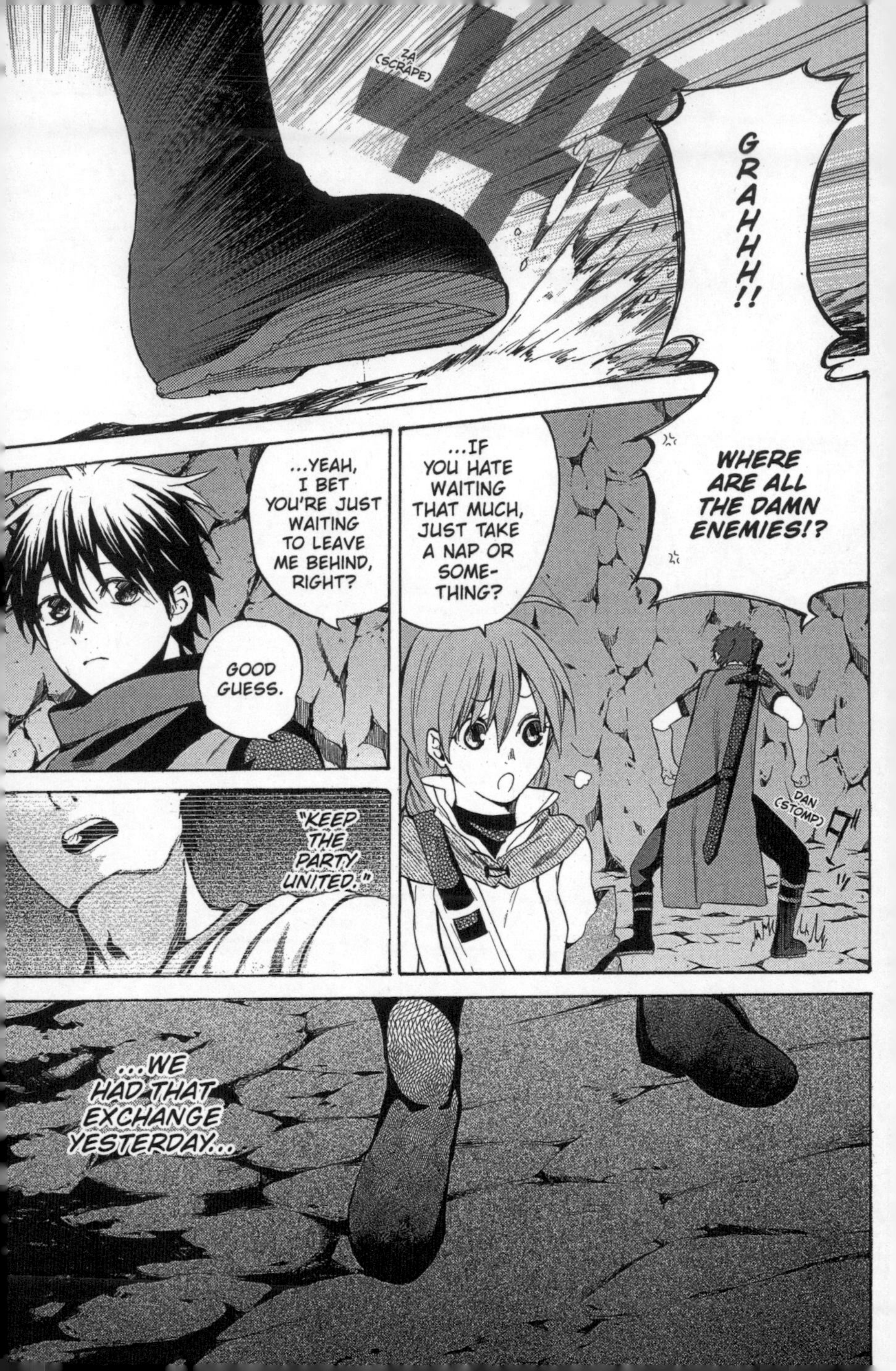
GRAHHH!!
ZA (SCRAPE)
WHERE ARE ALL THE DAMN ENEMIES!?
...IF YOU HATE WAITING THAT MUCH, JUST TAKE A NAP OR SOME-THING?
DAN (STOMP)
...YEAH, I BET YOU'RE JUST WAITING TO LEAVE ME BEHIND, RIGHT?
GOOD GUESS.
"KEEP THE PARTY UNITED."
...WE HAD THAT EXCHANGE YESTERDAY...

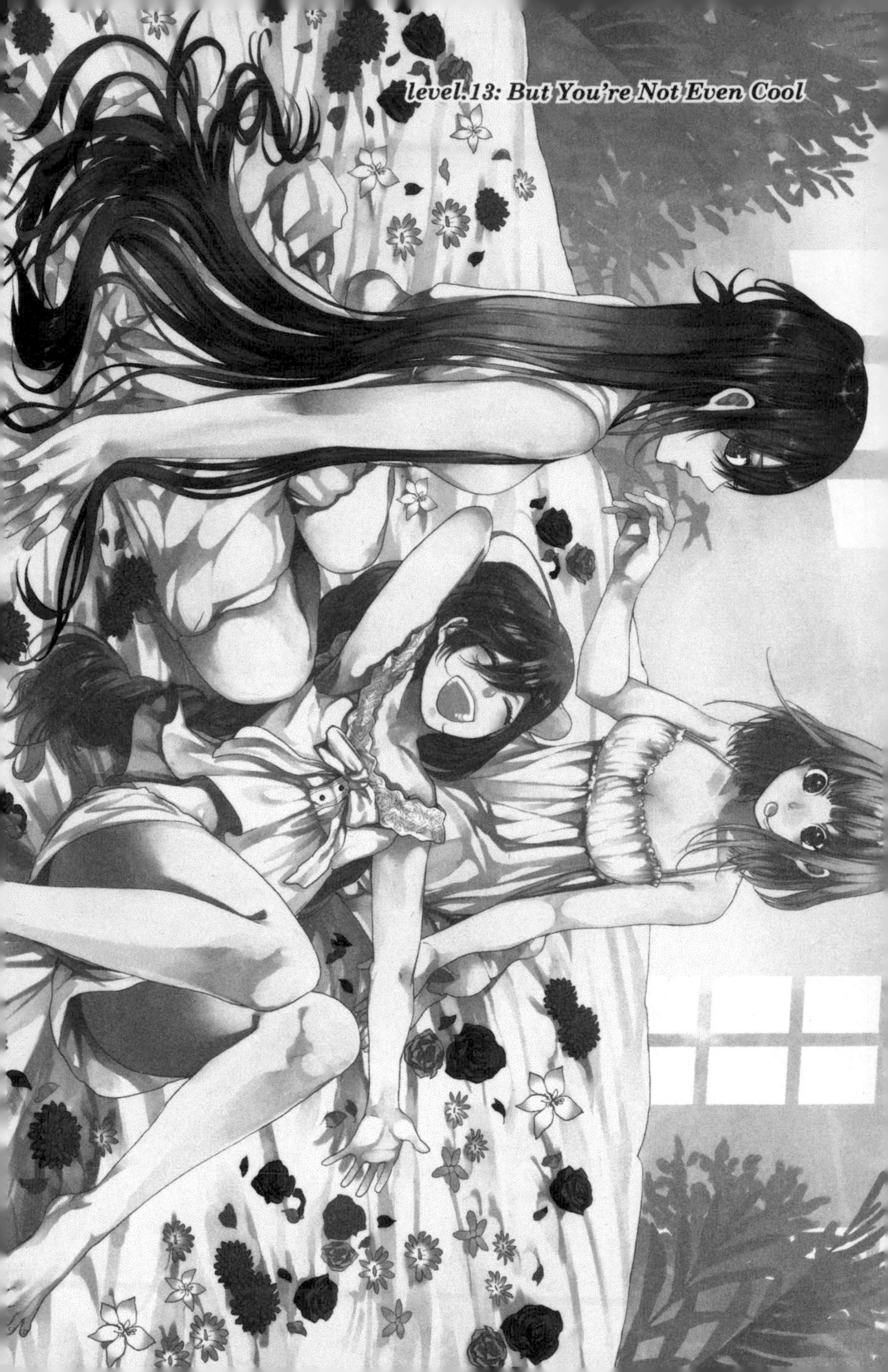
level.13: But You're Not Even Cool

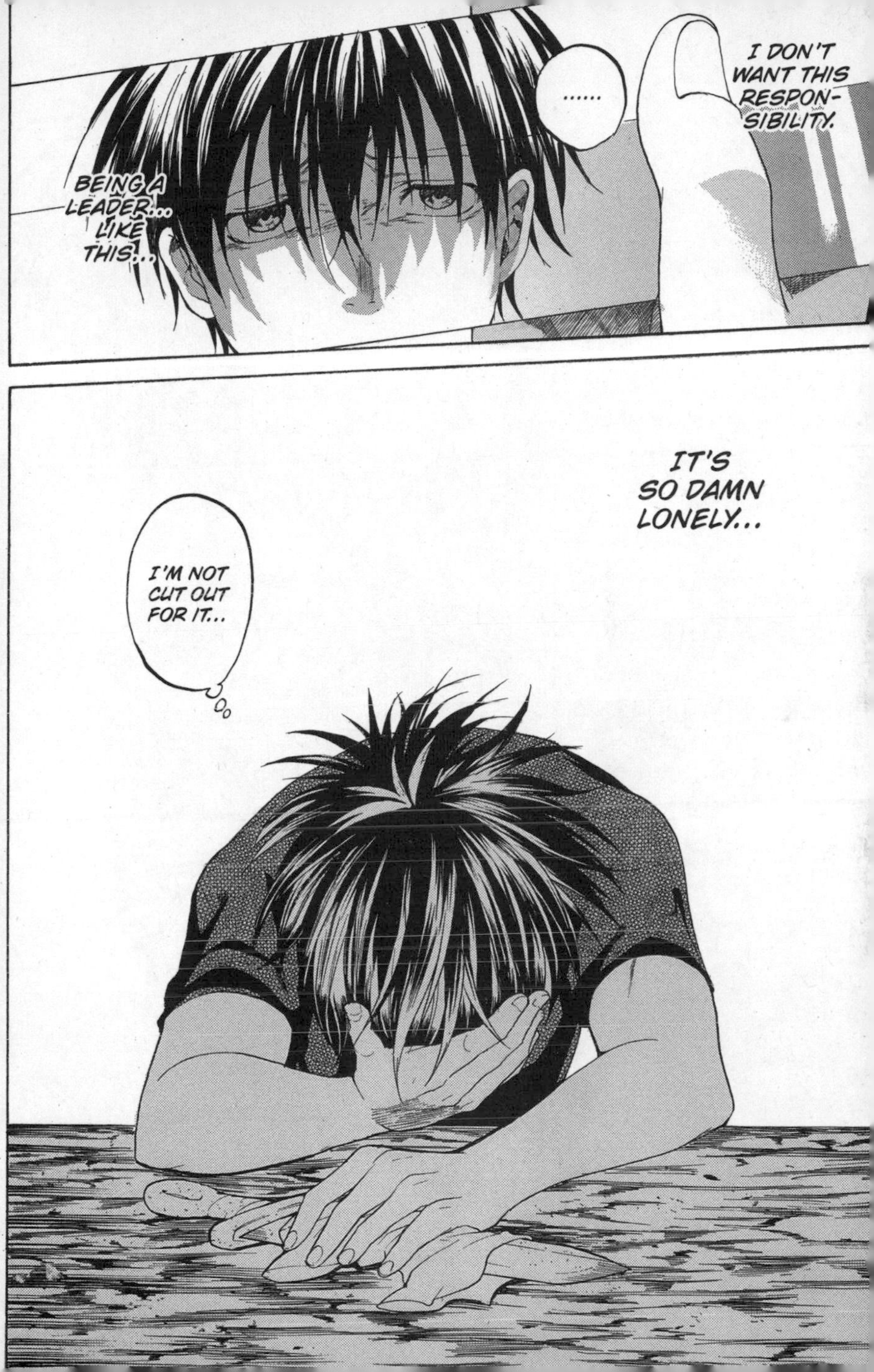
I DON'T WANT THIS RESPON-SIBILITY.
......
BEING A LEADER... LIKE THIS...
IT'S SO DAMN LONELY...
I'M NOT CUT OUT FOR IT...

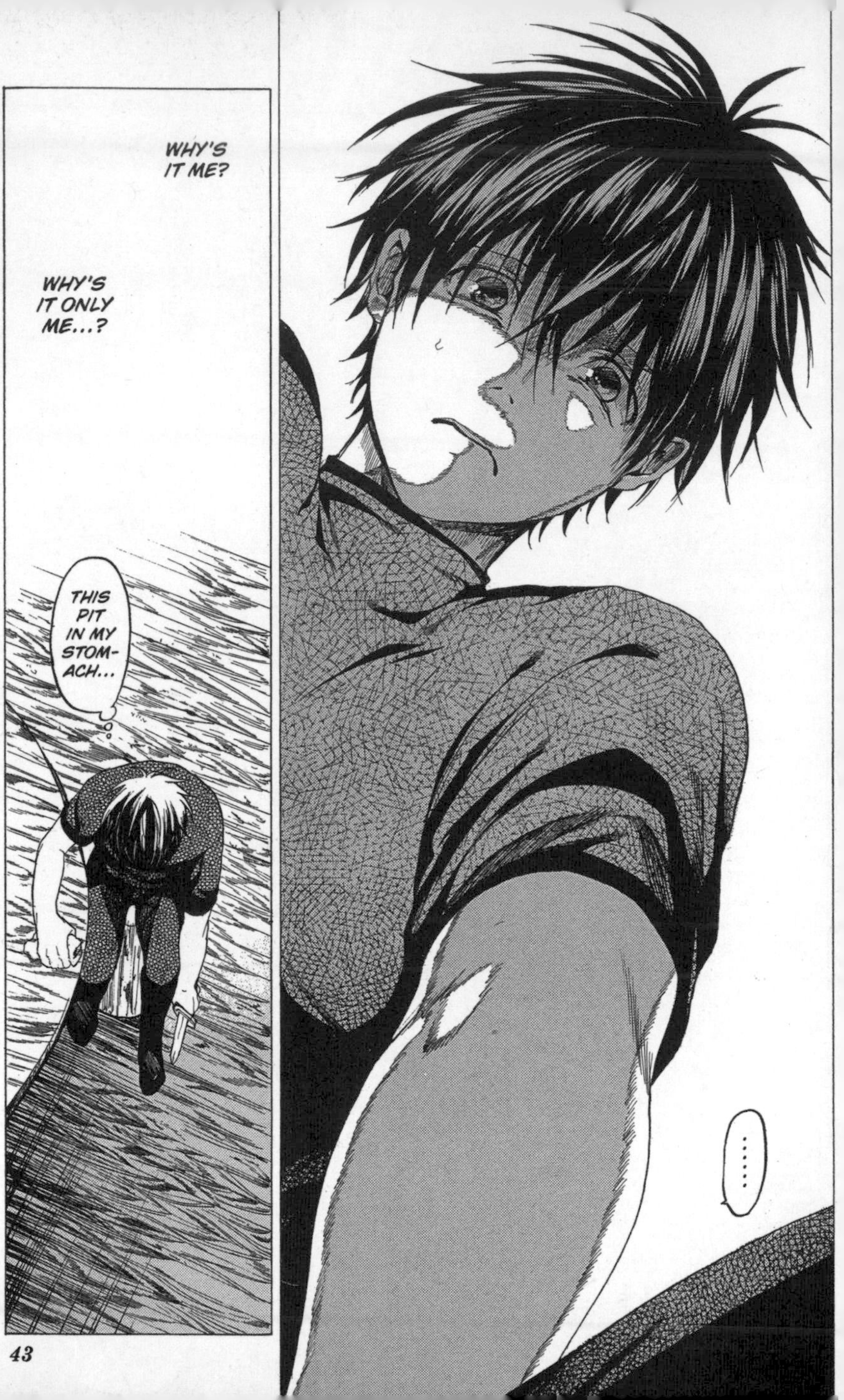
......
WHY'S IT ME?
WHY'S IT ONLY ME...?
THIS PIT IN MY STOMACH...

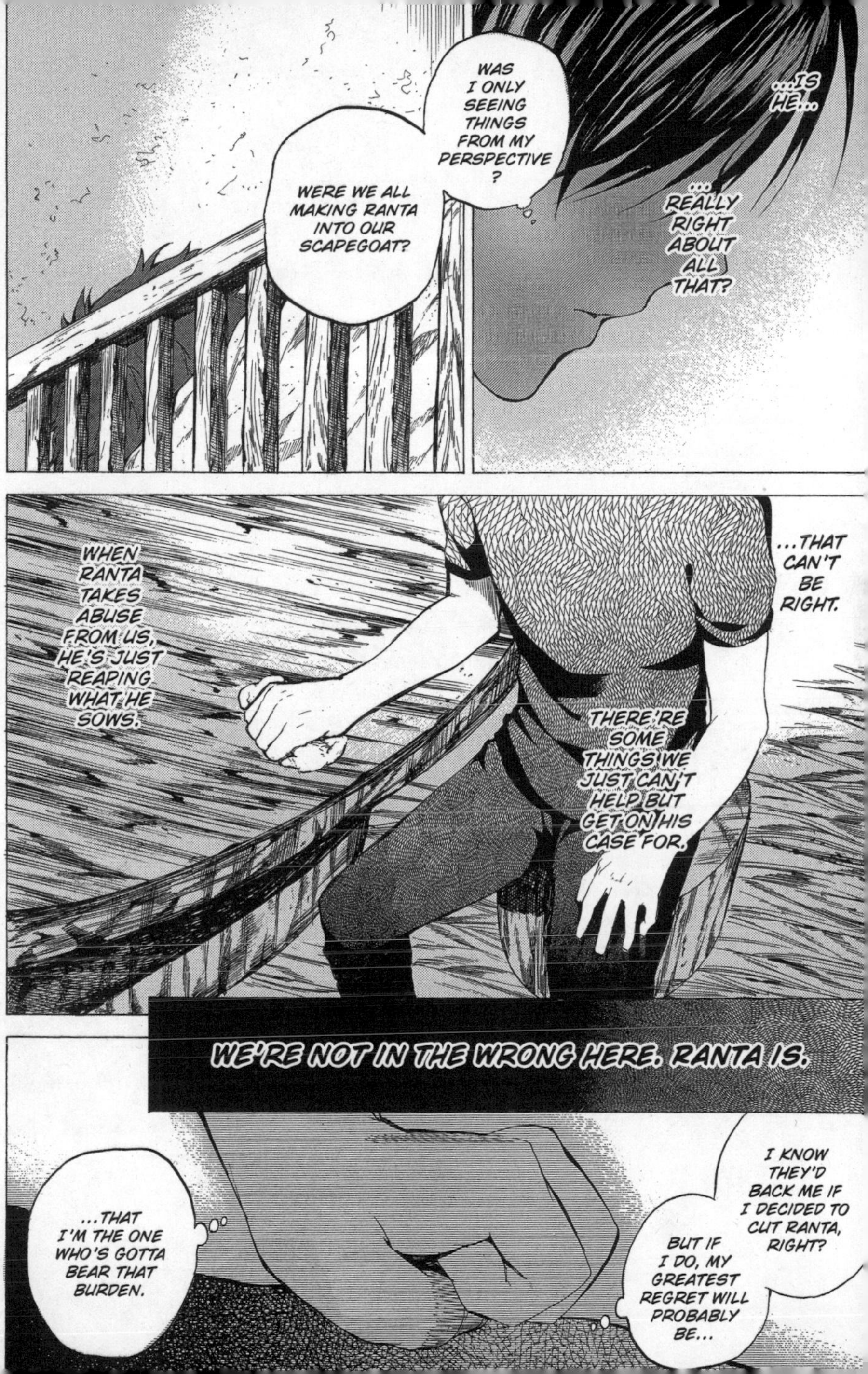
...IS HE...
...REALLY RIGHT ABOUT ALL THAT?
WAS I ONLY SEEING THINGS FROM MY PERSPECTIVE?
WERE WE ALL MAKING RANTA INTO OUR SCAPEGOAT?
...THAT CAN'T BE RIGHT.
WHEN RANTA TAKES ABUSE FROM US, HE'S JUST REAPING WHAT HE SOWS.
THERE'RE SOME THINGS WE JUST CAN'T HELP BUT GET ON HIS CASE FOR.
WE'RE NOT IN THE WRONG HERE. RANTA IS.
I KNOW THEY'D BACK ME IF I DECIDED TO CUT RANTA, RIGHT?
BUT IF I DO, MY GREATEST REGRET WILL PROBABLY BE...
...THAT I'M THE ONE WHO'S GOTTA BEAR THAT BURDEN.

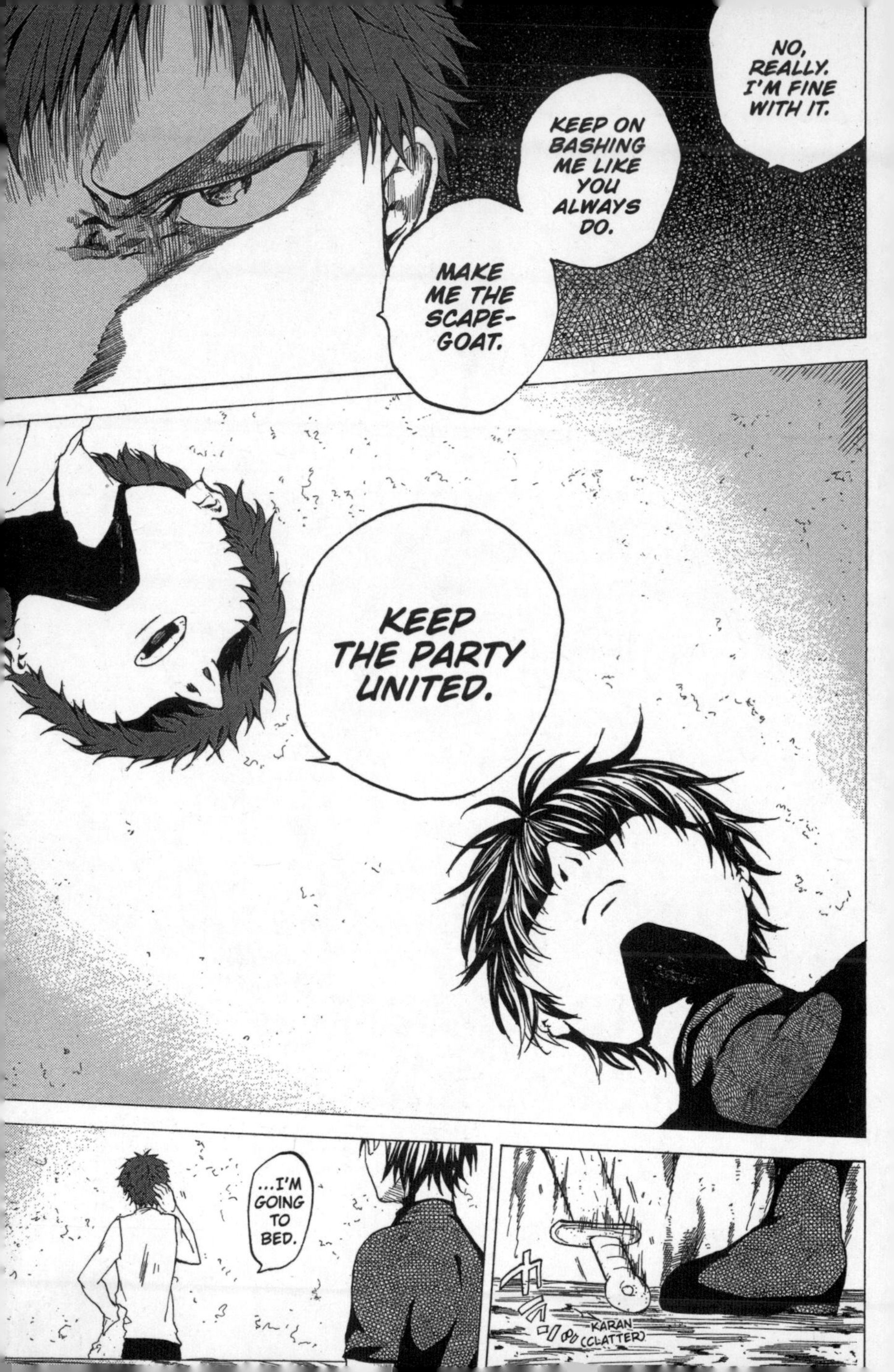
NO, REALLY. I'M FINE WITH IT.
KEEP ON BASHING ME LIKE YOU ALWAYS DO.
MAKE ME THE SCAPE-GOAT.
KEEP THE PARTY UNITED.
KARAN (CLATTER)
...I'M GOING TO BED.

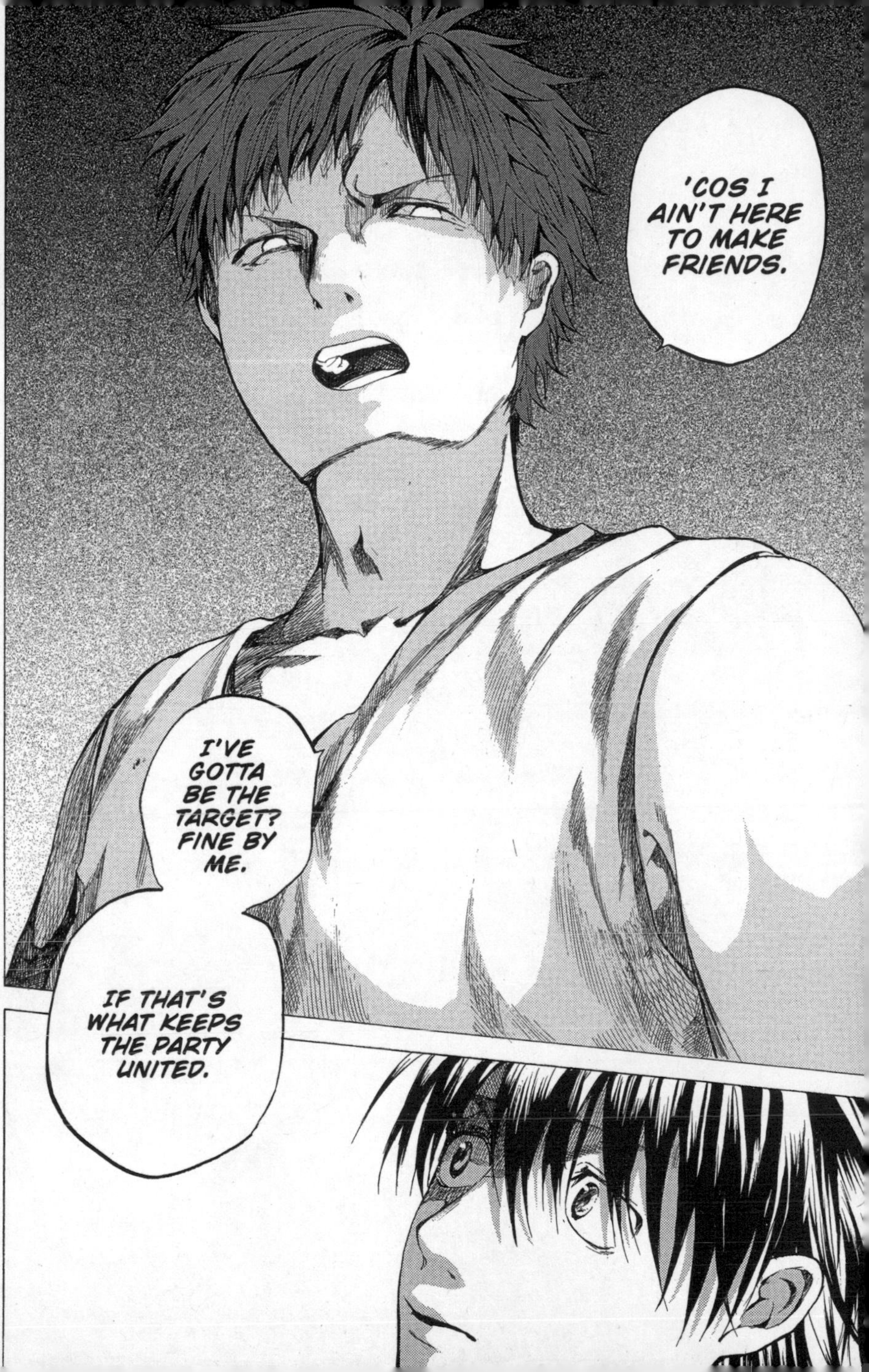
'COS I AIN'T HERE TO MAKE FRIENDS.
I'VE GOTTA BE THE TARGET? FINE BY ME.
IF THAT'S WHAT KEEPS THE PARTY UNITED.

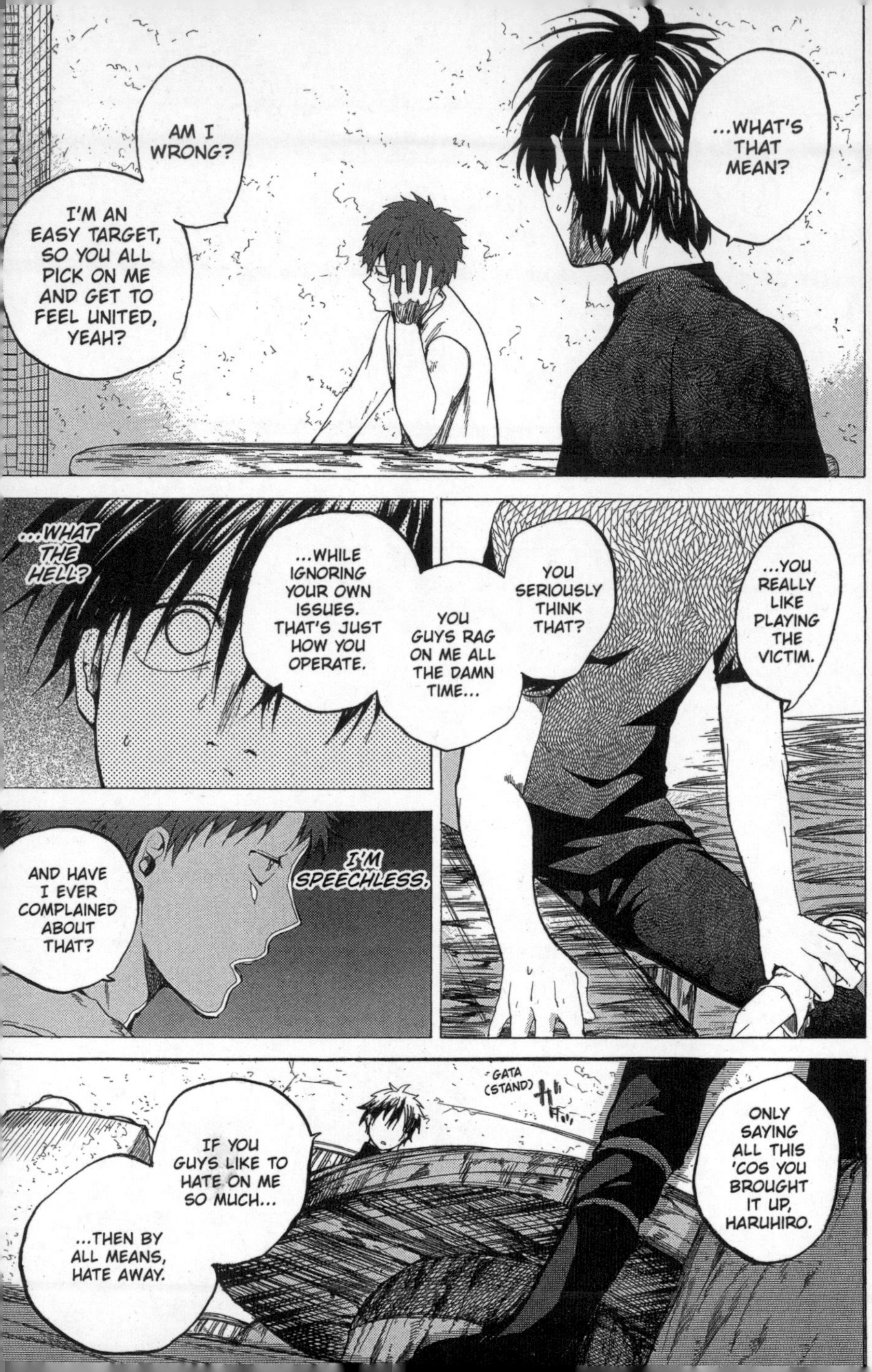
...WHAT'S THAT MEAN?
AM I WRONG?
I'M AN EASY TARGET, SO YOU ALL PICK ON ME AND GET TO FEEL UNITED, YEAH?
...YOU REALLY LIKE PLAYING THE VICTIM.
YOU SERIOUSLY THINK THAT?
YOU GUYS RAG ON ME ALL THE DAMN TIME...
...WHILE IGNORING YOUR OWN ISSUES. THAT'S JUST HOW YOU OPERATE.
...WHAT THE HELL?
I'M SPEECHLESS.
AND HAVE I EVER COMPLAINED ABOUT THAT?
GATA (STAND)
ONLY SAYING ALL THIS 'COS YOU BROUGHT IT UP, HARUHIRO.
IF YOU GUYS LIKE TO HATE ON ME SO MUCH...
...THEN BY ALL MEANS, HATE AWAY.

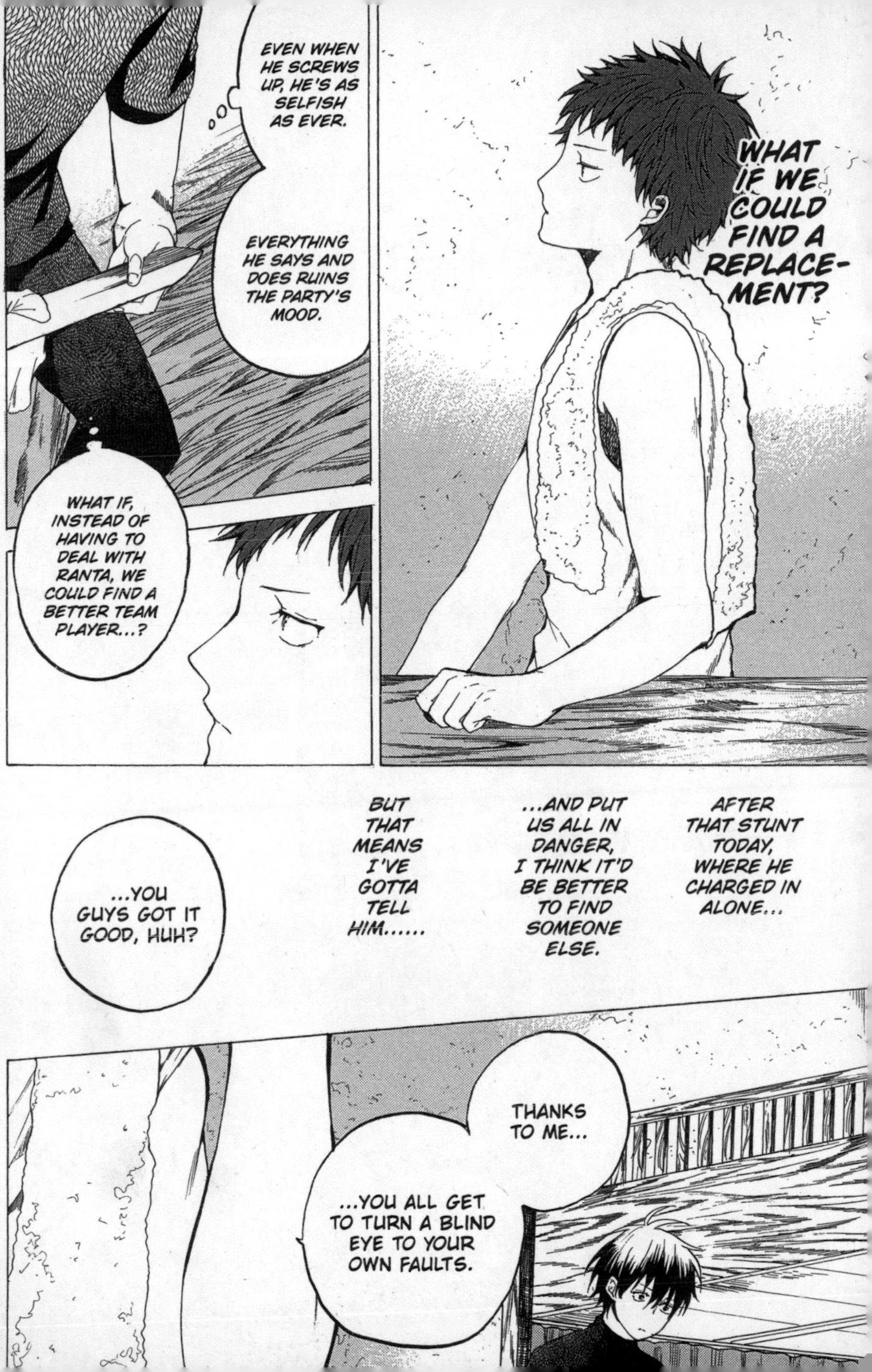
WHAT IF WE COULD FIND A REPLACE-MENT?
EVEN WHEN HE SCREWS UP, HE'S AS SELFISH AS EVER.
EVERYTHING HE SAYS AND DOES RUINS THE PARTY'S MOOD.
WHAT IF, INSTEAD OF HAVING TO DEAL WITH RANTA, WE COULD FIND A BETTER TEAM PLAYER...?
AFTER THAT STUNT TODAY, WHERE HE CHARGED IN ALONE...
...AND PUT US ALL IN DANGER, I THINK IT'D BE BETTER TO FIND SOMEONE ELSE.
BUT THAT MEANS I'VE GOTTA TELL HIM......
...YOU GUYS GOT IT GOOD, HUH?
THANKS TO ME...
...YOU ALL GET TO TURN A BLIND EYE TO YOUR OWN FAULTS.

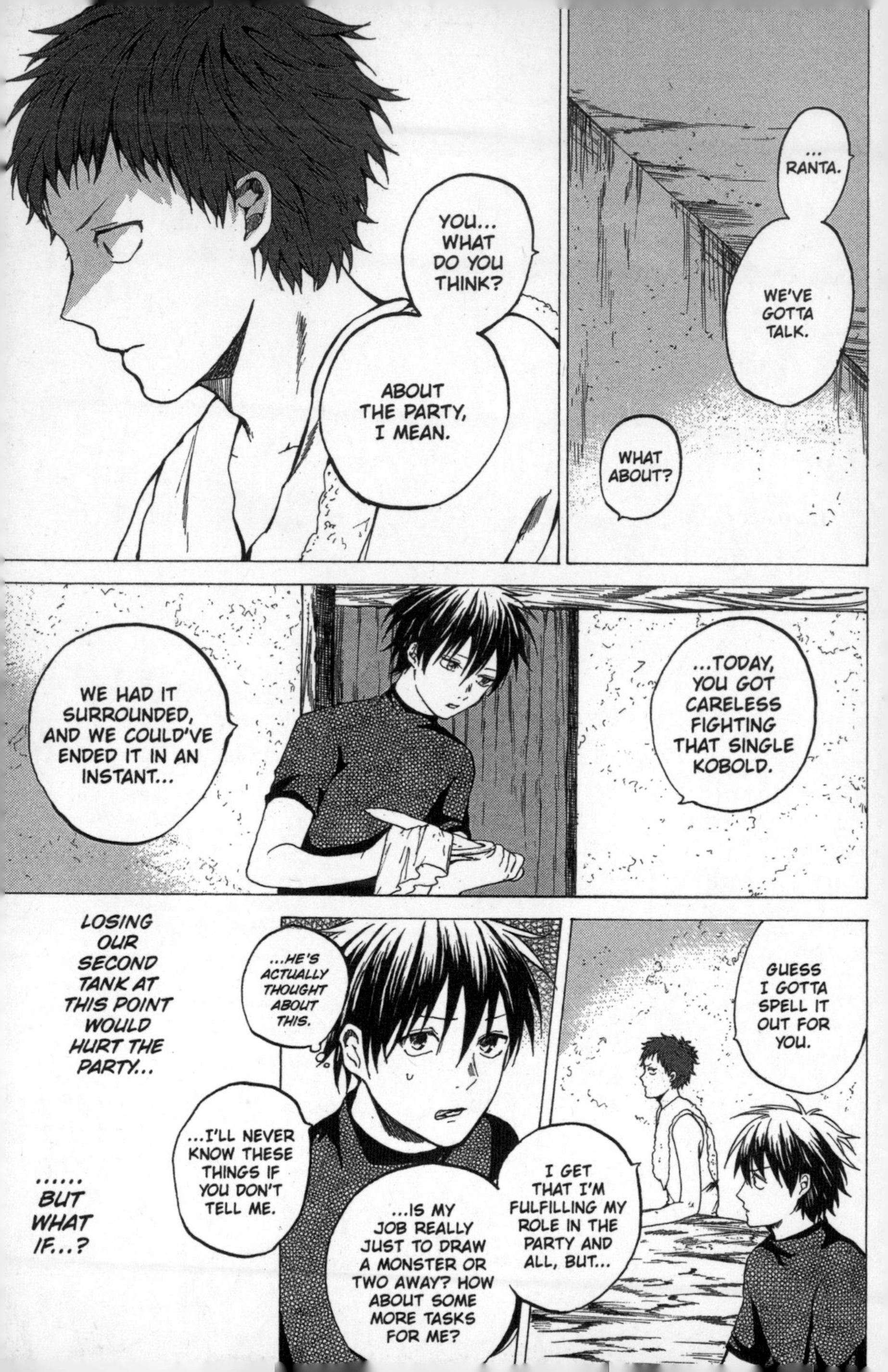
...RANTA.
WE'VE GOTTA TALK.
WHAT ABOUT?
YOU... WHAT DO YOU THINK?
ABOUT THE PARTY, I MEAN.
...TODAY, YOU GOT CARELESS FIGHTING THAT SINGLE KOBOLD.
WE HAD IT SURROUNDED, AND WE COULD'VE ENDED IT IN AN INSTANT...
GUESS I GOTTA SPELL IT OUT FOR YOU.
I GET THAT I'M FULFILLING MY ROLE IN THE PARTY AND ALL, BUT...
...IS MY JOB REALLY JUST TO DRAW A MONSTER OR TWO AWAY? HOW ABOUT SOME MORE TASKS FOR ME?
...HE'S ACTUALLY THOUGHT ABOUT THIS.
...I'LL NEVER KNOW THESE THINGS IF YOU DON'T TELL ME.
LOSING OUR SECOND TANK AT THIS POINT WOULD HURT THE PARTY...
...... BUT WHAT IF...?

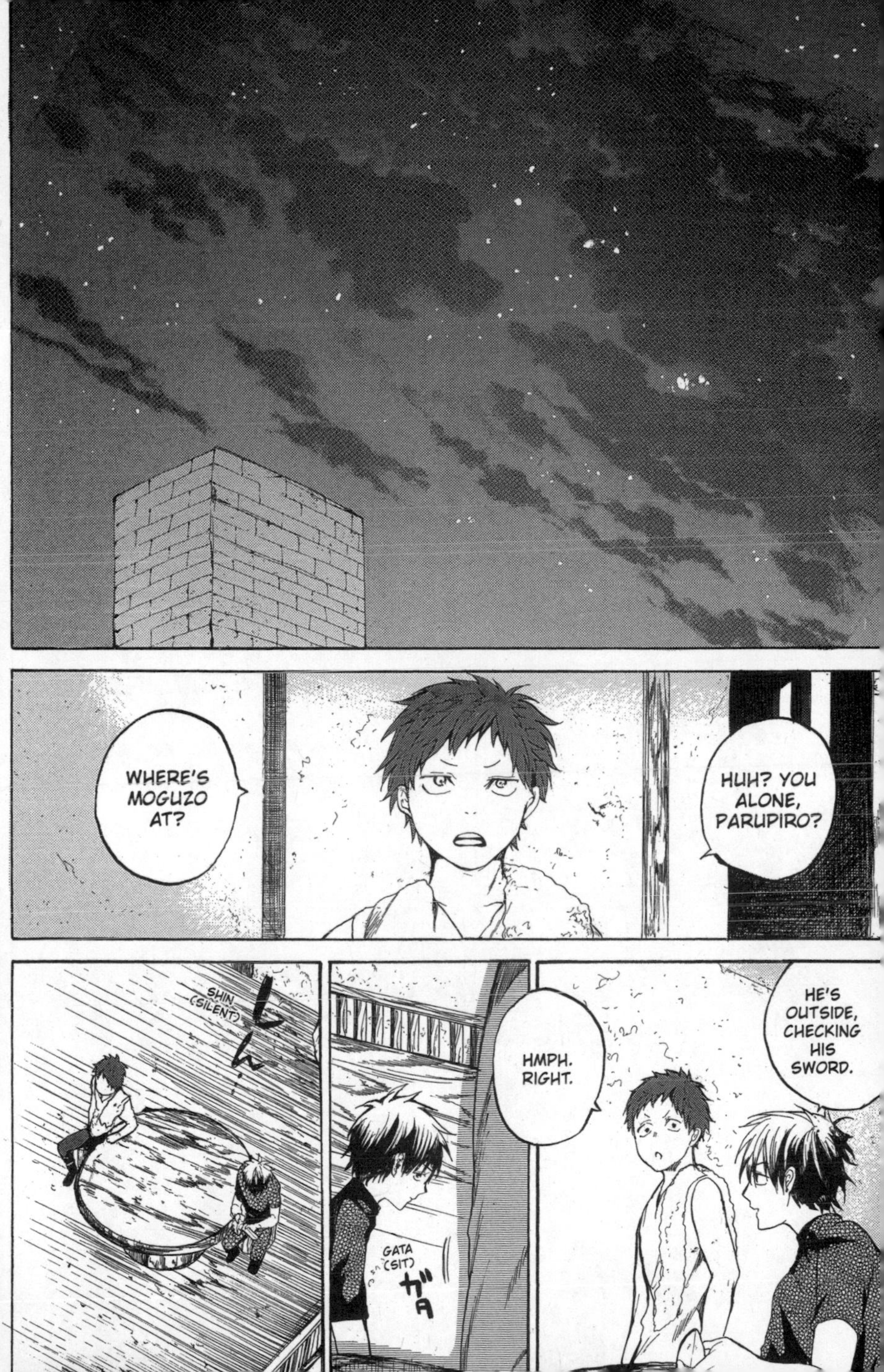
HUH? YOU ALONE, PARUPIRO?
WHERE'S MOGUZO AT?
HE'S OUTSIDE, CHECKING HIS SWORD.
HMPH. RIGHT.
GATA (SIT)
ガタ
SHIN (SILENT)
しん…

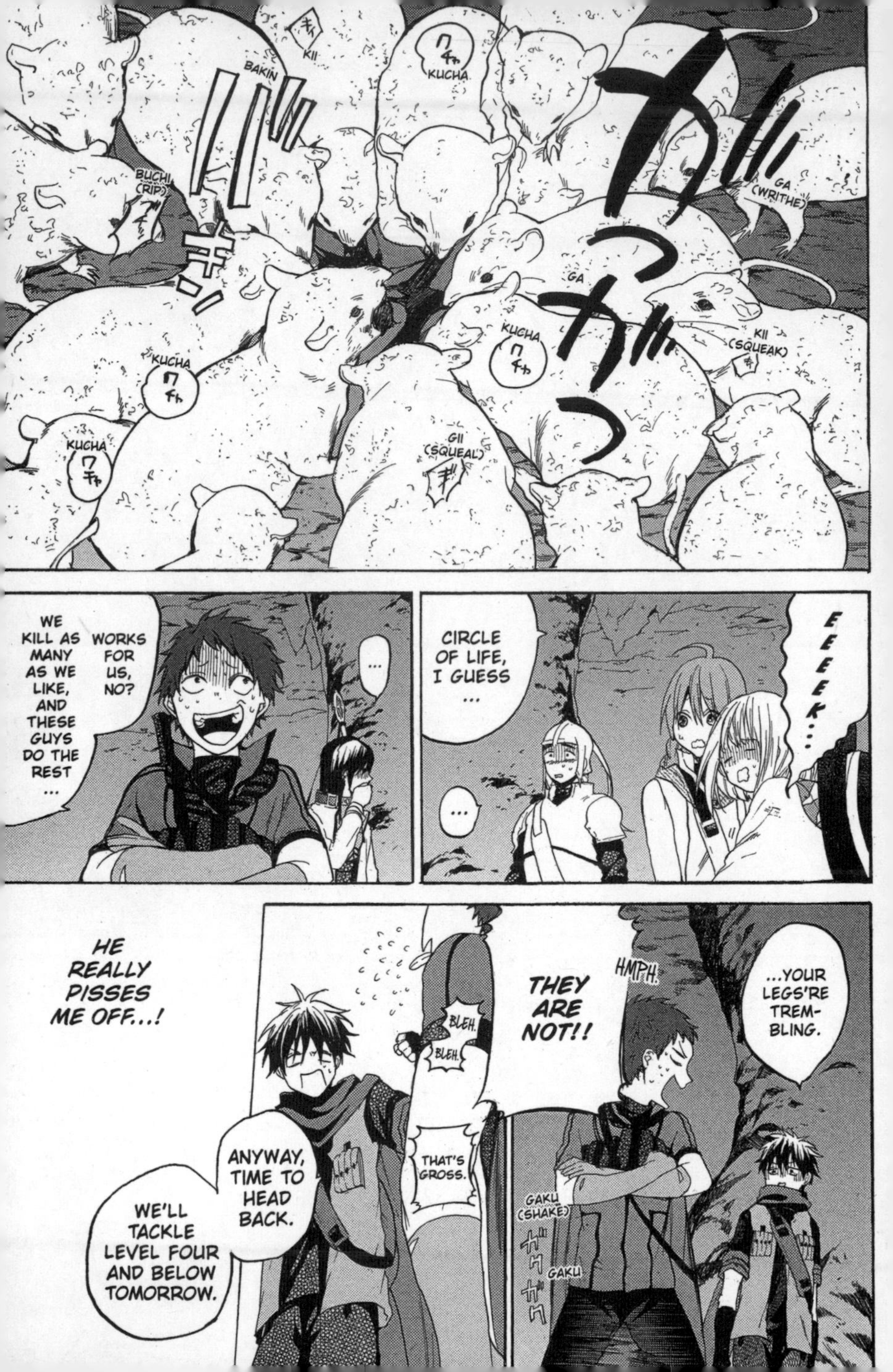
KII
KUCHA
BAKIN
BUCHI (RIP)
GA (WRITHE)
GA
KUCHA
KII (SQUEAK)
KUCHA
KUCHA
GII (SQUEAL)
CIRCLE OF LIFE, I GUESS ...
EEEEEK...
...
WE KILL AS MANY AS WE LIKE, AND THESE GUYS DO THE REST ...
WORKS FOR US, NO?
...
...YOUR LEGS'RE TREM-BLING.
HMPH.
THEY ARE NOT!!
BLEH.
BLEH.
THAT'S GROSS.
HE REALLY PISSES ME OFF...!
ANYWAY, TIME TO HEAD BACK.
WE'LL TACKLE LEVEL FOUR AND BELOW TOMORROW.
GAKU (SHAKE)
GAKU

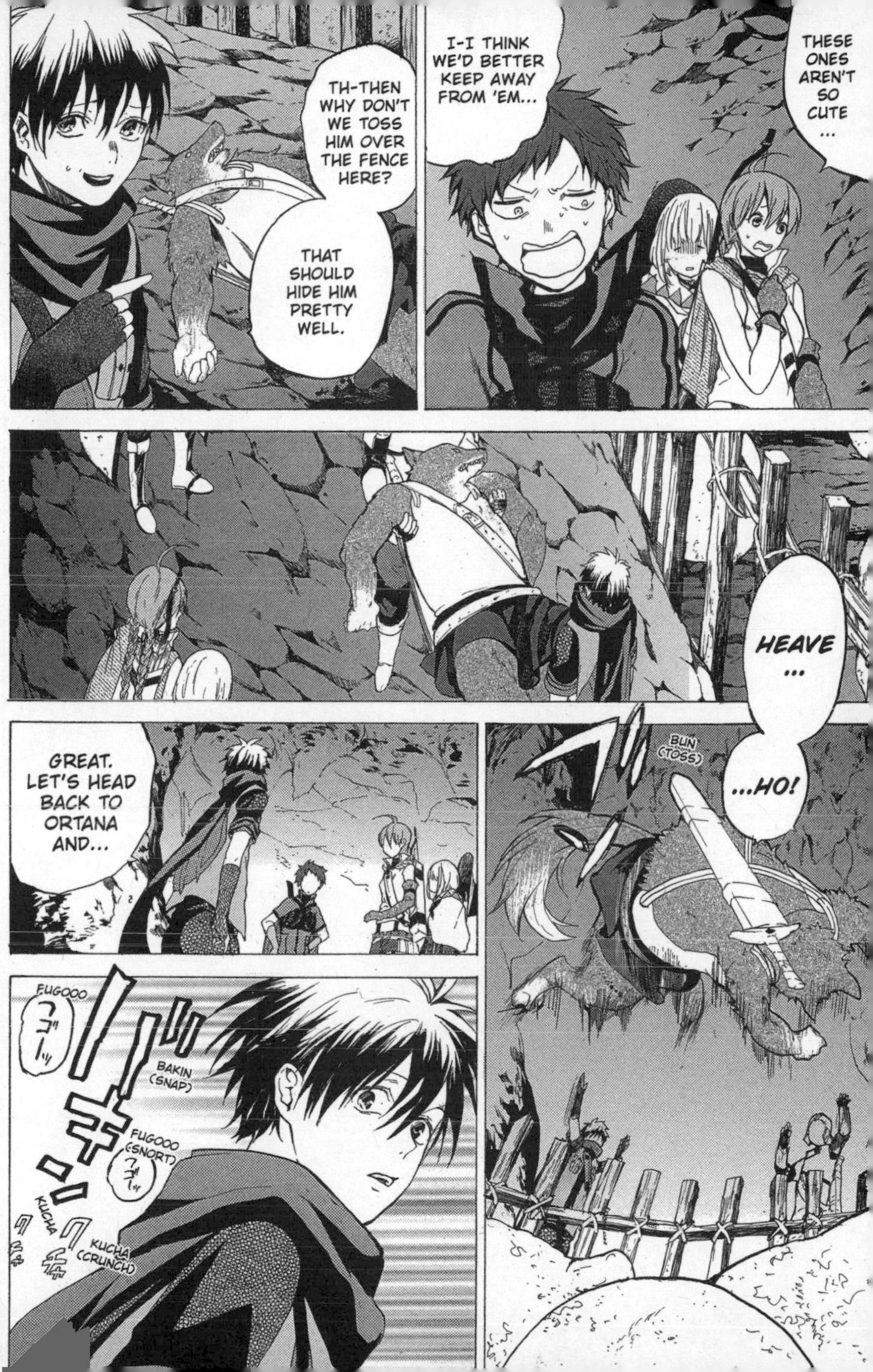

THESE ONES AREN'T SO CUTE ...
I-I THINK WE'D BETTER KEEP AWAY FROM 'EM...
TH-THEN WHY DON'T WE TOSS HIM OVER THE FENCE HERE?
THAT SHOULD HIDE HIM PRETTY WELL.
HEAVE ...
...HO!
BUN (TOSS)
GREAT. LET'S HEAD BACK TO ORTANA AND...
FUGOOO
BAKIN (SNAP)
FUGOOO (SNORT)
KUCHA
KUCHA (CRUNCH)

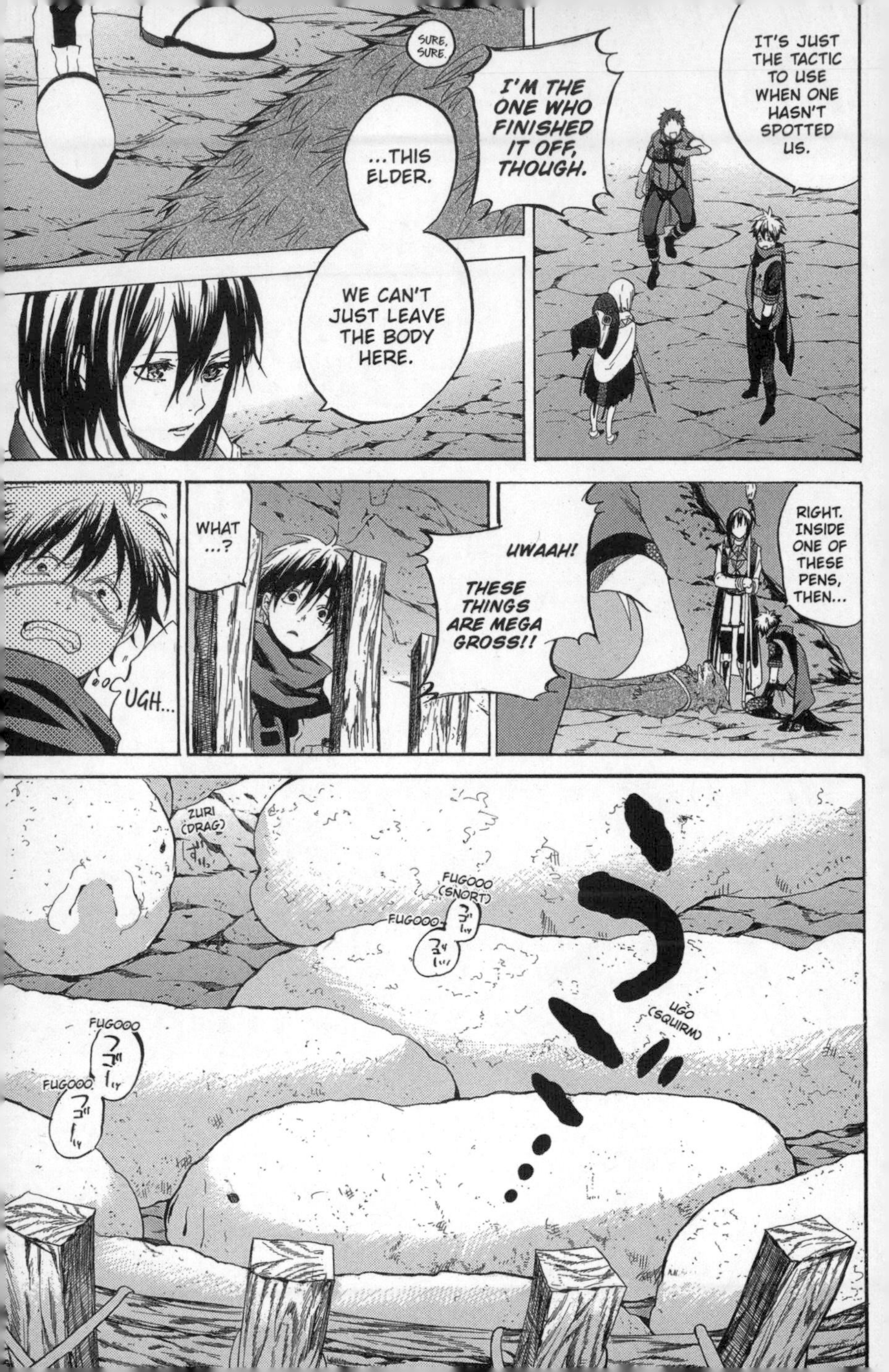
IT'S JUST THE TACTIC TO USE WHEN ONE HASN'T SPOTTED US.
I'M THE ONE WHO FINISHED IT OFF, THOUGH.
SURE, SURE.
...THIS ELDER.
WE CAN'T JUST LEAVE THE BODY HERE.
RIGHT. INSIDE ONE OF THESE PENS, THEN...
UWAAH!
THESE THINGS ARE MEGA GROSS!!
WHAT ...?
UGH...
ZURI (DRAG)
FUGOOO (SNORT)
FUGOOO
UGO (SQUIRM)
FUGOOO
FUGOOO

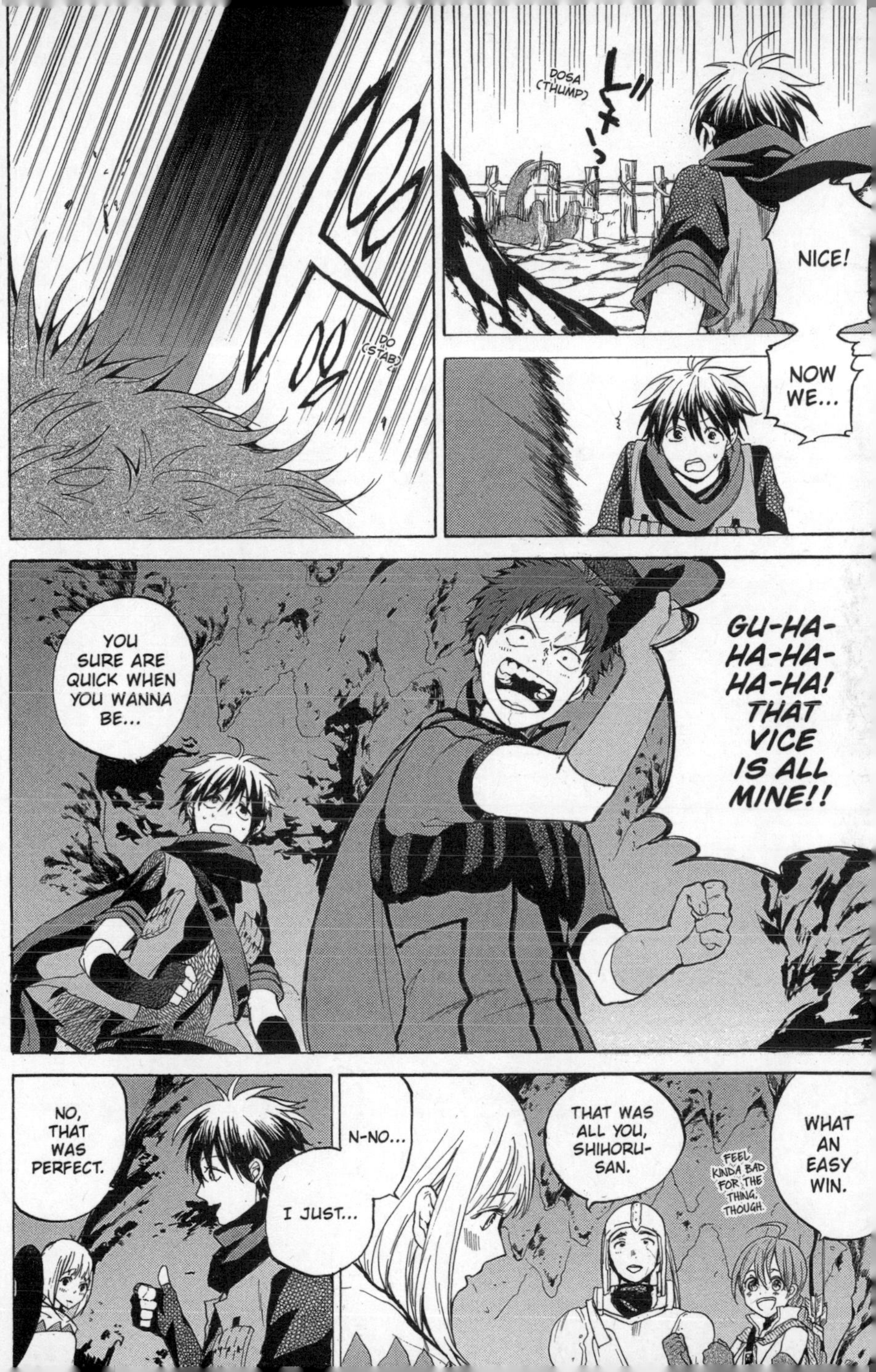
DOSA (THUMP)
NICE!
NOW WE...
DO (STAB)
GU-HA-HA-HA-HA-HA! THAT VICE IS ALL MINE!!
YOU SURE ARE QUICK WHEN YOU WANNA BE...
WHAT AN EASY WIN.
FEEL KINDA BAD FOR THE THING, THOUGH.
THAT WAS ALL YOU, SHIHORU-SAN.
N-NO...
I JUST...
NO, THAT WAS PERFECT.

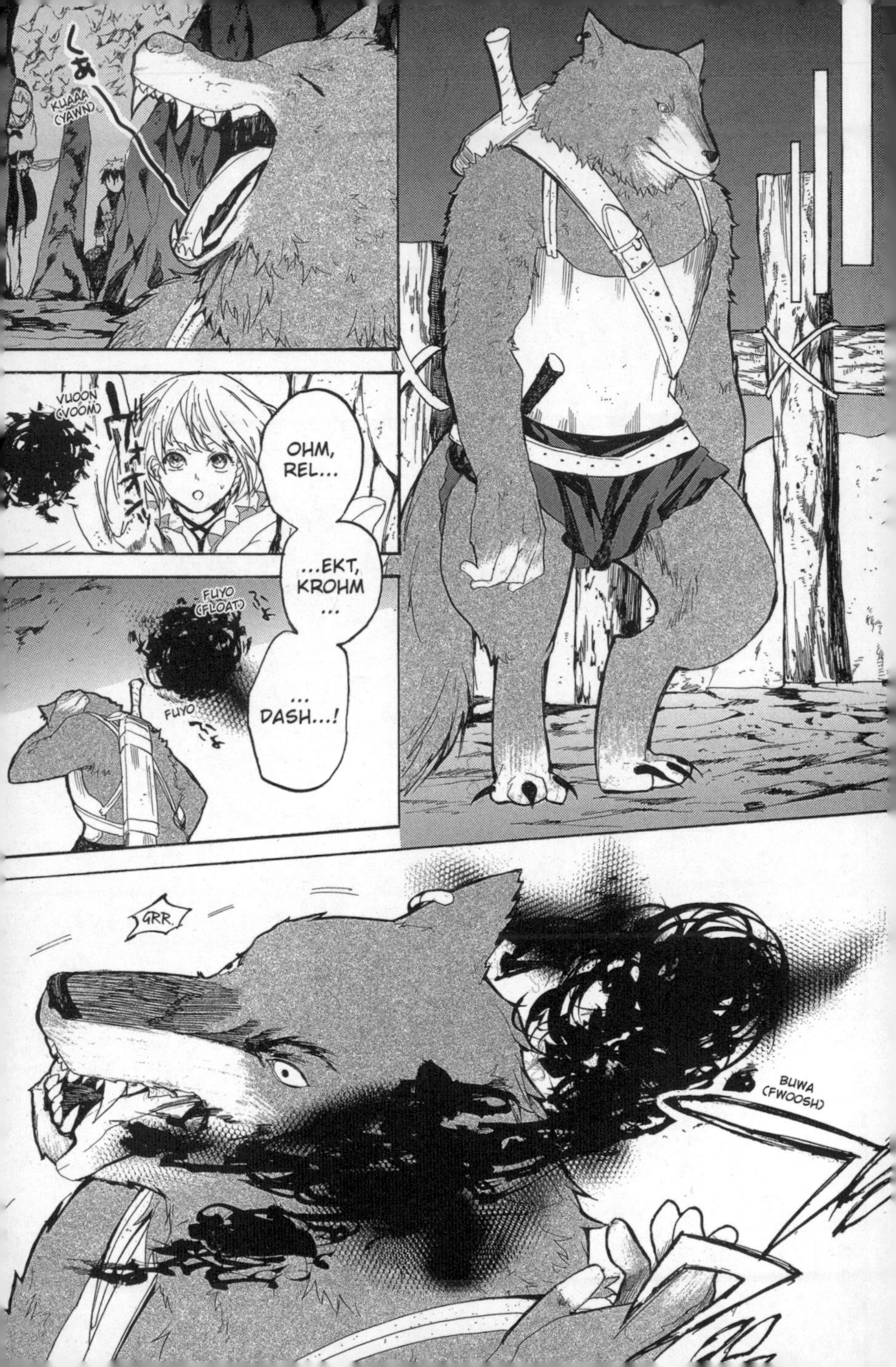
くあ
KUAAA (YAWN)
VUOON (VOOM)
ヴォオン
OHM, REL...
...EKT, KROHM...
... DASH...!
FUYO (FLOAT)
ふよ
FUYO
ふよ
GRR.
BUWA (FWOOSH)

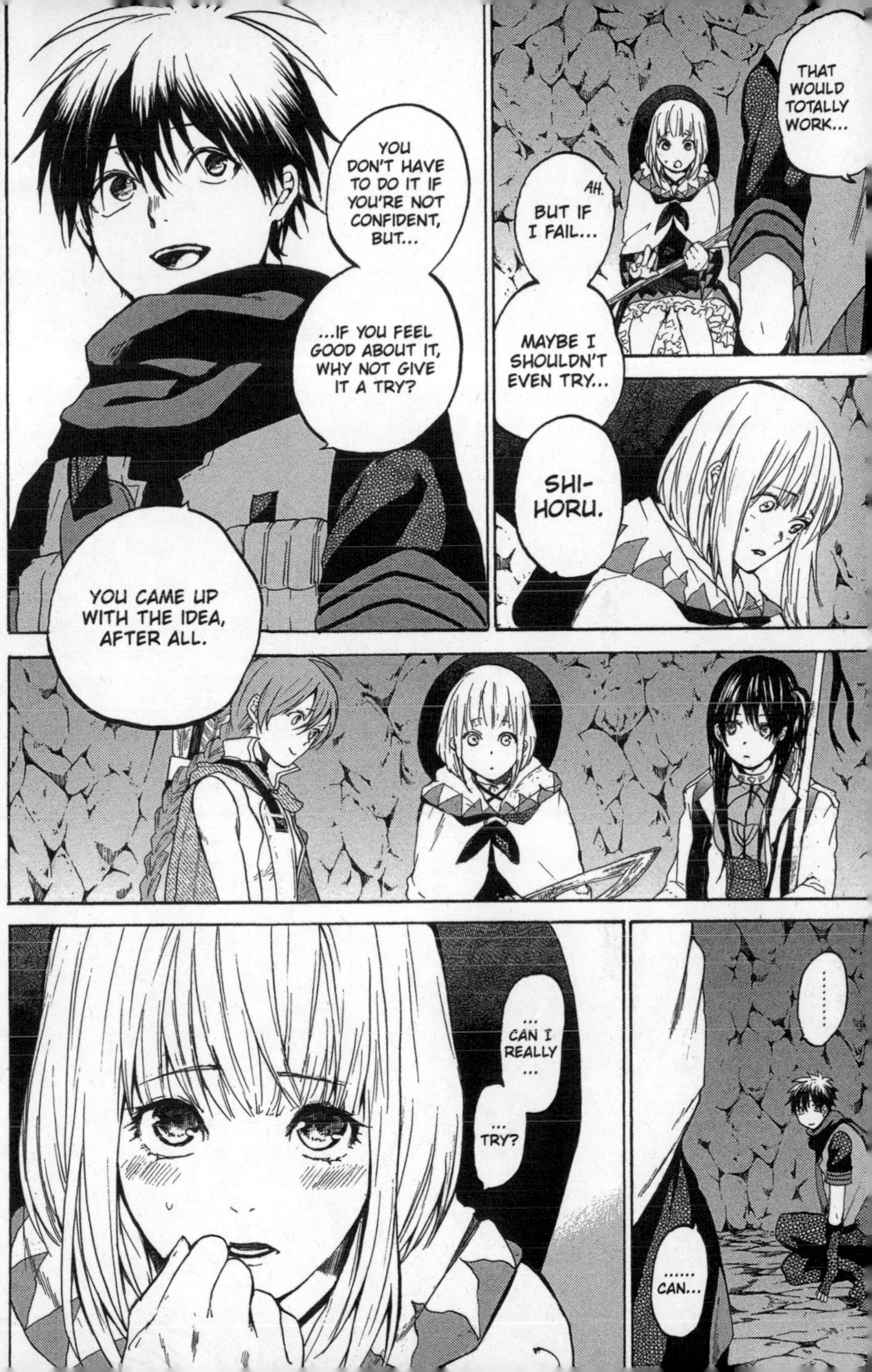
THAT WOULD TOTALLY WORK...
AH.
BUT IF I FAIL...
MAYBE I SHOULDN'T EVEN TRY...
YOU DON'T HAVE TO DO IT IF YOU'RE NOT CONFIDENT, BUT...
...IF YOU FEEL GOOD ABOUT IT, WHY NOT GIVE IT A TRY?
SHI-HORU.
YOU CAME UP WITH THE IDEA, AFTER ALL.
....
......CAN...
...CAN I REALLY...
...TRY?

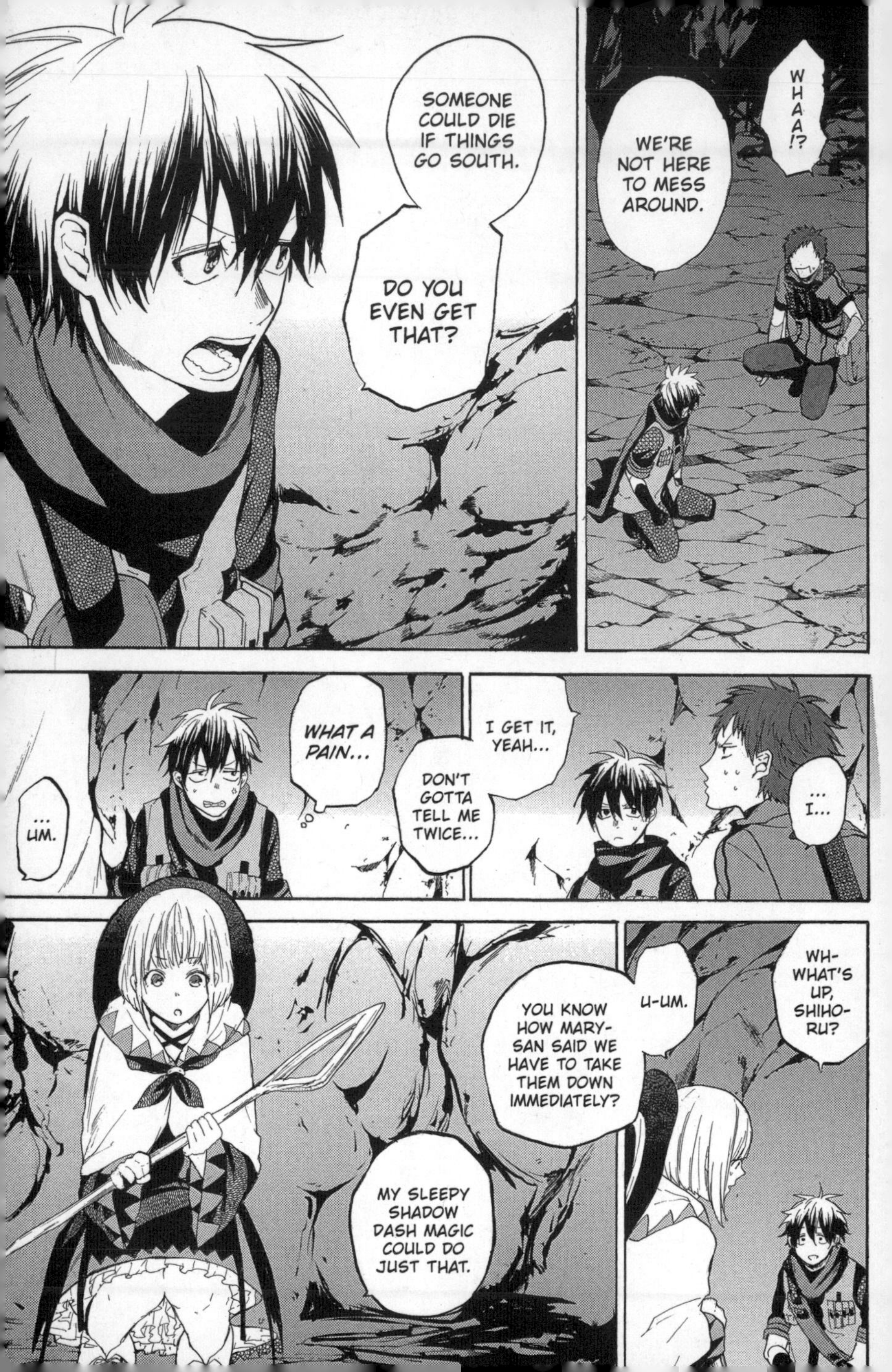
WHAA!?
WE'RE NOT HERE TO MESS AROUND.
SOMEONE COULD DIE IF THINGS GO SOUTH.
DO YOU EVEN GET THAT?
... I...
I GET IT, YEAH...
DON'T GOTTA TELL ME TWICE...
WHAT A PAIN...
... UM.
WH-WHAT'S UP, SHIHO-RU?
U-UM.
YOU KNOW HOW MARY-SAN SAID WE HAVE TO TAKE THEM DOWN IMMEDIATELY?
MY SLEEPY SHADOW DASH MAGIC COULD DO JUST THAT.

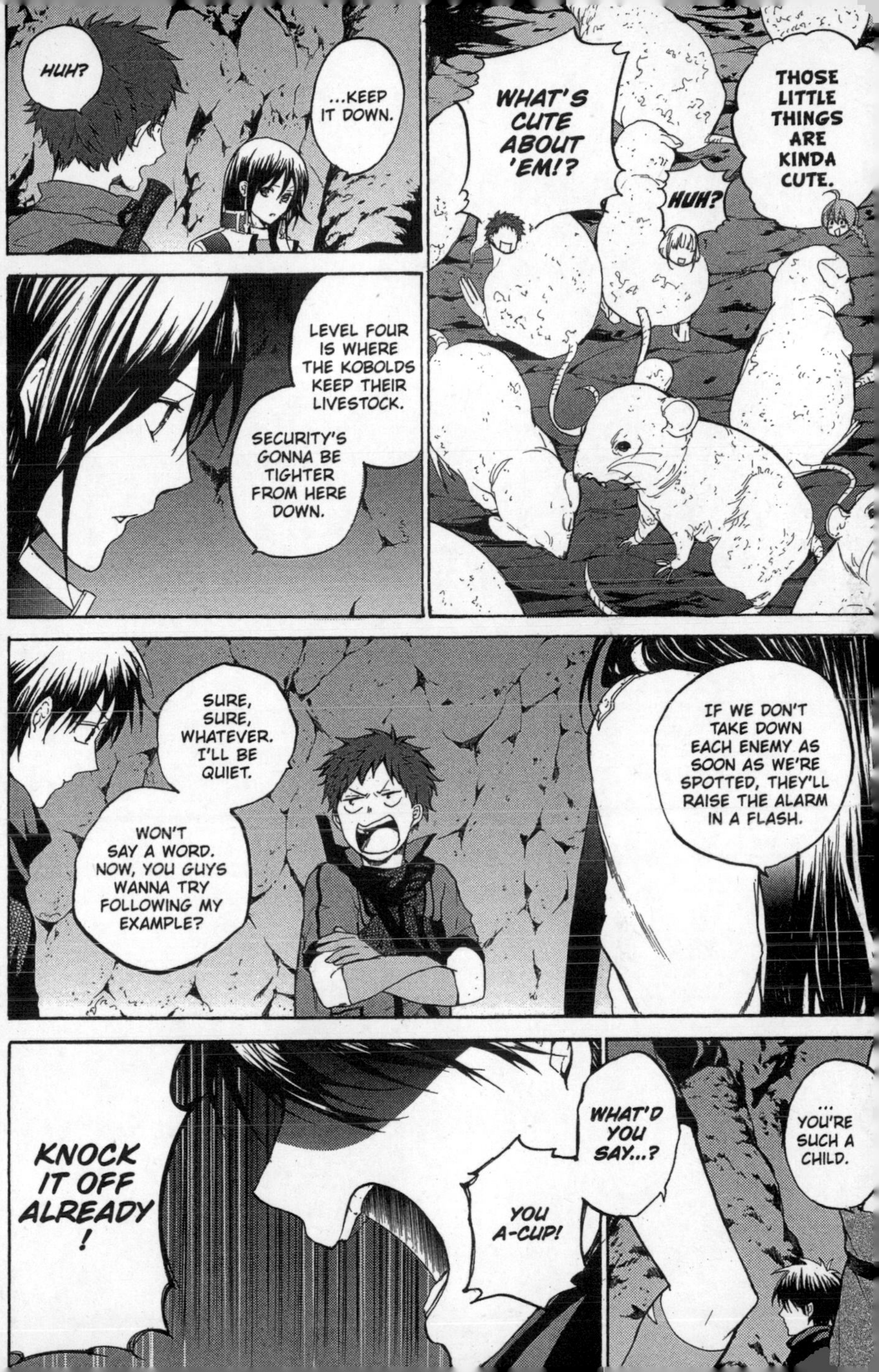
THOSE LITTLE THINGS ARE KINDA CUTE.
HUH?
WHAT'S CUTE ABOUT 'EM!?
...KEEP IT DOWN.
HUH?
LEVEL FOUR IS WHERE THE KOBOLDS KEEP THEIR LIVESTOCK.
SECURITY'S GONNA BE TIGHTER FROM HERE DOWN.
IF WE DON'T TAKE DOWN EACH ENEMY AS SOON AS WE'RE SPOTTED, THEY'LL RAISE THE ALARM IN A FLASH.
SURE, SURE, WHATEVER. I'LL BE QUIET.
WON'T SAY A WORD. NOW, YOU GUYS WANNA TRY FOLLOWING MY EXAMPLE?
...YOU'RE SUCH A CHILD.
WHAT'D YOU SAY...?
YOU A-CUP!
KNOCK IT OFF ALREADY!

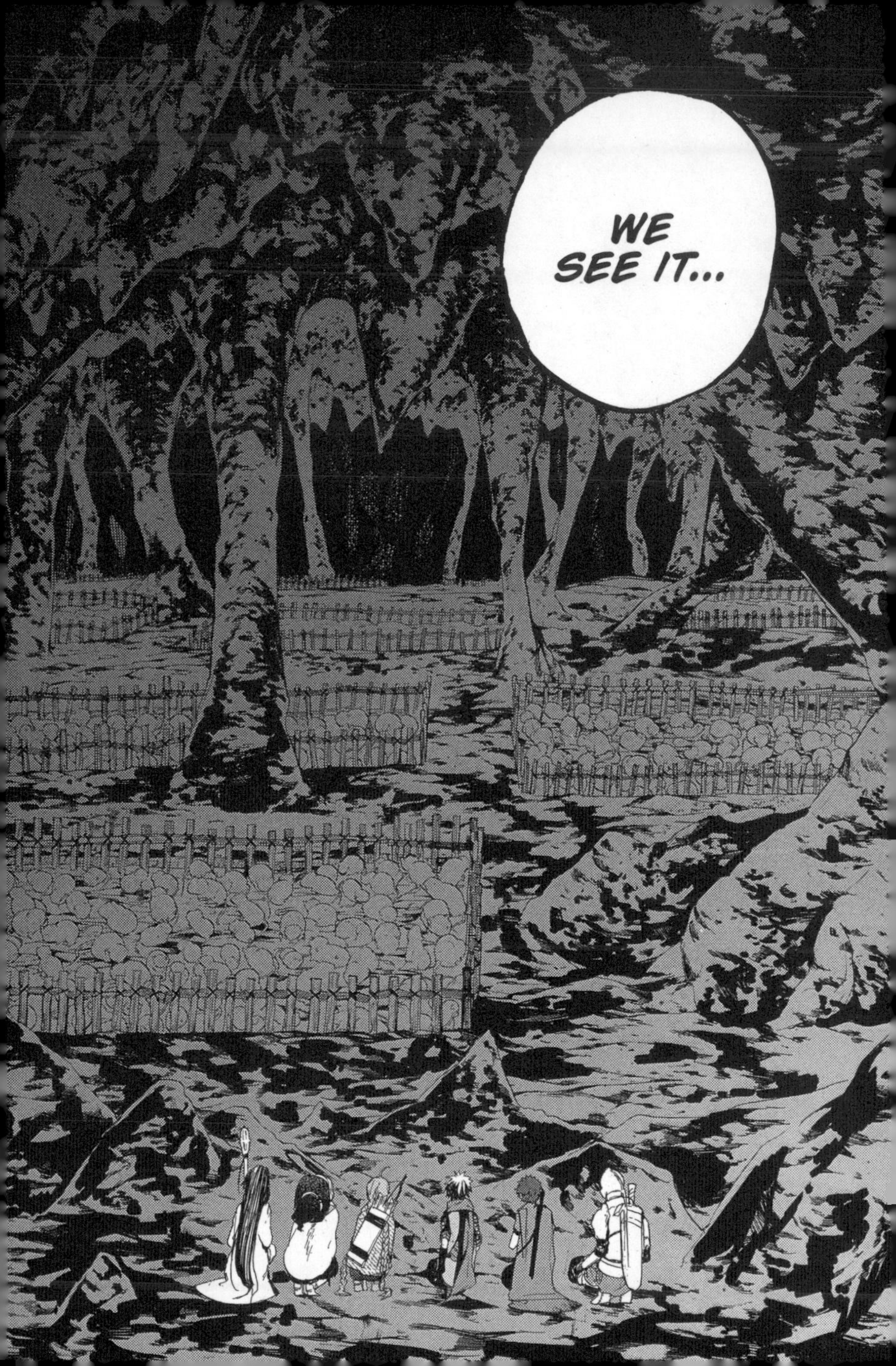
WE SEE IT...

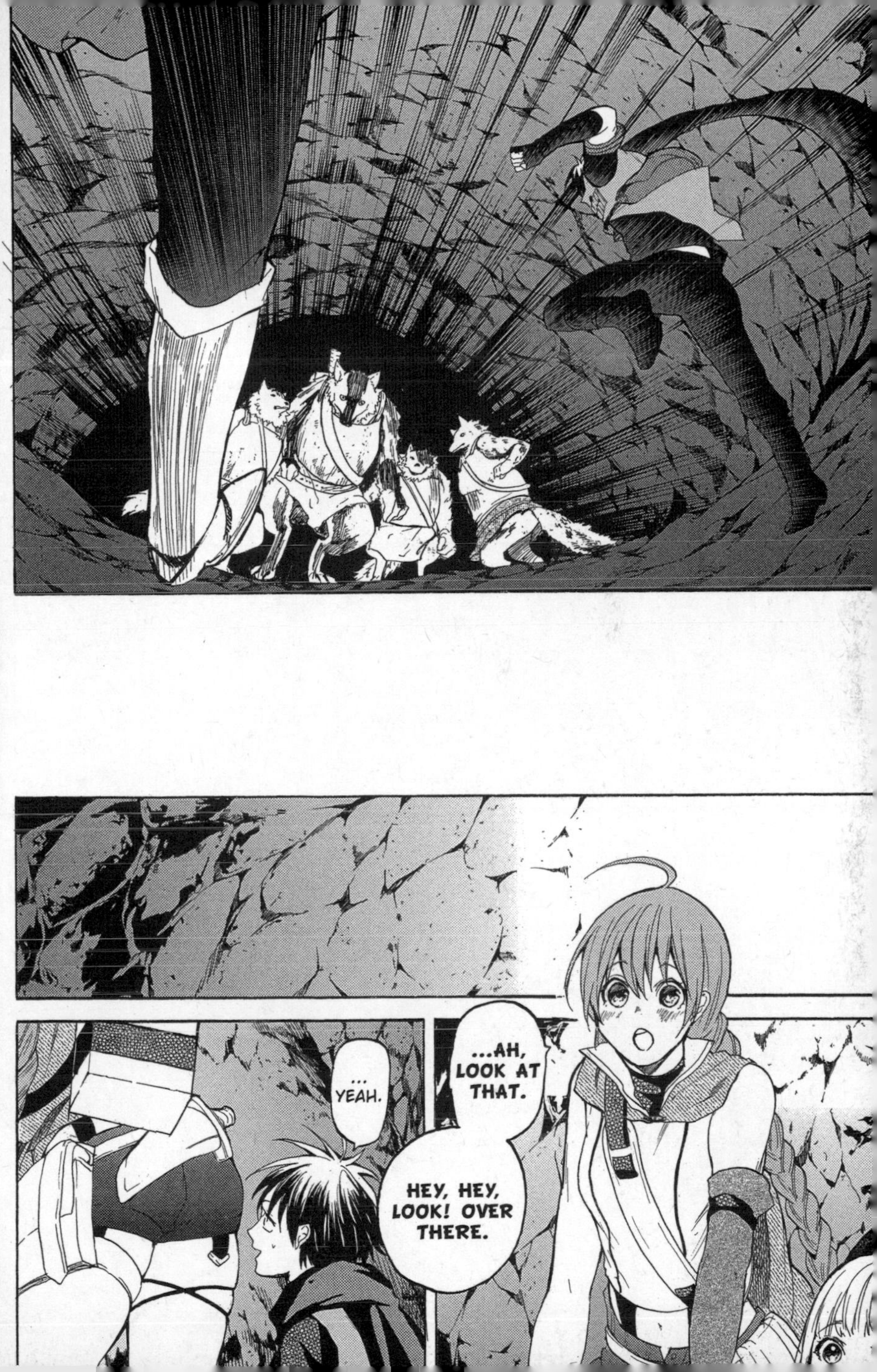
...AH, LOOK AT THAT.
HEY, HEY, LOOK! OVER THERE.
... YEAH.

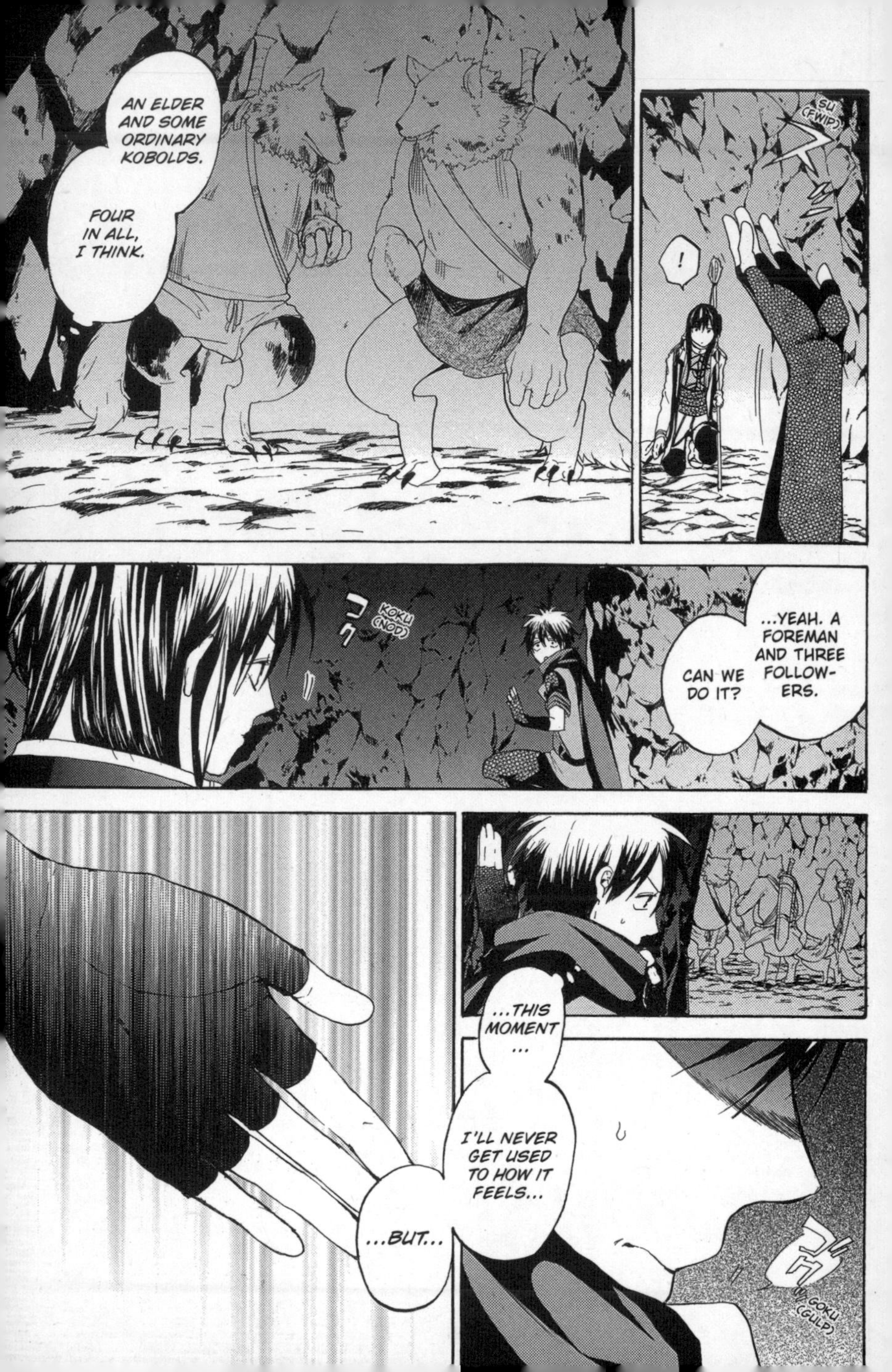
SU (FWIP)
!
AN ELDER AND SOME ORDINARY KOBOLDS.
FOUR IN ALL, I THINK.
...YEAH. A FOREMAN AND THREE FOLLOW-ERS.
CAN WE DO IT?
KOKU (NOD)
...THIS MOMENT...
I'LL NEVER GET USED TO HOW IT FEELS...
...BUT...
GOKU (GULP)

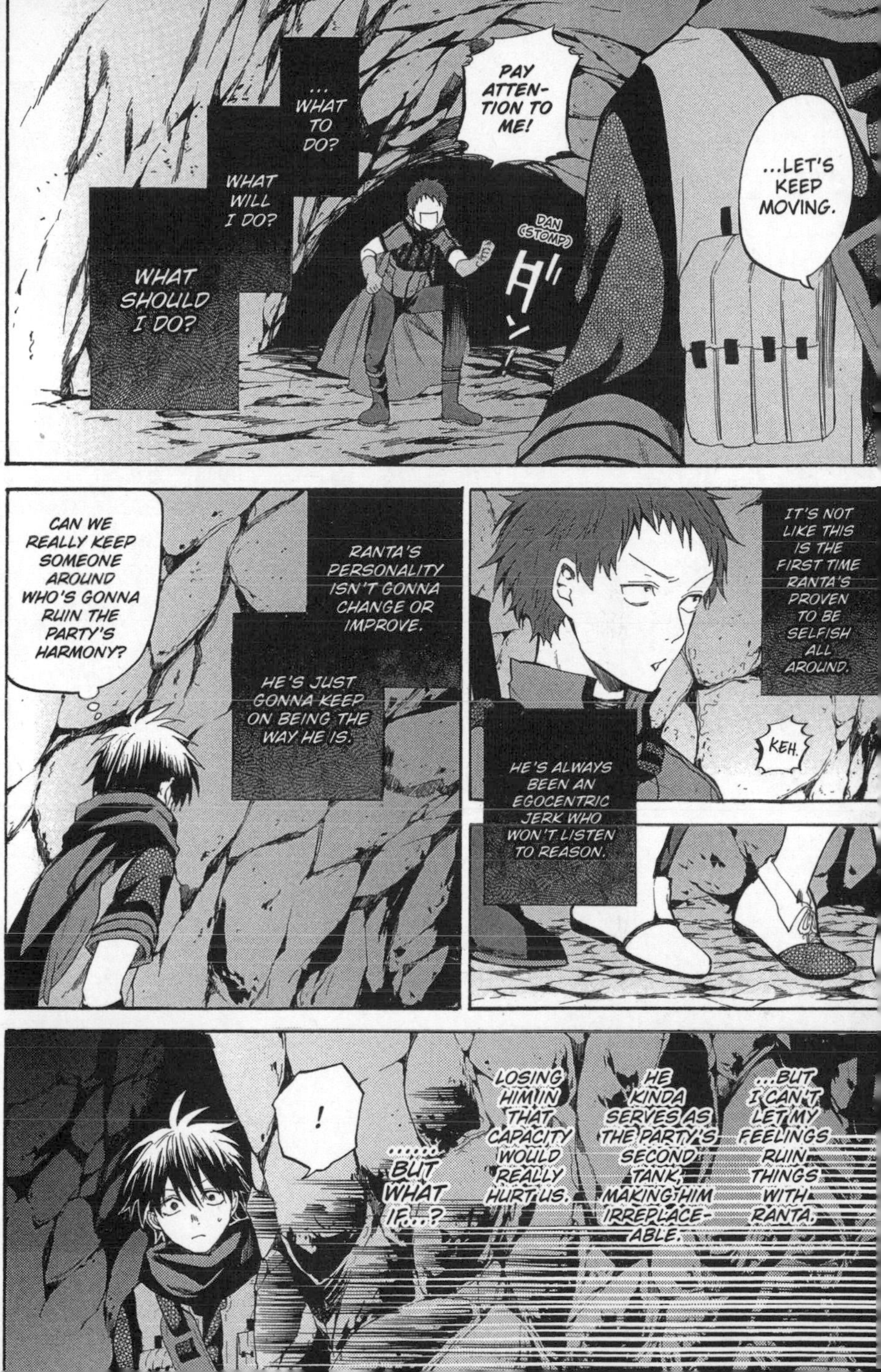
...LET'S KEEP MOVING.
PAY ATTENTION TO ME!
DAN (STOMP)
...WHAT TO DO?
WHAT WILL I DO?
WHAT SHOULD I DO?
IT'S NOT LIKE THIS IS THE FIRST TIME RANTA'S PROVEN TO BE SELFISH ALL AROUND.
KEH.
HE'S ALWAYS BEEN AN EGOCENTRIC JERK WHO WON'T LISTEN TO REASON.
RANTA'S PERSONALITY ISN'T GONNA CHANGE OR IMPROVE.
HE'S JUST GONNA KEEP ON BEING THE WAY HE IS.
CAN WE REALLY KEEP SOMEONE AROUND WHO'S GONNA RUIN THE PARTY'S HARMONY?
...BUT I CAN'T LET MY FEELINGS RUIN THINGS WITH RANTA.
HE KINDA SERVES AS THE PARTY'S SECOND TANK, MAKING HIM IRREPLACE-ABLE.
LOSING HIM IN THAT CAPACITY WOULD REALLY HURT US.
......BUT WHAT IF...?
!

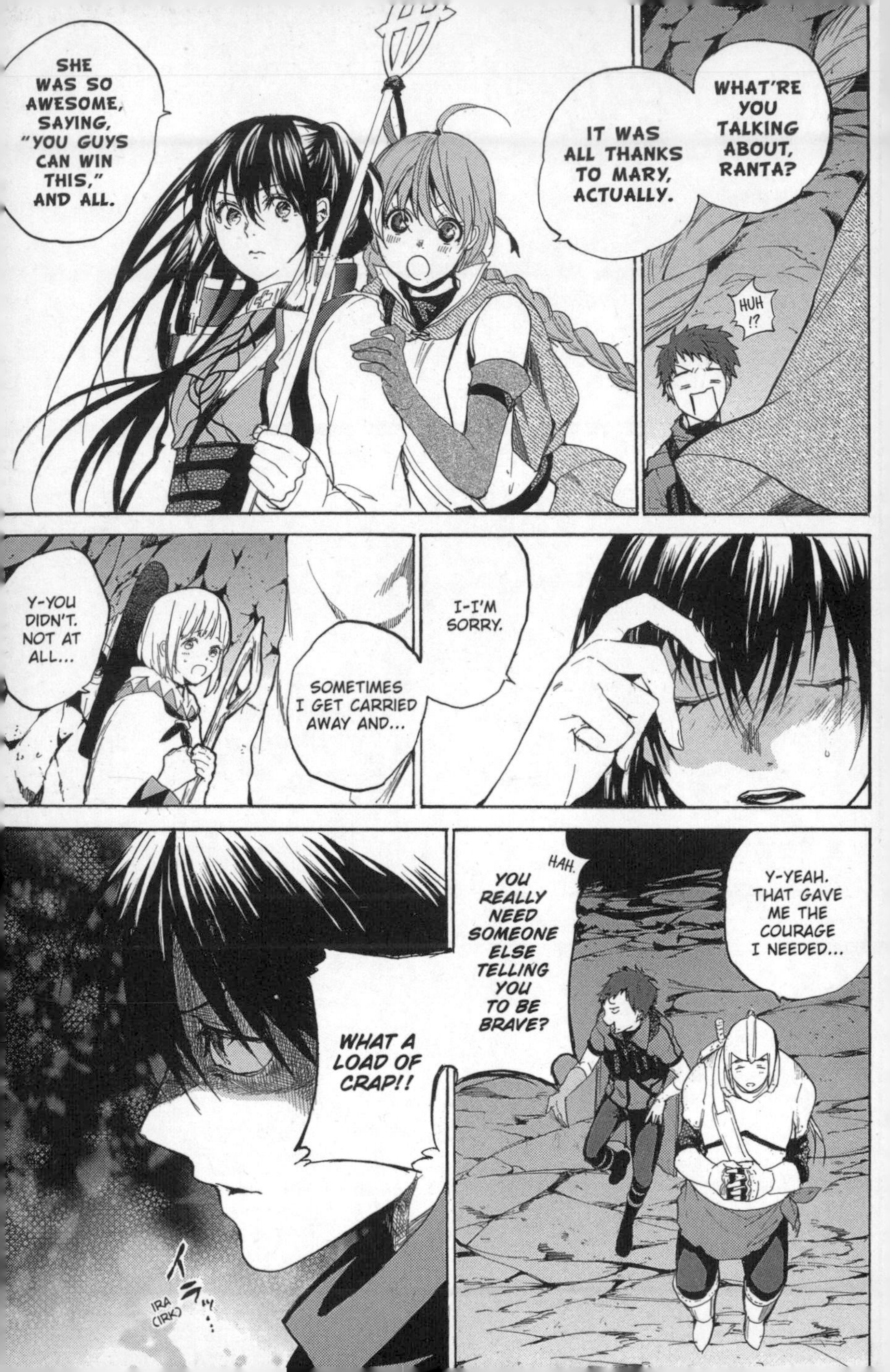
WHAT'RE YOU TALKING ABOUT, RANTA?
IT WAS ALL THANKS TO MARY, ACTUALLY.
HUH!?
SHE WAS SO AWESOME, SAYING, "YOU GUYS CAN WIN THIS," AND ALL.
I-I'M SORRY.
SOMETIMES I GET CARRIED AWAY AND...
Y-YOU DIDN'T. NOT AT ALL...
Y-YEAH. THAT GAVE ME THE COURAGE I NEEDED...
HAH.
YOU REALLY NEED SOMEONE ELSE TELLING YOU TO BE BRAVE?
WHAT A LOAD OF CRAP!!
IRA (IRK)

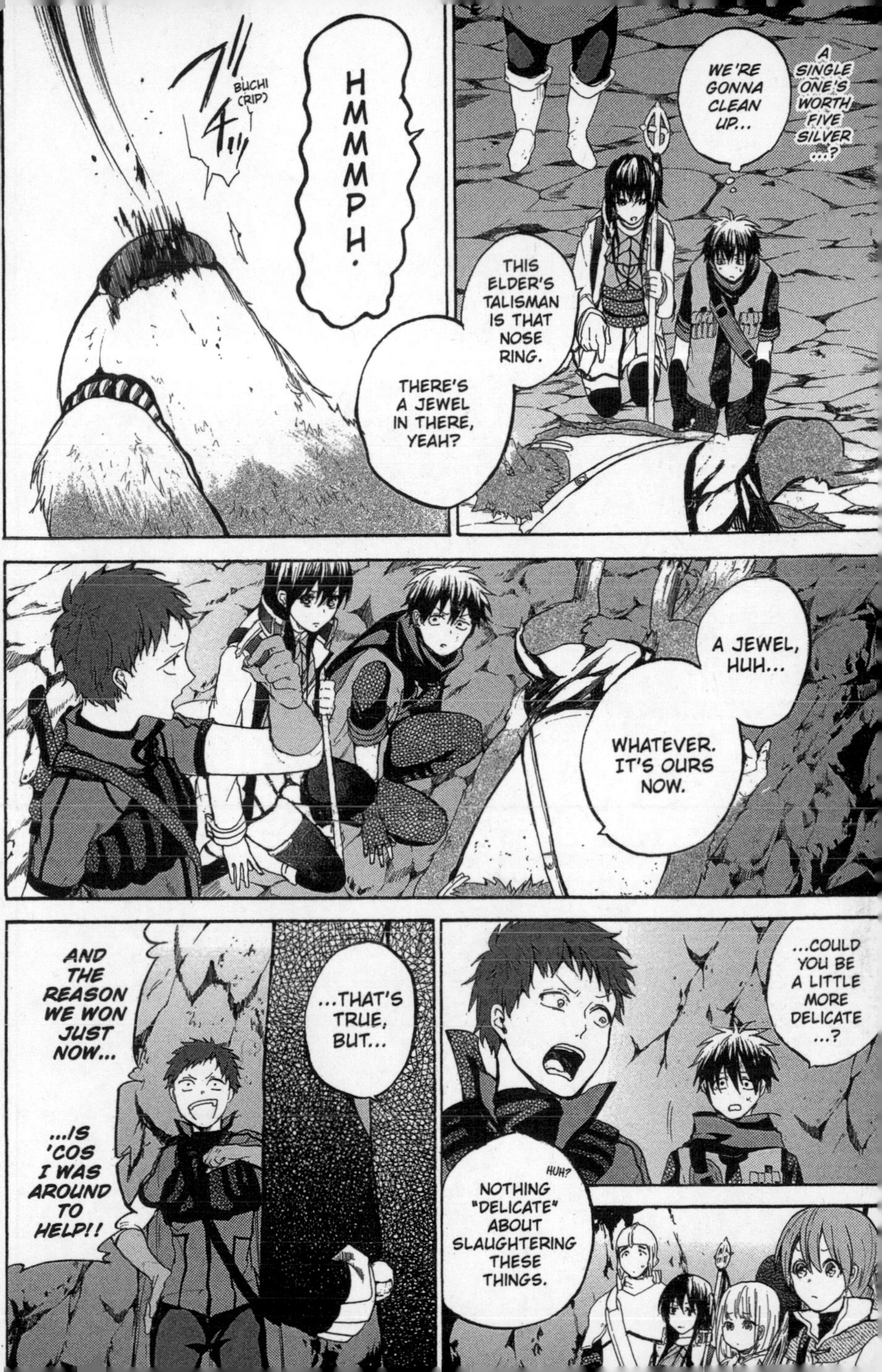
A SINGLE ONE'S WORTH FIVE SILVER ...?
WE'RE GONNA CLEAN UP...
THIS ELDER'S TALISMAN IS THAT NOSE RING.
THERE'S A JEWEL IN THERE, YEAH?
HMMMMPH.
BUCHI (RIP)
A JEWEL, HUH...
WHATEVER. IT'S OURS NOW.
...COULD YOU BE A LITTLE MORE DELICATE ...?
HUH?
NOTHING "DELICATE" ABOUT SLAUGHTERING THESE THINGS.
...THAT'S TRUE, BUT...
AND THE REASON WE WON JUST NOW...
...IS 'COS I WAS AROUND TO HELP!!

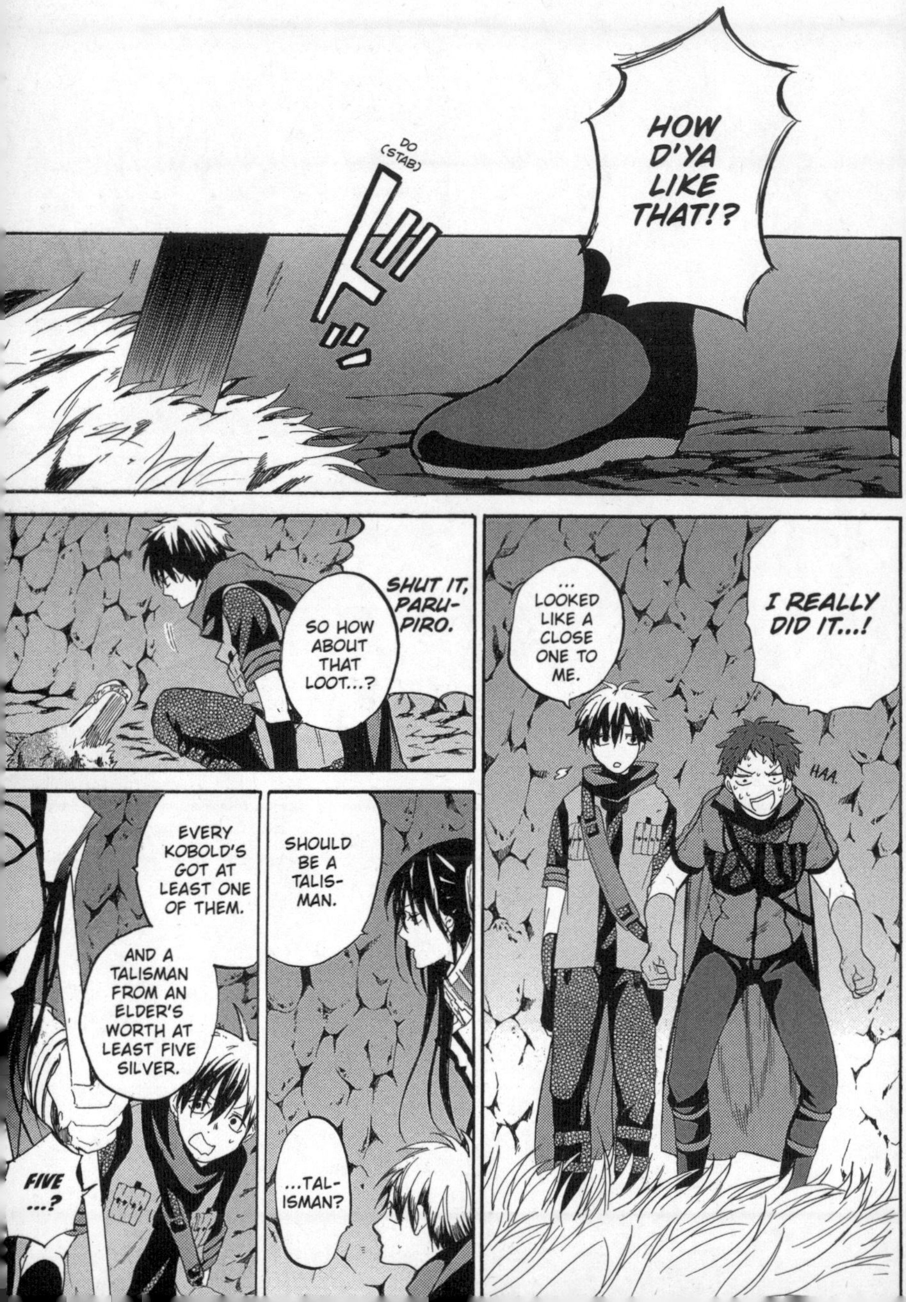
HOW D'YA LIKE THAT!?
DO (STAB)
I REALLY DID IT...!
... LOOKED LIKE A CLOSE ONE TO ME.
HAA.
SHUT IT, PARUPIRO.
SO HOW ABOUT THAT LOOT...?
SHOULD BE A TALISMAN.
...TALISMAN?
EVERY KOBOLD'S GOT AT LEAST ONE OF THEM.
AND A TALISMAN FROM AN ELDER'S WORTH AT LEAST FIVE SILVER.
FIVE ...?

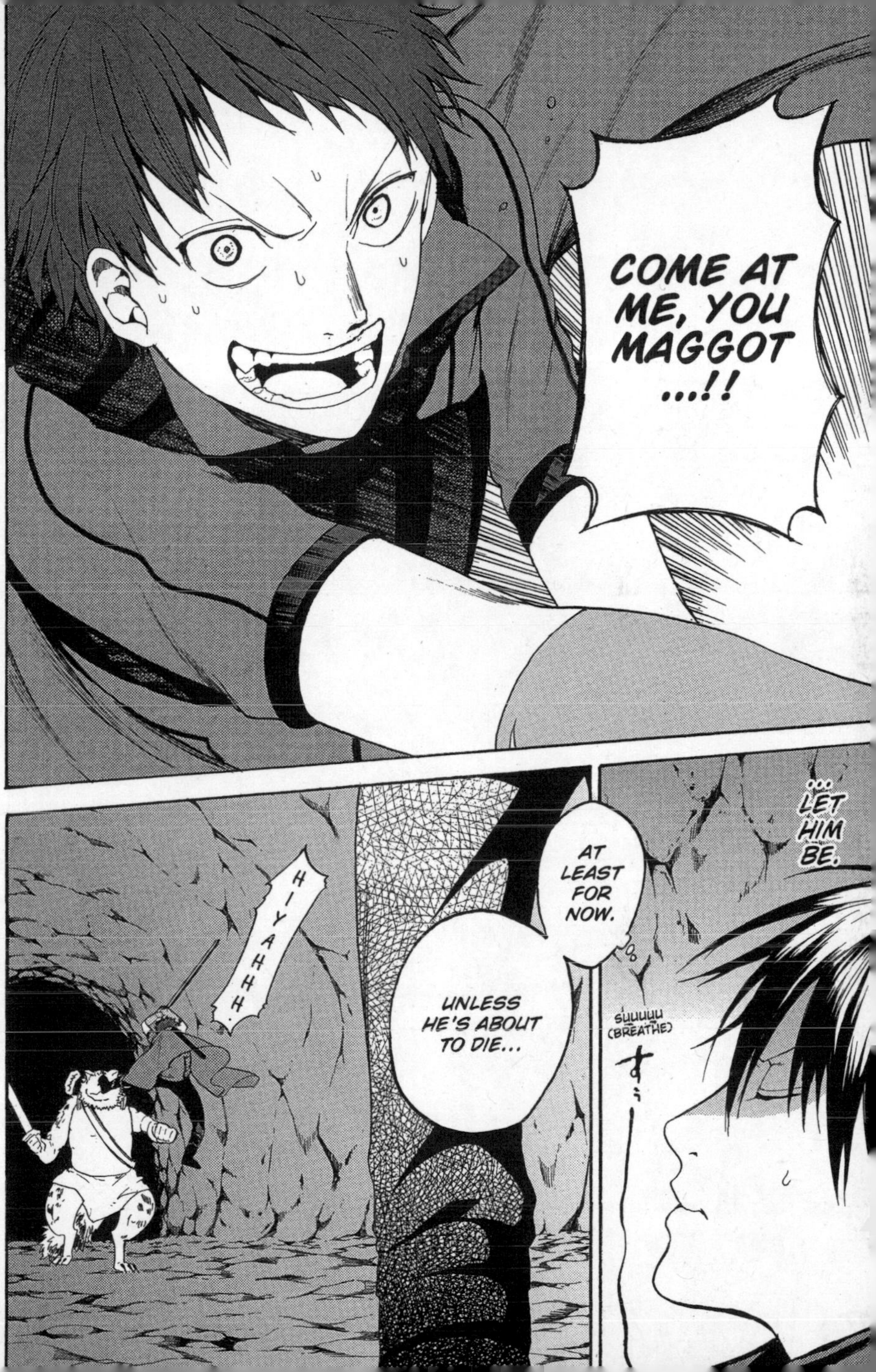
COME AT ME, YOU MAGGOT ...!!
...LET HIM BE.
AT LEAST FOR NOW.
UNLESS HE'S ABOUT TO DIE...
SUUUUU (BREATHE)
HIYAHHH

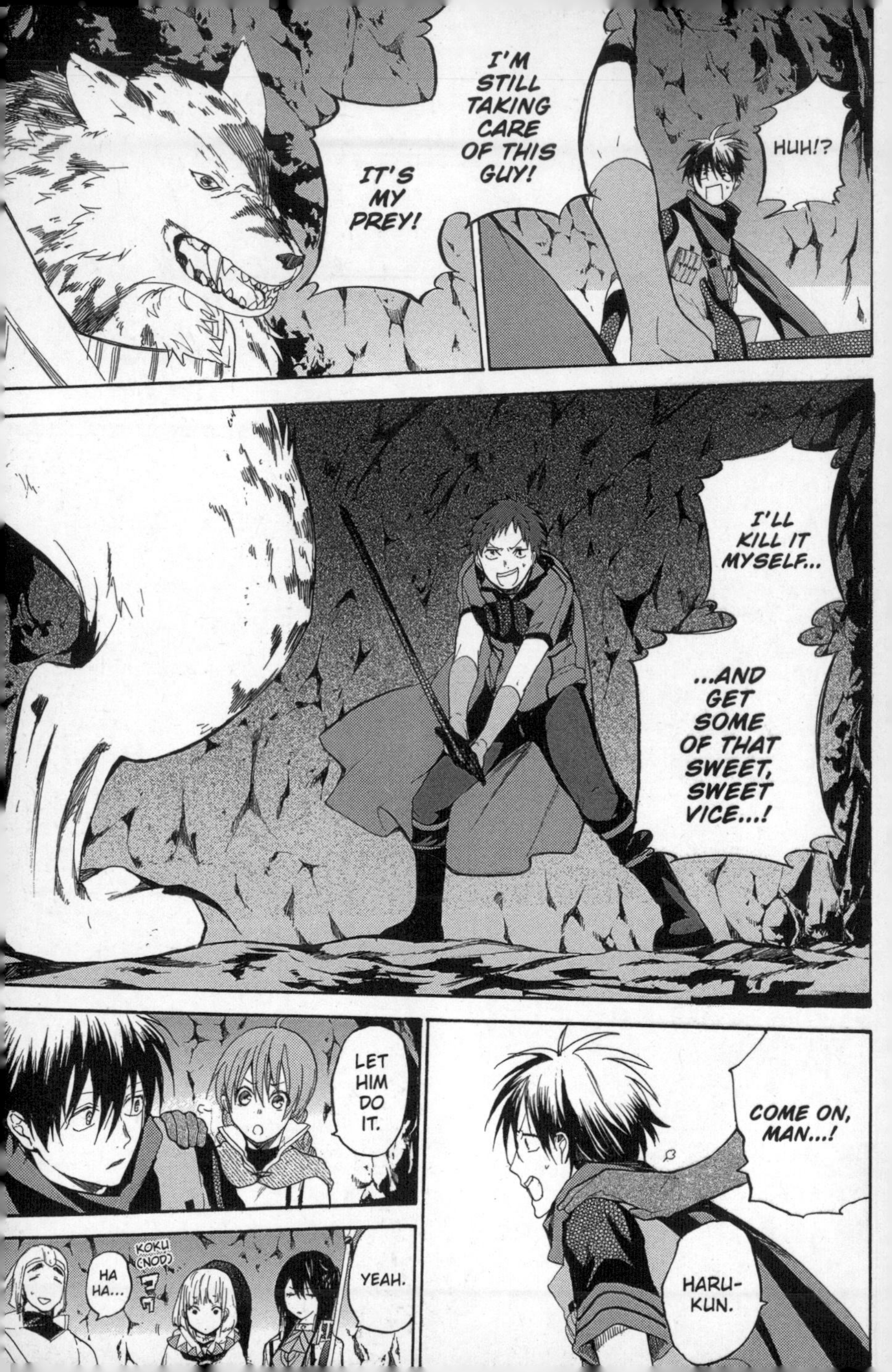
HUH!?
I'M STILL TAKING CARE OF THIS GUY!
IT'S MY PREY!
I'LL KILL IT MYSELF...
...AND GET SOME OF THAT SWEET, SWEET VICE...!
COME ON, MAN...!
HARU-KUN.
LET HIM DO IT.
YEAH.
KOKU (NOD)
HA HA...

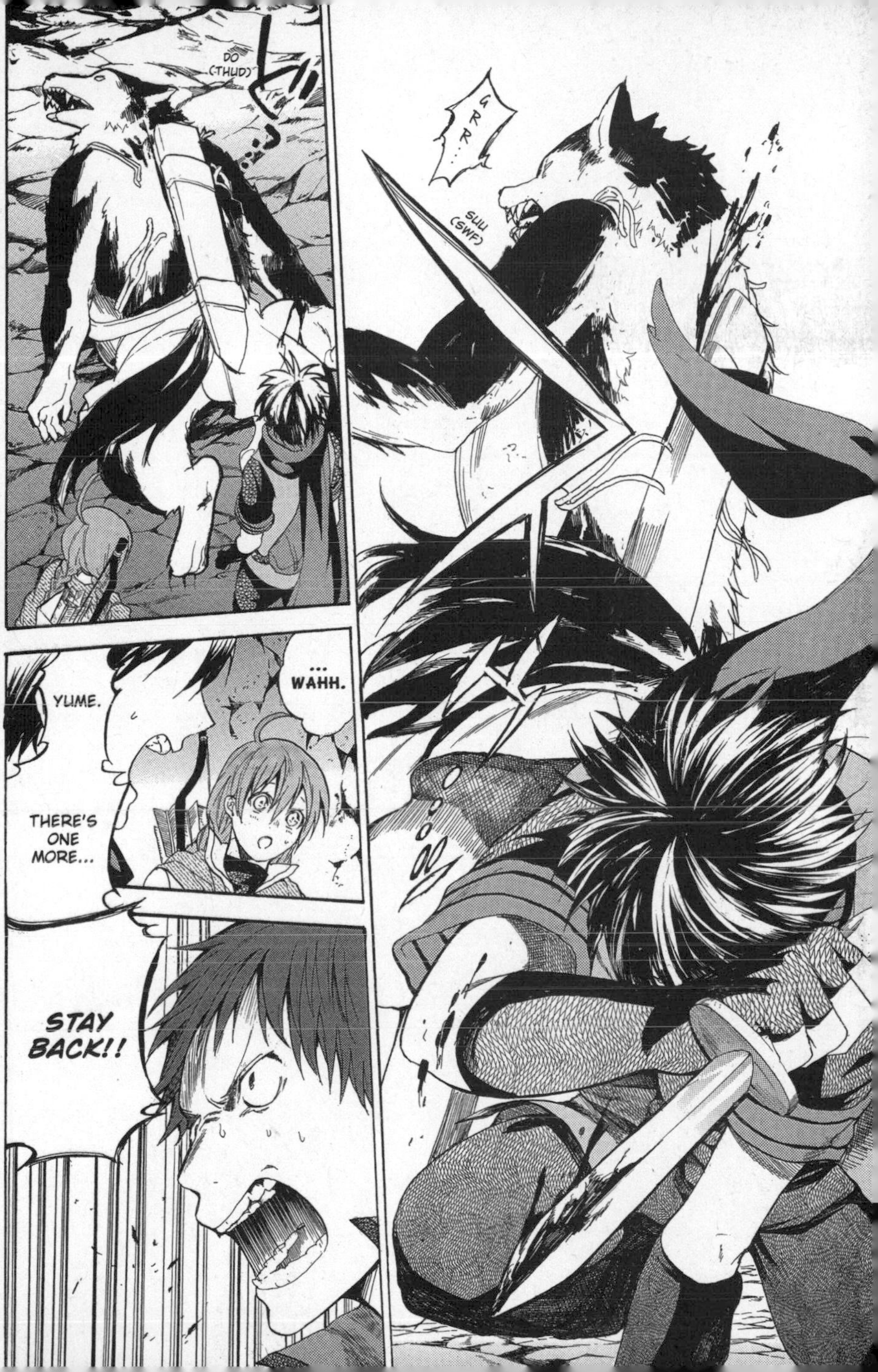
GRR...
SUU (SWF)
DO (THUD)
...WAHH.
YUME.
THERE'S ONE MORE...
STAY BACK!!

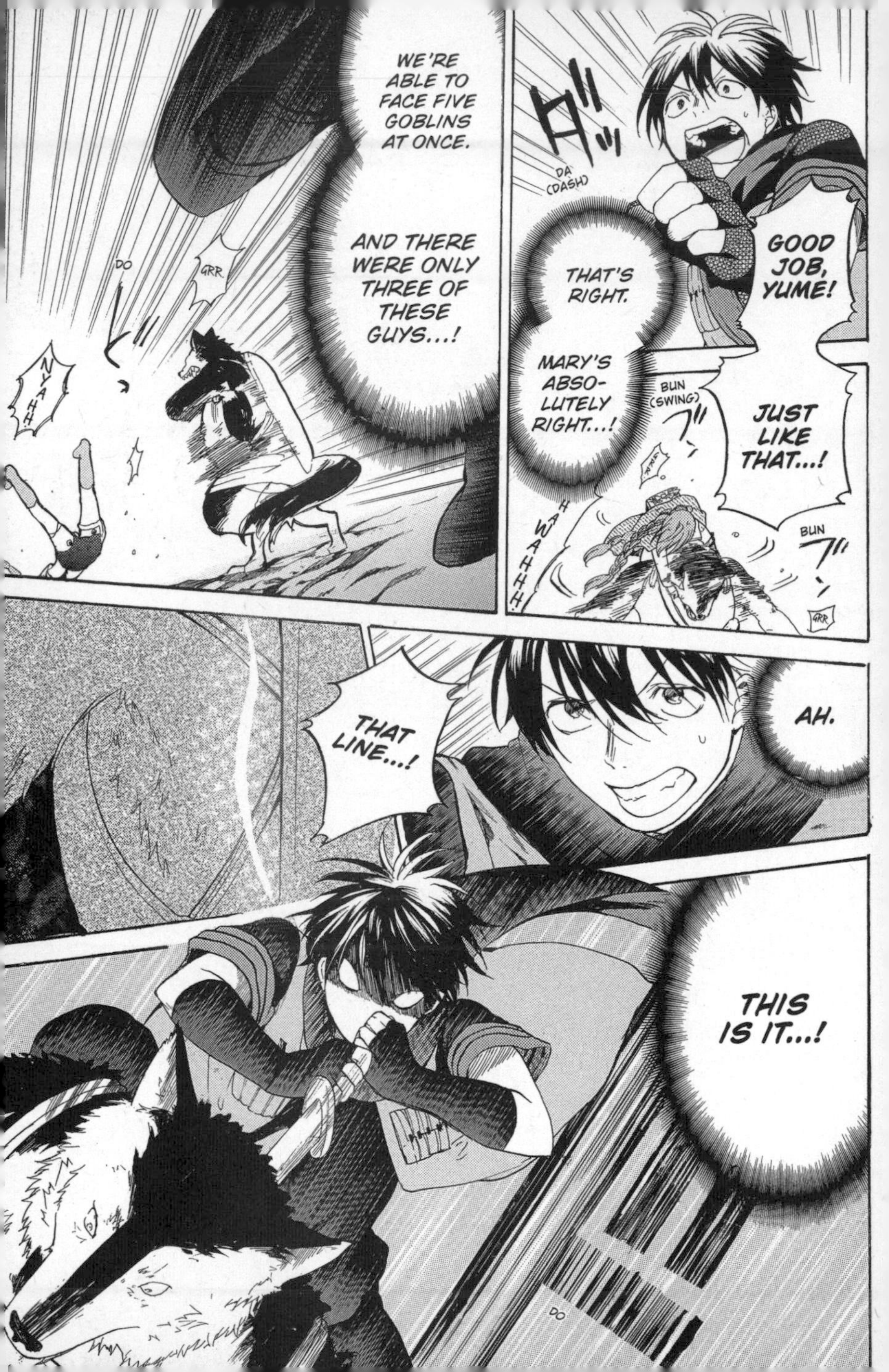
DA (DASH)
GOOD JOB, YUME!
THAT'S RIGHT.
MARY'S ABSOLUTELY RIGHT...!
BUN (SWING)
JUST LIKE THAT...!
HAWAHHH
BUN
GRR
WE'RE ABLE TO FACE FIVE GOBLINS AT ONCE.
AND THERE WERE ONLY THREE OF THESE GUYS...!
GRR.
DO
NYAHH
AH.
THAT LINE...!
THIS IS IT...!
DO

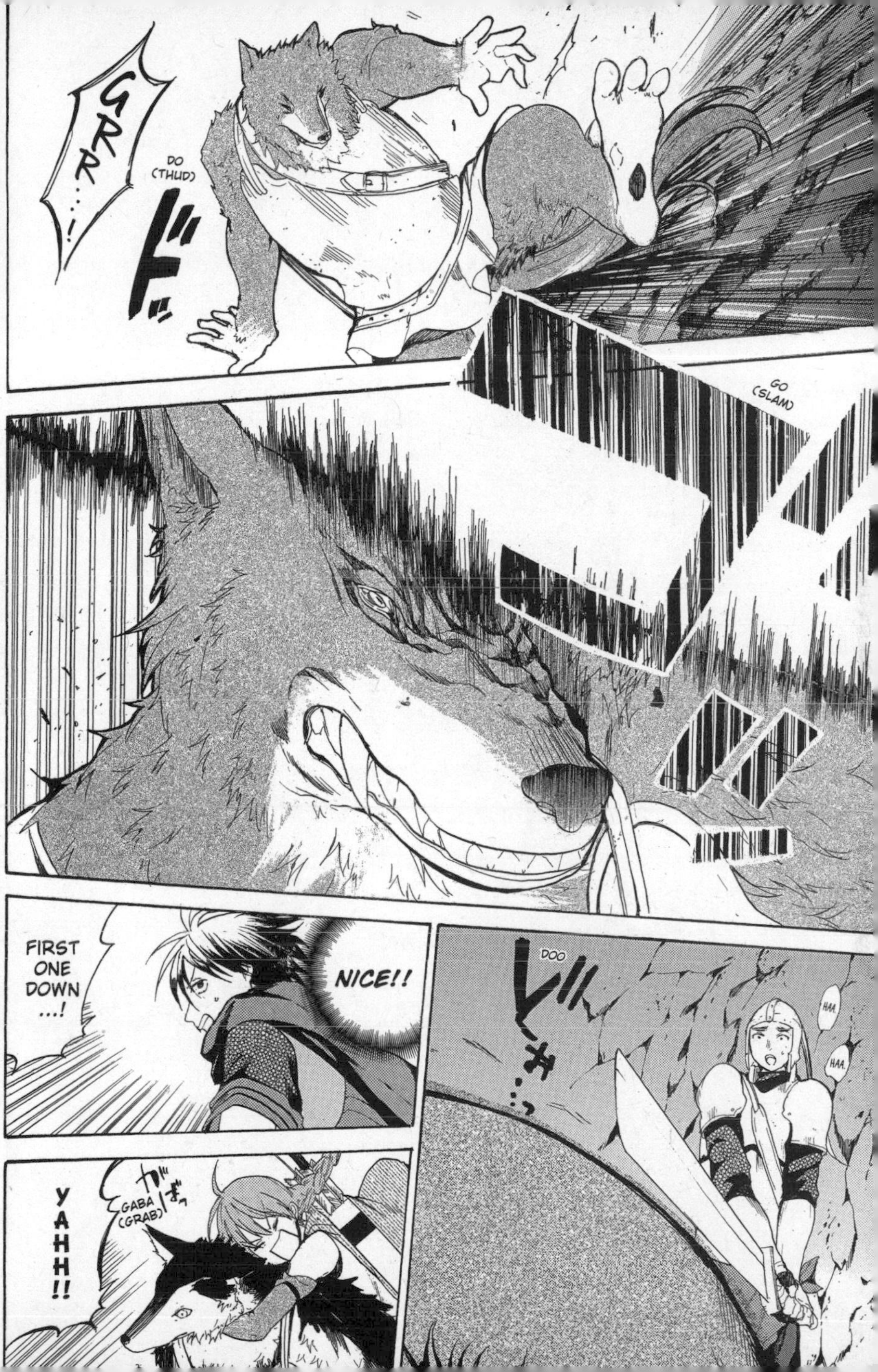
GRR...!!
DO (THUD)
ドッ
GO (SLAM)
DOO
HAA.
HAA.
NICE!!
FIRST ONE DOWN ...!
がばっ
GABA (GRAB)
YAHH!!

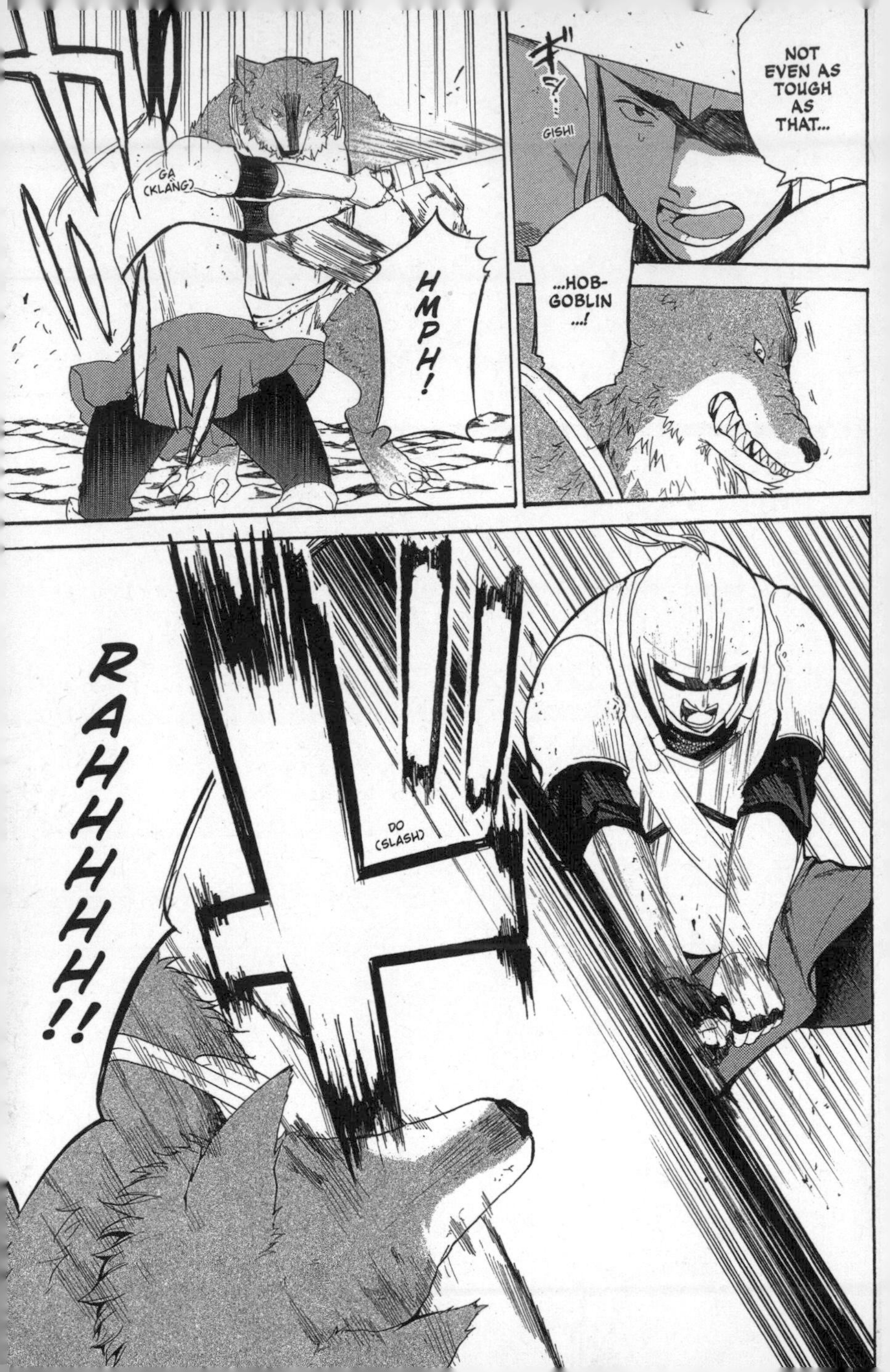

NOT EVEN AS TOUGH AS THAT...
GISHI
GA (KLANG)
HMPH!
...HOB-GOBLIN ...!
DO (SLASH)
RAHHHHHH!!

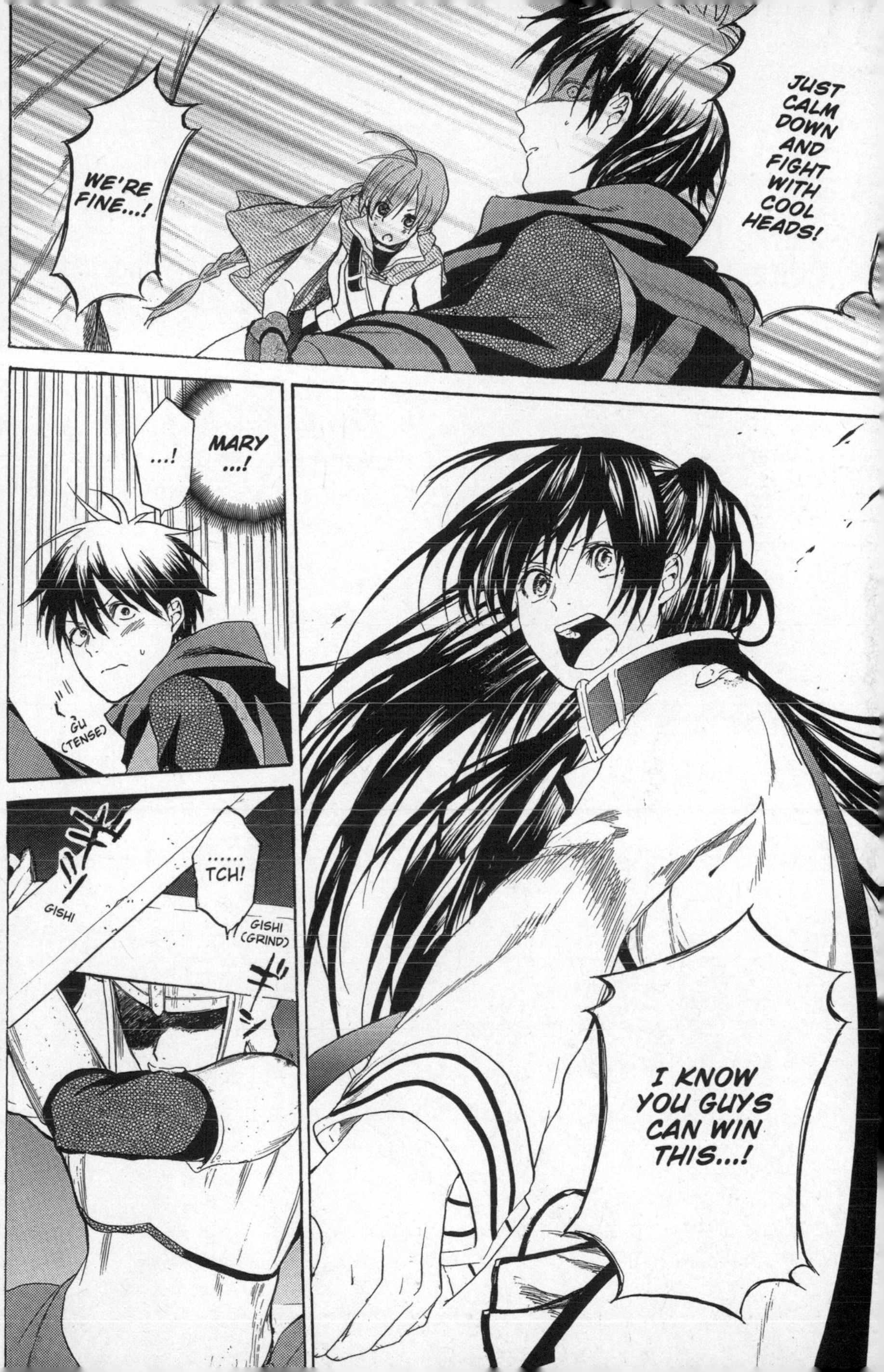
JUST CALM DOWN AND FIGHT WITH COOL HEADS!
WE'RE FINE...!
MARY...!
...!
GU (TENSE)
I KNOW YOU GUYS CAN WIN THIS...!
......TCH!
GISHI (GRIND)
GISHI

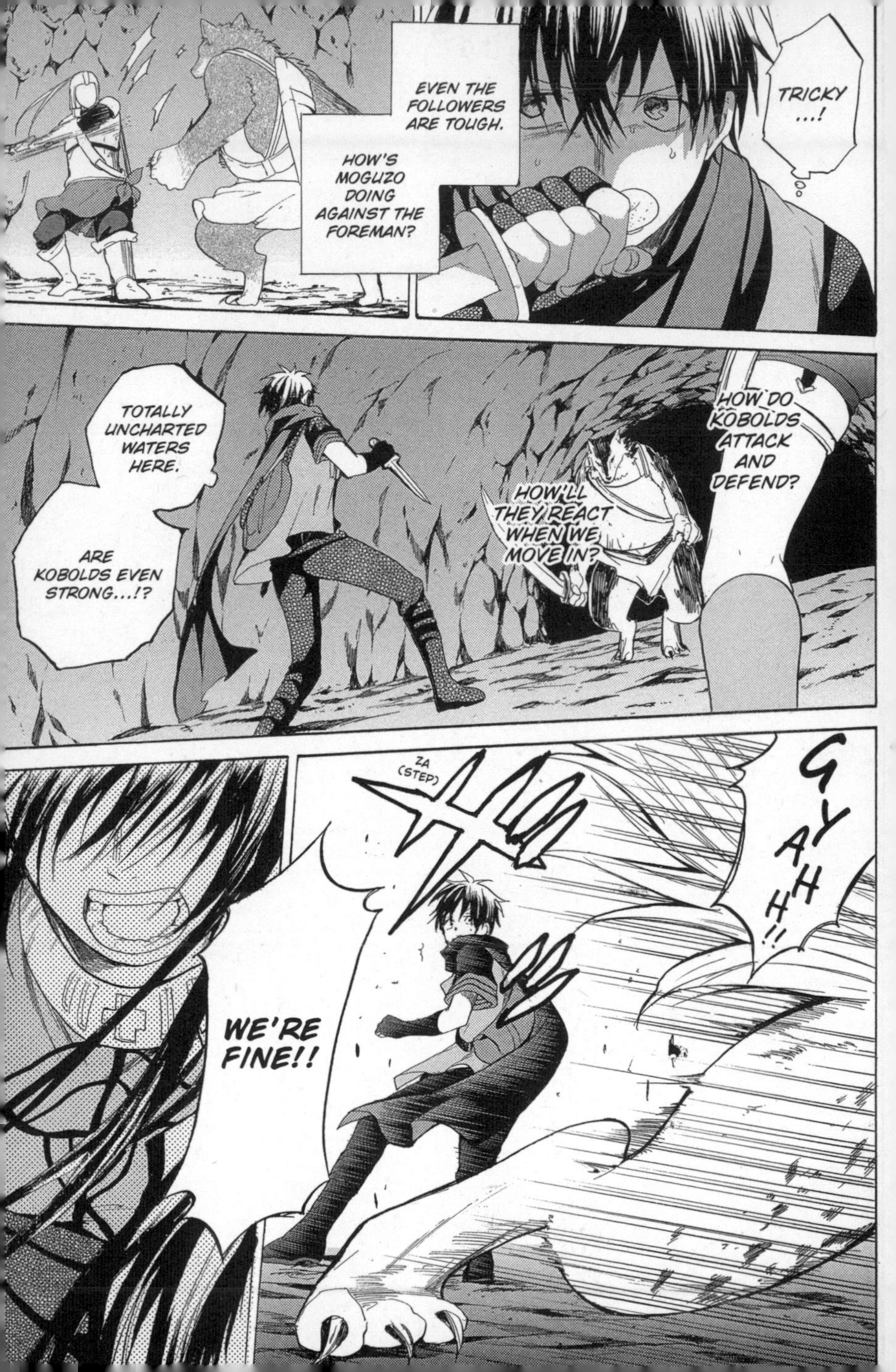
TRICKY ...!
EVEN THE FOLLOWERS ARE TOUGH.
HOW'S MOGUZO DOING AGAINST THE FOREMAN?
HOW DO KOBOLDS ATTACK AND DEFEND?
HOW'LL THEY REACT WHEN WE MOVE IN?
TOTALLY UNCHARTED WATERS HERE.
ARE KOBOLDS EVEN STRONG...!?
GYAHH!!
ZA (STEP)
WE'RE FINE!!

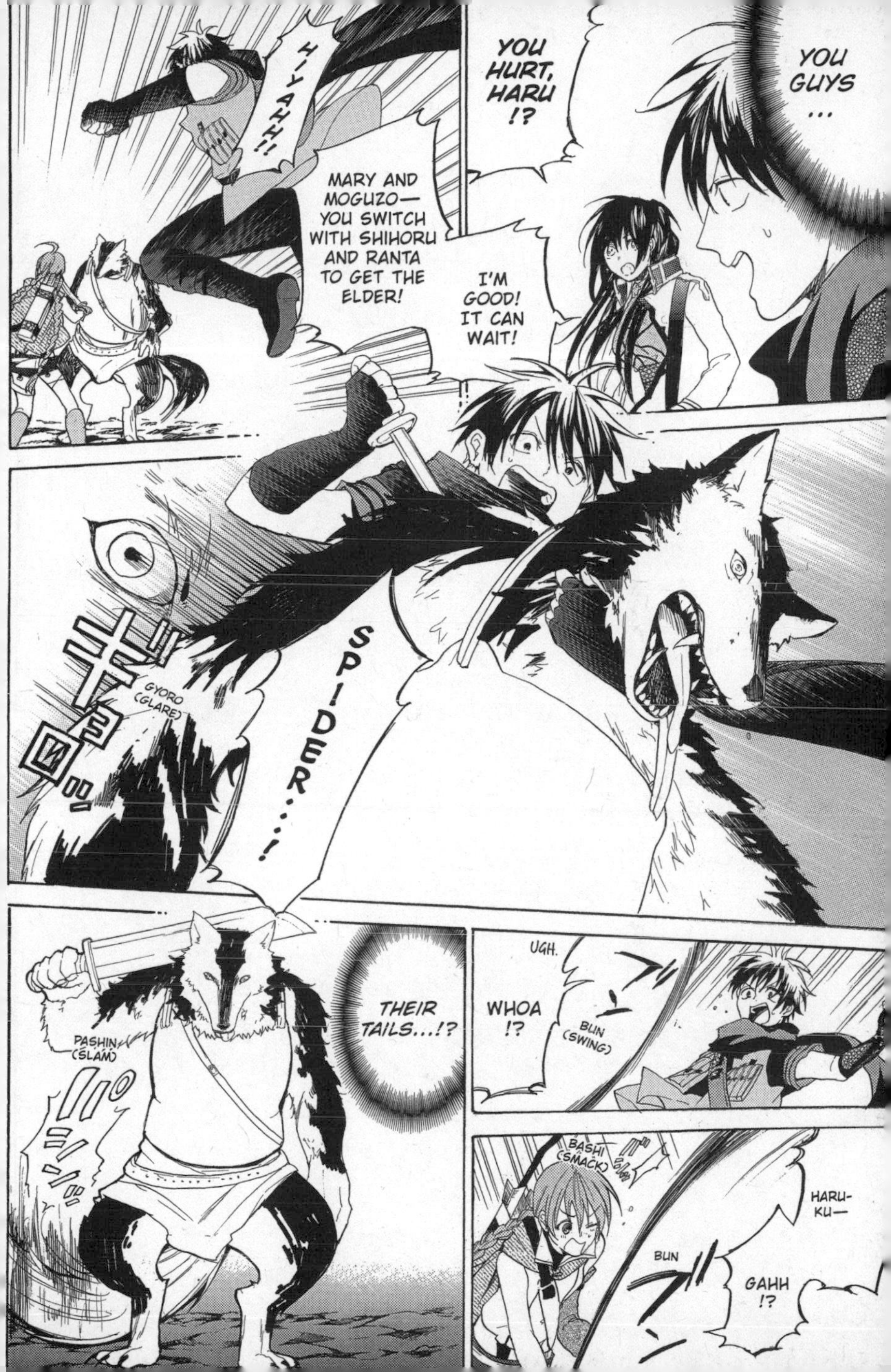
YOU GUYS ...
YOU HURT, HARU !?
I'M GOOD! IT CAN WAIT!
MARY AND MOGUZO— YOU SWITCH WITH SHIHORU AND RANTA TO GET THE ELDER!
HIYAHH!!
SPIDER...!
GYORO (GLARE)
UGH.
WHOA !?
BUN (SWING)
THEIR TAILS...!?
PASHIN (SLAM)
BASHI (SMACK)
HARU-KU—
BUN
GAHH !?

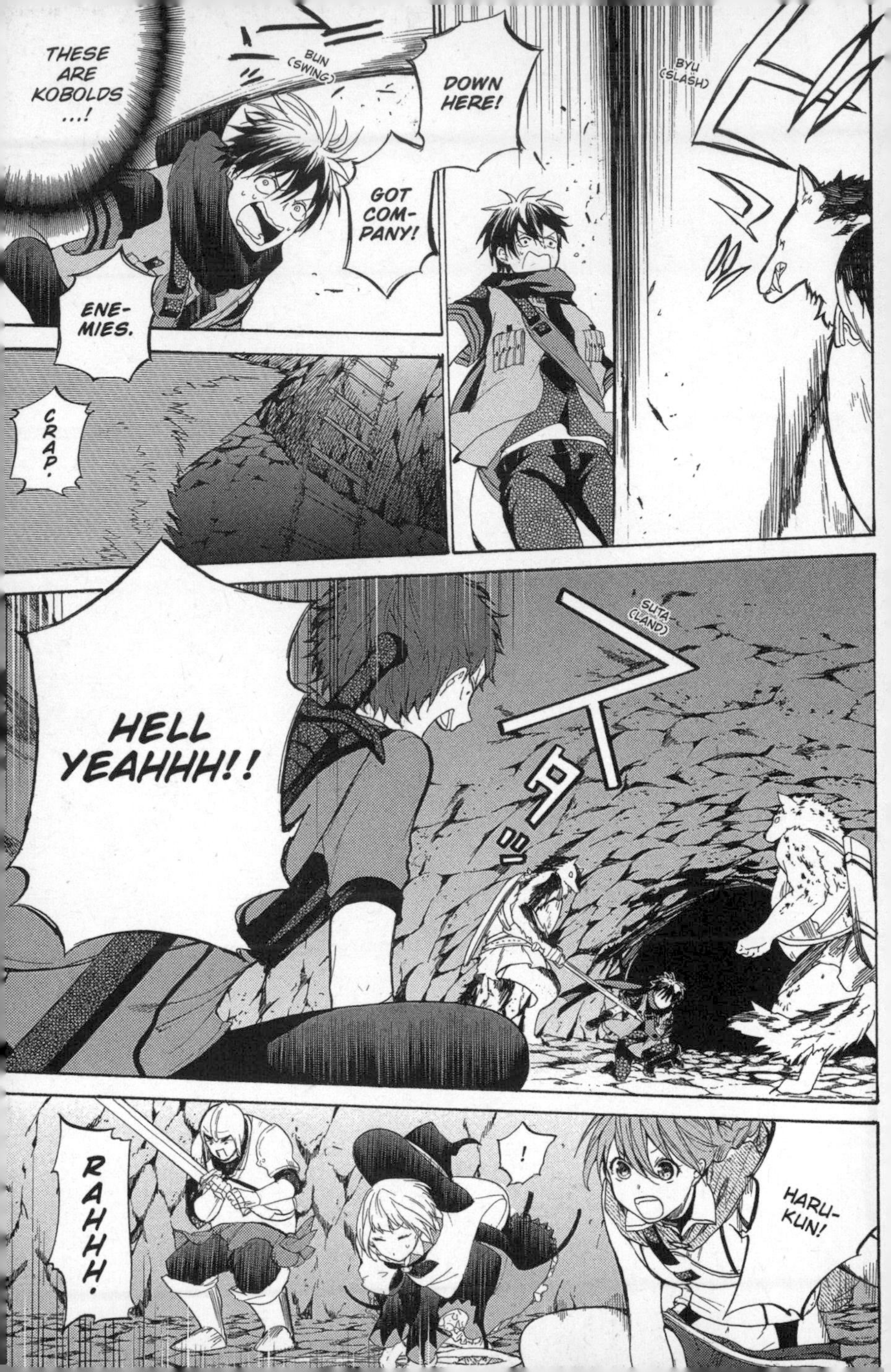

BYU (SLASH)
DOWN HERE!
GOT COM-PANY!
BUN (SWING)
THESE ARE KOBOLDS ...!
ENE-MIES.
CRAP.
SUTA- (LAND)
HELL YEAHHH!!
HARU-KUN!
!
RAHHH!

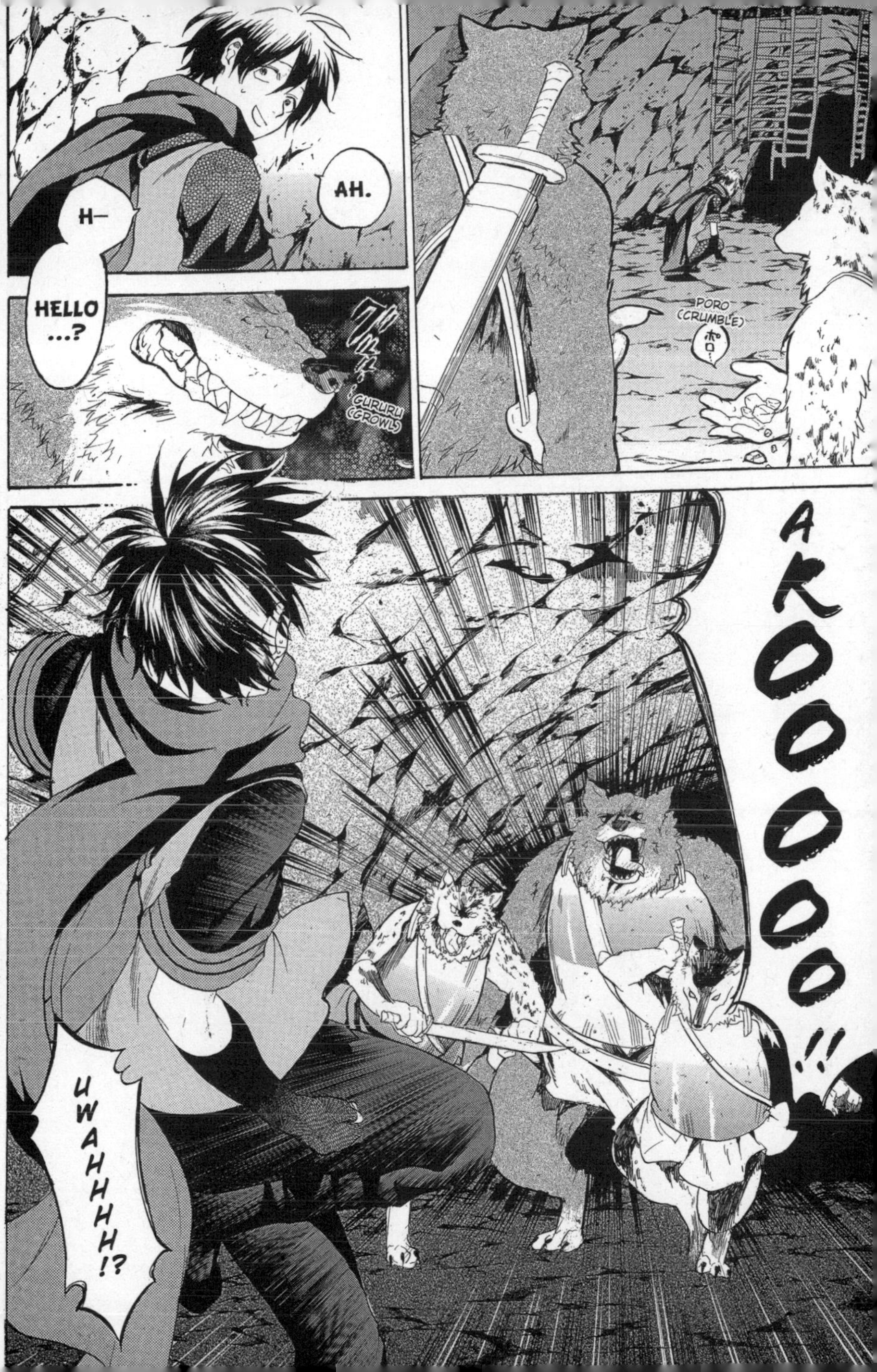

PORO (CRUMBLE)
ポロ…
AH.
H—
HELLO …?
GURURU (GROWL)
AROOOOOO!!
UWAHHHH!?

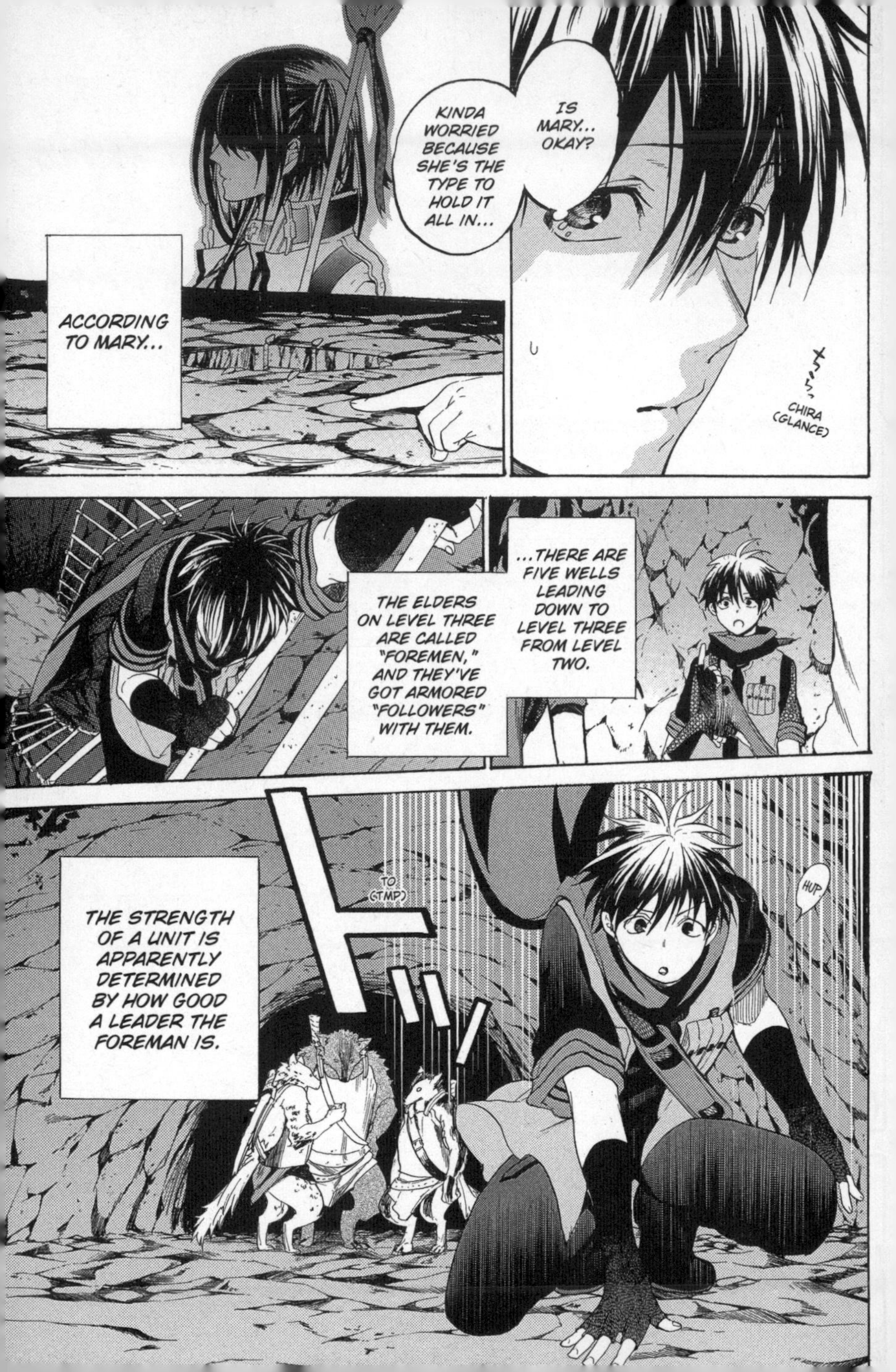
IS MARY... OKAY?
KINDA WORRIED BECAUSE SHE'S THE TYPE TO HOLD IT ALL IN...
CHIRA (GLANCE)
ACCORDING TO MARY...
...THERE ARE FIVE WELLS LEADING DOWN TO LEVEL THREE FROM LEVEL TWO.
THE ELDERS ON LEVEL THREE ARE CALLED "FOREMEN," AND THEY'VE GOT ARMORED "FOLLOWERS" WITH THEM.
HUP
TO (TMP)
THE STRENGTH OF A UNIT IS APPARENTLY DETERMINED BY HOW GOOD A LEADER THE FOREMAN IS.

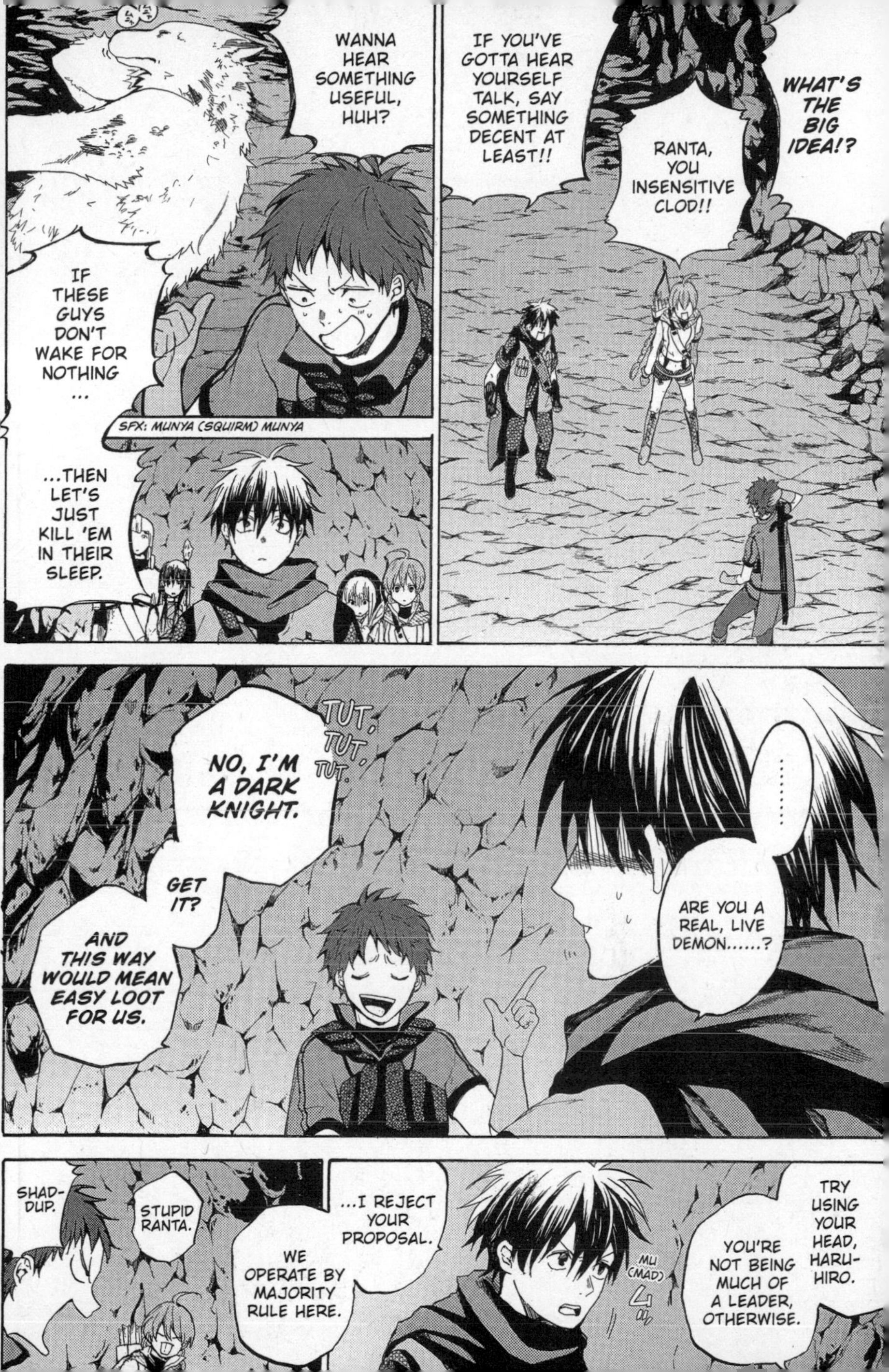
WHAT'S THE BIG IDEA!?
RANTA, YOU INSENSITIVE CLOD!!
IF YOU'VE GOTTA HEAR YOURSELF TALK, SAY SOMETHING DECENT AT LEAST!!
WANNA HEAR SOMETHING USEFUL, HUH?
IF THESE GUYS DON'T WAKE FOR NOTHING...
SFX: MUNYA (SQUIRM) MUNYA
...THEN LET'S JUST KILL 'EM IN THEIR SLEEP.
......
ARE YOU A REAL, LIVE DEMON......?
TUT, TUT, TUT.
NO, I'M A DARK KNIGHT.
GET IT?
AND THIS WAY WOULD MEAN EASY LOOT FOR US.
TRY USING YOUR HEAD, HARUHIRO.
YOU'RE NOT BEING MUCH OF A LEADER, OTHERWISE.
MU (MAD)
...I REJECT YOUR PROPOSAL.
WE OPERATE BY MAJORITY RULE HERE.
STUPID RANTA.
SHADDUP.

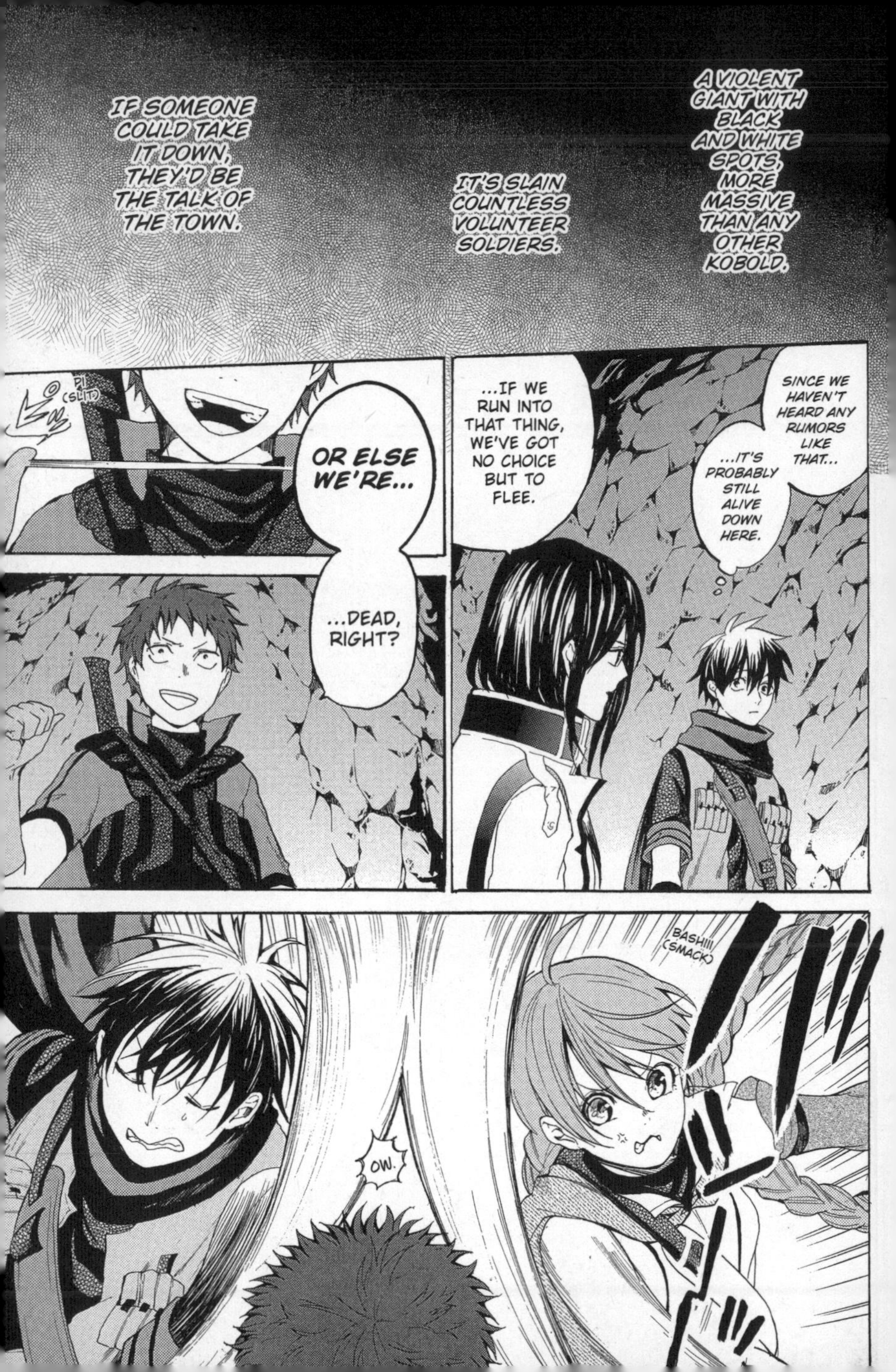
A VIOLENT GIANT WITH BLACK AND WHITE SPOTS, MORE MASSIVE THAN ANY OTHER KOBOLD.
IT'S SLAIN COUNTLESS VOLUNTEER SOLDIERS.
IF SOMEONE COULD TAKE IT DOWN, THEY'D BE THE TALK OF THE TOWN.
SINCE WE HAVEN'T HEARD ANY RUMORS LIKE THAT...
...IT'S PROBABLY STILL ALIVE DOWN HERE.
...IF WE RUN INTO THAT THING, WE'VE GOT NO CHOICE BUT TO FLEE.
PI (SLIT)
OR ELSE WE'RE...
...DEAD, RIGHT?
BASHIII (SMACK)
OW.

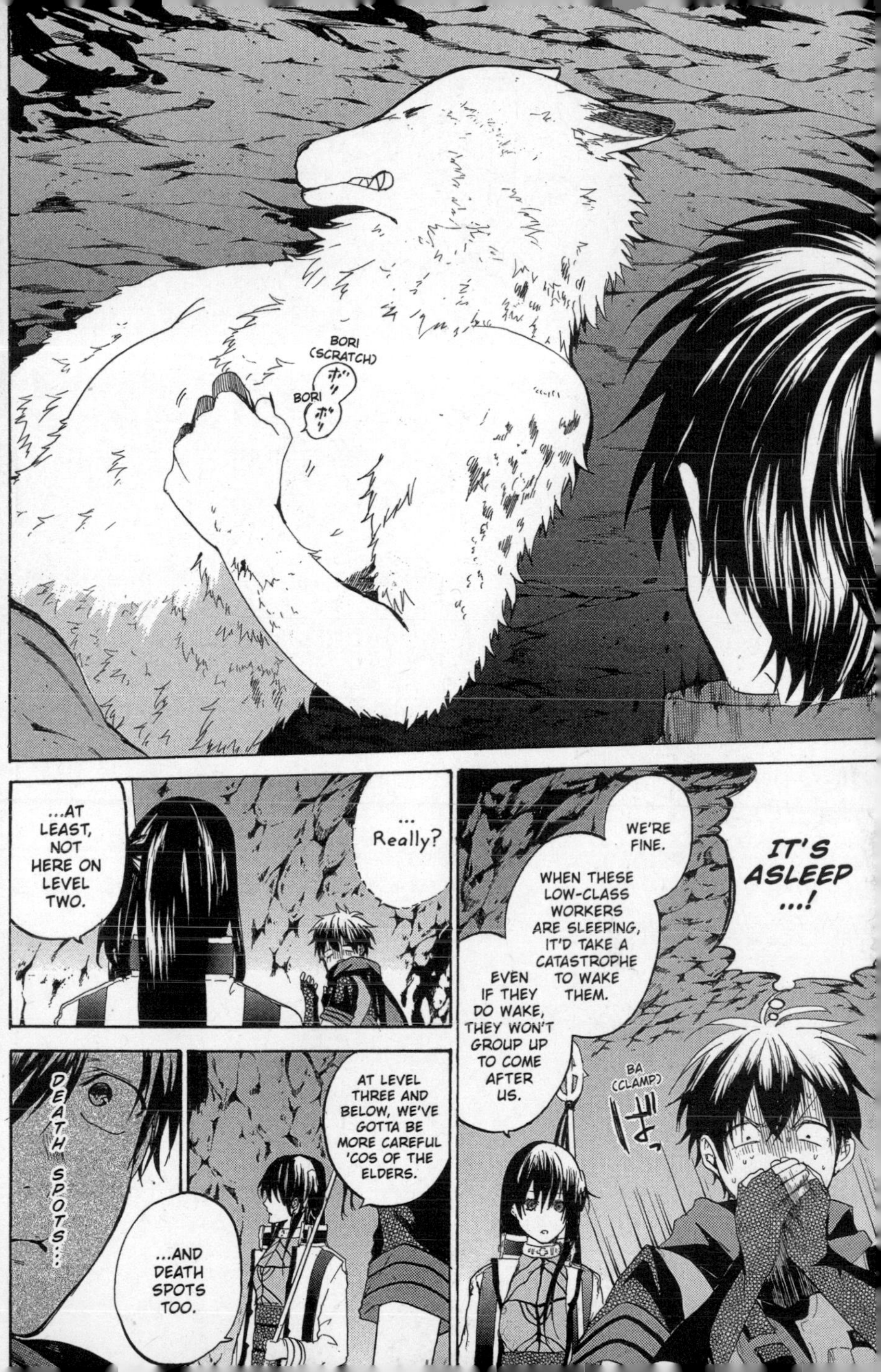
BORI (SCRATCH)
BORI
IT'S ASLEEP ...!
WE'RE FINE.
WHEN THESE LOW-CLASS WORKERS ARE SLEEPING, IT'D TAKE A CATASTROPHE TO WAKE THEM.
EVEN IF THEY DO WAKE, THEY WON'T GROUP UP TO COME AFTER US.
... Really?
...AT LEAST, NOT HERE ON LEVEL TWO.
BA (CLAMP)
AT LEVEL THREE AND BELOW, WE'VE GOTTA BE MORE CAREFUL 'COS OF THE ELDERS.
...AND DEATH SPOTS TOO.
DEATH SPOTS...

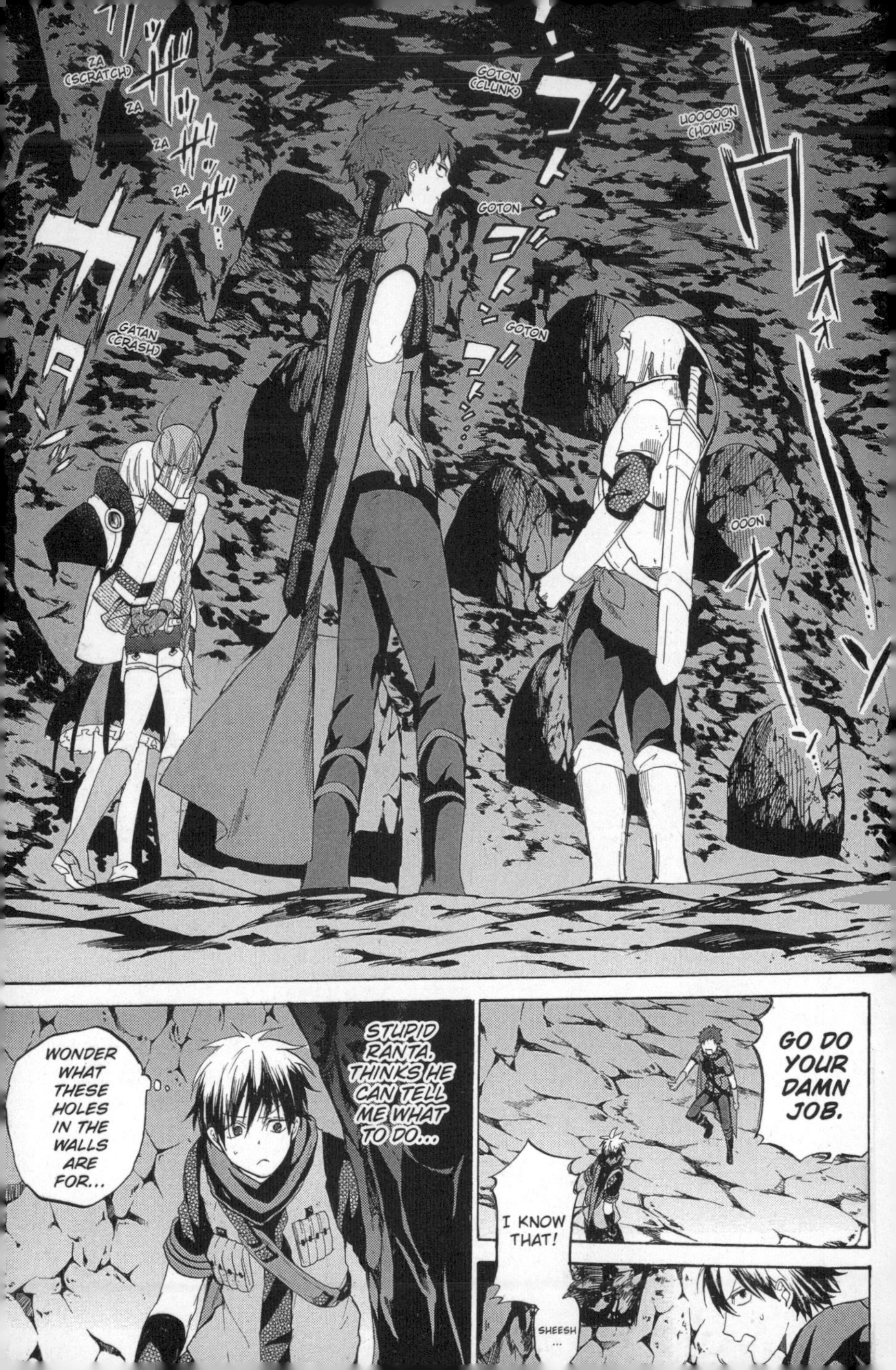
UOOOOON (HOWL)
OOON
GOTON (CLUNK)
GOTON
GOTON
ZA (SCRATCH)
ZA
ZA
ZA
GATAN (CRASH)
STUPID RANTA. THINKS HE CAN TELL ME WHAT TO DO...
WONDER WHAT THESE HOLES IN THE WALLS ARE FOR...
GO DO YOUR DAMN JOB.
I KNOW THAT!
SHEESH ...

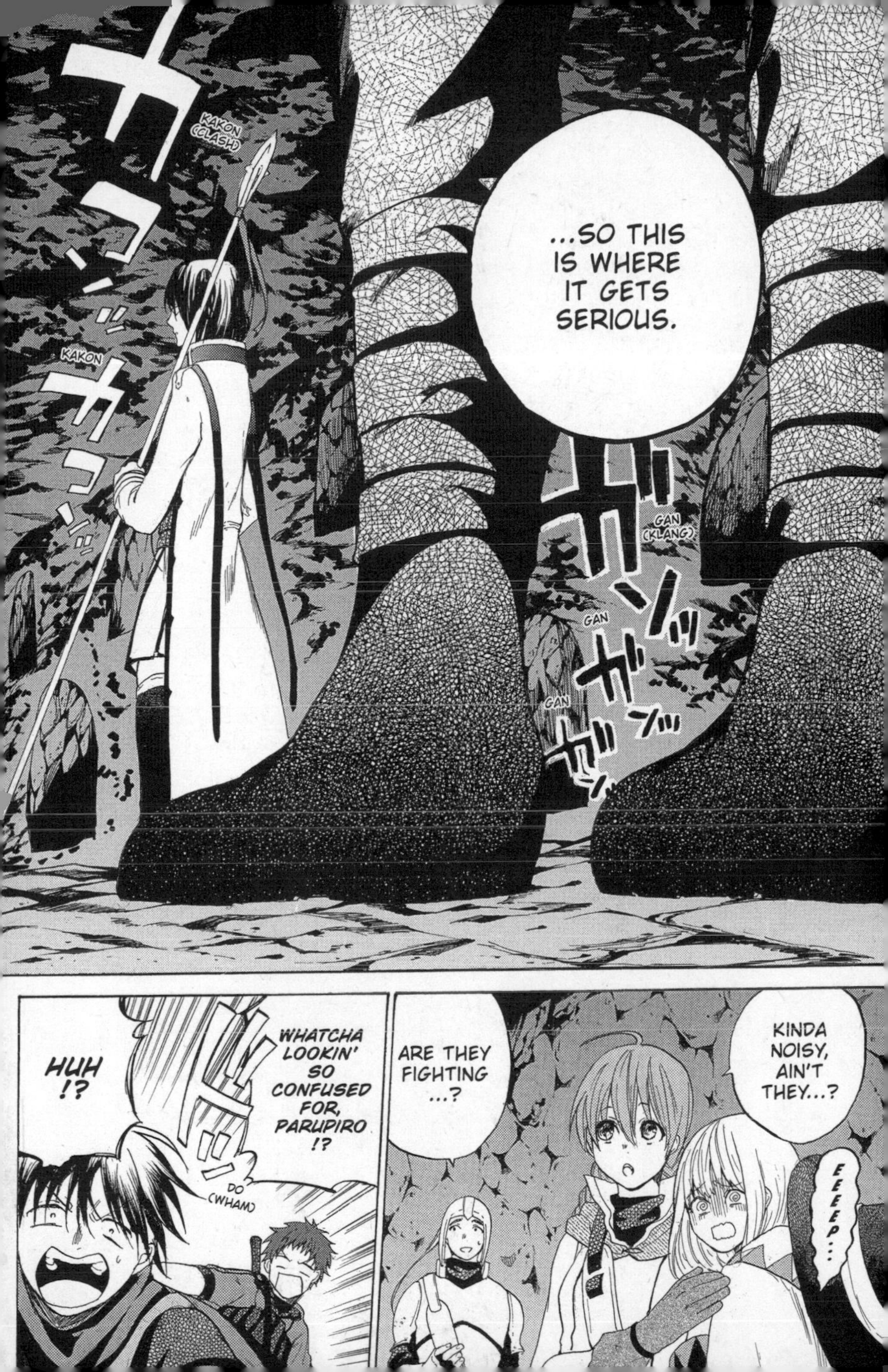

...SO THIS IS WHERE IT GETS SERIOUS.
GAN (KLANG)
GAN
GAN
KAKON (CLASH)
KAKON
KINDA NOISY, AIN'T THEY...?
EEEEP...
ARE THEY FIGHTING ...?
WHATCHA LOOKIN' SO CONFUSED FOR, PARUPIRO !?
DO (WHAM)
HUH !?

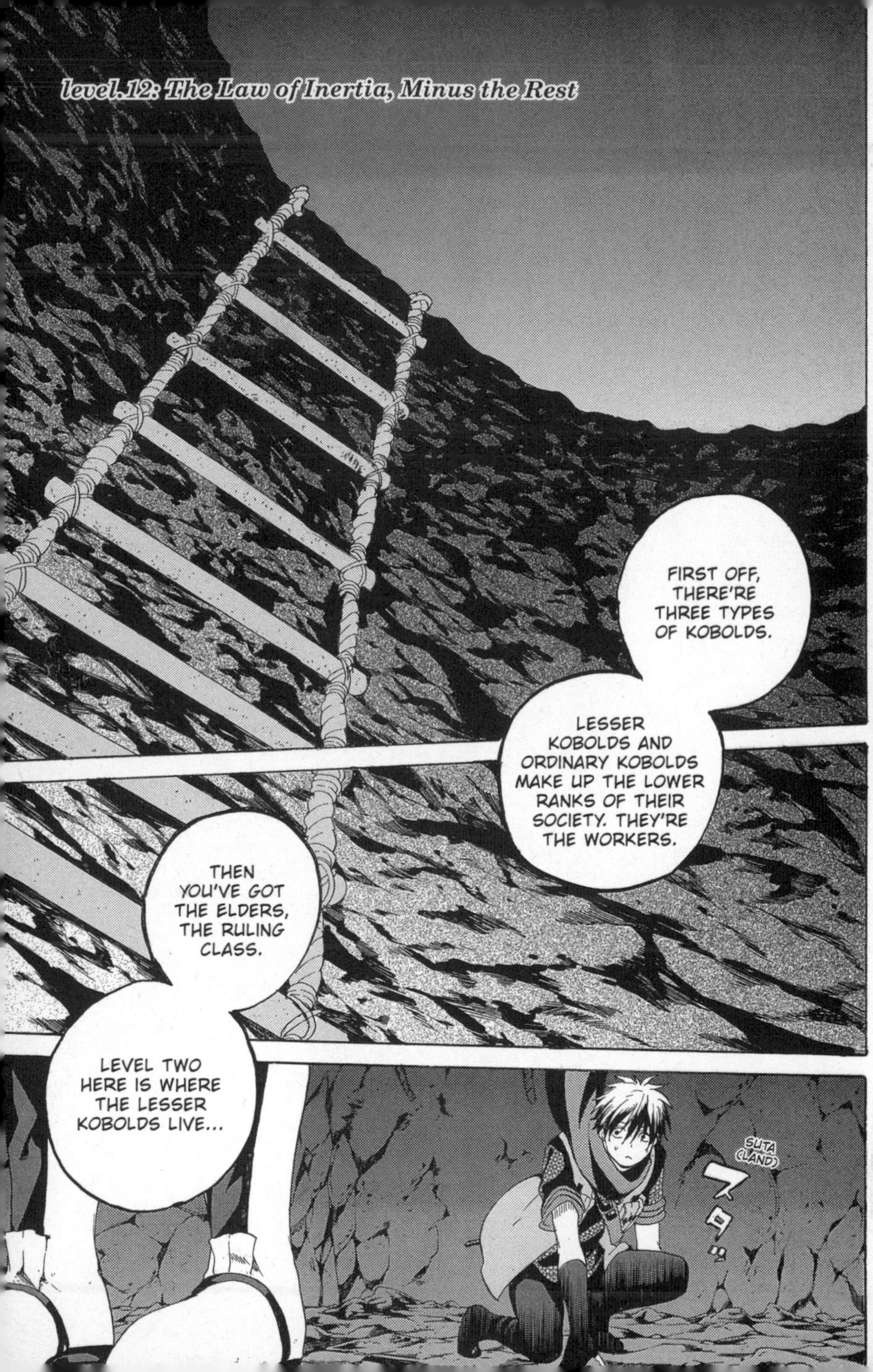
level.12: The Law of Inertia, Minus the Rest
FIRST OFF, THERE'RE THREE TYPES OF KOBOLDS.
LESSER KOBOLDS AND ORDINARY KOBOLDS MAKE UP THE LOWER RANKS OF THEIR SOCIETY. THEY'RE THE WORKERS.
THEN YOU'VE GOT THE ELDERS, THE RULING CLASS.
LEVEL TWO HERE IS WHERE THE LESSER KOBOLDS LIVE...
SUTA (LAND)

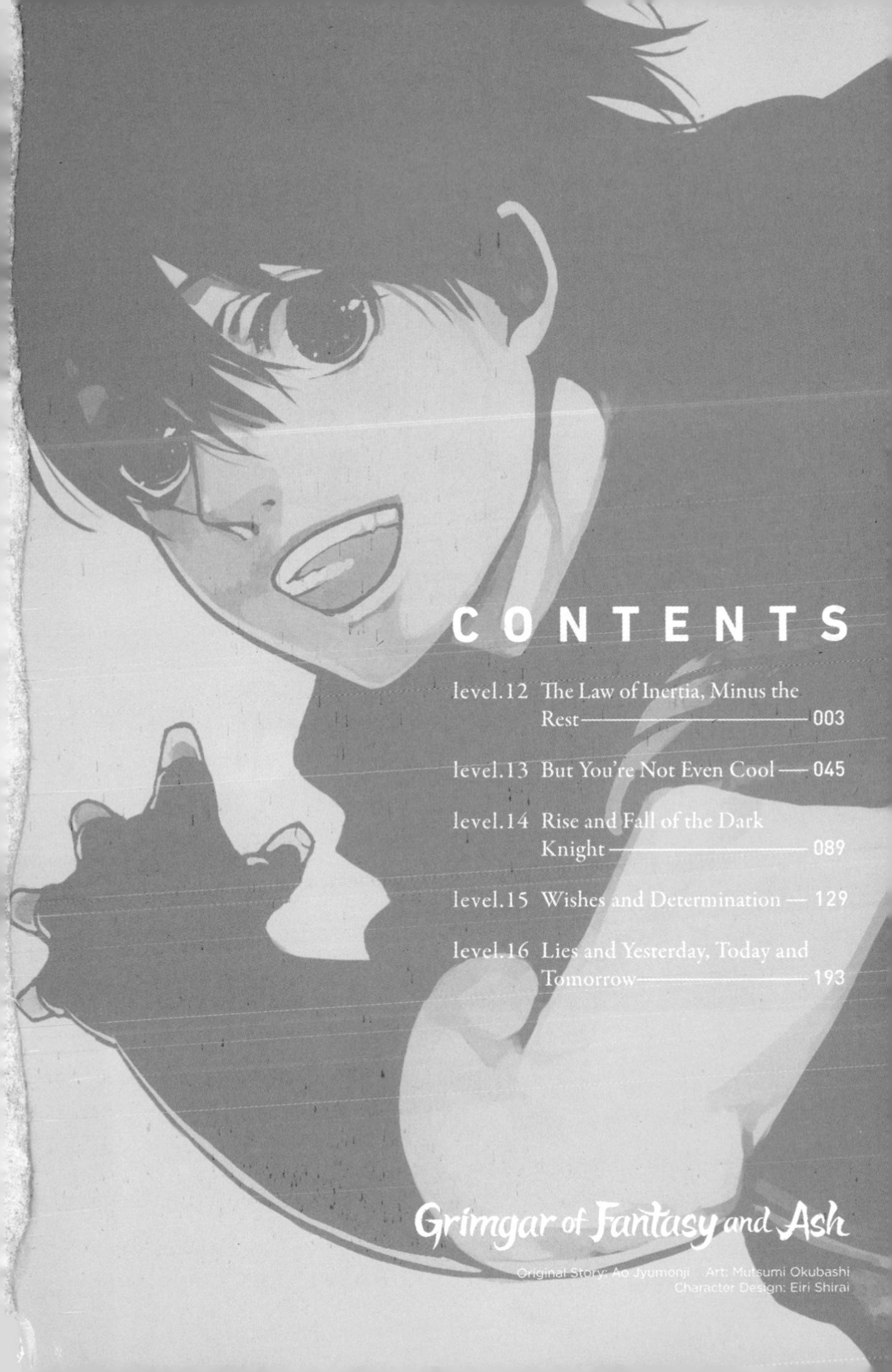

CONTENTS

Grimgar of Fantasy and Ash

Original Story: Ao Jyumonji   Art: Mutsumi Okubashi
Character Design: Eiri Shirai

Grimgar of Fantasy and Ash

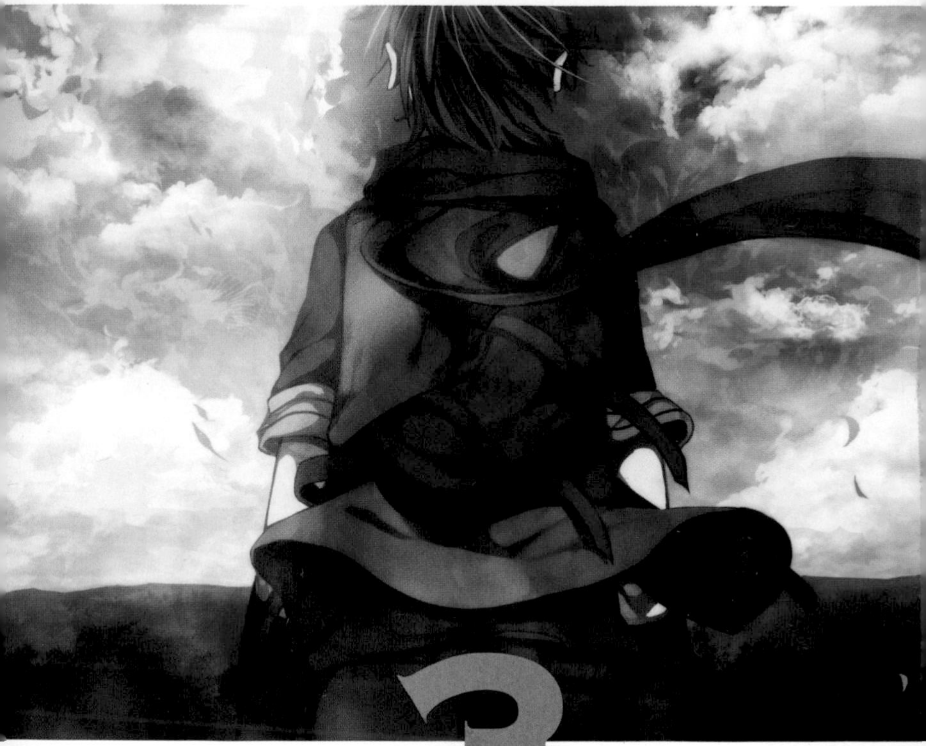

3

LEVEL.3

ORIGINAL STORY
AO JYUMONJI

ART
MUTSUMI OKUBASHI

CHARACTER DESIGN
EIRI SHIRAI